THE DEEP ECOLOGY OF RHETORIC IN MENCIUS AND ARISTOTLE

SUNY series in Chinese Philosophy and Culture
———————
Roger T. Ames, editor

THE DEEP ECOLOGY
OF RHETORIC IN
MENCIUS AND ARISTOTLE

A SOMATIC GUIDE

DOUGLAS ROBINSON

Published by State University of New York Press, Albany

© 2016 State University of New York

All rights reserved

Printed in the United States of America

No part of this book may be used or reproduced in any manner whatsoever without written permission. No part of this book may be stored in a retrieval system or transmitted in any form or by any means including electronic, electrostatic, magnetic tape, mechanical, photocopying, recording, or otherwise without the prior permission in writing of the publisher.

For information, contact State University of New York Press, Albany, NY
www.sunypress.edu

Production, Ryan Morris
Marketing, Fran Keneston

Library of Congress Cataloging-in-Publication Data

Names: Robinson, Douglas, 1954– author.
Title: The deep ecology of rhetoric in Mencius and Aristotle : a somatic guide / Douglas Robinson.
Description: Albany : State University of New York Press, 2016. | Series: SUNY series in Chinese philosophy and culture | Includes bibliographical references and index.
Identifiers: LCCN 2015027115 | ISBN 9781438461076 (hardcover : alk. paper) | ISBN 9781438461069 (paperback : alk. paper) | 9781438461083 (e-book)
Subjects: LCSH: Mencius—Criticism and interpretation. | Rhetoric, Ancient. | Aristotle—Criticism and interpretation. | Persuasion (Rhetoric)—History—To 1500.
Classification: LCC B128.M324 R63 2016 | DDC 181/.112—dc23
LC record available at http://lccn.loc.gov/2015027115

10 9 8 7 6 5 4 3 2 1

Contents

Preface — vii

1 Mencius and Aristotle as "Deep-Ecological" Theorists of Rhetoric — 1

2 The Group Subject of Persuasion — 51

3 Energy Channeled through Body Language — 107

4 The Circulation of Social Value — 157

5 Conclusion: Aristotle and Mencius on Ecosis — 247

Notes — 259

Glossary — 283

References — 297

Index — 307

Preface

Scope of the Study

This book explores a confluence of five different fields of study, namely rhetoric, deep ecology, somatic theory, Aristotle and ancient Greek philosophy, and Mencius and early Confucianism:

rhetoric (§1.1) is traditionally the study of persuasion, and specifically of the structures and forms of persuasive discourse; the deep ecology of rhetoric suggests a broader and more holistic understanding of persuasion, or "persuasivity" (*to pithanon*), as part of the circulation through groups of evaluative affect-becoming-conation (see the Glossary)

deep ecology (§1.1): as founded by the Norwegian philosopher Arne Naess, deep ecology is the study of the "Self-realization" of the ecological self, a concept derived from a number of sources, including Zen Buddhism, Spinoza, and Gandhi; lurking behind his conception of Self-realization as "realizing inherent potentialities," however, is Aristotle's notion of the *entelekheia* or entelechy; *qì*-driven moral maturation or self-realization is also Mencius's focal concern

somatics (§1.2): somatic theory studies the circulation of evaluative affect through groups as the primary channel of social regulation; to the extent that the deep ecology of rhetoric is an affective social ecology, it is specifically a somatic ecology, or what I call in §4.12 a somatic exchange

> *Aristotle* (§1.2–3, §1.5): the Athenian philosopher (384–322 BCE), considered the most important Platonist thinker after Plato himself, and in many ways more important, as he turned his master on his head—in ways that are remarkably reminiscent of Mencius, his near-contemporary
>
> *Mencius* (§1.3–5): the Chinese philosopher (ca. 372–ca. 303 BCE), considered the most important Confucian thinker after Confucius himself, and in many ways more important, as he expanded and complicated the basic Confucian concepts in salutary ways

The sequence in which those fields appear in the list reflects something like my expertise and argumentative priorities in this book: I admire Mencius and Aristotle, consider myself something of a follower of both, but I am very far from being an expert in either, or in classical Chinese or Attic Greek; I mostly construct the two thinkers as guides to my main concern, namely the deep somatic ecology of rhetoric. I do firmly believe that my reading of the two contemporaries is fundamentally on target—that I am not willfully distorting their thought to suit my argumentative purposes—but I am not a trained Sinologist, Hellenist, or Sino-Hellenist. I have put in the requisite time with the bilingual dictionaries and other lexical tools designed specifically for the study of classical Chinese and Attic Greek, as well as with the last few decades of scholarship (in English) on both thinkers; my research assistant Rico Chung and various Chinese friends and colleagues have tracked down and in some cases translated important scholarly sources for me in Chinese; I have engaged the various English translations critically, even perhaps tenaciously, reading them stereoscopically against both the originals and (here and there) their classical commentators; and my Acknowledgments record my great debt to the scholars of ancient Greek, classical Chinese, and both philosophical traditions who have checked my claims about both the meanings of words and phrases in context and the philosophical positions both thinkers adopt. My readings of specific passages are on the whole tendentious, and perhaps lean more toward the radical than toward the conservative; but I would not call them idiosyncratic. My reading of Aristotle is closely aligned with the readings offered by Nancy Sherman (1989) and Jeffrey Walker (2000, 2008), for example; and my reading of Mencius is closely aligned with those offered by Roger T. Ames (1991, 2002a), Shun Kwong-loi 信廣來 (1997, 2002), Huang Junjie 黃俊傑 (2001), and James Behuniak Jr. (2005). I also occasionally find the temerity to disagree with these experts—but only, it seems to me, on occasions when I think they have not pursued their own lines of interpretation consistently or insistently enough. Even so, my claims about the thought of Aristotle and Mencius are not intended, and should not be taken, as authoritative (let alone exhaustive) interpretations. They are, rather, strongly suggestive of a radically new theorization of rhetoric—and, more broadly, of what I call "ecosis/icosis" (§1.1; see the Glossary).

I'm certain that readers with expertise in either Mencius, classical Chinese, and Confucian thought or Aristotle and Attic Greek will find much to pick at in my claims; and the usual acknowledgments disclaimer applies *a fortiori* here, that any egregious errors in my readings of the two thinkers or their wordings should be attributed to my own stubbornness rather than any gaps in the knowledge of the scholars who checked them for me. I'm hoping, however, that the light those readings shed on the deep somatic ecology of rhetoric will be bright enough and novel enough that readers will be able to set any reservations they may harbor about my Mencian and Aristotelian expertise aside.

In fact my deepest expertise lies in somatic theory, especially somatic theories of translation, literature, and rhetoric and composition, on which I have published extensively for over two decades, beginning with *The Translator's Turn* (Robinson 1991) and running more recently to *Estrangement and the Somatics of Literature: Tolstoy, Shklovsky, Brecht* (Robinson 2008), *Translation and the Problem of Sway* (Robinson 2011), *First-Year Writing and the Somatic Exchange* (Robinson 2012), *Displacement and the Somatics of Postcolonial Culture* (Robinson 2013a), *Feeling Extended* (Robinson 2013b), and *Schleiermacher's Icoses* (Robinson 2013c). What I have found in Mencius and Aristotle in researching and writing this book is not only kindred somatic theorists from more than two millennia ago but deep somatic ecologists whose understanding of human social interaction everywhere complicates and occasionally derails my own.

Acknowledgments

I originally wrote this book on Aristotle's conception of rhetoric—no Mencius—at the University of Mississippi, where my colleague in Classics, Jonathan Fenno, read the whole manuscript carefully once, and then met with me several more times to discuss various new claims I wanted to make about Aristotle's Greek. Many of the subtler philological points I make in my discussion of Aristotle are thanks to Jonathan; and after he had pointed me toward the phonological convergence in Attic Greek between *oikos* and *eikos*, I had a long conversation at the Nida School of Translation Studies in Misano, Italy, with John Schwandt, classics professor at New Saint Andrews College, who honed my understanding of the phonology behind the convergence.

When I moved to Hong Kong and decided to rewrite the book as a comparative study of Mencius and Aristotle, I ended up receiving a lot of help from scholars of Chinese philosophy, Chinese-English translation, and Chinese-English comparative literature, from both Hong Kong and the Mainland. Especially helpful while I was researching the classical Chinese were Zhu Lin (朱琳) of Hengshui University (衡水学院), John Wang (王瓊) of Jinan University (暨南大學), and, from the English department at Lingnan University (嶺南大學), my colleague Ding Ersu (丁爾蘇) and my M.Phil. student Franziska Cheng (鄭安儀); all four also read the entire manuscript and made helpful comments. Rachel Lung (龍惠珠) in the Lingnan Translation department and Wang Chunhong (汪春泓) in the Lingnan Chinese department also commented usefully on the entire manuscript. Shun Kwong-loi (信廣來), Chair Professor of Chinese philosophy and head of New Asia College (新亞書院) at the Chinese University of Hong Kong (香港中文大學), read and commented on a conference paper I built around his tracing of the three historical phases of interpretations of *xìng* 性 (condensed here into §4.3).

As the new comparativist version of the book began to take more or less coherent shape, I began to present bits and pieces of it in guest lectures and conference talks, specifically in the context of problems faced when translating specific Mencian concepts into English; the audience members at Hong Kong Baptist University (香港浸會大學), Henan Normal University (河南师范大学), and Guangdong University of Foreign Studies (广东外语外贸大学), as well as the professors and associates at the Nida School of Translation Studies in Misano and the Translation Research Summer Seminar at HKBU, asked many pointed questions and made many useful suggestions. Thanks especially to the late Martha Cheung (張佩瑤), who heard several versions of these talks, both in Hong Kong and in Italy, and gave me a good deal of tough-minded feedback.

Prof. Chan Sin-wai (陳善偉) at Chinese University of Hong Kong (香港中文大學) invited me to present a condensed version of §2.1–3 at the Translation and Asian Studies conference in late April, 2011, and then published the paper in the conference proceedings ("Problems in Translating 'Circulatory' Terms from Aristotle's Greek and Mencius's Chinese: *pistis* 'persuading/being persuaded' and 治 *zhì* 'governing/being governed' in

English." In Chan Sin-wai, ed., *Two Voices in One*, 159–74. Newcastle Upon Tyne: Cambridge Scholars, 2014.) Thanks to Prof. Chan for permission to reprint the paragraphs that appear both there and here.

A Note on Romanization Conventions

The romanization system used for transliterating standard (Pǔtōnghuà 普通话) Chinese in the People's Republic of China since 1958, and increasingly among Western Sinologists as well—and in this book—is called *pinyin* (拼音). It replaces the nineteenth-century Wade-Giles romanization system, which is still found in books published in English about China around the turn of the millennium. Shun Kwong-loi's *Mencius and Early Chinese Thought*, for example, is still using Wade-Giles in 1997; James Behuniak Jr's *Mencius on Becoming Human* in 2005 has switched to *pinyin*; but at this writing early in the second decade of the new millennium, some American Sinologists are still vowing never to switch to *pinyin*.

Four illustrative examples of the differences between these two romanization systems might be the names of Mencius himself and three of the most influential scholars of his work:

Chinese characters	孟子	朱熹	戴震	唐君毅
Wade-Giles	Meng Tzu	Chu Hsi	Tai Chen	T'ang Chüni
pinyin without tone markers	Mengzi	Zhu Xi	Dai Zhen	Tang Junyi
pinyin with tone markers	Mèngzǐ	Zhū Xī	Dài Zhèn	Táng Jūnyì

The advantage of pinyin over Wade-Giles for the non-Chinese-speaker, even without tone markers, is that its romanizations of many phonemes are closer to the actual Chinese pronunciation than the Wade-Giles. As a general rule, Wade-Giles tends to devoice Chinese voiced consonants: 戴 begins with a voiced [d], not a voiceless [t] (it's "die," not "tie"); 朱 and 震 begin with a voiced [dʒ] (朱 is pronounced "jew," not "chew," and 震 is pronounced "jun," rhyming with "done," not "chen," rhyming with "when"); 子 begins with a voiced [dz] (like the consonant in English *adze*), not a devoiced [tz]. It's rather strange, in fact, that the voiceless and aspirated [t] that begins 唐 is pronounced almost exactly like the voiceless and aspirated English [t] (as in "tong"), but because Wade-Giles has reserved the letter "t" for [d], it has to represent [t] as "t.'" The "u" in Tzu, too, is the Wade-Giles approximation of the Chinese [ə] (what we would call a schwa); Mengzi is actually pronounced not [meng tsu:], as the Wade-Giles romanization tends to make non-Chinese-speakers say it, but [mʌŋdzə] (the first syllable like the italicized part of "a*mong*," the second syllable like the italicized part of "ki*ds a* lot").

Since as part of my comparative approach I assume that many of my readers will have no knowledge of Chinese, I've also (except with proper names!) provided tone markers: Zhū Xī (first tone, high flat), Táng (second tone, rising), zǐ (third tone, falling-rising), and Mèng (fourth tone, falling). There is also a neutral tone that is sometimes called the fifth tone, as in the second syllable of *miànzi* 面子 "face"; it takes no diacritic at all.

In standard Chinese every syllable has not only a possible five different tonalizations, but a potentially very large number of different characters for the same tonalization, each with a different historically organized cluster of meanings. To avoid confusion, I have also provided the actual Chinese character in every case.

Since Greek has a phonetic script that can be represented in Roman characters without confusion, however, I have not used Greek characters. The only possible source of confusion in Roman transliteration is the existence of two different vowel-pairs that are close to a single English vowel, one in each longer, the other shorter. In transliterating these I follow the conventions of Hellenist studies in English:

    Εε *epsilon* (short *e*) > e
    Ηη *eta* (long *e*) > ē
    Οο *omicron* (short *o*) > o
    Ωω *omega* (long *o*) > ō

This means that the same diacritic over ē and ō will signify *syllabic tone* (high flat first tone) in Chinese romanizations and *vowel length* (long) in Greek transliterations.

1

Mencius and Aristotle as "Deep-Ecological" Theorists of Rhetoric

1.1 Rhetoric and Deep Ecology

To the extent that this book draws on the philosophy of deep ecology to study rhetoric, it implies an expansion of our understanding of rhetoric past rationalistic conceptions focused on the form and content of rhetoric (arguments, claims, proofs, etc.) to ecological conceptions focused on rhetorical situation—the affective and conative *flows* of persuasivity through groups that make rhetorical persuasion possible. The former conception of rhetoric is the one that dominated the field in the West for two thousand years, and lingers on as the default definition; the latter shifts the conceptual focus from argumentative structures to what Jenny Edbauer (2005, p. 9) calls "a framework of *affective ecologies* that recontextualizes rhetorics in their temporal, historical, and lived fluxes." Troping rhetorical situation as a network (Shaviro, 2003; Edbauer, 2005, pp. 9–10), as a "radically *distributed* act" (Syverson, 1999; Edbauer, 2005, p. 12), as a verb, and as a viral economy, Edbauer (ibid., p. 14) suggests that "a given rhetoric is not *contained* by the elements that comprise its rhetorical situation (exigence, rhetor, audience, constraints). Rather, a rhetoric emerges already infected by the viral intensities that are circulating in the social field. Moreover, this same rhetoric will go on to evolve in *aparallel* ways: between two 'species' that have absolutely nothing to do with each other. What is shared between them is *not* the situation, but certain contagions and energy."

This passage adumbrates my main concerns as a theorist and intellectual historian of rhetoric: rhetorical situation as an ecology; persuasivity (*to pithanon*) as the circulation of "viral intensities" or energies through groups; that circulation specifically as an energy-exchange, a circulatory or reticulatory flow of energy-transfers that in §4.12 I call the *somatic exchange* (see the Glossary). In addition, however, I bring to bear on the affective ecologies of persuasivity the specific philosophical articulation of ecological theory offered by Arne Naess (1995, p. 33):

> N1: Self-realization!
> H1: The higher the Self-realization attained by anyone, the broader and deeper the identification with others.
> H2: The higher the level of Self-realization attained by anyone, the more its further increase depends on the Self-realization of others.
> H3: Complete Self-realization of anyone depends on that of all.
> N2: Self-realization by all living beings!
>
>   (N = norm; H = hypothesis)

As we will see in §2.2, what Naess here calls empathy-based "identification" *is* the becoming-communal movement of rhetoric ecologically understood; and though Naess does not mention Kenneth Burke's name or work, it is at least historically grounded in Burke's (1950/1969) radical reading of Aristotle's rhetorical theory. Naess (ibid., pp. 15–16) gives the example of intense affective identification with a flea that falls into acid and dies in agony; Mencius (1A7) illustrates precisely the same collectivizing disposition through the story of King Xuan of Qí (齊宣王, r. 342–324 BCE), whose empathetic identification with an ox being led to slaughter he praised (though he also goes on to chide the king for caring more about the ox than about his subjects; and in 7A45 he says specifically that an exemplary person will experience intimacy [*qīn* 親] with family members, fellow-feeling [*rén* 仁] with all humans, and a lower level of "love" [*ài* 愛] for animals and other living things).

Because I am primarily interested here not generally in deep ecology but in the deep ecology specifically of rhetoric, this is as far as I follow Naess; I will not be exploring his next set of norms and hypotheses (ibid., p. 35):

> H4: Diversity of life increases Self-realization potentials.
> N3: Diversity of life!
> H5: Complexity of life increases Self-realization potentials.
> N4: Complexity of life!

H6: Life resources of the Earth are limited.
H7: Symbiosis maximizes realization potentials under conditions of limited resources.
N5: Symbiosis!

This would be the bioecosophical application of Naess's philosophical intervention; my concern is with affective ecologies.

Still, thinking affective ecologies more deeply will suggest some ways in which a concern with affective deep social ecologies only keeps bringing us back into the vicinity of the kind of global or planetary deep-ecological thinking that Naess engages:

[1] Let the primary affective ecology be an ecology of social value that reticulates evaluative affect through the community in a becoming-conative form.

- Since the evaluative affect is circulating through a group—since it is an affective *ecology*—it reflects not individuated but collective value, and:

- Since as Aristotle insists we are social animals, so that we care so much about group approval and disapproval that the mere *feeling* of evaluation becomes by default conative pressure, therefore:

[1a] Let the becoming-conativity of affect mean that evaluative affect begins as a *feeling* of value—approving or disapproving, honoring or dishonoring, praising or condemning—that is then *used-and-taken* as social pressure (collective conation) to conform to group norms.

[1b] Let this affective-becoming-conative ecology also be understood as becoming-cognitive, in the sense that it is always moving toward conscious awareness, without necessarily depending for its effectiveness on such awareness (both individuals and groups may participate in such ecologies without recognizing or being able to articulate their doing so).

[2] Let the key social subecologies at work in this ecology of value be organized around the three foci of the philosophi-

cal tradition emerging out of Plato and Aristotle, namely, the good, the just, and the true.

- Since, unlike Plato, for whom these ideals are transcendental abstractions, pure and stable universals descending to us from the Realm of Forms, demanding only that we learn to discern them accurately, Aristotle theorizes them as *communal* virtues—which is to say, in the terms I'm using here, social ecologies—therefore:

[2a] Let the good be what the community decides is good.

[2b] Let the true be what the community decides is true.

[2c] Let the just (or the fair, or the equitable) be what the community decides is just or fair or equitable.

[2d] Let the community decide these things through (1a) the affective-becoming-conative(-becoming-cognitive) ecology of social value: by circulating or reticulating evaluative affect-becoming-conation through the group.

[2e] Let rhetorical theory (and other social theories) emerge out of (1b) the becoming-cognitive of the affective-becoming-conative-becoming-cognitive ecology of social value.

- Since the communal determination of the good was aimed specifically at the building of good character(s), and since for Aristotle the good was therefore determined ecologically by the community, therefore:

[3] Let (2a) "the good" be a collective social ecology/entelechy of *becoming-good*.

[3a] Let *becoming-good* also mean *becoming-normal*, in the sense of gradually coming to conform to communal norms, or, in the term Behuniak (2005) takes to be the key concept in Mencius's philosophy, *becoming-human*, in the sense of coming to embody what the community takes to represent the human (transbestial) ideal.

[3b] Let a more inclusive term for (3) be *becoming-communal*—an apposite umbrella term for becoming-good not only because the community regulates the process but because in that process the community itself (potentially) becomes good as well.

- Since the Attic Greek word for community is *oikos* (pronounced [yikos], with tightly pursed lips on the front diphthong [yi], like the diphthong in French *nuit*[1]), from which we derive our Latinized terms economy (*oikos* + *nomos* "communal law") and ecology (*oikos* + *logos* "communal study" or "communal reason"), therefore:

[3c] Let *ecosis* signify the entelechial ecology of becoming-good or becoming-normal or becoming-human or becoming-communal, or what Arne Naess calls the self-realization of the ecological self (ideally for Naess and deep ecology, ecosis would be the becoming-good/becoming-communal of the entire planet).

- Since Aristotle does not define the true or the just transcendentally either, as something fixed by or in a spiritual realm, but rather as determined communally, therefore:

[4] Let (2b) "the fair" be a collective social ecology of *becoming-fair*, and (2c) "the true" be a collective social ecology of *becoming-true*.

- Since when Aristotle writes about the communal determination of truth he tends to deal less with *alētheia* "truth" and more with *ta eikota* "the probable, the likely," from *eikos* (pronounced [i:kos], with the initial front diphthong collapsed into a long front [i:]), which Stephen Colbert might want to translate as "truthy," and:

- Since Aristotle's word for fairness or equity was also derived from *eikos*, namely *epieikeia*, and:

[4a] Let the communal ecologies of *becoming-fair* and *becoming-true* collapse into one, comprising the commu-

nity's emerging ecotic sense of what is fair because it seems true (seems probable or plausible or likely to be true, and therefore "truthy"), and of what is truthy because it seems fair.

- Since communal becoming-fair and becoming-true are steeped in *persuasion,* or what Aristotle calls persuasivity (*to pithanon*), therefore:

[4b] Let *icosis* (Latinizing *eikos* as *icos*) be a collective social ecology/entelechy of *becoming-persuasive* and *becoming-real-seeming* or *becoming-truthy.*

[5] Let the primary affective ecology of social value take the form(s) of two closely intertwined subecologies, two collective entelechies or self-realizations: (3c) *ecosis* (moving toward the communal good or the good community) and (4b) *icosis* (moving toward the communal determination/construction of truth and fairness through persuasivity).

- Since, given their extremely similar pronunciations, *oikos* and *eikos* were often either confused or punningly compared in Attic Greek, and at various times folk etymologies have been developed deriving *eikos* from *oikos*, leading Plato, Aristotle, and Xenophon to pun on the two words,[2] and:

- Since the aural convergence that Attic Greeks heard in *oikos* and *eikos* ties each closely to the other, therefore:

[5a] Let icosis be ecotic to the extent that becoming-persuasive works through normalization, the circulation of affective-becoming-conative pressures to adhere to group norms.

[5b] Let ecosis be icotic to the extent that becoming-communal works through communication, the verbal telling-and-hearing of opinions as truths (realities, identities) or as an emerging collective sense of justice.

- Since for Aristotle (3) ecosis or becoming-communal is also a process of developing good character(s), and:

- Since the Attic Greek for "character" is *ēthos* (which is why a concern with the good is traditionally the concern of "ethics"), therefore:

[5c] Let *ethecosis* signify ethical ecosis, simultaneously the becoming(-individual-and-becoming)-communal of good character and the becoming-good of communal character.

- Since icosis is grounded in *doxa*, which in the Attic Greek of Plato and Aristotle means both opinion and reputation (and specifically opinion-*becoming*-reputation), therefore:

[5d] Let *doxicosis* signify the communal becoming-persuasive (becoming-truthy, becoming-fair, becoming-real-seeming, becoming-identity) of people's opinions.

Or, to put that in simpler English: icosis/ecosis is the process by which social life is organized ecologically out of group dynamics; by "organized ecologically" I mean emerging out of situated group relationships and interactions without being overtly directed by a leader, or following a rational plan. The group dynamics that wield the "ecological" organizing power begin as interactive/shared affect, especially evaluative affects like approval and disapproval; because we are social animals who care very much about group belonging, those shared evaluative affects tend to be experienced as conative *pressures* to conform to group norms. (If the whole group disapproves of my actions, I will tend to feel shame and a determination to change my behavior in future. I can resist that pressure, and even—if the group is small enough—sometimes change their minds; but even in a small group that kind of counterpressure is extremely difficult to bring successfully, and almost impossible in a whole population.) Within that broad socio-ecological framework, then, "icosis" is the rhetorical process by which opinions are plausibilized as truths and realities, so that a socially constructed world view comes to seem like "the way things are"; and "ecosis" is the rhetorical process by which values are plausibilized as morals and laws, so that a socially constructed morality comes to seem like "God's will" or the like.

In both Aristotle's *Rhetoric* (which I will abbreviate *TR*, for *tekhnē rhetorikē*) and the *Mencius* (which I will abbreviate *MZ*, for *Meng zi*), the deep ecology of rhetoric is (4b) icotic or (5d) doxicotic, and the deep ecology of ethical growth or maturation in both writers is (3c) ecotic or (5c) ethecotic. Since this book is a study of the deep ecology of *rhetoric*, my focus will be on the former, doxicosis—although, like Aristotle in the *Nicomachean* and *Eudemian Ethics*, Mencius is most often read as primarily an ecotic rather than an icotic thinker. (The question of whether Mencius can or should be read as an icotic or rhetorical theorist as well is the topic of §1.3.)

But ultimately, I suggest, it is impossible to separate the two subecologies: Aristotle is everywhere in the *TR* an ecotic thinker and everywhere in the ethical books an icotic thinker; Mencius is everywhere both as well. Issues of rhetorical persuasion, plausibility, emotion, disposition, and the verbal/communal construction of truth can only be isolated from ethical questions of character with great analytical violence.

Yet another way to think affective ecologies more deeply: in both Mencius and Aristotle scholars have discerned a fruitful and ecologically definitive tension between *disposition* (*xìng* 性 in Mencius, *hexis* in Aristotle) or *character* (*dé* 德 in Mencius, *ēthos* in Aristotle) on the one hand and *circumstances* or *conditions* (*mìng* 命 in Mencius, *kath' hekaston* in Aristotle) on the other. As Sherman (1989, pp. 3–4) writes, "Pursuing the ends of virtue does not begin with making choices, but with recognizing the circumstances relevant to specific ends. In this sense, character is expressed in what one sees as much as what one does. Knowing how to discern the particulars, Aristotle stresses, is a mark of virtue." And again: "Before we can know how to act, we must acknowledge that action may be required. And this reaction to circumstances is itself part of the virtuous response. It is part of how the dispositional ends of character become occurrent" (ibid., pp. 5–6). And Behuniak (2005, p. 118) writes: "Just as the 'force of character' of a ruler is always in tension with the 'mandate' (*ming* 命) and thus, in Tang Junyi's words, 'a mutual giving and receiving,' the force of character of those who perform sacrifices with integrity can also be understood as in tension with conditions (*ming* 命). Sacrifices boldly deny the finality of mortal death, an irrevocable *ming*."

On the one hand, circumstances do condition action, form the constraining conditions of possibility within which action becomes thinkable and realizable; on the other hand, people of great force of character can often successfully resist or minimize the limiting effects of conditions. This tension implies a kind of mutual circulation of ecosis through icosis and of icosis through ecosis. In rhetorical terms, one can think of what the rhetor brings to the rhetorical situation as *strength of character and disposition,* and the doxicotic currents into which the rhetor must insert his or her character in order to effect persuasion as the situational or ecological *conditions* under which persuasion becomes possible; but Aristotle also sees the characters, emotions, and dispositions of the rhetor's audience as part of those conditions, as *to endekhomenon pithanon* or "the available persuasivity." To persuade his or her audience the rhetor must muster a convincingly "good" (communally shared) *ēthos*, a character with which the audience can identify; the only way the rhetor can accomplish this task successfully is by entering into the ethecotic-becoming-doxicotic ecology of social value. S/he has to *feel* the affective ecosis of character as an affective icosis of truthiness and fairness, and both as conative pressure to become part of the becoming-communal.

1.2 Somatics

Somatic theory posits that individual members of any group (a) see, hear, remember, or imagine other people's body language and simulate those other people's body states in their own, and in so doing (b) circulate becoming-normative evaluative affects through the group, thereby (c) generating a group body-becoming-mind or group agency that wields regulatory power over the group but also "is" the group, and in some incompletely transpersonal sense "is" each member of the group. Because the somatic model is based on the almost simultaneous (within 300 milliseconds) neural representation and simulation of other people's body states, I call it "somatomimetic" (see the Glossary)—as opposed to competing neurophysiological modelings of the same phenomenology that are based on chemical (pheromonic) entrainment, like that offered by Teresa Brennan (2004).

Those who know Mencius know that the driving force behind his ethecotic ecology is *xīn* 心, which in Chinese is both "heart" and "mind," and which I argue in §2.6 might best be translated "heart-becoming-mind" or "feeling-becoming-thinking"; the primary argumentative burden of my first chapter is to show that Mencius's key concept *rén* 仁 is specifically (c) a *group* heart-becoming-mind, or what I translate there as "fellow-feeling." My topic in chapter 3 is the driving vitalistic force behind the Mencian *xīn* 心/*rén* 仁 ecology, namely *qì* 氣 "configurative energy"—a viral intensity that Brian Massumi (2002) would also want to associate with affect. Reading Mencius somatically, therefore, seems almost supererogatory. How else *could* one read him? (As we'll see in §1.3, there have historically been other influential readings; and one, which dominated Chinese Confucian scholarship for six centuries, until the eighteenth century—that formulated by Zhu Xi 朱熹—stands in stark opposition to my somatic reading, which really only seems unavoidable in the context of the last two and a half centuries of Mencius scholarship. Strikingly, however, one of the most recent translations of the *MZ*, Bryan W. Van Norden's (2008), is based explicitly on Zhu Xi's commentary.)

It may still seem odd, however, to include Aristotle too in a somatic study of rhetoric, since many scholars still read him as the cold-minded king of reductive-rationalist abstraction. To be sure, Aristotle was interested in emotion (*pathos*), especially but not exclusively in the *Rhetoric*, and famously and influentially included emotional appeals as one of three major *pisteis* (arguments, proofs, modes or means of persuasion, *TR* 1356a3), the other two being ethical appeals to the speaker's character and logical appeals based on the "words" or arguments themselves. But surely that alone isn't enough to warrant a somatic reading of Aristotle? After all, Aristotle himself seems decently embarrassed about pathetic persuasion, as a vulgar strategy unfortunately mandated by democracy, which puts deliberative power into the hands of the riffraff who can't manage the philosophical purification of their thought processes into pure reason. And as Gretchen Flesher Moon (2003) notes, most treatments of Aristotelian argumentative *pathos* in contemporary writing textbooks still tend to brand it fallacious reasoning, with a certain uneasiness or even outright embarrassment that such a thing even exists, let alone gets theorized by the great abstract formalist Aristotle. Larry Arnhart (1981, p. 3) reflects this attitude openly in noting that "rhetoric also has a darker side. Does not the rhetorician sometimes employ emotional appeals and deceptive arguments to move his listeners to whatever position he wishes?" Arnhart is actually very balanced and fair-minded on Aristotle's psychology of the emotions, so maybe what he means here is not that emotional appeals are *necessarily* rhetoric's dark side but that they *can* be used to darker ends; but then why not ask whether the rhetor does not also sometimes employ *logical* appeals and deceptive arguments to manipulate listeners and readers?

Let me begin to flesh out what I mean by somatic theory by taking a look at what appears to be Aristotle's "idealism" about the rhetor "working from truth" rather than manipulating the audience's emotions—as summarized here, for example, by Amélie Oksenberg Rorty (1996, pp. 2–3):

> Ideally, the best oratory addresses the minds as well as the psychology of its audience. Aristotle chides the authors of earlier handbooks on rhetoric for concentrating primarily on techniques for

swaying the emotions of judges and legislators, instead of first and primarily considering the best modes of persuasion. Enthymemes and metaphors are most convincing when their assumptions are reasonable (1355a4–1355b7). Aristotle wryly complains that addressing the emotions of a judge is like warping a ruler before using it. The best orator does not manipulate beliefs in order to make the worse appear to be the better course, but rather presents the best case in a way that is comprehensible and moving to each type of character (1113a30 ff.). In suiting his arguments to his audience—presenting a course of action as gloriously noble to the young and as prudent to the elderly—the rhetorician need not be lying. Aristotle's ethical words are meant to show that the best life is—in principle, under ideal circumstances, and in the long run—also the most pleasant, the most expedient, and the noblest (1140a25–28, 1142a1–11, 1359a30–1363b4). As long as his rhetoric is also constrained by what is true and what is best, the rhetorician will not "warp the ruler."

. . . Since even a debased audience aims at the opaque objects of its desires—at the real (and not merely the apparent) good—it implicitly wants its rhetoricians to be, and not merely to seem, good. It is for these functional normative reasons that the rhetorician must know how to present himself as substantively intelligent and virtuous, rather than merely as cleverly skilled at rhetoric. He must not only convince his audience that his arguments are sound, but also that, like the physician, he has their real interests—and not merely their surface desires—at heart. (101b5 ff.)

What are we to do with this? Is Aristotle just being naïve here? Is it patently silly to assume that it's even possible for a rhetor to present sound arguments, with his or her audience's "real interests . . . at heart," and *not* "manipulate beliefs in order to make the worse appear to be the better course"—*not* warp the ruler by appealing to his audience's emotions? Is there some sense in which it is not outright contradictory, perhaps a disturbing example of bad faith, to warn against emotional appeals in *TR* 1 and then devote ten chapters in *TR* 2.2–11 to a careful study of the best ways to appeal to an audience's emotions?

Let's imagine a methodomachy for dealing with this set of assumptions in Aristotle, a dialectical model or myth that is grounded in the history of such methodological wranglings but here conveniently narrativized:

Thesis: moralizing/objectivizing methods. The assumption here is that there exists a moral or ethical code that is not socially constructed or maintained but objective, stable, universal, received from God, and inscribed either in a Book (the Law, the Bible) or in the minds of all right-thinking people. So far from being understood as socially constructed, in fact, this method may even be seen (and in Christian thematizations typically is seen) as oppositional to society: the right-thinking moralist obeys the objective Law even in the face of widespread social chaos or immorality, surrounded on all hands by liars and swindlers, sophists and casuists, spin doctors and snake-oil salesmen. The righteous moralist is conceived as an individual, normatively male, who is free to make rational choices in accordance with morality and other objective codes, but equally free to deviate or "fall" from those rational choices into sin and degradation.

We like to call these methods "conservative," of course, but they are really only one of many conservativisms—as it happens, one associated in academic circles these days with a now mostly retired generation of colleagues and institutionalized in the National Association of Scholars. From this point of view, Aristotle's method is the only acceptable one; indeed, it is one of the founding models for this approach, along with Paul's in the New Testament epistles, Augustine's in *On Christian Doctrine*, Thomas's in the *Summa*, and so on. As his method is constructed by this group, Aristotle preaches adherence to moral/ethical models of truth-telling, honesty, and integrity even when all the other rhetors are lying and manipulating their audiences for personal or collective gain. Even if these various immoral rhetorics are so widespread as to dominate the scene, so that the Aristotelian rhetor actually does himself (not herself) a grave practical or political disservice by adhering to what is right, he continues to act in accordance with the true and the good.

Antithesis: discursivizing/constructivizing methods. The assumption now becomes that all such "codes" posited by moralizing and objectivizing methods are in fact ideological apparatuses that are socially constructed and maintained and discursive in nature, based on regimes of signs that impose meaning on both objects and the human subjects that are "interpellated" into them. The discursive subject is no longer an individual but a shaped functionality, what Massumi (2002, p. 2) calls "a subject without subjectivity: a subject 'constructed' by external mechanisms." He also notes that bodies are radically foreclosed in this approach: "This thoroughly mediated body could only be a 'discursive' body: one with its signifying gestures. Signifying gestures make sense. If properly 'performed,' they may also unmake sense by scrambling significations already in place. Make and unmake sense as they might, they don't *sense*" (ibid.). The model is insistently mentalist: in it everything is organized by the abstract logic of verbal language, or more generally discursive signs, semiosis. Anything unmediated by mind and mentalized language—say, affect—is theoretically dangerous and must be either methodologically repressed or retheorized as ultimately just another discursive functionality (see Terada, 2001).

For roughly the last two decades of the twentieth century we associated these methods with a left-leaning cultural theory that we thought of as politically radical, but methodologically they too have now become another conservatism, desperately engaged in a rearguard action against the vast stretches of human experience that their discursivist doctrines cannot explain or reduce. In this approach, obviously, Aristotle becomes hopelessly naïve, an idealistic objectivist who retains a childish faith in discredited ideological abstractions like Truth and the Right and actually thinks he is an individual with free choice—and, more perversely still, presents himself as electing to use that bogus "free choice" in the service of ideological state apparatuses. For this approach, in other words—see Haskins (2004a, 2004b)—Aristotle becomes one of the leading representatives of the thetic conservatism against which this antithetic radicalism is launched.

To some small extent, as Haskins (2004a) herself admits, Aristotle can be seen as a discursivist himself, attuned to the linguistic nuances of the received opinions from which he derived his philosophical categories; from a cultural-studies perspective, however, he is such a naïve, even primitive, objectivizing discursivist that he jumps straight from "what is said" to "what is," from *endoxa* to *pragmata*, with no lingering over "social and cultural markers" (ibid., p. 7). He is also wildly and disturbingly reactionary, uncritically supporting the exclusive rule of noble well-educated males and arguing that women and barbarians make natural slaves (ibid., pp. 9–11). Rather than seeking out and articulating the tiny opportunity for resistance that ideological apparatuses inadvertently but inevitably leave open, then, Aristotle wholeheartedly aligns himself with the state and its repressive discursive regimes, including objectivism.

Synthesis: somatizing methods. Somatic theory has one kind of beginning in the attempt to synthesize the discursivist theory of social construction with the phenomenology of objectivism—to explain the conflicting facts that human belief systems are demonstrably constructed but that one's own belief system nevertheless typically *feels* so objectively grounded in reality as to be virtually impossible to change. The Foucauldian assumption brought to bear on this objectivist phenomenology by discursivists, that we are corporeally trained or disciplined to believe in the reality of our own social constructs, in a sense only defers the problem: *How* are we so trained? What is it in us that is trained, what is disciplined, and how does the training or discipline take such a fierce hold on our orientation to the world that it comes to feel to us like the world itself? I say "in a sense" because the problem is really only deferred in highly selective discursivist readings of Foucault; Foucault himself, in *Discipline and Punish* (1975/1977) and elsewhere, is very clear: we are trained through the kinesthetic and affective programming of our autonomic nervous systems. It is only when Foucault is read through Kafka's "In the Penal Colony"—by Judith Butler (1989), for example—to be talking about "writing on the body," the inscribing of discursive codes on the "paper" of the skin, that it remains difficult to explain our overwhelming continuing attachments to philosophically discredited orientations like objectivism. How exactly does inscribing objectivism on my skin make me *feel* that what I believe is really real?

According to somatic theory, social construction operates much more powerfully at a kinesthetic-becoming-affective-becoming-conative level than it does at the discursive, which latter is itself in fact a corporeal-becoming-mental remapping of "ideosomatically" (group-affectively-becoming-conatively) organized/organizing feelings (see the Glossary). That ideosomatic regulation of groups is something like what Rorty (1996, p. 3) seems to be hinting at in "these functional normative reasons": the Aristotelian rhetor has to convince his audience that he has their real interests at heart by *truly* (normatively, ecotically) having them at heart (*en* "in" + *thumos* "passion, spiritedness," see §2.8). This is to say that s/he has to speak and feel (as Jeffrey Walker notes in 1994, 2000, pp. 173–74, and 2008, p. 85) "enthymematically" *as them*, doxicotically as them, through what Kenneth Burke calls the consubstantiality of identification (§2.2), as a member of the collective, but as an influential member whose speaking also shapes their real interests "at heart," which is to say, *as felt*, so that, as they are persuaded, their felt-and-believed real interests *become* what the rhetor is suggesting, and also, as that (e)merging of consensus occurs, they feel themselves being affectively and cognitively persuaded. Persuading and being persuaded, in other words, are both collective activities, corporeal-becoming-mental activities performed by the group in and through the *persons* of "the audience" and "the rhetor." The rhetor, to put that differently, is the embodied voice through which the audience discovers its real interests. Aristotle's voice as the author of the *TR* is the supervoice through which the Attic Greek community and countless communities of rhetorical scholars and practitioners since discover their real interests in the field of rhetoric as well. As Nancy Sherman (1989, p. 4) reminds us, "Aristotle himself urges us to take this role seriously: time (and future generations), he says, must be co-workers and co-discoverers in the development of his theory (1098a22)." Aristotle, after all, is not merely *describing* rhetoric; he is persuading us. And, as I will be attempting to show throughout the book, his persuasion operates as much through affective channels as it does through cognitive ones—or, more precisely, his persuasion is always entelechially affective-becoming-cognitive.

As I explain in §4.12, in somatic theory this group ecological (affect-homeostatic, ecotic/icotic) regulation of behavior, belief systems, language, and constructions of identity and reality is called the "somatic exchange." It is based on the mimetic transfer of somatic response from body to body in a group, through what has come to be called the Carpenter Effect (Carpenter, 1874), the unconscious mimicking of other people's body language in our own. This effect has been studied more recently by several groups of scholars in terms of the mimesis not merely of body *language* (the outward expressions of body states) but of the actual body states themselves. The idea, theorized and lab-tested most recently by Antonio R. Damasio's neurological research team at the University of Iowa (see Adolphs, 2002; Damasio, 2003), is that in mimicking other people's body language we actually simulate their body states in our own: hence, for example, the famous contagiousness of yawns, or of high (or low) spirits, or, most relevantly for our purposes here, of social approval and disapproval. Ultimately the somatic exchange regulates group realities by circulating ideosomatic (group-affective-becoming-conative) impulses of approval and/ or disapproval. This circulation may be set in motion by one person, by a rhetor—a group leader, or even a disruptive heckler or bully—but often seems phenomenologically to appear out of nowhere, without an instigator, as if launched more or less simultaneously by the whole group, or by a significant portion of the group; and certainly each member of the group contributes to it, circulating approval or disapproval responses through his or her body, feeling them and passing them on, and inevitably also adding her or his own slight spin (what Derrida [1971/1988] calls an "iteration") on them. This phenomenology may be largely preconscious: the somatic exchange very often operates regulatorily just below the conscious arousal levels of those involved, being mapped as feeling but not quite as thought.

This is not quite what Massumi (ibid., 35) calls "the autonomy of affect":

> Affects are *virtual synesthetic perspectives* anchored in (functionally limited by) the actually existing, particular things that embody them. The autonomy of affect is its participation in the virtual. *Its autonomy is its openness*. Affect is autonomous to the degree to which it escapes confinement in the particular body whose vitality, or potential for interaction, it is. Formed, qualified, situated perceptions and cognitions fulfilling functions of actual connection or blockage are the capture and closure of affect. Emotion is the most intense (most contracted) expression of that *capture*—and of the fact that something has always and again escaped. Something remains unactualized, inseparable from but unassimilable to any *particular*, functionally anchored perspective. That is why all emotion is more or less disorienting, and why it is classically described as being outside of oneself, at the very point at which one is most intimately and unshareably in contact with oneself and one's vitality. If there were no escape, no excess or remainder, no fade-out to infinity, the universe would be without potential, pure entropy, death. Actually existing, structured things live in and through that which escapes them. Their autonomy is the autonomy of affect.

Affect for Massumi is the vitality of the body, its "potential for interaction" with other bodies—this is specifically a Deleuzean vitalist model, with an Aristotelian entelechial concern for potentiality and actualization mixed in—but it also insistently escapes the body, and in that escape is (forever becoming) autonomous. "*Its autonomy is its openness*" in the sense of not being enclosed in the body. Affect is "captured" and "closed" in the body, and its "most intense (most contracted) expression" of that "capture and closure of affect" is emotion; but "something remains unactualized, inseparable from but unassimilable to any *particular*, functionally anchored perspective," which is to say that affect always remains partly uncaptured by and unenclosed within the individual body. Even though emotion is "the very point at which one is most intimately and unshareably in contact with oneself and one's vitality," because it is also the captured/enclosed aspect of affect, which always escapes the body, we *experience* it as disorienting, as being outside ourselves. In that extrapersonal disorientation lies our vitality, our life, our autonomy as individuals who are not entirely trapped inside embodied individuality.

Several things bother me about this formulation, though. One is Massumi's series of binarisms based metaphorically on the prison break: capture/escape, openness/(en)closedness, confinement/autonomy, emotion/affect, inside/outside, death/life. What he's doing with those binaries, obviously, is underscoring the importance of the transpersonal: we only live insofar as something that we feel escapes the prisons of our individual bodies. But why the prison metaphor? Why is it necessary to trope the body as capture, (en)closure, as an imprisoning space from which life must escape?

Massumi is enough of a poststructuralist not to enforce rigid boundaries between his binary poles—his model is all about leakage or escape across the boundary between, about "excess or remainder," and of course for him "actually existing, structured things live in and through that which escapes them"—but the very fact that his basic binary is prison/freedom conditions him to define affect as vitality as *autonomy*. This is extremely problematic. The vitality or "potential for interaction" with other bodies of affect is only autonomy, clearly, from the perspective of the individual body as the jail cell from which affect escapes. The inevitable effect of this perspective is to thematize everything outside the individual body as sheer freedom, escape-as-vitality, the prisoner's dream of total freedom outside the prison walls, which is to say as sheer negativity, the negation of confinement—leaving us no positive image of what affect actually does outside the body that so vitalizes that body. Presumably, if "potential for interaction" is any indication, what it does is interact with other bodies—that would be the actualization of the "potential for interaction"—but Massumi insists on trapping actualization too inside the individual body, so that escape from the body (and thus autonomy) is thematized as "something remain[ing] unactualized." Affect's vitality, which is also the individual body's vitality, is a potential for interaction with other bodies; but then "something remains unactualized" and affect escapes. Surely that escape *is* the actualization of the body's potential for interaction? Surely it is an escape not into vague random freedom but into interaction?

In somatic theory, the individual body is not a prison cell from which affect escapes but the communicative (ecological) medium through which affect circulates; and it is also, recursively, the collective agency that vitalizes individual bodies affectively by *guiding* the ecological circulation of affect through the other bodies in the group. Every "transformission" of affect through a body is also an *organizing* event. The body is not merely a communicative medium through which social affects pass as through air or water, but an evaluative ethecotic agency that takes the social affect coming in—notably some form of approval or disapproval—and transforms (retonalizes, reiterates) it slightly or significantly in the act of retransmitting it.

To put that differently, every transmission of affect through a body is a *rhetorical* event. It is an event grounded specifically in the purposeful organization of bodily-becoming-mental (affective-becoming-cognitive, corporeal-becoming-discursive) meaning in order to have a specific impact on an audience—namely, the other members of the group. At the moment that evaluative affect is passing through any individual member, in other words, s/he is "the rhetor" who is (in Rorty's terms) "suiting his [or her] arguments to [her or] his audience," who is "constrained by what [the group believes] is true and what [the group believes] is best," and who "must not only convince [her or] his audience that his [or her] arguments are sound, but also that, like the physician, [s/]he has their real interests—and not merely their surface desires—at heart."

Note here however that this rhetorical event is really only a freeze-frame moment in an ongoing process—that the somatic exchange consists of a continuous flow of such events, all interacting with all others, all generating collective guidance out of the interactions of all those rhetorical events. This is not rhetoric-as-persuasion, in other words, so much as it is doxicosis, the deep social ecology of persuasivity. It is what has been thought of as Aristotle's communicative triangle—"a speaker and a subject on which he speaks and someone addressed" (*TR* 1.3.1, 1358b; Kennedy, 1991/2007, p. 47)—sped up and virally decentered and affectively intensified into a telling-and-hearing becoming-communal, as each member of the group cycles through all three apices of the triangle at virtually every moment of the conversation.

1.3 Mencius as a Theorist of Rhetoric

The title of this section, and of the book, may seem strange to readers who are familiar with Mencius, as he is not generally read as an ancient Chinese theorist of rhetoric—or even as an ancient Chinese philosopher who had anything at all to say about rhetoric. What little ancient Chinese philosophers had to say about rhetoric, so the usual narrative goes, was said by Xunzi 荀子 and Han Fei 韓非, not by Mencius. In my terms from §1.1, Mencius is normally taken to be an "ethecotic" thinker, concerned with collective guidance for ethical growth, not a "doxicotic" thinker, concerned with persuasivity.

To be sure, the character 說, voiced either *shuì* and translated into English "persuade" or *shuō* and translated "say, speak," appears 21 times in the *MZ*; and in two of those occurrences, in 2A2, D. C. Lau 劉殿爵 (Lau, 1970/2003, pp. 63, 65) translates it "rhetoric": "Zai Wo and Zi Gong excelled in rhetoric [*shuì* 說]; Ran Niu, Minzi and Yan Yuan excelled in the exposition of virtuous conduct. Confucius excelled in both and yet he said, 'I am not versed in rhetoric'" (Lau's Wade-Giles romanizations pinyinized; Van Norden, 2008, p. 41 follows Lau's lead here). The original Chinese (宰我、子貢善為說辭， 冉牛、閔子、顏淵善言德行; 孔子兼之, 曰：『我於辭命, 則不能也。』[2A2]) would also allow a less obviously rhetorically oriented translation like "Zai Wo and Zi Gong were excellent teachers; Ran Niu, Minzi, and Yan Yuan were excellent teachers of virtue. Confucius excelled at both and yet he said he was not able [*zé bù néng yě* 則不能也]." And in any case the passage says nothing at all about what it might mean to excel at speaking, or at speaking persuasively, or at rhetoric. In two other chapters (5A7, 6B4) Lau (ibid., pp. 211, 267, 269) translates *shuì* 說 as "persuade," but again in neither section does Mencius specifically theorize persuasion. This is obviously far too desultory a terminological trajectory to justify studying Mencius as a theorist of rhetoric.

What this approach to the *MZ* misses, however, is the heavy emphasis the book places on advice to political leaders—various rulers and the high scholar-officials in their administrations—regarding how to govern. This is especially clear in what Brooks and Brooks (2002) regard as the "authentic core" of the *MZ*, namely 12 of the 23 chapters in Book 1: 1A1, 1A3:1–3, 1A5:1–3, 1A6, 1B1, a resequenced 1B16, 1B9, 1B10, 1B12, 1B13, 1B14, and 1B15. Eleven of those twelve chapters are addressed explicitly to rulers, and the twelfth (1B1) is addressed explicitly to a high-ranking minister or official, giving advice on how to advise the ruler most effectively. This means that the *entire* core of the *MZ*, the part that Mencius presumably either wrote himself or helped edit into something like its current form, consists of advice on how to govern the people. In only one of the 12 core chapters is his advice not addressed explicitly to a ruler; and in that single exception the focus is still on effective government.

Since according to Brooks and Brooks 2A2 was compiled around the time of Mencius's death, based on extensive interviews with his disciples, and the rest of the *MZ* was compiled by his disciples many years later, it is understandable—though not perhaps the most robust example of what Ames (2002, p. 96) calls the "resolutely historicist and genealogical" thinking of the ancient Chinese—that after the 12 core chapters of *MZ* 1 the stories told about Mencius should become shorter and more aphoristic, and his sayings increasingly decontextualized:

> 153 (62%) of the 248 chapters that make up the later parts of *MZ* 1 and *MZ* 2–7 are addressed to no one in particular (they typically begin *Mèngzǐ yuē* 孟子曰 "Mencius said")

56 (23%) narrate a (probably fictionalized or reconstructed) conversation between Mencius and one of his disciples, most commonly with the disciple asking for clarification on some point of the Mencian world view (sometimes apparently seeking to catch him out in a contradiction) and Mencius responding

MZ 4 and 7 in particular consist almost exclusively of very short chapters, each for the most part made up of a single Mencian aphorism without rhetorical context. 3A6, 6A1–6, and 6B1 consist of disputations with philosophical opponents, contributing to the impression modern readers may take away from the *MZ* that it is a series of universally applicable philosophical statements.

Still, 29 (12%) of the later chapters of the book (especially the inserted chapters of *MZ* 1 and *MZ* 2, 3, and 5) retain the form of what Brooks and Brooks call the "genuine" core of *MZ* 1, with Mencius in conversation with a ruler or a high scholar-official, giving advice on how to govern. In addition, the decontextualization process that has led to the impression that the *MZ* consists entirely of Mencius giving advice to anyone who happens to read it has also left traces of the original rhetorical situations in which Mencius supposedly gave the reported advice, with 57 chapters implicitly addressed to rulers, 23 to high scholar-officials, and 7 to a small elite group potentially including rulers, high scholar-officials, and the exemplary persons from whose ranks rulers and scholar-officials were (at least ideally) recruited. If we add the numbers from the *MZ* 1 core to these, 41 (18%) of the total 260 chapters are explicitly and 87 (33%) are implicitly addressed to rulers or high scholar-officials and aimed at giving "doxicotic" advice on how to govern. Even allowing for the natural decontextualization that would have resulted from the passage of time after Mencius's death, in other words, *more than half* of the *MZ* chapters are primarily organized around the offering of advice to governmental policymakers.[3] And, since most of the chapters that are implicitly addressed to anyone who happens to be reading the book are very short aphorisms, the proportions are even clearer in a character count: chapters explicitly or implicitly offering governmental advice to rulers or high scholar-officials account for just over 33,000 characters; chapters implicitly addressed to anyone who happens to pick up the book in search of an "ethecotic" guide to virtuous living for just over 6,000.

Historically, however, this policy-wonk rhetorical situation has been problematic for scholars of the *MZ*, especially during the many centuries of despotic rule in China. As Huang (2001, pp. 256–57) notes, readings of the *MZ* have tended to take one or more of three hermeneutical lines, the personal, the political, and the apologetic—the personal line aimed at "ecotic" development of virtuous self-cultivation in ordinary individuals and groups, the apologetic at defending the Confucian tradition against Daoism and Buddhism. The political line, Huang (ibid., p. 257) adds, has traditionally faced the most resistance from above: "Chinese politics was monarchical, centered on the ruler, while the political ideal of Confucianism was centered on the people. In desperation, many Confucian scholars devoted themselves to ostensibly pure scholarship," which is to say, to the personal and apologetic lines. Given that Mencius was the most radically influential proponent in the Confucian tradition of placing the people at the center of politics and (even in his advice to rulers) regarding the ruler as peripheral, commentaries on the *MZ* have been especially fraught in this political sense; and as Huang (ibid., p. 2–7) also notes, the Confucian scholars most interested in advancing explicitly political readings of the *MZ* have typically been political reformers.

Zhu Yuanzhang (朱元璋, 1328–1398, r. 1368–1396), founder of the Ming Dynasty (明朝, 1368–1644), ran the whole gamut of attitudes toward the *MZ*. Born to an impoverished peasant family, at 24 he became an insurgent fighting against the unraveling Mongol empire, and quickly rose through the ranks until he was commanding the rebel forces struggling to unite China. At that time he revered Mencius. Even after conquering Nanjing (南京) in 1356 and hearing a lecture on Mencius's populist notions of government, he was favorably impressed. But when he assumed the imperial throne in 1368, his attitudes underwent an abrupt about-face. Reading "If a prince treats his subjects as mud and weeds, they will treat him as an enemy" (Lau, 1970/2003, p. 128), he exploded with wrath and banned the *MZ*. When a minister bravely appealed the decision, the emperor assigned Chancellor of the Hanlin Academy Liu Sanwu (劉三吾, 1312–ca. 1399) the task of expurgating it, leading to the 1394 publication of the abridged *MZ*; the removed passages were restored two decades later by the third Ming emperor Yong Le (永樂, 1360–1424, r. 1402–1424).

The original canonization of the *MZ* by Zhu Xi (朱熹, 1130–1200) as one of the Four Books of Confucianism (along with *The Great Learning*, the *Doctrine of the Mean*, and the *Analects of Confucius*), was partly driven by this political tension as well. (Neo-)Confucian scholar-officials in the Song Dynasty (960–1279) found themselves in a political situation similar to Mencius's own in the Warring States period and hoped to instigate political changes along Mencian lines; the *MZ* was frequently used in political rhetoric to justify specific policies. Many Song emperors, too, proclaimed themselves patrons of the *MZ*. But somehow, as if coincidentally, the understanding of Mencius that established the MZ as one of the Four Books and dominated Mencian studies for six centuries—Zhu Xi's own—was based on a rationalistic and dualistic misreading of Mencius that justified despotic rule (see Huang, 2001, p. 217). Zhu was also for many centuries the most influential voice arguing that the *MZ* was addressed not to rulers and scholar-officials, as the Han commentator Zhao Qi 趙岐 (d. 201) had earlier argued, but to ordinary people, to teach them how to grow ethically toward sagehood (Martinich and Xiao, 2010, p. 93).

Dai Zhen's (戴震, 1724–1777) successful deconstruction of Zhu's Neo-Confucian misreading effectively established for the modern era the philologically and philosophically more defensible integrated (nondualizing) reading of the book, theoretically opening the door to new protodemocratic or populist readings of Mencius; but in fact Dai's intellectual legacy has largely been apolitical as well, leading to major "personal" or ecotic readings of the *MZ* by such influential twentieth-century Mencian commentators as Tang Junyi (唐君毅, 1909–1978) and Mou Zongsan (牟宗三, 1909–1995), both of whom fled the PRC in 1949 for Hong Kong, where Tang was instrumental in creating (and Mou later taught at) New Asia College, which eventually expanded into the Chinese University of Hong Kong. More politically activist readings of the *MZ* have been offered as well, from Huang Zongxi (黃宗羲, 1610–1695) in the early Qing Dynasty (see de Bary, 1993) to Kang Youwei (康有為, 1858–1927) in the late Qing, and in the revolutionary period from Sun Yat-sen (Sun Zhongshan 孫中山, 1866–1925) to Xu Fuguan (徐复观, 1903–1982), advisor to Dr. Sun's successor Chiang Kai-shek (Jiang Zhongzheng 蔣中正, 1887–1975) until 1946. But this was very much a minority approach to the *MZ*, and for obvious reasons considered a political powderkeg. The Qing Dynasty *MZ*-based advocacy of constitutional ideals from Huang to Kang met with fierce opposition from the various emperors, and those Mencian ideals were never put into play politically; and to the extent that twentieth-century revolutionary politics were influenced by Mencian thinking, the results were invariably less than Mencian-utopian, repeatedly embittering Xu and others.

There is another reason as well for the tendency in Mencius studies to focus on personal growth: the default audience is obviously going to be larger for such ethexegetics than it is for a focus on governmental policy decisions. An ecotic reading of the MZ that treats Mencius's advice as addressed to anyone who wants to live more virtuously tends to make the book "universally" relevant to contemporary readers. Indeed, since its Confucian canonization in the late twelfth century, the *MZ* in China has hegemonically been read as a guide to virtuous living for ordinary people. Until the revolutionary upheavals of the twentieth century, key passages from it were assigned to Chinese schoolchildren to memorize, precisely as that sort of ecotic guide for their future lives. In that historico-philosophico-pedagogical context, the fact that more than half of the book's chapters (accounting for 85% of the book's characters) revolve around very specific advice to rulers and their advisors on how to rule may even seem like a distraction from its contemporary (or "universal") relevance.

It is perhaps in this sense that Huang (2001), on whose history of Chinese Mencius-hermeneutics my discussion in the previous five paragraphs relies heavily, and who devotes considerable space in his book to political readings and applications of the *MZ*, says that of the three hermeneutical "lines" in Mencius studies, the personal, the political, and the apologetic, "the first is most important" (257–58). The personal line is, obviously, the most important for the large audience. Behuniak (2005) too, after devoting four long chapters to the study of Mencius's ethecotic advice to ordinary people on how to "become human"—how to aspire to greater virtue and so fuller humanity—devotes a three-page section in his final chapter to "The Conditions for Political Legitimacy." Most of that very brief section is devoted to an unpacking of key passages in the *Zhōngyōng* 中庸 and *Guōdiàn Chǔ* strips (郭店楚簡), but he also pauses briefly to summarize Tang's (1962) reading of *tiān mìng* 天命 "heavenly ordinance" in the *MZ*:

> In the *Mencius*, the conditions that facilitate moral and political legitimacy are brought about as a result of the associated humanity (*ren* 仁) exhibited by the ruler. Through the personal cultivation of associated humanity, the ruler's "force of character" (*de* 德) becomes authoritative in its influence on the sociopolitical realm: "forces" then turn in favor of the ruler. (Behuniak, 2005, p. 110)

Having covered political legitimacy, then, he returns to consider individual aspiration to "the human way" in the context of "the conditions" (see §4.5)—"There is nothing that is without conditions [*feiming* 非命]" (7A2; Behuniak, 2005, p. 113)—and the importance of "getting the most out of one's disposition," "cultivating one's person in solitude if need be" (ibid.). And then, by way of concluding the chapter and the book, he adds, almost parenthetically: "For those who hold political power, however, this is not enough. Rulers must do more: they must establish socioeconomic conditions that promote the novel expression of human experience collectively" (ibid., p. 123). The *MZ*, this implies, is for all of us as private individuals; but we should not forget, however belatedly, that it also has special implications for rulers.

Yet another recent example is Birdwhistell (2007, p. 105), whose central claim is that, "despite his position of political superiority and power, the ruler is urged [by Mencius] to behave in two new ways—first like a subordinate in the position of a son, younger brother, and wife toward the aged, and second, like one who is a moral superior as a good mother, as a father and mother, or a motherly kind of father to the young." This is a book, in other words, that is primarily focused on Mencius's advice to rulers, and in particular the radical way in which Mencius appropriates maternal thinking as a model for rule while still peripheralizing mothers as model family members; and yet she insists that "Mencius is interested in the behavior of the ruler because it affects the lives of the people, who are his ultimate concern" (59). That is certainly how the book has traditionally been read; but, given that we have no way of determining "his ultimate concern," it is at the very least no less likely that Mencius is interested in the lives of the people because they are so powerfully impacted by the behavior of rulers. (Yes, Mencius is widely known to be a populist philosopher who puts the people ahead of the ruler; but this might be read as primarily a lesson in humility for the ruler.)

Zhang (2010) offers yet another twist: his reading is that Mencius means two very different things by *rén* 仁 (see chapter 2), one when he is talking about the individual's ethical growth toward full *humanity*, quite another when he is advising rulers on how to achieve *rén zhèng* 仁政, which is usually translated "*benevolent* government." 仁-as-humanity, Zhang argues, is based on a recognition of and respect for the humanity of other people; 仁-as-(the-ruler's-)benevolence, on the other hand, seems predicated on a conception of the people as small children or domesticated animals, helpless not-quite-humans who need a benevolent ruler to protect and shelter them because they are incapable of doing so on their own. Zhang's argument is that, while it is quite understandable that Mencius had to present his advice to rulers in this antipopulist mode in Warring States China, it is a philosophical error of considerable magnitude, one that continues to shape domestic policy in the PRC today.

Let us construct these different readings of the *MZ* as three different takes on its relevance to us, its readers in the present:

> [a] The traditional "personal growth" interpretation tends [1] to read Mencius's advice to rulers as advice to ordinary people

and [2] to ignore or downplay any passages that don't lend themselves to that reading.

[b] Birdwhistell's gender-based interpretation tends to find contemporary relevance in Mencius's risky but praiseworthy expansion of patriarchal masculinity, which involves [1] advising rulers and other elite men on how to become more compassionate (and thus more motherly) while [2] continuing to exclude mothers and wives from patriarchal philosophizing.

[c] Zhang's political-science interpretation finds two kinds of relevance: [1] one (a salutary one) for personal growth, [2] the other (a disastrous one) for Chinese politics.

There [c1] is at least structurally congruent with [a1]; what Zhang adds to the debate is a new attention to the moments in the *MZ* that were glossed over in [a2], yielding a much more critical assessment of the book in [c2]. By the same token, Birdwhistell's contribution particularizes the "personal growth" reading by noting that it is advice not to all human beings but to men alone, and specifically to elite men—and insists that while it is *good* advice, and thus potentially relevant to readers today, the fact that it excludes lower-class men and women of all classes either diminishes its contemporary relevance or requires of readers the kind of inattentive "soft focus" that would allow [b1] advice to elite men to be taken as [a1, c1] advice to anybody.

In addition to these three approaches, however, I suggest that there is another way of reading the *MZ* that makes its political advice equally relevant to contemporary "ordinary" (non-policy-wonk, non-elite-male, non-PRC) readers: we can treat the political advice on how to govern not as *ethecotic* advice on how to grow in virtue but as *doxicotic* advice on how to persuade. Behuniak (2005, p. 123) seems to preclude such an approach by reducing the *MZ*'s advice to rulers to helping them "establish socioeconomic conditions"; but he goes on to note that rulers must be taught to "bring about order without coercion by facilitating the free intercourse of associated humanity (*ren* 仁)"—and what is involved in "bring[ing] about order without coercion" if not rhetoric? How does the ruler "facilitat[e] the free intercourse of associated humanity" except rhetorically?

The reason we don't automatically associate those facilitations with rhetoric may be that they aren't necessarily verbal. They don't necessarily involve arguments, enthymemes, proofs, tropes, *topoi,* all the painstakingly labeled and classified persuasive structures that we in the West, based on narrow readings of Aristotle's *TR* and its many successors (by Cicero, Quintilian, etc.), take to constitute the "art of rhetoric." They undeniably involve the mobilization of some sort of collective will to act, and thus action-directed persuasion as collective conation; but because the persuasion in question consists of nudges and pressures that are not always verbal, or even clearly structured, we have been disinclined to associate the whole process with rhetoric.

My brief in this book is that rhetoric properly understood—and here I am thinking primarily of Kenneth Burke's (1950/1969) approach in *A Rhetoric of Motives* (see §2.2)—is broad enough to include the kinds of pressures with which Mencius is centrally concerned, namely, how to get people to do things that are good for themselves and others, but may be unattractive because they involve too much hard work. We might tabulate Mencius's philosophical priorities like this:

[1] First in importance for him is the issue of what a ruler should do in order to rule more indirectly, with less coercion—which is to say, how the ruler should *persuade* his subjects rather than simply commanding and then doling out rewards for compliance and punishments for noncompliance. (This obviously constructs the *MZ*'s advice to rulers differently from Zhang, for whom Mencius sees rén zhèng 仁政 not as persuasive government but as paternalistic government.) *Governance at the highest levels as a doxicotic becoming-persuasive.*

[2] Second in importance is how that ruler's advisors should talk to him so as to persuade him to rule more indirectly. *Political advice at the highest levels as a doxicotic becoming-persuasive.*

[3] Third is how potential and actual advisors to that ruler should themselves be trained to think about their job, so as to maximize their effectiveness in persuading the ruler to take their advice. Which scholars should take the job of advisor to the ruler, and what should be the criteria they should follow in deciding whether to accept the job if offered, or in staying on in the job if appointed, or in giving the ruler incidental

advice after leaving if such advice is solicited? (Note that all of Mencius's disciples are, like their Master, themselves potential future advisors to (1) rulers and (2) scholar-officials as well as (4) the people.) *The training of an entire intellectual class as a doxicotic becoming-persuasive.*

[4] Fourth and last in importance is the issue of how "the common people" should be persuaded to grow toward virtue—that which many commentators have made the work's primary concern. As Zhang (2010) also shows, Mencius certainly does believe that anyone can become a sage (6B2), but the *MZ* does not devote significant attention to this fourth concern. When the common people are mentioned (e.g., 1A7, 2B4, 3A3–4, 7A5), it is typically in an "understanding" (sympathetic but condescending, even infantilizing) tone that is explicitly oriented toward the extreme unlikelihood of their ever rising much above animal status. *The rhetorical training of the ethecotic trainers of ordinary people as a doxicotic becoming-persuasive.*

The passages from the *MZ* that are cited by commentators as support for (4) "universal" (everyman's and everywoman's) growth toward virtue are in fact very often addressed either to (1) a ruler or to (2–3) a high government scholar-official, and, as we saw in [a2], above, are read "modernizingly" by readers today through the more or less unconscious stratagem of bracketing the high position of the explicit or implicit governmental addressee—or perhaps of [a1] unconsciously democratizing that high position, so that advice to an autocrat in Warring States China is tacitly reframed as advice to any member of a democratic society today.

My point here is not that readers should refrain from such "modernizing/democratizing" readings of the *MZ*. Reconstructions of what the *MZ* must have been in its original historical context are valuable, of course, but I do not believe that they are the only valuable way of reading the book. All I am suggesting is that, when we modernize and democratize the book, when we read advice to rulers as if it were advice to us as "commoners," or advice to elite men as if it were advice to human beings of both sexes/genders and all classes, we not *radically reduce* [RR] Mencius's advice all the way down to advice on "how to live virtuously," or "how to become (more) virtuous," or even, in Behuniak's terms, "how to become human."

Backing off that radical reduction one small but significant notch [RR-1], we might also reduce the book to advice on "how to live virtuously *with others*," or "how to treat others more virtuously"—after all, *rén* 仁 is specifically a collectivist virtue, a culturally organized inclination to live effectively and harmoniously with others.

But I am recommending backing off the radical modernizing/democratizing reduction yet another notch [RR-2], to something like advice on "how to give advice to others in order to move the group most effectively toward harmonious living together," or, more subtly, "how to nudge others in order to bring about the most harmonious group life"—or, in the technical terms I coined and preliminarily theorized in §1.1, doxicotic advice on ethecosis (see §4.15–16 for further theorization). In other words, to the extent that we identify with the rulers and advisors and other high officials and elite males to whom Mencius addresses his advice, we should take that advice to be not just *moral instruction* but *moral meta-instruction*, and thus as *applied rhetorical theory*—advice not just on aspiring to greater individual virtue but on pushing the group, including oneself, rhetorically (doxicotically) to aspire to greater collective (ethecotic) virtue.

This displaced (modernized/democratized, RR-2) understanding of the *MZ* as a study of rhetoric is remarkably close, I suggest, to Aristotle's express purpose in the *TR*: to help members of a democratic society learn to "rule" (or guide) it through persuasive speech. Athens in Aristotle's day was a democracy, something that did not give Aristotle, an aristocrat himself, a great deal of satisfaction; nevertheless, as a philosopher and teacher he recognized the importance of theorizing, and training his students for, rhetorical participation in democratic (collective self-)rule, which is to say a doxicotic becoming-persuasive. China in Mencius's day was a collection of autocracies at seemingly perpetual war with one another;[4] as a would-be "protodemocrat,"[5] as it were, a philosopher-sage and sometime advisor to rulers who was dedicated to the spread of virtue as harmonious group living and thus to the transformation of autocratic rule in a more persuasion-based direction, Mencius had a far less obvious mandate for his theories of rhetoric than had Aristotle. A rhetorical approach to rule was a potentially revolutionary idea that, as Zhang (2010, p. 67) also notes, he had to smuggle into his advice to rulers, typically in the form of history lessons (the Former Kings ruled this way) and pragmatic appeals to opportunistic power lusts (this is the best way to consolidate and protect your power). Aristotle, an aristocrat at heart, is driven by political pragmatism to give his students democratic advice; Mencius, a populist (*rén*-ist 仁

者) at heart, is driven to present his Confucian Way to rulers as political pragmatism.

1.4 The "Historical" Mencius and the "Literary" Mencius

To what extent are the claims I make here about "what Mencius said" and "what Mencius meant" true of the actual historical Confucian sage, and to what extent do they merely take the literary representation of Mencius in the text named for him at face value? Or, to put that rather more tendentiously, to what extent am I guilty of reifying a literary character as an actual historical philosopher on a par with Aristotle?

These nagging worries arise from the speculative but on the face of it quite persuasive periodization of the composition of the *MZ* that we've just seen being offered by Brooks and Brooks (2002); they do after all explicitly divide the various chapters and sections of the book into "genuine" texts written by or in conjunction with the historical Mencius and "spurious" texts written by two later Mencian schools that in effect invent Mencius as an authenticating literary character. The more tendentious second question in the previous paragraph reflects the strong negativity implied in their adjective "spurious": the upshot of Brooks and Brooks's periodization would appear to be that any attempt to understand the philosophy of the historical "Mencius" by reading anything outside of 12 chapters in *MZ* 1 and possibly 2A2 is meretricious.

The fact that I look closely at none of those 12 chapters, which Brooks and Brooks speculate were based on actual interviews with Mencius and composed ca. 320–310 BCE, when Mencius was in his fifties and early sixties, and so that I derive exactly *none* of my key Mencian theorizations from the "historical" Mencius, obviously means that my understanding of the deep ecology of rhetoric in Mencius is based on analysis of Mencius as a literary construct, not of the "real" or "true" historical Mencius. If Brooks and Brooks are right, all my claims are about the "spurious" or literary Mencius.

I wonder, though: does a speculative periodization of the text's composition make the Mencius who speaks in those specific chapters in *MZ* 1 any less literary? Even if it were possible to establish that only those chapters are "genuine" in the sense that the historical Mencius actually wrote them, or worked on them—and of course Brooks and Brooks freely admit that it isn't possible, that their periodization is at best a "hypothesis," and will always be—the ontology of that "historical Mencius" in the *MZ* is still literary, still a construct. He is still a character in a series of more or less contextualized dialogues. The same would have been true of the historical Socrates in Plato's dialogues had Socrates actually co-written or edited one or two before his death. The same is true when the author of a novel names a character or the narrator after him/herself—and, students of autobiography emphatically agree, when the author of a memoir or autobiography does the same. Creating oneself as a character in a written text effectively fictionalizes that self.

More: while reading a memoir, or a novel that is clearly a thinly veiled autobiography, or a philosophical dialogue co-written by someone named in it, any attempt one makes to separate specific "true" or "genuine" or "historically accurate" details out from lies and distortions and "spurious" claims is an act not of forensic science, but of literary criticism. There is nothing any reader of the *MZ* can do to any specific dialogue in it that can transform the literary Mencius in it into "the historical Mencius." All one can do is try to persuade one's own readers to *act as if* (they believed that) one's historicized Mencius-construct were actually the historical Mencius. The fact that "Mencius" as a literary character is internally inconsistent, and that the inconsistencies in that character can usefully be explained through a speculative periodization of its composition, emphatically does not sort the sayings of Mencius into "genuine" historical documents and "spurious" literary fictions; it simply means that, like any problematic literary construct, it is open to many different kinds of interpretation, all of which proceed by seeking out and attempting to explain patterns. Brooks and Brooks's periodization is one such interpretation—an intriguing and persuasive one, but still just an interpretation.

So how do I construct a coherent literary/philosophical Mencius-construct? Brooks and Brooks (2002, p. 273) depict the long chapter 2A2, dealing with *zhī yán* 知言 "knowing speech" and *yǎng qì* 養氣 "cultivating energy," as based on "composite remembered Mencian conversations" from around the time of his death in 303 BCE. I devote considerable attention in chapter 3 to the implications of *zhī yán* 知言 "knowing speech," especially the energizing of speech through body language, and the use of the flood-like *qì* 氣 to *read* the dispositional traces left by that energizing of speech on and in the body. Brooks and Brooks would accord that discussion of Mencius relatively more historical credibility than my discussions of *MZ* 3–7, based on their speculation that 2A2 was composed when memories of the actual conversations that fed it were still fresh in the Mencian disciples' minds; but I find close parallels with the 2A2 passages I discuss in 4A15, 6B15, and especially 7A21, which they tentatively assign to early, middle, and late northern-school strata, from around 300, 286, and 250 BCE, respectively.

In my discussion, the idealized image of the good ruler, based on a compassionate and persuasion-based participation in *rén* 仁 "fellow-feeling," derives from chapters in *MZ* 2 and 4 that Brooks and Brooks assign to both schools' early period, around 300 BCE. From the northern school, according to the Brooks and Brooks model, this would include the notions that only people who participate in fellow-feeling should be allowed to rule (4A1–3); that if you try to govern (*zhì* 治) others and they aren't governed (*zhì* 治), you should look back at your own wisdom (4A4); that it's important (but difficult) for ministers to get non-fellow-feeling rulers to "participate in words" (*yǔ yán zāi* 與言哉: 4A8); and that fellow-feeling has attractive powers (4A9). From the southern school, it would include the notion that honor follows from fellow-feeling and disgrace follows from its lack (2A4), the discussion of the four hearts (2A6, but also 6A6, the parallel passage from possibly around two decades later in the northern school), and the more panegyric version of 4A9 in the Confucian paean to the beauty of the hometown full of fellow-feeling (2A7).

As I develop it here, the Mencian doctrine of "human nature" (in the broad sense of "what humans are like and how they got to be that way") is mostly a product, in Brooks and Brooks's periodization, of the northern school in the middle period: the disputation with Gaozi (6A1–6), Ox Mountain (6A8), the notion that fellow-feeling is human feeling (*rén, rén xīn yě* 仁, 人心也: 6A11), the notion that when feeling becomes thinking, it engages (6A15), and the discussion of body language mentioned above (6B15).

The late period, according to Brooks and Brooks, runs from the appointment of Xunzi 荀子 as Magistrate of Lanling (蘭陵令) in 255 BCE to the conquest of Lu (魯國) by Chu (楚國) in 249 BCE; the northern school's contribution to my understanding of Mencius here, on their hypothesis, would include the notion that the best way to "get the most" out of one's heart (*xīn* 心) is to know and follow one's own inclinations (*xìng* 性), and to know/follow one's own inclinations is to know/serve *tiān* 天 (7A1); the rooting of the four shoots (*sì duān* 四端) in the heart and *xìng* 性 as something one gradually learns to embody (7A21); and the inspiring of people by *dào* 道 when the world is "on the way" (7A42). The southern school's late contribution to my Mencius, if Brooks and Brooks are right, would tend to be focused on *lǐ* 禮 (ritual propriety): the five relationships

(3A4) and the somatic signaling (breaking out in a sweat) to the ancient Chinese that they needed to bury their dead (3A5).

Brooks and Brooks (2002, p. 274n3) argue rather strenuously against what they call "the integral view of the *Mencius*," especially the old idealized assumption that "the text was written by Mencius in retirement, in collaboration with several disciples." They react with incredulity to the opinion voiced by one of the external evaluators for the University of Hawai'i Press to the effect that no one believes in this old fairy tale any more, and that therefore Brooks and Brooks have nothing new to offer—and it seems to me that they are right to be incredulous. Nearly every Mencius scholar I've read, including all the other articles in Chan (2002), has constructed a unified or integrated Mencius as the "author" or perhaps collectivized authorial consciousness behind the text. The only exception in my reading has been Birdwhistell (2007), who tends to take the periodization in Brooks and Brooks (2002) as simple historical fact, rather than as the provocative and highly speculative hypothesis as which they themselves present it.

It's true that their hypothesis might be used to put to rest certain long-standing debates, such as the one between Roger T. Ames (1991, 2002a) and Irene Bloom (1994, 1997, 2002) over *xing* 性 (see §4.3), which flares up again in Chan (2002b); Brooks and Brooks (2002, p. 269) suggest that their dispute may be explained by the fact that Bloom tends to focus on *MZ* 6, from the middle northern period, and Ames tends to focus on *MZ* 7, from the late northern period, and the northern school seems to have changed their minds (perhaps through responding to critiques) over the intervening three or four decades. But does this really mean that *imposing* a unified mentality on Mencius—interpreting the literary text in terms of its unity rather than its disunity, constructing it as a coherent philosophy rather than deconstructing it in terms of its inconsistencies—is now a retrograde, uncritical activity? Grounded as my thought is in American pragmatism, which is grounded in turn in German Idealism going back to Kant, I tend to assume that all texts, including the *MZ* and its many philosophical and philological commentaries, and including Brooks and Brooks (2002), are interpretive constructs imposed on disparate and contested (and ultimately inaccessible) facts. As I say, I find Brooks and Brooks extremely persuasive; but the historical disparity they hypothesize, so far from obviating any unified claims I or anyone else might want to make about "what Mencius thought," simply complicates the process of imposing a unified interpretation on it—an ongoing project in which they themselves are manifestly and brilliantly engaged.

1.5 Sino-Hellenism

To the extent that the book is a comparative study of Mencius and Aristotle, it situates itself in the long and somewhat problematic tradition of Sino-Hellenist studies—problematic not just because of its Orientalist origins and some surviving Orientalist undertones, but because of tensions in the West between Sinologists and comparative philosophers, who bring their very different sets of expectations and methodological orientations to the comparative project. Obviously if one is mainly interested in Greek philosophy or science or storytelling and uses early China as a point of comparison, one is likely to see the Chinese texts as secondary, even inadequate in some way; and contrariwise, if one is mainly interested in Chinese philosophy or science or storytelling and uses early Greece as a point of comparison, one is likely to see the Greek texts as secondary and even inadequate. Most Sino-Hellenists work very hard not to lean in either direction, to find a balance, and thus to portray both traditions as equally interesting and intelligent; but of course the very need to *try* and achieve a balance implies an inclination to lean one way or the other.

What makes this book somewhat different from the Sino-Hellenist mainstream is that I am mainly interested in neither early China nor early Greece—in neither Mencius nor Aristotle—but in rhetoric, and specifically in somato-ecological theories of rhetoric. As it happens—or at least so I claim here—both Mencius and Aristotle explore the *deep social ecology* of rhetoric, and both ground their understanding of that ecology in the ecotic/icotic circulation of evaluative affect(-becoming-conation) through groups. As rough contemporaries who articulate similar but not quite convergent ecological theories of rhetoric, they are both about equally interesting to me. (To put that differently: I'm interested in *constructing* or *consolidating* through a close comparative look at Mencius and Aristotle a single unified deep ecology of rhetoric.)

As a result, I tend to construct Mencius and Aristotle more in terms of their similarities than in terms of their differences. This approach to the Sino-Hellenic juxtaposition differs markedly from the standard views in the field, according to which the Greeks are more "analytical" and "decontextualizing," the Chinese more "resolutely historicist and genealogical," and thus "resistant to articulation in theoretical and conceptual terms that presupposes unfamiliar notions such as objectivity and strict identity, notions that have underwritten dualistic thinking as a Western cultural dominant" (Ames, 2002, p. 96). Depending on how one feels about analytical decontextualization, objectivity, and strict identity, or the other items Ames (ibid.) lists as "of central importance in Western epistemology" and minimally relevant in China—"principles, univocal meanings, correspondence between propositions and states-of-affairs, and a sense of reference"—this standard comparison can go either way, either making the Greeks look scientific and the Chinese primitive or making the Chinese look attentive to situational and historical complexity and the Greeks look cut off from everyday pragmatic reality.

In setting up his persuasive ecological reading of Mencius, for example, Behuniak (2005, p. xii) works hard to distinguish Mencian thinking from "Aristotelian" misreadings of the *MZ* among Western Sinologists:

> Many of the most qualified interpreters of classical Chinese thought incline towards such an understanding in treating what is commonly understood to be the notion of "human nature" (*renxing* 人性) in the *Mencius*. Benjamin Schwartz [1985: 175] understands *xing* 性 to be "an innate tendency toward growth or development in a given, predetermined direction." Robert Eno [1990: 121] considers "Heaven" (*tian* 天) itself a "teleological force" that engenders a good "nature" (*xing* 性) in human beings and thereby "indicates what man's purpose, or 'final cause,' is to be." In the same vein, P. J. Ivanhoe [1997: 156] submits that for Mencius, to follow one's nature (*xing*) is "the way to both understand and fulfill heaven's plan." A. C. Graham [1989: 136], at one point in his career, considers *xing* to be a notion developed "on lines rather suggestive of Aristotelian teleology." Throughout the secondary literature, the default understanding of *xing* is "nature" with a predetermined end. The botanical metaphor [that informs Mencian thinking] is usually understood as reinforcing the fixity of this end.

Behuniak's critique here is that Western Sinologists have assimilated Mencian thought too radically to Aristotelian thought; his book is a salutary attempt to explore the *MZ* in its own Chinese light, as radically different from "Aristotelian teleology." I will be relying heavily on Behuniak's reading of the *MZ* in what follows; but I want also to suggest that his juxtaposition of an ecological Mencius over against a teleological Aristotle rests in part on a (well-established) misreading of Aristotle.

As Cheng Zhongying 成中英 (Cheng, 1991, p. 6) puts the standard juxtaposition between Chinese and Western philosophy, broadly:

Chinese Philosophy and Western Philosophy
Contrast in Development and Possible Integration

Chinese Philosophy	Western Philosophy
Basic Orientations	
1. Harmonizing human experience with human thinking	1. Overcoming human experience by human thinking
2. Nonreductive naturalism	2. Reductive rationalism
Development and Possible Integration	
1. Naturalization (nature and naturality in Chinese philosophy: *I Ching/Tao Te Ching*)	1. Rationalization (reason and rationality in Greek philosophy: Socrates/Plato/Aristotle)
2. Humanization (classical Confucianism)	2. Transcendentalization (Judeo-Christianity)
3. Interplay between naturalization and humanization (Neo-Confucianism)	3. Interplay between rationalization and transcendentalization (modern science and modern rationalistic philosophy)
4. Future development in light of interaction with Western orientation	4. Future development in light of interaction with Chinese orientation
5. Possible rationalization of naturalization	5. Possible naturalization of rationalization

Cheng there obviously seeks not only a delicate value-balance between Chinese and Western philosophy but a convergence, an integration; still, his sense of the two traditions as occupying neatly opposed positions reflects most thinking in the field.

But not all. Schaberg (2002, pp. 159–60), for example, identifies an often forgotten current in Aristotle's thought that is far more similar to Chinese thought than is often recognized:

> It is true, as Lloyd has argued, that Aristotle's systematic analysis of the techniques of logic and rhetoric has no Chinese counterpart.

The fragmentary advice on argumentation writers such as Xunzi and Han Fei [韓非] give bears on the psychology of persuasion and the selection of materials, but never compasses the science of the syllogism. Aristotle, on the other hand, presented in the *Organon* a comprehensive account of the syllogism as an inductive and deductive means of establishing truth. Yet that the *Organon* (especially the *Topics* and the *Sophistical Refutations*) and the *Rhetoric* also address the means of establishing merely apparent truths is remarkable. As he systematized the mechanisms of truth, Aristotle also took pains to describe the tools of nontruth; the needs of public debaters and orators were never far from his mind. By embedding syllogistic in a comprehensive guide to public argumentation, Aristotle himself cleared the way for a different sort of comparison, one that focuses not on the presence or absence of instruments of infallibility, but on the probable and specious things that, for historical and cultural reasons, could pass for truth in most practical argumentation. On this level, the practical rhetoric of fourth-century Athens and the literary reflections of rhetoric in Warring States Chinese texts have much in common, and certain of the Greek writer's observations have unexpected resonances in the Chinese texts. Formalizations of logic, whether Aristotle's syllogistic or the Later Mohists [*sic*] system of definitions and propositions, are comparable in that they are purified precipitations from within the arts of persuasion.

This is an important corrective: it is not so much that Chinese and Greek conceptions of rhetoric (and everything else) are fundamentally philosophically opposed, as Ames and Cheng and many others suggest, as it is that more rationalist formulations tend to emerge out of the less clearly crystallized pushes and pulls of practical rhetoric. Nor is Schaberg implying, I think, that "formalizations of logic" as "purified precipitations from within the arts of persuasion" represent a kind of inevitable and laudable teleology in both Athens and Warring States China; his brief is merely that something like this "precipitation" happened, and even, more realistically still, that it was *one* thing that happened, among many.

This book arises out of the conviction that, salutary as Schaberg's intervention is, it does not go far enough. His contrast between syllogistic and enthymematic reasoning in Aristotle recognizes the important differences in Aristotle's own conceptions of rhetoric between pure abstract logic and the realities of the rhetorical "marketplace" (actually the courts and the legislative assemblies), but still tends to privilege the *form* and *content* of rhetoric without taking into consideration rhetoric's socio-ecological conditions of possibility. Schaberg's formulation takes as its implicit norm *how the rhetor constructs arguments,* and so tends to rule beyond the rhetorical pale considerations of "the psychology of persuasion and the selection of materials," which as he says is all the "fragmentary advice on argumentation" given by Xunzi 荀子 and Han Fei 韓非 amounts to. But of course a very large portion—arguably the bulk—of the *TR* is devoted to "the psychology of persuasion and the selection of materials" as well. *TR* 2:2–11 on the emotions and 2:12–19 on the dispositions offer the first comprehensive psychology in history; and the lengthy discussions of *topoi* in *TR* 1:4–14 and 2:19–23 and elsewhere in the *TR* and other treatises (especially the *Topics*) are explicitly focused not just on the selection of materials but the processes by which the rhetor converts "found" materials like topics, probabilities, and signs into enthymematic arguments.

Schaberg's reading of Aristotle and Warring States Chinese conceptions of rhetoric might be schematized like this:

Syllogistic argumentation		*Enthymematic argumentation*
pure logic "mechanisms of truth" "instruments of infallibility"	emerges (or is "purified" or "precipitated") out of	practical persuasion "tools of nontruth" probabilistic and specious arguments that may be taken for truth

As noted in §1.1, the contrast I offer here is a more radical one between rationalistic and ecological conceptions of rhetoric—between rhetoric as argument and rhetoric as the viral circulation of affective intensities, as an energy-exchange. As we've seen in Ames's and Cheng's formulations, many Sino-Hellenist comparativists identify something like the contrast between rationalism and this ecological approach to the world as the very core of the comparison between Greece and China: the Greeks are rationalists, the Chinese ecologists; the Greeks care about abstract conceptual frameworks, the Chinese about situated interactions. What I want to argue, to the contrary, is that both orientations are strongly and ubiquitously present in the Greeks as well, or at least in Aristotle:

Rationalistic conceptions of rhetoric:	*Ecological conceptions of rhetoric:*
are interested in the rational argumentative structures that will predictably persuade, with an implied direct object—"audiences in general"—that is so highly idealized as to be theoretically dispensable: the structures are said to be "persuasive" whether they actually persuade or not	are interested in the social (affective-becoming-conative) ecologies that make persuasion possible in specific social situations, driven by specific social goals and needs as felt by specific situated interactants
understand Aristotle's psychological chapters in *TR2* to be a taxonomy of *types* of emotion and disposition	understand emotions as arising situationally out of dispositions, dispositions out of social interactions
take the rhetor as seeking to master a rhetorical situation with abstract reason	take the rhetor as seeking to enter a rhetorical situation with attentiveness to the flows of social value
privilege hierarchized analytical knowledge	privilege situationally sensitive and flexible knowledge
take enthymemes to be truncated syllogisms (the universalizing premise left implicit)	take enthymemes to be collectively directed channels of feeling and pressure (conation)

As Schaberg shows, the rationalistic conceptions in that left-hand column are not absent from Warring States Chinese philosophy—they emerge in Later Mohist thought—but without question the intellectual traditions emerging out of early Chinese philosophy have tended to dwell more insistently in the right-hand column. And while I am going to be tracing the ecological conceptions in the right-hand column to specific passages in Aristotle's *TR*, it is equally without question that the intellectual traditions emerging out of Plato and Aristotle have tended to dwell more insistently in the left-hand column. In the aggregate, perhaps, with a focus on large historical trends, Sino-Hellenic comparatists like Cheng have been justified in labeling something like the left-hand column as "Greek" or "European" or "Western" and something like the right-hand column as "Chinese" or "Asian" or "Eastern." Still, the aggregate view undeniably misses a lot.

Another interesting reframing of the Sino-Hellenist comparative paradigm is offered by Robert Wardy (2006). Wardy is interested specifically in a single translation history, an early-sixteenth-century Jesuit project that translated selected passages of Aristotle's *Organon* into Latin and provided an extensive commentary on the whole that effectively Christianized Aristotle, and a late-sixteenth-century translation of the *Categories* section of that work into Chinese undertaken by a Chinese Christian in collaboration with a Portuguese Jesuit missionary. More broadly, Wardy (pp. ix, 1) tells us, he is interested in "the relation between language and thought," and specifically, in his first of two chapters, in "the presumption that there is something distinctively Chinese about Chinese philosophy taken more or less in its entirety; that this feature (or these features) set(s) the path of its development; and that it (or they) must be invoked to account for whatever large and deep contrasts are perceived between it and that other strange monolith, Western philosophy." Invoking Geoffrey Lloyd's (1990; see also Lloyd, 1996, 2002, 2005, 2006; and Lloyd and Sivin, 2002) trenchant attack on the "mentality" mentality in comparative studies—the highly questionable assumption that each culture has a single stable mentality that can be identified across centuries of thought—Wardy (2006, pp. 2–3) notes that the most defensible form this totalization of mentality takes explores the mentality not of a given *culture* (like "classical Greece" or "Warring States China") but of a given *language group* (like "Attic Greek" or "classical Chinese"); but that even that totalization is highly problematic:

> We begin far beyond the range of dialectal differences, diachronic linguistics, the relation between spoken and written language, or the proprietary modes of expression of given cultural groupings. We begin with the structure of the language itself, as it were with *langue* rather than *parole*; structure must be understood as so fundamental as not to be subject to any of the enormous variations I have enumerated, on pain of losing that putative unitary theoretical entity, *the* language. So here is the first shift of comparative linguistic hypotheses outside the narrow circle of the mentalities debate: their favoured terms of comparison are less vulnerable to the accusation of being mere figments of the theoretical imagination. Second, champions of linguistic comparativism do not always regard thought as intrinsically linguistic. But they *do* happily claim both that linguistic structure is to some significant extent isomorphic with major thought-patterns and that it is necessarily language which imposes those patterns on thought, not the other way around. Third, this isomorphism is supposed to be apparent in the articulation of reason called

philosophy, and philosophical development is judged to be positively guided and negatively constrained by the language in which it is done.

This hypothesis "that basic linguistic structure at once encourages and constrains the development of philosophical tendencies and doctrines" Wardy (ibid., p. 3) calls "the guidance and constraint hypothesis." He is mostly concerned to critique this hypothesis negatively, his main target A. C. Graham's *Disputers of the Tao* (1967/1999), which claims that certain Western philosophical notions simply "cannot be reproduced in Chinese" (quoted in Wardy, ibid.). Graham certainly admits that coinages and various circumlocutory glosses are possible, but stipulates that semantic and syntactic innovations designed to reproduce a Western philosophical concept do not constitute legitimate translation; his assumption seems to be that the Chinese (or any) language simply and stably *is* thus and such, and any change in response to foreign pressure (for example through translation) is simply and stably "not Chinese."

It is undeniable, Wardy agrees, that the impact of any given habitualized but still situational convergence of linguistic or philosophical practices will be conditioned to some fairly significant extent by the past practices of the community that regulates them; his critique is aimed at the idealizing notion that those habitualizing/habitualized practices should or can be rigidly hypostatized as "the language." And in his second long chapter on the Chinese translation of Aristotle's *Categories* he adds that his chapter 1 discussion of Sino-Hellenist relativism/comparativism has ignored one important consideration: that Aristotle too might have been guided and constrained by his language; "that his thought is permeated throughout by a variety of linguistic influences rarely recognized as such by Aristotle himself" (Wardy 2006, p. 69).

My discussion of Aristotle here could of course be read resistively as uncovering not so much actual theoretical orientations in Aristotle as simply the sort of unrecognized "permeations" Wardy mentions. These "permeations" would include the fact that thinking *pistis* in Greek "automatically" disposes one to think both persuasion and belief, and indeed to think both *pisteis* "arguments" and *to endekhomenon pithanon* "the available persuasivity" (chapter 2); or the fact that thinking *doxa* and *dokeō* in Greek "automatically" disposes one to think not only my opinion becoming your reputation but personalized *dokeō* "I think/feel" becoming depersonalized *dokei* "it seems/is" (chapter 4). This counterreading might continue that, while Aristotle is perhaps arguably predisposed to an ecological understanding of rhetoric by the pre-epistemic *doxai* circulating through Athenian culture and given expression by the Greek language, he is definitively and characteristically and indeed celebratedly working very hard to "raise" such *doxai* to the "philosophical" (reductive rationalist) level of the *epistēmē*. And while it is perhaps true that he didn't entirely succeed at that epistemic undertaking, he is justifiably best known for the areas in which he did succeed, because they represent the highest and truest (most Aristotelian) aims of his work. He left, admittedly, everywhere in the *TR*, traces of a prerationalist understanding of human social interaction; but, this resistive reading might conclude, those traces are not so much affirmed and tracked and theorized by Aristotle the rationalist philosopher as they are unconsciously reticulated through his thinking "by" the Greek language.

I only have one qualm about that counterreading of my take on Aristotle—but that qualm is a fairly significant one. It arises out of the fact that Aristotle himself constantly pushes past the arguably unconscious influence of such semantic habits by coining new terms—most famously his *en-* coinages, *entelekheia, energeia, enthumēma*—that point insistently "back" from the reductive rationalist surface of his conceptualization into the socio-ecological realm that is supposedly foreclosed by his explicit theorizing, and that supposedly only survives in his discourse through unnoticed and unprocessed semantic atavisms.

If his philosophy is end-driven, teleological, all processes somehow rigidly dominated by the potential perfection toward which they strive, why does he coin a term for those processes signaling the *having of an end within* (*entelekheia* as *en* "in" + *telos* "end" + *ekhein* "to have")?

If his philosophy is mechanistic, all motion on earth somehow perfectly impelled and coordinated by a transcendental Unmoved Mover, why does he coin a term for the force or "energy" behind such motion signaling an immanent *working within* (*energeia* as *en* "in" + *ergon* "work")?

And if his philosophy is reductively rationalistic, moving decisively toward the suppression of the body and its passions by mind, why does he coin a term for the typical argumentative form taken by practical reasoning signaling an *inner passion* (*enthumēma* as *en* "in" + *thumos* "passion, spiritedness, anger")?

One might be tempted to insist, conservatively, that

- just as *doxa* is the practical pre-epistemic public opinion that is ideally superseded by the rationalist *epistēmē*, so too is the enthymeme the practical pre-epistemic argumentative form that is ideally superseded by the syllogism;

- Aristotle devotes the attention that he does to both *doxa* and the enthymeme precisely in order to show us how to supersede them; and
- his entelechial conception of the process by which *doxa* becomes *epistēmē* and the enthymeme becomes the syllogism is effectively dualistic rather than processual, a model in which the *telos* (*epistēmē* or the syllogism) does not constantly and flexibly and situationally arise out of actuality but rather dominates it from Plato's ideal Realm of Forms.

But if that is truly the core of Aristotle's thought, why does he imagine the entelechy not only as powered by a vitalistic energy but as synonymous with it?

Aristotle of course is on record as characterizing the Europeans to the cold north as having great spirit or passion (*thumos*) but little intelligence (*dianoia*), and therefore being free but incapable of ruling others, and the Asians to the east as "intelligent and inventive, but . . . wanting in spirit [*thumos*], and therefore they are always in a state of subjection and slavery" (*Politics* 7.7, 1327b26–27); and only the Greeks, who occupy the geographical middle ground between Europe and Asia, as having both passion and intelligence. In that light, one Orientalist reading of the socio-ecological impulses that I tease out of Aristotle might be that Mencius and the Chinese tradition(s) in philosophy that he represents in my argument here stand as the pre-epistemic *thumos* that Aristotle sublates in his entelechial movement toward the *telos* of pure reason.

Given my emphatic rejection of that reading, what *is* the relationship between Mencius and Aristotle in my juxtaposition of the two?

It is in fact more heuristic than genetic: I use each to direct attention to nuances in the other that might otherwise be missed. Kenneth Burke calls a somewhat similar analytical method "perspectives by incongruity"; the only hitch in applying Burke's term to my approach here is that there is so *little* incongruity between Mencius and Aristotle. The main incongruity, in fact, may be that they are *thought* to be wildly incongruous, and thus read dualistically by Prof. Cheng and others as opposites.

In fact there are striking similarities between the two books—the *TR* and the *MZ*. Both were written/compiled over a number of decades, and neither was published in its author's/compiler's/eponymous hero's lifetime; each author or compiler wrote or compiled the initial document while teaching at his predecessor's school (Mencius at the school founded by Confucius in the state of Lu 魯國, Aristotle at Plato's Academy); both were completed and published by disciples. Both books were written with a practical political purpose in mind: to help rulers rule better and their subjects be better subjects (*MZ*); to help young aristocrats persuade (and thus run the democracy) more effectively (*TR*). To some extent these practical purposes are at cross-purposes, even within each book. *MZ* 1–3 consists primarily of mostly supportive advice to the emperor, while *MZ* 4–7 is notoriously populist, even incipiently democratic, based on the revolutionary notion that the people are more important than the emperor and that it is the people's duty to remove a bad ruler. In *TR* 1.1 and the odd later moment Aristotle follows Plato in rejecting and lamenting the use of rhetoric for the purpose of convincing people of things that are not true, though most of the rest of the book is dedicated to teaching precisely that skill; and while he clearly knows that rhetoric is important to his students because the "rulers" of a democracy are effective persuaders, not autocrats, he also rails repeatedly against that state of affairs. Even so, in the *Politics* (1288a15–19) Aristotle expressed strong reservations about monarchy, insisting—very much along the lines of Mencius—that a king and his family must be more virtuous than all of the king's subjects put together.

Of course there are also important differences. The *MZ* is all we have of Mencius under his name; the *TR* is one of nearly three dozen treatises written by Aristotle, most of which are arguably far more reductively rationalist or "scientific," and thus far less Mencian. In isolating the *TR* from Aristotle's extensive oeuvre for comparison with the *MZ*, therefore, I am manifestly foregrounding the similarities between the two thinkers and backgrounding the differences in the shape of their careers as a whole. In addition, there are obvious differences between the *TR* and the *MZ* in their own right. The *TR* is almost entirely written by Aristotle; the *MZ* is compiled by Mencians, probably with some input from Mencius himself during his lifetime, but mostly by his followers after his death, and, if Brooks and Brooks (2002) are to be believed, reflecting schisms between two different groups of followers. The *TR* is a third-person scholarly treatise in which the author does not appear as a character or speaker; the *MZ* is a series of brief narrative vignettes featuring dialogues between Mencius and various others. In that sense the *MZ* more closely resembles Plato's Socratic dialogues, the multiply voiced genre that Aristotle himself reputedly plied in his (presumably lost) "exoteric" works and arguably "reduced" or "purified" into depersonalized academic discourse in his (surviving) "esoteric" works.

Aristotle and Mencius were contemporaries, of course, Aristotle born twelve years before Mencius in 384 BCE and dying in his late fifties in 322 BCE, while Mencius, probably born around 372 BCE, lived a long life, dying toward the end of the fourth or the beginning of the third century. Aristotle drafted the *TR* in Athens, in two different periods: between 367 and 347 BCE, from his arrival at Plato's Academy at the age of 23 until Plato's death twenty years later, by which time Aristotle had become his Number Two; and between 335 and 322 BCE, from his return from Macedonia and founding of his own school, the Lyceum, until his own death. As we've seen, Brooks and Brooks (2002) speculate that the original interviews that make up what they deem the "authentic" chapters of *MZ* 1 were conducted and possibly written up in 320–310 BCE, his last years at the Confucian school in Lu; *MZ* 2A2: 1–23 was based on composite remembered Mencian conversations around the time of his death in 303 (though many others have him dying around 289); and *MZ* 3–7 was written and compiled by his followers in the early to mid-third century.

1.6 The Structure of the Book

In "The Meaning of Body in Classical Chinese Philosophy," Roger T. Ames (2002) sets up his reading of three classical Chinese terms for the body, *shēn* 身, *xíng* 形, and *tǐ* 體, in two introductory steps.

The first is to offer a methodological principle for the study of the philosophy of a whole culture or epoch: he quotes F. M. Cornford (1907, p. ix) to the effect that "in every age the common interpretation of the world of things is controlled by some scheme of unchallenged and unsuspected presupposition; and the mind of any individual, however little he may think himself to be in sympathy with his contemporaries, is not an insulated compartment, but more like a pool in one continuous medium—the circumambient atmosphere of his place and time" (quoted in Ames 2002, p. 157). Local contemporary consciousness of individual differences, in other words, should be superseded by later scholarly attention to unconscious commonalities. Ames goes on to cite Alfred North Whitehead's (1925, p. 71) urging that in studying the philosophy of an epoch we direct our attention not to "those intellectual positions which its exponents feel it necessary to defend" but to the "fundamental assumptions which adherents of all the variant systems within the epoch unconsciously presuppose" (quoted in Ames 2002, pp. 157–58).

Ames's second step, then, is to adduce David L. Hall's (1982) distinction between the *dualistic* philosophies that have dominated Western thought and the *polaristic* philosophies that have tended to prevail in Chinese thought. As Ames amplifies the distinction, dualistic thinking tends to arise in cultures that imagine the world as having been created by a transcendental deity or spirit that is utterly unlike his or its creation: spiritual rather than physical, nondependent rather than dependent, eternal rather than mortal; hence the importance in Western thought of dualisms like natural and supernatural, mind and matter, subject and object, self and other. By polarism Hall means a symbiotic relationship in which each "pole" or related entity is at once "of itself" (autogenerative and self-determinate) and "for the other"—each stands alone *and* requires a reciprocal relationship with its polar opposite as its condition of possibility.

For example, self and other in a dualistic worldview tend to become not only radically but hierarchically distinct: not just *subject* (agent, capable of thought) and *object* (nonagent, incapable of thought) but *right* (possessing the truth, and therefore better) and *wrong* (mired in confusion and error, and therefore worse). In a polaristic worldview, by contrast, self and other become mutually defining, like left and right, up and down, east and west: just as west is defined as not-east and east is defined as not-west, and as indeed one can go to the East by traveling west and to the West by traveling east, so too you are my self's other and I am your self's other. Martin Buber's (1936/1970) I-You relation is an attempt in precisely that polaristic spirit to tilt against the dualistic hegemony of the I-It in Western thought; a similar project can be found in Mikhail Bakhtin's (1970/1986, p. 7) notion that in responding dialogically to you I incorporate your view of me into my self-concept, see myself through your eyes, and that your view of me also contains something of my view of you.

Now the interesting question here is not whether dualism truly is endemic to Western thought. Obviously it is. I use the Cervantean term "tilt" for these twentieth-century projects because in Western thought antidualism always feels a bit quixotic, like fighting a battle that one cannot possibly hope to win. The interesting question, I suggest, arises out of the observation that dualism is not exactly the kind of "scheme of unchallenged and unsuspected presupposition" that Cornford urges us to look for. In fact it is arguably the chief intellectual position which Plato and Aristotle and their legion of Western followers "feel it necessary to defend," and thus precisely what according to Cornford and Whitehead we should *not* be studying.

So what else is going on in Western thought? Specifically, here, what "scheme of unchallenged and unsuspected presupposition" is at work in the rhetoric of Aristotle's *TR*?

The two "unchallenged and unsuspected presupposition[s]" in (Plato and) Aristotle that I propose to examine in some detail in this book in fact both emerge out of polaristic concepts supplied to those two thinkers by the language they spoke, Attic Greek:

- *pistis* as both what I do to you in order to *pressure* you to believe something (persuasion) and what you do in *responding* to my pressure (being persuaded, believing)
- *doxa* as both my view of you (opinion) and the "character" or "name" or "fame" or "face" you possess as a result of how I and others see you (reputation)

Just how problematic the prevailing dualizing view of Western thought is for understanding these polar concepts in Plato and Aristotle can perhaps best be illustrated by Eric Havelock's (1963, pp. 250–51) "explanation" of *doxa* in *Preface to Plato*:

> Both the noun [*doxa*], and the verb *doko*, are truly baffling to modern logic in their coverage of both the subjective and objective relationship. The verb denotes both the 'seeming' that goes on in myself, the 'subject,' namely my 'personal impressions,' and the 'seeming' that links me as an 'object' to other people looking at me—the 'impression' I make on them. The noun correspondingly is both the 'impression' that may be in my mind and the 'impression' held by others of me. It would appear therefore to be the ideal term to describe that fusion or confusion of the subject with the object that occurred in the poetized performance and in the state of mind created by this performance. It is the 'seeming show of things,' whether this panorama is thought of as within me or outside of me.

This association with "the poetized performance" is important for Havelock's conception of Plato's understanding of *doxa* because his brief is that in the *Republic* Plato is arguing not so much against poetry per se as against "the act of memorization through identification in the poetic performance which to him is inseparable from the poem itself, and which constitutes a total act and condition of *mimesis*" (Havelock, 1963, p. 244)—specifically, against the pedagogical culture that grounded education in having pupils memorize long passages from ancient poems and identify psychologically with the characters, which, he says, "constituted the content of the Greek mind before Plato" (Havelock, 1963, p. 251). If then the *doxa* that Plato associates with this educational tradition, and thus with the philosophically untrained mind, is an irrational and vaguely poetic (indeed "dreamlike": *Republic* 476cd) frame of mind in which subject and object blur together, the binary for Plato is clear: clear rational scientific thinking (*epistēmē*) bars the gates to this prescientific murk of opinion (*doxa*) by banishing the poetry it rode in on.

What this analysis suggests in Hall's terms, of course, is that the polarism of *doxa* is prescientific specifically in the sense of being predualistic; hence Havelock's complaint that it "cover[s] both the subjective and objective relationship." The prevailing scholarly understanding of both Greek thinkers' understanding of *doxa* follows roughly this line: that philosophy for both Plato and Aristotle entails the principled move from the prescientific disorganization of public opinion (*doxa*) to the scientific organization of *epistēmē*. Polarism, in other words, is perceived by dualists as "disorganized." My challenge to this prevailing view is twofold: that [a] Aristotle is far more interested than Plato in *doxa* in its own right, as an empirical social phenomenon, and devotes significant energies especially in the *TR* to its investigation; and [b] for Aristotle *pistis* and *doxa* as markers for social interaction are far more than polar: they are ecological, emerging out of the *flows of persuasivity* through a culture.

Aristotle wants to know, specifically, how the social circulation of value that is implicit in *doxa* conditions the entelechial movement toward *ta eikota*, that which the community (*oikos*) takes to be probable or likely or "truthy" (*eikos*). And he wants to know how rhetoric—the loose and constantly emerging collection of communal persuading/being-persuaded speech acts that is implicit in *pistis*—participates in the social ecology by which certain things come to seem likely or plausible enough to be as good as true. He doesn't always seem to be aware that he wants to know these things; his interest in them is often implicit in his argumentation. But they don't have to be read into his sentences. It requires no special interpretive cleverness or inventiveness to "find" them there. Indeed I submit that it requires extremely effective guidance from the neo-Aristotelian tradition for us *not* to find them there. Look carefully at how he uses *pistis, doxa, timē,* and *eikos,* and try to make sense of the complexities and "confusions" that result from reading him through a certain conventional set of lenses, and you can't help but see them there.

Each of the book's three main chapters is organized around a single main concept-pair: persuasivity (*pistis*/*zhì* 治) in chapter 2, energy (*energeia*/*qì* 氣) in chapter 3, and reputation (*doxa*/*wén* 聞) in chapter 4. Each chapter also ranges fairly widely, sweeping up associated concepts that bring psychosocial depth and nuance to the core concepts: *rén* 仁 "fellow-feeling" and its constituents and rough synonyms in chapter 2, *hupokrisis* or "acting" (body language) in chapter 3, and *timē/zūn* 尊/*róng* 榮 (honor) and *aiskhunē/xiūwù* 羞惡 (shame) in chapter 4.

Chapter 2, then, is framed by a concern with the nature of persuasion, which, by the end of the chapter, is revealed to emerge out of *to pithanon*, literally "persuasivity." Given the circular nature of the Greek word *pistis*, which means both what I do in persuading you and what you do in being persuaded by me, I argue that persuasion is in fact a group speech act, performed by a group subject that I tentatively identify as the collective heart-becoming-mind that circulates and organizes fellow-feeling in what Mencius calls *rén* 仁. En route to that claim, I first consider the similarity of the Mencian term *zhì* 治, which means both what the ruler does in governing and what his subjects do in being governed, to Greek *pistis*—which makes sense, because the Mencian ideal for government is a governing-by-persuading based on fellow-feeling, in which the ruler feels what the people are feeling and the people feel what the ruler is feeling. Since *rén* 仁 is almost always translated into English with terms for the individual's ethical disposition like "benevolence" and "humaneness" that are conceptually quite alien from my focus on fellow-feeling, I devote most of the chapter to a careful unpacking of what Mencius and his commentators say about *rén* 仁, moving through *bùrěn* 不忍 (the inability to endure someone else's suffering), and *xīn* 心 as the heart-becoming-mind that is collectivized in *rén* 仁, to *xuèqì* 血氣 or "blood *qì*" as parallel in interesting ways to Aristotle's conception of *thumos* "valor." The deep-ecological flows in chapter 2 are defined through the concept of "identification" developed independently by Kenneth Burke and Arne Naess.

Given that Gary Snyder (1994/1995) reflects on deep ecology as powered by "energy-exchanges," it is appropriate to devote chapter 3 to energy, derived from a Greek word (almost certainly coined by Aristotle) meaning in-work or at-work; one of the key terms of early Confucianism, *qì* 氣, is often translated "energy" or "vital energies" or "configurative energies." The chapter ranges through Aristotle's conception of *energeia* as functionally synonymous with *entelekheia*, George Kennedy's (1992) concept of rhetoric as energy, Susan Miller's (2008) reinterpretation of Kennedy's thesis in terms of "charismatic signifiers," and Jeffrey Walker's (2008) reinterpretation of that thesis in terms of the energizing or "presencing" of rhetoric-as-words through body language. After exploring a possible connection in Mencius between *zhī yán* 知言 "knowing speech" and *yǎng qì* 養氣 "cultivating energy," specifically through the energizing effects body language has on speech, I end the chapter with a look at *lǐ* 禮 "ritual propriety" as the organization of group behavior around shared norms.

Chapter 4 is a study of the circulation of social value through groups, first in terms of *doxa* in Aristotle and *wén* 聞 in Mencius, the slow collective transformation of telling-and-hearing into news, knowing the news, and being known in and by the news (reputation, fame); then, through Mencius on *xìng* 性 as a learned disposition, the four hearts, and the "external" forces (*tiān* 天) and conditions (*mìng* 命) over which we have no control; then, through Erving Goffman (1955/1967) on face (another possible translation of *doxa*), in terms of honor and shame; and finally, through a close look at key Aristotelian discussions of *ta dokounta* (seeming), *ta eikota* (truthiness), and *to pithanon* (persuasivity), in terms of doxicosis or the becoming-communal of persuasivity.

The Conclusion brings the argument full circle, returning from doxicosis to ecosis or ethecosis, the becoming-good of the community—and so also to deep ecology, and the tension between giving priority to the ecological self and its absorption into the natural environment (Arne Naess) and focusing primarily on the social self and the improvement of social interaction (Murray Bookchin). While Mencius and Aristotle are very close to the deep-ecological thought of Naess, I argue, ultimately they remain firmly in the camp of Bookchin: their primary concern is with the functionality of the sociopolitical sphere.

2

The Group Subject of Persuasion

2.0 Introduction

The study of rhetoric is the study of persuasion: this much is easy. Complications only arise when we ask what persuasion *is*. Western rhetorical theory, relying heavily on readings of Aristotle's *Rhetoric* (*TR*), has tended to define persuasion as a speech act performed by the rhetor as a discrete individual: the speaker or writer builds, out of the various building materials Aristotle identifies (enthymemes and examples, *topoi*, analyses of the audience and other aspects of rhetorical situation), an argumentative structure—makes a "case," or offers a "proof." Persuasion is something *one person does*.

But even on the face of it this is a problematic assertion. If I claim to have "persuaded" you, and you insist that you are not persuaded, have I or have I not performed the act of persuasion? Is unsuccessful persuasion still persuasion? Should we include under the rubric of persuasion *attempted* persuasion?

Or, more radically still, should an argument or a proof be counted as "persuasive" if it possesses a certain structure that is commonly believed to be *likely* to have a persuasive effect, regardless of whether it actually has that effect on actual audiences? Western rhetoricians, obviously, have tended to say *yes*. Hegemonically in Western thought, idealized abstract structures are assumed to have certain attributes in the so-called null context: a text is said to have "narrative" structure whether or not anyone is actually narrating, "persuasive" structure whether or not anyone is actually persuaded, and so on. What I am calling here the deep ecology of social interaction has long been constructed as a secondary "real-world application" that is of only peripheral (and certainly nonrestrictive) relevance to the true nature of the ideal structure.

And indeed given the hegemony of the *TR* in this Western intellectual tradition, it is not at all surprising that the book's central term, the keyword that most pithily sums up what Aristotle is attempting to do in the handbook, is *pistis*, which means not only "persuasion" but "means of persuasion," and thus "proof" or "argument." To the extent that the book is a practical guide to persuading people, therefore, it is—and has traditionally been read as—about *pisteis* as the specific argumentative strategies and devices that the rhetor should learn to use to that end. This plural noun *pisteis* appears throughout the *TR* in just this sense, and is translated with great semantic consistency by the best-known twentieth-century English translators of the *TR*: as "proofs" by Freese (1926), as "proof [persuasion]" by Cooper (1932), and as "modes of persuasion" or "means of persuasion" or "means of effecting persuasion" by Roberts (1941/1984). (Kennedy, 1991/2007, calques it as *pisteis*, often with explanatory notes.)

The problem with this long-dominant approach to the *TR*, however, is that in Attic Greek *pistis* is not only persuasion; it is also belief, the *result* of persuasion. If *pistis* is persuasion, then persuasion—and thus rhetoric—is something performed not by a single individual, the rhetor, but by at least two people, a speaker and a listener, a writer and a reader, and very often by an entire group. If the subject of rhetorical study as we derive it from Aristotle's *TR* is the study of *pistis*, the true topic of rhetoric is arguably not persuasive form, nor even specific persuasive acts performed by a rhetor, but broad collective acts of *persuading-and-believing*.

But of course this is conceptually rather problematic, at least for English-speakers. If we follow the English semantic pattern and take persuading and believing to be the reciprocal acts of a two-party transaction, using the same term for both would be like using the same verb for paying and receiving payment, or for attacking and defending a city, or for warning someone who is about to step into traffic and that person responding by not taking the fateful step. The cognitive contortions we experience in attempting to subsume both sides of such transactions into a single term are akin to trying to see the famous ambiguous image as a duck and a rabbit at once: it seems to us so overwhelmingly and indeed so mind-paralyzingly natural to apprehend persuading and believing as two separate and reciprocal actions performed by different people that we may attempt to conflate them by speeding up our semantic oscillations between them. Or we may take the tack of imagining persuader and believer to be the same person, either in the same body (talking oneself into doing something, feeling persuaded by one's own spin) or, more radically, in two or more bodies, yielding lurid science-fantasy scenarios in which the humans present in the *pistis*-event are all bee-like hive creatures controlled by a single collective will.

Given the dominant dualizing tendencies in Western thought, of course, the fact that my reading of Aristotle and Mencius on persuasion is deep-ecological and therefore rather more "collectivistic" than "individualistic" will be taken by some readers to mean that I am indeed arguing for something like this hive or swarm mentality: if it is not individualistic in the established Western sense, which is to say an action performed by discrete individuals controlled separately by reason-centers in individual heads, it must be the exact opposite of individualistic. It must be an action performed by whole groups controlled collectively by a single group mind, a collective reason.

What I want to carve out in this book, however, is a deep-ecological middle ground between the "one-mind-one-body rationalism" of radical individualism (*the good self* in this standard Western dualism) and the "one-mind-many-bodies rationalism" of the hive mind or swarm intelligence (vilified and banished as *the evil other*), or what we might call "nightmare collectivism"—the dualized kind of scare-tactic bogeyman construction of collectivism dreamed up by "panicked individualists" (to adapt Judith Butler's 1991 term "panicked heterosexuality"; see §4.10 for discussion). The middle ground I envision is, as I say, more collectivistic than individualistic; but it is also one that does not subsume individual reason into the working of a hive rationalism. In fact it is strictly speaking not rationalistic at all—it operates largely at the level of feelings and feeling-based dispositions, and is often described in terms of the "energies" driving it—but it does not exclude rational thought. The feelings and the dispositions and the energies that power it are always at least potentially becoming-rational—what I call feeling-becoming-thinking. Individuals becoming aware of their own feelings and feeling-based dispositions make significantly rational contributions to the working of what I will persist in calling the "group mind": the deep-ecological model of rhetoric that I tease out of Mencius and Aristotle affirms the important role played in group persuasion-becoming-believing by conscious perception and logical analysis. But conscious perception and logical analysis in this model are constantly *emerging out of* more inchoate (icotic) social forces that are primarily affective and largely shared.

I begin, then, with the translation problems arising out of the "circularity" of the Attic Greek concept of *pistis* (§2.1), and offer a tentative collectivist explanation of that circularity through the related concepts of identification developed independently by Kenneth Burke and Arne Naess (§2.2), before delving deep into key concepts in Mencius: *zhì* 治 "(be) govern(ed)" as a circulatory concept that works very much in the same way as Greek *pistis* (§2.3), *rén* 仁/*bùrěn* 不忍/*xīn* 心 as a collective heart-becoming-mind or fellow-feeling (§2.4–2.6, §2.9), Mencius's (bio-)

ecological metaphors for this embodiment of virtue (§2.7), *xuèqì* 血氣 or "blood *qì*" as parallel in interesting ways to Aristotle's conception of *thumos* "valor" (§2.8), and *rén zhèng* 仁政 as "fellow-feeling"-based persuasive government (§2.10). I close the chapter by returning to Aristotle on persuasion, specifically to his radically doxicotic notion of *to endekhomenon pithanon*, literally "the available persuasivity" (§2.11).

2.1 Aristotle: The Headaches *pistis* Gives Translators

The semantic polarity mapped out by *pistis* in Attic Greek obviously makes things a bit tricky for the *TR*'s English translators, who, given that English does not have a single term that would cover both the act of persuading and its desired effect, are faced with the unenviable task of rendering the term more or less consistently.

For example, in *TR* 1.2 Aristotle tells us that *tōn de dia tou logou porizomenōn pisteōn tria eidē estin* (1.2.3, 1356a2; see also 1.9.1, 1366a25–26), or as Kennedy (1991/2007, p. 38) translates that, "of the *pisteis* provided through speech there are three species." The calqued word *pisteis* in that rendition does stand in for something like the semantic complexity at which Aristotle is hinting; but in the very next sentence Aristotle complicates things for Kennedy's calquing strategy, implicitly back-referring to the *tōn . . . pisteōn* that Kennedy calqued as "of the *pisteis*" and then giving us two more *pistis*-words, *axiopistos* "worthy of belief" and *pisteuō* "to believe." Such are the transformations of *pistis* there that Kennedy cannot track them for us in English: "[There is persuasion (Kennedy's interpolation)] through character whenever the speech is spoken in such a way as to make the speaker worthy of credence [*axiopiston*]; for we believe [*pisteuomen*] fair-minded people to a greater extent and more quickly [than we do others]" (1.2.4, 1356a4–6; Kennedy, 1991/2007, p. 38). Kennedy's bracketed explicitation of Aristotle's implicit back-reference as "[There is persuasion]" obviously fails to mark "persuasion" as referring back to *pisteis*; and *axiopistos* and *pisteuō*, later in that same sentence, get translated with "belief" words. Other translators fare no better (I've numbered and bolded the keywords):

> The orator [1] **persuades** by moral character when his speech is delivered in such a manner as to render him [2] **worthy of confidence**; for we [3] **feel confidence** in a greater degree and more readily in persons of worth in regard to everything in general. (Freese, 1926, p. 17)

The character of the speaker is a cause of [1] **persuasion** when the speech is so uttered as to make him [2] **worthy of belief;** for as a rule we [3] **trust** men of probity more, and more quickly, about things in general. (Cooper, 1932, p. 8)

[1] **Persuasion** is achieved by the speaker's personal character when the speech is so spoken as to [2] **make us think him credible.** We [3] **believe** good men more fully and more readily than others. (Roberts, 1941/1984, p. 2155)

In each case there, (1) is the implied *tōn . . . pisteōn* ("of the *pisteis*") that Kennedy was unable to mark; (2) is *axiopistos* ("believable," morphologically "worth believing" or "worth being persuaded by," or Cooper's "worthy of belief"); (3) is *pisteuomen* ("we believe"). In attempting to render these, Freese gives us "confidence" twice (2–3), but the first *pistis* in (1) remains "persuasion"; Cooper and Roberts give us three separate words each, though in each case the translations in (2–3) ("credible"/"believe" and "belief"/"trust") are at least roughly synonymous. Cooper could have brought (3) into line with (2) by giving us "we *believe* men of probity"; but the resulting terminological belief-cluster would not have hinted at the connection with (1) persuasion. Roberts likewise could have given us (2) "believable" and (3) "believe," but again this would not have brought the implied *pisteis* in (1) into line. Not one translator is able even to hint that behind all three of the keywords in the passage is the book's central concept, *pistis*. Note also that in (2) Freese and Cooper follow Aristotle's morphology in rendering *axiopistos* adjectivally, as a produced property of the speaker; Roberts marshals a verb and shifts point of view to the listeners, who "think [the speaker] credible." This rotating perspectivism—the sense in which *axiopistos* is at once (or alternately, or "becomingly") an attribute of the speaker and a character that is attributed to the speaker by the listeners—is part of what I want to identify as the ecological circularity/polarity in Aristotle's conception, closely related to the circular/reticular conceptions of reputation, face, and honor that are the focus of chapter 4. (Freese also produces a secondary semantic field in moving from "worthy of confidence" to "persons of worth": *worthies* are *worthy*.)

Is this shoddy translation? Since translators, especially of major philosophical texts, are often (perhaps somewhat pedantically, and unrealistically) expected to use the same target-language equivalent for every incidence of a single source-language term, the pedantic answer would be yes, this is very shoddy—especially given the fact that *pistis* is not some random noun but arguably the book's defining keyword. But in this case I think the translators are justified. Given the fact that we lack a single word (or group of words derived from the same semantic root) for persuasion, belief, credibility, and trust, and that the three concepts cannot and should not be reduced to a single simplified equivalent like "make-believe," Aristotle's English translators are forced to keep jumping around semantically, trying to capture whatever aspect of *pistis* that Aristotle seems to be working with at any given moment.[1]

Or consider another passage from later in *TR* 1.2, where Aristotle writes that *pantes de tas pisteis poiountai dia tou deiknunai ē paradeigmata legontes ē enthumēmata* (1.2.8, 1356b6–7)—which is literally, if we replace the problematic *tas pisteis* with X, "and all [speakers] make X through proving, speaking either examples or enthymemes." What exactly are all speakers *making* by proving with examples and enthymemes? If *pantes de tas pisteis poiountai* "everyone makes X" had not been modified with *dia tou deiknunai* "through proving," Aristotle's translators would probably have rendered it "make/construct proofs," since *pisteis* do often seem to be specific argumentative structures, and are often translated "proofs." Obviously, though, making X *through* proof renders X problematic. What is X? The two obvious choices are "persuasion" and "belief," and our translators give us both, Cooper, Roberts, and Kennedy choosing the former, Freese alone the latter: "men in speaking effect persuasion" (Cooper, 1932, p. 10), "every one who effects persuasion" (Roberts, 1941/1984, p. 1330), "all [speakers] produce logical persuasion" (Kennedy, 1991/2007, p. 40), but "Now all orators produce belief" (Freese, 1926, p. 19). But of course we don't *produce* persuasion in English, and it is not much more idiomatic to say that "orators produce belief," either. Cooper's and Roberts's shift from "produce" to "effect" works better with "persuasion," and suggests some of the same circulatory semantics as the Greek, since "to *effect* persuasion" is to achieve a "persuasion-*effect*" in one's audience.

Indeed J. L. Austin (1962/1975) would probably want to say that in normal circumstances persuading is the illocutionary *force* of the speaker's speech act, what s/he does *in* speaking, and believing or being persuaded is the perlocutionary *effect* of that act in or on the listener; but in fact Aristotle's sentence seems to suggest that the persuasive speech act's illocutionary force in this case is not persuading at all but *proving*. This would appear to make persuading the perlocutionary effect of the illocutionary act of proving—and believing or being-persuaded simply a listener-phenomenology of that same perlocutionary effect. The speaker proves in order to "effect persuasion" or "produce belief" in the listener. Proving is at once something the speaker does [a] *logically* or *empirically* (as demonstration) to a claim or a case or an argument and [b] *rhetorically* (as persuasion) to an audience; while it can be construed in isolation from social interaction ("in the prover's head," like the proverbial tree falling in a forest with no one there to see or hear it) as (a) a logical structure, it depends rhetorically for its success on (b) the listener's acceptance or believing/being-persuaded, so that (b) persuading the listener (effecting persuasion or belief in the listener) is the success condition for proving. But note how this makes persuading both part of the speech act's illocutionary force (speaking/proving *in order to persuade*) and part of its desired perlocutionary effect (effecting persuasion or producing belief) on the listener. This shifter-status would make Aristotle's conception of persuading at the very least a mediatory/transitional third term *between* illocutionary force and perlocutionary effect, and possibly even a higher-level third term that *contains* illocutionary force and perlocutionary effect and effects the shift from the one to the other (except when it doesn't, quite).

What makes this conceptually difficult—and as I've shown (Robinson, 2003, pp. 95–99), it was a massive and ultimately insurmountable stumbling block for Austin himself, in defining the relationship between illocutions and perlocutions—is that the shifter-status of persuasion locates it, as Western dualism would insist, "inside" two different social actors. The speaker proves; the listener believes. Persuasion contains or channels both acts, encompassing and organizing both the speaker-phenomenology that wants to convince a listener and the listener-phenomenology that vets proof as successful by believing.

Or, I'm suggesting, the shifter-status of persuasion locates it ecologically in an emergent "icotic" reciprocity between speaker and listener. This would obviously make persuasion a powerful example of the kind of "polar" thinking that is supposedly alien to Aristotle (see §1.5). Polar persuading-becoming-believing is an unpredictable and ultimately uncontrollable ecological consequence or byproduct of the speaker's illocutionary act of proving—which itself emerges, as we'll see in §2.11, below, ecologically out of the speaker's observation of and participation in *to endekhomenon pithanon,* the available persuasivity.

2.2 Burke on Aristotle: The Group Mind as Identification

Aristotle's translators' difficulties are caused by Attic Greek semantics, obviously—by what from an English standpoint seems like a semantic anomaly. Even in English, however, persuading is a speech act that cannot be performed by a single individual: *I* cannot persuade *you* unless *you* are persuaded. If I claim I have persuaded you, but you insist that you remain unpersuaded, at best we've got ourselves an is-so/is-not situation, and at worst I'm deluded. Persuading, as I've suggested elsewhere of such speech acts as intimidating, warning, and annoying (Robinson, 2003), is definitively performed by the *group*, by the "group mind" of at least two people.

I noted in §1.1 that Arne Naess (1995, p. 34) theorizes "Self-realization" as a conduit of "ecotic" or becoming-communal maturation in the context of identification:

> Considering the widening scope of identification as internally related to increased Self-realization, this increase depends on the Self-realization of others. This gives us H1 [hypothesis 1: "The higher the Self-realization attained by anyone, the broader and deeper the identification with others." (ibid: 33)]. It implies that "the others" do not lose their individuality. Here we stumble upon the old metaphysical set of problems of "unity in diversity." When the human being A identifies with B, and the wider self of A comes to comprise B, A is not supposed to reject the individuality of B. Thus, if A and B are persons, the self of A comprises that of B and vice versa.

As I also mentioned there, however, the most famous theory of identification, Kenneth Burke's in *A Rhetoric of Motives* (1950/1969), is almost identical to Naess's, but precedes it by several decades and is grounded specifically in a close reading of Aristotle's *TR*. In Burke's theory, the speaker persuades the listener not just by creating sound proofs (*logoi*), projecting an attractive persona (*ēthos*), and appealing to the listener's emotions (*pathē*), but by *identifying* with the listener—in some imaginary but nevertheless powerfully transformative sense *becoming* the listener. As Naess puts it, "the wider self of A comes to comprise B." As in Naess's later theory, too, the Burkean identification that results is not unidirectional: by identifying with the listener, and in some sense becoming the listener, the speaker also encourages the listener to identify with and in some sense become him or her as well. As Naess puts it, "if A and B are persons, the self of A comprises that of B and vice versa." More than that, the speaker's identification with the listener is rendered both possible and potentially powerful by the listener's identification with the speaker—and vice versa. Identification is not so much something that one individual does to another, a transitive action, as it is an ecotic exchange in which people simultaneously do things to others and have things done to them by those others—in which, to put that differently, "doing" circulates through individual bodies, and the "doer" is a collectivized everybody and nobody, as well as, in a potentially infinite proliferation of brief moments that largely go unnoticed by individuals, a fleeting each-body.

In this light *ēthos* and *pathos* together become not so much a living mask—a strategic persona fitted out with appropriate emotions—that the rhetor dons in order to enhance his or her credibility, but rather a kind of permeable shared identity, built and inhabited collaboratively by the rhetor and his or her audience. Burke tropes identification as consubstantiality, as "one body" or "shared body," but specifically as the *experience* of a shared body, the circulation of an ecotic *feeling* of shared embodied self through a group. "For substance," Burke (1950/1969, p. 21) writes, "in the old philosophies, was an *act*; and a way of life is an *acting-together*; and in acting together, men have common sensations, concepts, images, ideas, attitudes that make them *consubstantial*" (emphasis Burke's). What is shared or circulated in identification, in other words, is not physical but *affective* substance. Hence the social phenomena that Virginia Holland (1959, p. 27) describes, in her book on Burke's radical unpacking of Aristotle, as "groups 'magically' persuad[ing] other groups," or "social cohesion result[ing] without the external action of a critic who attempts to persuade."

In an important sense, in fact, Burke's unpacking of Aristotle is only radical in the sense of rethinking the Aristotle that has been constructed for us by Aristotelian scholarship by returning to the Aristotelian roots. If we take "radical" to mean the transformation of Aristotle in ways that he himself would not have been able to imagine, Burke's reading is not radical at all. As Nancy Sherman (1989, ch. 4) points out, Aristotle's conception of the good life centers around friendship (*philia*) and friendly feeling (*to philein*), so that happiness (*eudaimonia*), for Aristotle the greatest and most definitive good in the good life, means the happiness not (just) of the individual but of the group—or, to put that differently, the happiness of the individual as not just augmented by but *constituted* in and by the happiness of the group. As Aristotle puts it in the *Nicomachean Ethics*, happiness as the *energeia* (energy as the in-working or en-acting) and the *entelekheia* (energy as the actualization) of human life requires not merely virtue but virtuous action, and specifically virtuous *interaction with others*:

> Yet evidently, as we said, it [happiness] needs the external goods as well; for it is impossible, or not easy, to do noble acts without the proper equipment. In many actions we use friends and riches

and political power as instruments; and there are some things the lack of which takes the luster from happiness, as good birth, goodly children, beauty; for the man who is very ugly in appearance or ill-born or solitary and childless is not very likely to be happy, and perhaps a man would be still less likely if he had thoroughly bad children or friends or had lost good children or friends by death. (1.8, 1099a31–b6; Ross, 1941/2001, p. 945)

While recognizing that this dependence of happiness on friends-as-resources might be read to mean that friends are the external *tools* of the individual's happiness, like money or political connections, Aristotle also insists that friends are more than just instrumentalities; they are co-agents with us of our happiness. We collaborate with our friends in the actualization or energization of our happiness. The key ecotic (inter)activities constitutive of happiness are simply not available to loners—people without friends, lovers, spouses, children, etc. Aristotle also notes that it is not possible for an individual to be happy if his or her friends are unhappy, which effectively makes *my* happiness a *group* happiness, the happiness of my group of friends (including me). As Sherman (1989, p. 128) puts it, "Happiness or good living is thus ascribable to me, not as an isolated individual, but as a self extended, so to speak, by friends." As she goes on to note, Aristotle stresses the importance for good living of "self-sufficiency," but specifically, "since friends are among the goods which make a life self-sufficient, self-sufficiency is relational and the good life a life dependent upon and interwoven with others" (ibid.). "By self-sufficient," Sherman (ibid.) quotes from the *Nicomachean Ethics*, "we do not mean for a solitary individual, for one living a life alone, but for parents, children, and wife, and in general for all friends and fellow citizens since a human being is by nature political and social" (1.7, 1097b9–11; Sherman also directs us to *NE* 1169b18–19). This conception of the good life stands in stark contrast to the ascetic ideal Aristotle had learned from Plato (*Phaedo* 64e–66b), according to whom the problem with depending on one's affection for (and the affection of) other people for happiness is akin to that of depending on one's appetites: because those factors are not subject to the individual agent's control, depending on them exposes the individual agent to risk, vulnerability. For Plato, therefore, the only way to ensure happiness is to protect the individual agent against such risk by isolating him or her from factors over which s/he has no control. Aristotle implicitly likens this conception of asceticism or affective self-sufficiency to a divine state—"we are not investigating the self-sufficiency of a god, but of human beings" (*Magna Moralia* 1218a8);

"for us well-being has reference to something other than ourselves [*kath' heteron*], but in [a god's] case he is himself his own well-being" (*Eudemian Ethics* 1245b18–19; Rackham, 1935/1996, p. 445)—in order to insist that the agent of *human* happiness is not the individual but the group. This does mean risk and vulnerability, Aristotle recognizes—this is why we value what he calls "virtue friendship" so highly, where the stability of the friendship is ensured by a shared interest not in specific activities but in virtue (see *MZ* 5B33)—but exposure to that sort of risk and vulnerability is part of the human condition, and seeking to flee it into ascetic isolation from others is simply not feasible for the social animals that we are.

What Kenneth Burke teases out of Aristotle is actually rather more complicated than a notion that can be summed up with a phrase like "the group mind." Burke (1950/1969, p. 22) specifically theorizes identification as "compensatory to division"—as "affirmed with earnestness precisely because there is division." "If men were not apart from one another," he adds, "there would be no need for the rhetorician to proclaim their unity" (ibid.): they would *be* unified. (By "apartness" Burke means specifically our biological division—for example, the fact that I cannot digest the food you eat. Because our bodies are individually wrapped, we see the world through different eyes, touch it with different fingers, channel it through different metabolic processes, and so on.) But neither would there be a need for the rhetor to proclaim our unity if we were totally apart. It would in fact hardly even be conceivable for identification, and thus persuasion, to exist if it were not for the partial merging of selves that Burke calls identification. Strife and persuasion are both possible and in some sense inevitable because we are neither entirely the same nor entirely apart. Identification is an imaginary oneness, but one that is often deeply felt—a shared *affective* self, as I noted above—and is thus both fragile and emotionally volatile. A calm conviction of loyalty and the intense pain of betrayal are both identificatory experiences: the one a feeling of consubstantiality, the other a feeling of its dissolution. One byproduct of identification is that "one body/one mind" sense that we sometimes have that we are part of a smoothly functioning whole that is greater than the sum of its parts—which is to say, more than just a collection of individual human beings. Another is war—"that most tragically ironic of all divisions, or conflicts, wherein millions of cooperative acts go into the preparation for one single destructive act," which for Burke is thus a "*disease* of cooperation" (ibid.). In some sense, in fact, war is ideally fought by one group mind against another—one group mind cooperating consubstantially to destroy another that is perceived as not only alien but inimical to it.

Implicit in Burke's notion of identification, then, is a distinction between the physical body and the affective self—or between what in Chinese might be called the *shēntĭ* 身體 (the organic body, made up of muscle and organs and skin wrapped around bones) and the *shēnxīn* 身心 (the psychosomatic body, made up of feeling-becoming-thinking, or heart-becoming-mind). In some cases the affective self may be coterminous with the physical body: my self ends at my skin. In others it may be smaller than the physical body, may withdraw into the mind (what Descartes calls the *res cogitans*) and view the body (the *res extensa*) as its big dumb ride. In cases of Burkean identification, or what Aristotle calls *philia* or *to philein* (friendship or friendly feeling), the affective self expands and extends and merges with others like it, forming a group mind, or a collective body-becoming-mind—but only transiently and imperfectly, because, as I say, that construct is fragile and emotionally volatile. This group body-becoming-mind or heart-becoming-mind is the collective subject of *pistis* "persuading-becoming-believing," and thus the hero of chapter 2; it is also the collective subject of *doxa* "opinion-becoming-reputation," and thus the hero of chapter 4 as well.

What Naess adds to Burke on this score is his recognition that while the collectivized affective self is often restricted to the *social* self—certainly it is that in Burke—there is also an affective self whose reach is far broader, which Naess calls the *ecological self*. Naess gives examples in which people identify with a specific mountain or river, and feel personally violated when ecological disaster is wreaked on it, or feel emotionally as well as geographically dispossessed when forcibly moved from proximity to the landscape with which they so strongly identify. This ecological identification is often linked with sacralization, and certainly some cultures do vest this phenomenology with the trappings of the sacred; but Naess's point is that the ecological self is far more widespread than this association with "sacred mountains" and the like might suggest. We all have it, to the extent that we identify with our homes (a home is a dwelling with which we affectively identify), our backyards, our neighborhoods, the views out our windows, the places and pathways we live in and walk through every day.

2.3 Mencius: *zhì* 治 "Govern" as Reciprocal

The *pistis* sort of term that in Eric Havelock's terms serves as both the subject and object of an action is quite common in Chinese; and the *MZ* has numerous passages exploring the resulting circulation of action through groups. For example, consider the rhetorical advice Mencius gives to a ruler in 4A4:

> Mencius said: "If others do not respond to your love with love, look into your own benevolence; if others do not respond to your attempts to govern them with order, look into your own wisdom; if others do not return your courtesy, look into your own respect. In other words, look into yourself whenever you fail to achieve your purpose. When you are correct in your person, the Empire will turn to you." (Lau, 1970/2003, p. 153)[2]

The organizing concept in this passage is *fǎn* 反, to reverse or invert, which Lau renders "look into"—more precisely "look *back* at/into." It is also to return from a place, to turn upside-down or inside-out, and to oppose or rebel against. Adjectivally it means "contrary" or "opposite," adverbially "against"; it can also be translated "anti-." It is also used for analogical expressions, since in Chinese these are thought to be inverted ways of saying a thing. Here it implies that the default directionality of the human gaze is outward, to other people, and indeed that gazes "circulate" through the bodies of those present; and that it is only when there is a break in that default circulation that one should "reverse" or "invert" one's gaze at oneself. What is notable is that *fǎn* 反 in this passage is itself the inverse of the default circulation: not a radically different action, but the same circulatory or reticulatory action turned inside-out, turned back on itself.

Related circulatory/reticulatory concepts in the passage include:

- *dá* 答 "answer, agree": here meaning (not) to respond to ritual propriety with ritual propriety, and thus (not) to reciprocate (Lau: "if others do not *return* your courtesy"). The social default for ritual propriety is reciprocity, and indeed somatic contagion, each ritual gesture not just requiring but invoking and conditioning its proper response; the failure to "answer" ritual propriety with ritual propriety signals a break in the flow that must be repaired.

- *guī* 歸 "to go back, to return": here referring literally to the return of "heaven-down" or "the land under heaven" (*tiān xià* 天下), or, as Lau more idiomatically translates that, "the

Empire will *turn* to you." The implication is that the Empire turns away from the immoral ruler and turns back to the ruler who has become moral.

In addition, of course, the whole passage deals with reciprocation, or more generally with reticulation, the contagious mirroring of emotion and behavior from one body or person (*shēn* 身, which means both body and person; Lau has "correct in your *person*," but the phrase *shēn zhèng* 身正 could have been rendered "upright in your body") to another, so that it is actually *transferred* from body to body. By implying that such reciprocation or reticulation is the default state in human society—that human beings naturally mirror each other's emotions and behavior—Mencius anticipates the Rizzolatti group's discovery of mirror neurons (Rizzolatti and Sinigaglia, 2008) by two thousand years. But of course the phenomenological "naturalness" of that mirroring has long been known; the Rizzolatti group merely identified the neural pathways through which it is channeled. What blocks that mirroring for Mencius is some sort of deficit in one (or more) of the participants in a social interaction; this passage identifies the specific kinds of deficits that can cause such blockages, and encourages readers to invert their gaze back at their own lacks or failings, in an attempt to identify and repair the blockage and restore the natural flows of feelings and behavior through groups.

Four of the major forms reciprocity takes in the passage, then, are:

[1] *The inversion of the gaze*: the default gaze is outward; the inversion is to pull it back from its outward movement to look back inward

[2] *The answer in kind*: the default response to ritual propriety is a mirroring with ritual propriety

[3] *Intimacy*: the default response to (and source of) love is *qīn* 親, which can mean "to draw close" or even "to kiss," but also parents and other close relations, intimates, and "dear." The idea is that love breeds not just kisses or other physical and emotional closeness, and not just love, but a whole complexly interconnected web of intimate relations

[4] *The return*: if the Empire has turned away from an immoral ruler, it will turn back if the ruler becomes moral

The circulation of (3) love (*ài* 愛) and closeness (*qīn* 親) through a family or a circle of friends is closely related to what we've seen Aristotle calling *to philein.* Mencius too, while primarily meaning family love here, places a high value on friendship. Indeed he associates the "relationship" (*lún* 倫: see note 5 on p. 263) of friendship with faithfulness or trust (*xìn* 信: 3A4 and 4A12, which latter also ties the ability to inspire faithfulness in one's friends to making one's parents happy and success in a job), and like Aristotle insists that what friends love in each other is their virtue (5B3, 5B7–8). For a discussion of (2), see §3.9.

The fifth is more complicated:

[5] *zhì rén bù zhì* 治人不治, literally "govern people not govern"

The interesting question to consider syntactically in reading [5] is whether the implicit (grammatical) subjects invoked by the two instantiations of the verb *zhì* 治 "govern" are one or two in number:

[a] One implicit subject:

[S₁ (ruler) +] V (govern) + DO (people) > Neg (not) + *[S₁ (ruler) +]* V (govern)[3]

[b] Two implicit subjects:

[S₁ (ruler) +] V (govern) + DO (people) > Neg (not) + *[S₂ (people) +]* V (govern)

In 5a, with a single subject, the ruler performs the actions named by both verb-instantiations, governs *and* fails to govern; in 5b, with two subjects, first the ruler governs the people and then the people do not "govern." 5a is obviously somewhat more attractive in English, since it relieves the translator of the need to look for (5b) a single transitive verb that might render both what the ruler does to the people ("govern") and what the people do in response (not "govern," but what?). In 5a, obviously, the ruler is simply trying to govern and not succeeding. The repeated if-then logic around which Mencius structures 4A4, however, is entirely in line with 5b: if *you* (the ruler) do something to *other people*—if you love and govern them and show them courtesy—and those *other people* don't do back to you what you expect them to, then your proper course of action is to look back at yourself.[4] It does seem likely, therefore, that Mencius means for *zhì* 治 to imply (5b) two subjects: to refer both to what the ruler does in ruling and what the people do in responding to that rule.

Here are some English translations, organized by how many implicit subjects they read into Mencius's subjectless clause:

(a) One subject:

> If he *is trying to* rule others, and his government is unsuccessful . . . (Legge, 1861/1970, p. 294; italics Legge's)

> If your rule over other people is unsuccessful . . . (Zhao et al., 1993, p. 263)

(b) Two subjects:

> If you rule men and they prove disorderly . . . (Collie, 1828, p. 99)

> If a man govern others, and they fail to respond . . . (Dobson, 1963, p. 145)

> If others do not respond to your attempts to govern them with order . . . (Lau, 1970/2003)

> If you try to govern people but they resist . . . (Hinton, 1998, p. 125)

> If one rules over others and they are unruly . . . (Van Norden, 2008, p. 91)

Whether we turn *bùzhì* 不治 "not govern" into an adjective, like Collie ("disorderly") or Van Norden ("unruly"), or a verb, like Dobson ("fail to respond"), Lau ("not respond . . . with order"), or Hinton ("resist"), it seems clear that in (b), with two subjects, the fundamental English sense of the second *zhì* 治 is a passive version of the first:

> If you govern the people and they are not governed . . .

> If you rule the people and they are not ruled . . .

This is, it should be clear, syntactically very close to Aristotle's *pistis* as both persuading and being persuaded. But then if you accept my suggestion that Aristotle's *pistis* might most effectively be read as a speech act performed not individually by the speaker (as persuasion) or by the audience (as belief) but by both at once, collectively, it will be quite clear that the same is *a fortiori* true of Mencius's *zhì* 治—*a fortiori*, because this sort of "circulatory" (ecotic) collectivism is widely recognized to be endemic to Mencian thought. After all, note the advisory context in which *zhìrén bùzhì* 治人不治 "govern people not govern" appears:

- *àirén bùqīn* 愛人不親, literally "love people not draw-close," more loosely "if you love people and they don't draw close," or "if you think you are showing love but the love you show doesn't engender a close loving family environment"—then look back at your *rén* 仁 (the "friendly feeling" to which we turn in §2.4)

- *zhìrén bùzhì* 治人不治, literally "govern people not govern," or "if your rule does not bring about an orderly political environment"—then look back at your own wisdom

- *lǐrén bùdá* 禮人不答, literally "accommodate people not respond," more loosely "if you are polite to people and they don't respond in kind," or "if your observance of the ritual proprieties does not create a social environment where everyone is inclined to observe those proprieties"—then look back at the respect you feel for other people

One important passing observation: 4A4 casts "the people" in a very different light from the construction Zhang (2010) argues Mencius puts on them. According to Zhang, Mencius is—perhaps unintentionally, or only opportunistically, in order to convince reluctant rulers—complicit in the then-standard infantilization of the people, whom he compares to the small child on the verge of the well (helpless to save itself, therefore dependent on adults to save it), or to domestic animals like the ox for whom King Xuan of Qi feels pity in 1A7. As Zhang (63) notes, this makes *rén zhèng* 仁政 (especially when mistranslated "benevolent government") a form of "pity ethics." In 4A4, however, what the ruler does and what the people do are explicitly constructed as not only reciprocal actions but *the same* action, circulated through the entire population (including the ruler) like love and intimacy through a family, or like ritual propriety through any other group. This does not change the fact that Mencius also portrays the people through infantilizing analogies; but it does offer a counterpoint that makes it possible for us to differentiate between the antipopulist advice Mencius gives recalcitrant rulers as opportunistic motivation and a more genuinely "humane" (protopopulist) political philosophy that he might be taken to believe "truly."

2.4 Mencius: The Group (Heart-Becoming-)Mind as *rén* 仁

Indeed I suggest that, in 4A4 and elsewhere in the *MZ*, governance is not just *like* persuasion in being a collective action performed by the group body-becoming-mind; for Mencius the ideal kind of governance *is* persuasion-based, precisely because it works in and through the group heart-becoming-mind or collective feeling-becoming-thinking. "Heart-becoming-mind" and "feeling-becoming-thinking" are my suggested translations of *xīn* 心 (explored in detail in §2.6); when *xīn* 心 circulates productively and harmoniously through a group, the result is what Mencius calls *rén* 仁.

Now *rén* 仁 is widely recognized as *the* key Confucian concept. As Chan (1955, 1963; see also Pang, 2009) tracks its history in Confucian thought, while in pre-Confucian texts it was occasionally used in a vague sense meaning the ruler's "kindness," it was only introduced for philosophical use by Confucius himself; it appears 105 times in the *Analects*, and 58 of the 499 chapters in that collection are dedicated to a discussion of that virtue (see also Jung, 1966, 1969; Hang, 1974; Tu, 1981; Chong, 1999). As Chan (1963, p. 16) notes, "No other subject, not even filial piety, engaged so much attention of the Master and his disciples." And what Confucius did with the concept specifically was to broaden its scope from a specific virtue, kindness or benevolence—which is how we've just seen Lau translating it, and until very recently was how most English translators tended to render it—to a general description of the "exemplary person" (*jūnzǐ* 君子). As Chan (ibid.) writes, the man of *rén* 仁 "is a man of the golden rule, for, 'wishing to establish his own character, he also establishes the character of others, and wishing to be prominent himself, he also helps others to be prominent'" (*Analects* 6.28). So all-encompassing was *rén* 仁 for Confucius and his later followers that it extended to nature as well—the Golden Rule applied to plants and water and soil and air—and even "heaven" (*tiān* 天), giving that concept what seems to thinkers in a Western dualizing/spiritualizing tradition a distinctly secular quality. Obviously, this is very much the same philosophical vein that Kenneth Burke and Arne Naess mine as well with their conceptions of identification—Naess in particular with his conception of identification as the key to the Self-realization of the ecological self.

The character *rén* 仁 appears even more frequently in the *MZ*, 158 times; in two-thirds (99) of those occurrences its meaning is left not only undefined but co-textually underdetermined:

- *rén rén* 仁人 (an X person: 1A7, 1B15, 3A3, 3A5, 5A3, 6B11, 7A22, 7B3)

- *rén zhèng* 仁政 (an X government: 1A5, 1B11–12, 2A1, 3A3–4, 4A1, 4A14)

- *rén yì* 仁義 (an X fittingness or X and fitting behavior: 1A1, 2B2, 6A16, 7A21; 3B9, 4B19, 6A1, 6A8, 6A17, 6B4, 7A33)
- *rén zhì* 仁智 (X and wisdom: 2B9)
- *rén xīn rén wén* 仁心仁聞 (an X heart and an X reputation: 4A1)

In each of these cases one either knows or does not know what Mencius means by the word; his co-text provides no guidance in settling on a precise meaning.

Examining English translations of *rén* 仁, we can distinguish two distinct periods:

(1) *Benevolent/benevolence*: from David Collie (1828) and James Legge (1861/1970) to D. C. Lau (1970/2003), the translators of the Shāndōng Friendship Press (山東友誼書社) edition (Zhao et al., 1993), and Bryan W. Van Norden (2008).

(2) *Humane/humanity*: from Chan Wing-tsit (1963) and W. A. C. H. Dobson (1963) to David Hinton (1998) and Irene Bloom (2009).

The move from (1) to (2) roughly traces the conceptual shift that Chan (1955, 1963) tells us Confucius effected in the Chinese understanding of *rén* 仁, from a specific individual *virtue* (benevolence) to a general characteristic of (exemplary) human social interaction (humaneness/humanity)—a quality of the interactive behavior of (good) people in groups rather than of discrete individuals. Significantly, given the fact that in English "humane" and "benevolent" can be synonymous virtues in the individual, in his translation of the *Analects* Chan (1963, p. 25) renders *rén rén* 仁人 not as "the humane man" but as "the man of humanity":

> 4:2. Confucius said, "One who is not a man of humanity [*rén rén* 仁人] cannot endure adversity for long, nor can he enjoy prosperity for long. The man of humanity [*rén rén* 仁人] is naturally at ease with humanity [*rén* 仁]. The man of wisdom cultivates humanity [*rén* 仁] for its advantage."

> 4:3. Confucius said, "Only the man of humanity [*rén rén* 仁人] knows how to love people and hate people."

4:4. Confucius said, "If you set your mind on humanity [*rén* 仁], you will be free from evil."

Clearly, there, *rén* 仁 is not so much a virtue like "benevolence" as it is an interactive phenomenology in which individuals *participate*. A *rén rén* 仁人 is not a person with a specific disposition so much as s/he is a person who allows *rén* 仁 to flow through his or her actions, thoughts, words, and relationships. If we used English translations of Aristotle's terminology to translate *rén rén* 仁人, it would be not "a friendly person" or "a person who feels friendly toward others" but "a person who partakes ecotically in friendly feeling."

Still, there remains among many English-speaking scholars in China today a strong attachment to the older translation "benevolence," despite both the slow shift away from it in more recent translations and the fact that in the older translations the resulting collocations often sound odd enough to ring alarm bells. For example, in 1B8 we find *zéi rénzhě wèi zhī zéi* 賊仁者謂之賊 translated as:

- "He who outrages the benevolence *proper to his nature*, is called a robber" (Legge, 1861/1970, p. 167)
- "He who mutilates benevolence is a mutilator" (Lau, 1970/2003, p. 43)
- "He who outrages benevolence is an outrager" (Zhao et al., 1993, p. 81)
- "One who mutilates benevolence should be called a 'mutilator'" (Van Norden, 2008, p. 26)

What exactly would it mean to outrage or mutilate *benevolence*? It is a bit difficult to imagine. But perhaps this is a problem in the translation not of *rén* 仁 but of *zéi* 賊? The core meaning of *zéi* 賊 is actually a thief or a traitor; if we stay with the traditional "benevolence" translation, literally the Chinese says that anyone who steals (or betrays) benevolence is called a thief (or a traitor). And obviously it doesn't make any more sense to steal or betray benevolence than it does to outrage or mutilate it. Legge's italicized interpolation in "the benevolence *proper to his nature*" makes the outrage he reports seem marginally more plausible, suggesting some manner of violation of the actor's own moral nature; even so, "benevolence" in his rendering remains difficult to parse. Collie (1828, 26) backs off his usual translation of *rén* 仁 here as "benevolence" to render this passage "he who injures (or robs) virtue, is called a robber"—but this too is difficult to understand. What is it about virtue that can be injured or robbed? But if *rén* 仁 is a collective phenomenology, a felt quality of caring human interaction like Aristotle's "friendly feeling," it is considerably easier to imagine someone "betraying" it. As we have seen (§2.3), two of the interactive phenomenologies that Confucians take to be constituent of *rén* 仁 are love (*ài* 愛) and trust (*xìn* 信); as we will see later (§2.8), another is loyalty (*zhōng* 忠): unlike benevolence, all three are quite obviously "things" that can be betrayed.[5]

Reading the various English translations stereoscopically against the Chinese originals turns up other problems as well. In 4A2–3, for example, Mencius quotes and then expands upon the Confucian notion that *dào èr: rén yǔ bùrén ér yǐ yǐ* 道二: 仁與不仁而已矣 (4A2), or as Lau (1970/2003, p. 153) translates that, "There are two ways and two only: benevolence and cruelty." Mencius's exfoliations of this contrast in 4A3 include: "The Three Dynasties won the Empire through benevolence [*rén* 仁] and lost it through cruelty [*bùrén* 不仁]" and "To dislike death yet revel in cruelty [*bùrén* 不仁] is no different from drinking beyond your capacity despite your dislike of drunkenness" (Lau, ibid.).

In the original Chinese, however, the opposite of *rén* 仁 in all these passages is not a specific immoral disposition like "cruelty"; it is simply "not *rén*." Confucius's words as quoted in 4A2 are *rén yǔ bùrén* 仁與不仁: not "benevolence and cruelty" but, as Van Norden (2008, p. 90) has it, "benevolence and nonbenevolence." The Three Dynasties lost the Empire through "a lack of benevolence"; the reveling that Mencius compares to liking death is a reveling in that same lack of benevolence. The problem with a translation like "not benevolence" or "lack of benevolence," obviously, as Lau clearly realized, and Collie, Legge, Zhao et al., and Van Norden did not,[6] is that in English a lack of benevolence does not seem like a particularly heinous kind of immorality; it would typically make a person morally *neutral*. From that observation we can in fact infer that benevolence is not an overwhelmingly praiseworthy attribute in English: morally positive, to be sure, but not positive enough to make its absence a critical problem for morality. It essentially means being *kind* to people, the colloquial sense of *rén* 仁 before Confucius took over the term; Confucius and Mencius here are talking about a much more serious (indeed more dangerous) moral flaw than simply failing to behave nicely, kindly, benevolently.

It is also telling that, no matter how meticulously Lau attempts to render *rén* 仁 as "benevolent/-ce," there are contexts where he finds that it does not convey a strong enough sense of moral force. In the line "After three years, Tai Jia repented and reproached himself, and, while in Tong, reformed and became a good and dutiful man" (5A6; Lau, 1970/2003, p. 209; names pinyinized), for example, the Chinese for "became a good and dutiful man" is *chǔ rén qiān yì* 處仁遷義, literally "behave *rén* become right." Lau clearly sensed that he needed a broader and stronger moral characterization than "benevolent" here; indeed he could as well have translated it "became a *moral* and dutiful man."[7] Like "benevolence," of course, "good" and "moral" are adjectives describing individual virtue—and thus lacking the pan-human connectivity that Confucius introduced and Mencius expanded.

The collocation of *rén* 仁 with *yì* 義 (rightness or fitting behavior) to form *rényì* 仁義 occurs 26 times in the *MZ*; Huang (2001, 71) notes that this compound is one of Mencius's core concepts. Moving exemplification and discussion of *rényì* 仁義 to an endnote,[8] let us consider here only two of the most famous passages in which it plays a central role. The first is in the disputation with Gaozi (6A1):

> Gaozi said, "Human nature [*xìng* 性—for discussion, see §4.3] is like the *qǐ* willow. Dutifulness [*yì* 義] is like cups and bowls. To make morality [*rényì* 仁義] out of human nature is like making cups and bowls out of the willow."
>
> "Can you," said Mencius, "make cups and bowls by following the nature of the willow? Or must you mutilate the willow before you can make it into cups and bowls? If you have to mutilate the willow to make it into cups and bowls, must you, then, also mutilate a man to make him moral [*rényì* 仁義]? Surely it will be those words of yours men in the world will follow in bringing disaster upon morality [*rényì* 仁義]." (Lau, 1970/2003, p. 241; names of first speaker and willow pinyinized)

This passage obviously invokes the implicit metaphorical context Mencius is alluding to in 1B8, where Lau tells us that "he who mutilates benevolence is a mutilator" (43); indeed semantic continuity with this metaphorical context is almost certainly why Lau used "mutilate" for *zéi* 賊 "thief, traitor, wily, evil" in 1B8, rather than, say, "injure (rob)" (Collie), "outrage" (Legge, Zhao et al.) or "steal" (Hinton).[9] Here Mencius makes it clear that in troping *rényì* 仁義 as carving bowls out of a tree Gaozi is rather disastrously troping the "path of morality" (the process of becoming-moral, which is also the process of becoming-human) as mutilation.

This is a theme to which Mencius returns again and again. In the well-known Ox Mountain chapter (6A8), for example, he tells a parable about the trees on Ox Mountain, which, because they were close to a great city, were "constantly lopped by axes. Is it any wonder that they are no longer fine?" (Lau, 1970/2003, p. 251). The people from the city do not cut off their branches every moment of the day, however, so with moisture from the rain and the dew, they put out new shoots (*duān* 端, which Mencius uses to trope the four virtuous dispositions [2A6]); but then the grazing livestock nibble those off too. Thus Ox Mountain comes to be deforested, "bald," and people think that "it never had any trees. But," Mencius asks, "can that possibly be the nature of a mountain? Can what is in man be completely lacking in moral inclinations [*rényì* 仁義]? A man's letting go of his true heart is like the case of the trees and the axes" (ibid.). As a person lets go of his or her true heart, s/he becomes dissipated, and the moisture in the night air can no longer nourish his or her new growth (the four shoots of dispositional virtue), which for Mencius also means that "what was originally in him" is lost; "when that happens, the man is not far removed from an animal" (ibid.).

Scholars generally agree that Mencius expanded significantly on the central concepts developed by Confucius; in order to begin to flesh out his conceptual expansions of *rén* 仁, I propose to make a longish digression into the web of related terms that support and help define it in the *MZ*: *bùrěn* 不忍 "to be unable to bear [other people's suffering]" in §2.5, *xīn* 心 "heart-becoming-mind" in §2.6, Mencius's (bio)ecological metaphors for this embodiment of virtue in §2.7, and Dai Zhen on *xuèqì* 血氣 "blood-*qì*, valor" in §2.8. Only after that digression will I return to define *rén* 仁 as group *xīn* 心 in §2.9, and to rethink *rén zhèng* 仁政 "*rén* government" as a *rhetorical* conception of government as/by persuasion in §2.10. I conclude the chapter in §2.11 by returning to Aristotle, with the concept *to endekhomenon pithanon*, which I translate "the available persuasivity."

2.5 Mencius: *bùrěn* 不忍 as the Inability to Bear Other People's Suffering

Shun Kwong-loi (1997, p. 49) notes that Chinese scholars relate *rén* 仁 to another tonalization of *ren*, namely *rěn* 忍 "to bear, to endure." This appears 17 times in the *MZ*, specifically in the negative form of *bùrěn* 不忍 "to be unable to bear," in the sense of "an inability to bear the pain and suffering of others" (ibid.). Mencius discusses this inability at considerable length in several sections, the most famous (1A7) being King Xuan's empathy for the suffering of an ox being led to slaughter that I noted was exactly parallel to Arne Naess's (1995, pp. 15–16) example of identification with the nonhuman suffering of a flea; others include 4A1, 4B24, 5B1, and 7B36. Mencius ties *bùrěn* 不忍 specifically to *rén* 仁 in two sections, the latter being the simpler case: "Mencius said, 'For every man there are things he cannot bear [*bù rěn* 不忍]. To extend this to what he can bear is benevolence [*rén* 仁]'" (7B31, Lau, 1970/2003, p. 323). The former is the famous "Child at the Well" scenario (2A6), which begins with implicit advice to a ruler:

> Mencius said, "No man is devoid of a heart sensitive to the suffering of others [*rén jiē yǒu bùrěnrén zhī xīn* 人皆有不忍人之心]. Such a sensitive heart [*bùrěnrén zhī xīn* 不忍人之心] was possessed by the Former Kings and this manifested itself in compassionate government [*bùrěnrén zhī zhèng* 不忍人之政]. With such a sensitive heart behind compassionate government, it was as easy to rule the Empire as rolling it on your palm." (ibid., p. 73)

Literally, what Lau translates there first as "a heart sensitive to the suffering of others" and then in abbreviated form as "a sensitive heart" is a "can't-bear-person's heart": what the person's heart can't bear, namely other people's suffering, is implicit in *bùrěn* 不忍 "can't bear" (for further discussion of the four hearts, see §4.4). What Lau translates as "compassionate government" is literally "can't-bear-person's government": precisely the same phrase with only the last character substituted, *zhèng* 政 "government" for *xīn* 心 "heart."

Mencius goes on:

> "My reason for saying that no man is devoid of a heart sensitive to the suffering of others is this. Suppose a man were, all of a sudden, to see a young child on the verge of falling into a well. He would certainly be moved to compassion, not because he wanted to get in the good graces of the parents, nor because he wished to win the praise of his fellow villagers or friends, nor yet because he disliked the cry of the child. From this it can be seen that whoever is devoid of the heart of compassion is not human [*wú cèyǐn zhī xīn, fēirén yě* 無惻隱之心, 非人也], whoever is devoid of the heart of courtesy and modesty is not human, and whoever is devoid of the heart of right and wrong is not human." (Lau, 1970/2003, p. 73)

And then he goes on to tell us that the "heart" or feeling of compassion *is* the dispositional "shoot" or "sprout" that is *rén* 仁, and so on. Shun (1997, p. 49) notes that the term Lau here translates as "compassion," *cèyǐn* 惻隱, literally "secret sorrow" and generally understood to mean "being moved by the suffering of others" (ibid.), is considered by most Chinese commentators to be synonymous with *bùrěn* 不忍, justifying Lau's two-step terminological shift from "a sensitive heart" (*bùrěnrén zhī xīn* 不忍人之心) to "compassionate government" (*bùrěnrén zhī zhèng* 不忍人之政) to "the heart of compassion" (*cèyǐn zhī xīn* 惻隱之心; see also 6A6).

Birdwhistell (2007, ch. 7) offers a trenchant gendered reading of this famous scene, noting that for philosophical impact the person who sees the young child on the verge of the well *has* to be male—that under patriarchy we would "naturally" tend to assume that a woman would respond compassionately to the sight of a young child in danger, making that particular scenario no news at all, nothing worth citing as a knock-down argument. Mencius's claim, Birdwhistell suggests, is that men have that compassionate heart as well—that it is not just a woman's heart, but a *human* heart. What Mencius is doing, Birdwhistell argues, is appropriating the compassion (and other relational affects, like love and trust) we associate with women for men as well, and thus—at least ideally—for all human beings. In actual fact, Birdwhistell notes, this "transgender ideal" only really applies for Mencius to sages and other exemplary persons—ordinary men (not women) are mostly beasts—and should ideally apply in the end to the ruler, who thus becomes father and mother to the people (*wéi mín fùmǔ* 為民父母, 1A4, 1B7, 3A3; *fùmǔ* 父母, 2A5).

The obvious dualisms that this cluster of associations suggests to us would, Birdwhistell warns, be simplistic—men as rational individuals, women as emotional floods that overflow the boundaries between individuals, or what Lacan calls the "undifferentiation" of the maternal Imaginary—but it does seem as if Mencius might himself be drawing on some such dualisms in his attempt to rethink them, to smuggle something like what we take to be "natural" maternal impulses into "standard" (elite) masculinity. In my ongoing attempt to thwart the simple mapping of such simple-minded dualisms onto Sino-Hellenic comparisons as well—the Greeks as rational individualists and therefore "masculine," the Chinese as emotional collectivists and therefore "feminine"—I will keep reminding the reader not only that Mencius indulges in rationalist and individualizing dualisms (and as Birdwhistell shows insists on the patriarchal dualism between men's and women's social roles), but that Aristotle too draws heavily on the "emotional flooding" that patriarchy assigns to women. In Birdwhistell's terms, the deep ecology of rhetoric in this book is metaphorically masculine-plus-feminine, based on a transgender ideal that leans strongly toward affective collectivism without blurring individuals out of the picture altogether; and because my models for that transgender ideal are the complexly but resolutely patriarchal Mencius and Aristotle (and I am obviously male myself),[10] my argumentation will retain a subtle orientation toward the universalization of (transgendered) male experience, with only the odd paragraph like this one to remind the reader of what my approach elides.

Arne Naess manifestly understood identification affectively, as a *feeling* of oneness with other living beings (see e.g., Naess, 2002, p. 20ff), but to my knowledge never referred in his writings to Mencius. In a paper entitled "Ecology, Place, and the Awakening of Compassion," however, Gary Snyder (1994/1995, pp. 239, 240)—sometimes referred to as "the poet-laureate of the deep ecology movement" (Bookchin, 1994, p. 25)—specifically mentions both "the Mind of Compassion" and "the heart of compassion" as interactive phenomenologies that the ecologically minded person must not lose. It is difficult to know whether Snyder had read Lau's 1970 translation of Mencius in the seventies, but in a 1977 interview with Peter Barry Chowka he notes that "the spiritual legacy of Chinese culture is essentially Zen (or Ch'an) Buddhism" but also mentions that a "secondary spiritual legacy of China" is "the aesthetics—the poetry and painting (Confucius, Lao-tzu, and Chuang-tzu are included in that; also Mencius, whose work will be appreciated more in time for its great human sanity, although it's deliberately modest in its spiritual claims)" (Chowka, 1977/1980, p. 104). Snyder is the deep ecologist who is best grounded in Asian philosophy and poetry, and he has translated extensively from both the Japanese and the Chinese; but clearly his expertise leans more toward Japan than China, and more toward poetry and spirituality than the secular political philosophy of Confucianism. Hence, perhaps, his inclination to read Confucius, Laozi (老子), Zhuangzi (莊子), and Mencius as poets rather than as philosophers, and his preference for the more overtly spiritualizing thought of *Laozi* to the more secular Mencius. Naess too gravitated to *Laozi* and Zen Buddhism.

2.6 Mencius: *xīn* 心 as Feeling-Becoming-Thinking

Now let us look more closely at Mencius's conception of *xīn* 心. Noting that the character 心 derives from a stylized drawing of the human heart, Behuniak (2005, p. 26) warns that translating the character as "heart" (as Lau does) often leads to "anatomical reification," and in many contexts to confusion. For example, in 2A6, when the man sees the child teetering on the verge of a well, Mencius describes what he experiences as *cèyǐn zhī xīn* 惻隱之心, literally "secret sorrow's heart"; obviously, Behuniak notes, "the heart" here means feeling, specifically in this case a feeling of distress, which as we began to see in §2.5 is generally understood to mean a vicarious distress, a participation in someone else's distress. Indeed, Behuniak (ibid.) adds, "In the *Mencius*, it proves adequate to translate *xin* as 'feeling' in crucial instances."

One of the "crucial instances" to which Behuniak turns in his very next paragraph, however, is at first glance problematic for the "feeling" translation: in 6A15 Mencius writes that the eyes and ears cannot think, and so are easily deceived, but *xīn zhī guān zé sī, sī zé dé zhī, bù sī zé bù dé* 心之官則思, 思則得之, 不思則不得, literally "The heart's office/function is to think, thinks and engages it, doesn't think doesn't engage." Drawing on a later extension of *guān* 官 as "organ," Lau (1970/2003, p. 259) translates the passage "The organ of the heart can think. But it will find the answer only if it does think; otherwise, it will not find the answer." It sounds a bit odd in English, of course, for the cardiac muscle to be thinking; Collie (1828, p. 151) and Legge (1861/1970, p. 418) solve this problem preemptively by shifting from heart to mind:

> It is the mind that can think. When one thinks, he finds the right way; but if he do not think, he will not find it. (Collie glosses this in a note: "It is only by the right employment of our rational powers, that we come to the knowledge of those principles on which our conduct should be formed in all our intercourse with the world.")

> To the mind belongs the office of thinking. By thinking, it gets *the right view of things*; by neglecting to think, it fails to do this. (Italics Legge's)

And indeed *xīn* 心 in many contexts can be translated "mind"; contemporary native speakers of Chinese with good English very often offer "mind" as their *first* translation of *xīn* 心. Chin and Freeman (1990, p. 62) point out that Dai Zhen (戴震, 1724–1777) identified two different "hearts" in Mencius, a feeling heart and a perceiving heart, or mind; the *xīn* 心 in 6A15 is clearly a perceiving heart. Obviously, if in Chinese the heart thinks, then it is itself a kind of mind, a heart-mind (as *xīn* 心 is also often translated) as opposed to the brain-mind.

In my literal translation above of the line about the heart thinking, I followed Behuniak in rendering *dé zhī* 得之 as "engage it"; Chinese-English dictionaries typically define *dé* 得 as "obtain, get, gain." As we saw, Collie, Legge, and Lau translated that predication expansively, unpacking *zhī* 之 "it" so as to give it a suitably cognitive meaning: "finds *the right way*," "get *the right view of things*," "find *the answer*." Van Norden (2008, 156) resists the temptation to identify the antecedent of *zhī* 之 "it": "But the function of the heart is to reflect. If it reflects, then it will get it. If it does not reflect, then it will not get it." He also adds Zhu Xi's commentary: "*What is the 'it' the heart will 'get' if it reflects? Zhu Xi says it is the Pattern of whatever things or affairs one encounters; to 'get it' is to understand how things are and how they should be*" (ibid.); Shun (1997, p. 150) cites similar constructions of the verb's direct object by other traditional Chinese commentators as well. Zhu Xi's dualizing idea, as many have suggested, is close to Plato's: in some dualistically different or opposite realm (spiritual as opposed to material, intellectual as opposed to corporeal) there is an "it" (for Zhu Xi *lǐ* 理 or "the Pattern," or in Plato's terms the "Ideal Form") that only the rational or reflective "heart" can "get." *lǐ* 理, which appears eight times in the *MZ*, can also be translated "reason, logic, science, inner principle or structure."

In Behuniak's (2005, p. 25) reading, Mencius distinguishes between the moral guidance provided by *xīn* 心 "feeling" and the moral indeterminacy of *qì* 氣 on the grounds that *xīn* 心 is the normative engagement with the world of things and people in and through which *qì* 氣 is configured as a moral force—specifically, in 2A2, the moral force that Mencius calls his "flood-like *qì*" (*hàorán zhī qì* 浩然之氣), of which more in §3.1. *qì* 氣 is not a stable preexisting force that influences certain actions or movements or changes from without; in fact in some sense, very like the Hegelian *Geist*, it is an ecotic force that can only be said to exist at all within—and above all to emerge transindividually through and out of—specific interactive worldly configurations. For Mencius *xīn* 心 is *qì* 氣 as configured through a habitualized moral disposition; as Behuniak puts it, it "is the outcome of a specific kind of disposition (*xing* 性) actually embedded in the world. Rule-based doctrines are more abstract and thus at a remove from the feeling (*xin*); they do not entail the quality of engagement that dispositions do" (ibid.).

Shun (1997, p. 150) notes further that in the *MZ* as well as in other contemporary Confucian texts, *sī* 思 "think" specifically means "to direct the attention to," especially to a thing that one regards favorably or an action one is contemplating undertaking. It is thus not generically "thinking" (which would include logical operations) but more narrowly "attending to," or in Perelman's (1982, pp. 36–40) term "presencing," or perhaps what Aristotle might call "energizing" (see §3.6)—activities that it is considerably easier to imagine "the heart" performing than, say, performing a cost-benefit analysis would be. Interestingly, Mencius makes this claim about "the heart attending to" things in 6A15 in the specific contrastive context with the eyes and ears, which, he says, cannot "think" (*sī* 思) in this same way. What makes this contrast striking is that the attentive/presencing powers of the eyes and ears are in English our primary metaphors for the attentive/presencing powers of thought, in phrases like "lend an ear to," "hearken to," "keep an eye on," and "see, note, notice, observe, regard, watch," and the like; indeed we often take the body language of sensory attentiveness (eye contact, full-facing body posture, etc.) as outward signs of inward (cognitive) attentiveness. But when one considers that *guān* 官 originally meant a government office, later a government officer, someone in charge of making decisions, *xīn zhī guān zé sī* 心之官則思 "the heart's office is to think" also hints at "the heart is the officer that manages thought." The affective directing/guiding/managing/commanding of thought/attention/perception/focus in effect *saturates* cognitive/conscious apperception of the world with managerial or "officious" affect. This is almost exactly Damasio's (1994) somatic-marker hypothesis.

The interesting question, however, is how to translate *xīn* 心 in *xīn zhī guān zé sī* 心之官則思. "The functioning of feeling, however, is thoughtful"? "But feeling is attentive"? I suggest that, *pace* Behuniak, for Mencius thinking or attentiveness is not exactly an *attribute* of feeling (Q: What is the functioning of feeling like? A: It is attentive). Rather, just as *qì* 氣 is configured ecotically as feeling (*xīn* 心), in order for feeling to be configured ecotically as disposition (*xìng* 性) it must first presence itself as guiding thinking (*sī* 思). That is to say, *xīn* 心 is not a "heart-mind" that is somehow distinct from a "brain-mind"; rather, feeling issues imperceptibly into thinking, *becomes* thinking by incremental steps. In my discussion of the *MZ*, therefore, I translate *xīn* 心 as "feeling-becoming-thinking" (or "heart-becoming-mind"), a perhaps somewhat cumbersome Hegelian or Deleuzean construction that I think far more accurately captures the ecotic flows of feeling into thinking in the *MZ*.

If according to Behuniak the temptation to render *xīn zhī guān* 心之官 as the cardiac muscle is a pitfall to be avoided, Lau's "The organ of the heart can think" falls headlong into that pit. But I submit that the danger of reducing *xīn* 心 to our own medical conception of the heart is not significantly greater than the danger of warding off that misreading by retreating to the disembodied world of philosophical abstraction. Mencius is not merely writing a moral philosophy, or a philosophical psychology of morality; he is also writing a physiology. He believes, or at least talks as if he believes—perhaps he believes as half-metaphorically as Westerners do today—that the heart is *also* an anatomical organ that feels and thinks.

Is it far-fetched, I wonder, to suggest that most Westerners today, even educated Westerners, still do "sort of believe" that the heart is the seat of emotion, and that feeling is a kind of knowing? We remember enough of high school biology classes to know that the heart is a muscle that pumps blood, and may even have picked up enough neurophysiology to know that the true seat of emotion is the brain's limbic system; but we so often *feel* strong emotion in the center of our chest, it still seems somehow physiologically accurate—or at least not entirely inaccurate—to refer to the heart as the seat of emotion. And some Westerners still like to say that the heart knows better than the head.

In fact modern neuroscientists, *mutatis mutandis,* might even agree with Mencius here—that is, once they had established that the autonomic nervous system, which regulates, channels, monitors, and signals emotional response, actually spans the central nervous system or CNS ("the brain") and the peripheral nervous system or PNS ("the body"), and has important signaling pathways running between the "head" and the "heart." Paying close attention to the region of the heart, for example—the center of the chest—may give us far more accurate information about what we truly feel about a thing than trying to analyze our feelings "coldly" "in the brain alone" (whatever that might mean). The autonomic nervous system often signals our feeling-based orientations to situations and courses of action by giving us a feeling of painful constriction, or hot swelling, or warm relaxation, in what feels like the heart. The feeling may technically "begin" in the head, in the limbic system (the amygdala or the hypothalamus, say), but may "begin to be felt" in the heart area (or the "stomach," where enteroceptive signals are perceived, or chills up and down the spine, or sweat on the palms of the hands, etc.). In other words, in the "wiring diagram" established by neurophysiologists, the CNS generates the feeling, then sends signals to the PNS, where they are read by the CNS—a head-heart-head loop, or head-stomach-head loop, or whatever. Phenomenologically, though, these loops *feel* like feeling-becoming-thinking.

Indeed the neo-Jamesian tradition in contemporary neurophysiology understands "feelings" to be becoming-cognitive mappings of body states called "emotions"; to map an emotion as a feeling is to become aware of it, to attend to it, to presence it, to become able to distinguish it from other body states. Feeling in that sense is the leading edge of the emergence of thinking from an organism's homeostatic self-regulation, and it does begin to emerge as directed attention, as an enhanced awareness of our priorities, of what is important, of what concerns us. As thinking continues to emerge from feeling, ever subtler maps are sketched in—comparing, remembering, imagining, and so on—until we reach what we in the West take to be the pinnacle of thinking, various logical operations (categorizing, sequencing, hierarchizing, and so on). In this scientific tradition emerging out of the work of William James (1890), cognition is always affective-becoming-cognitive; even at its most rarefied, its most coolly abstract and anti-emotional, it remains saturated in affect, which only rarely emerges into the stream of consciousness. The famous "somatic-marker hypothesis" of the neo-Jamesian neuroscientist Antonio Damasio (1994, 1999, 2003) postulated that somatic markers—neuroelectrical impulses measurable with a skin-conductance test, and experienced phenomenologically as various physiologically localized sensations of pleasure or pain, well-being or unease, like the kind of intense somatic sensations in the chest that make us trope emotion as "the heart"—powerfully condition and enable our decision-making processes, to the extent that patients with damage to the part of the autonomic nervous system that controls such "marking" are unable to perform very simple cognitive tasks such as prioritizing two courses of action.

Behuniak (2005, p. 28) implicitly draws a powerful parallel between the *MZ* and these neuroscientific findings:

> The world is engaged on many levels, one of the most important of which is the physical. In presenting feeling as a source of moral wisdom, Mencius intends to appeal to the empirical evidence of one's physical reactions, and these consummate in the body. The feelings of distress and concern that emerge upon suddenly spotting a child dangerously close to a well are visceral: increased heart rate, heightened tension, and shortness of breath. The physical dimension of feeling is illustrated throughout the *Mencius* in a manner consistent with the assumptions of a *qi* 氣 cosmology. For the body to fall or run, Mencius tells us, involves a reconfiguration of energy (*qi*) that registers directly as feeling. Tears and perspiration are understood to flow spontaneously from one's feelings through the face and eyes. There is no sharp distinction between feeling and its physical manifestations.

I am not suggesting, in other words, that Behuniak is inclined to neglect physiology in his exposition of Mencius; only that his determination to airbrush the cardiac organ out of *xīn zhī guān* 心之官 may be excessive.

2.7 Mencius: The Deep Ecology of Virtue

Mencius stresses the power of that *xīn zhī guān* 心之官 "the heart's organ" to "organ-ize" and direct human ethecotic (becoming-communal) growth through a (bio)ecological conceit ("human as plant" metaphor) that runs through the *MZ* like a scarlet thread. In 7A21, for example, he calls the heart-becoming-mind (*xīn* 心) the soil in which fellow-feeling, rightness, ritual propriety, and wisdom are *rooted* (*gēn* 根); in 2A6 he calls those four virtues *sì duān* 四端 "the four shoots." Every time this conceit appears in the *MZ* it takes a slightly different form, but always, Behuniak (2005) reminds us, with close attention to the environmental dependencies and contingencies of growth, in the sense in which dispositions depend on conditions (*xìng zì mìng chū* 性自命出):

- If there is a drought in the seventh or eighth month of a seedling's life, it will wither and die; but if it rains, it will perk up again (1A6)

- Some people, trusting their plants to grow on their own, don't weed them; a man from Sòng, wanting to hasten the growth of the seedlings he has planted in his orchard, makes the opposite mistake: he tries to stretch them by hand, and ends up pulling them all the way out of the ground, so that they shrivel up and die (2A2)

- Water can be dammed up so that it forms a lake on a mountaintop, or forced to spray straight up in the air, but it is best to channel and direct its natural tendency to flow downhill (6A2, 6B11)

- The trees on Ox Mountain are near a great city, whose inhabitants chop the trees down for firewood and send their cattle to nibble on the new shoots, so that eventually the mountain is deforested (6A8)

- Wisdom is like a plant that grows easily in the right conditions, but King Xuān of Qí is surrounded by advisors who are like a day of warmth and then ten days of frost, and in Mencius's absence they are always "freezing" the king's "sprouts" of wisdom (6A9)

- When they reach maturity, the domesticated grains are extremely valuable; before they reach maturity, however, even wild plants are more valuable (6A19)

- The exemplary person teaches others on the model of growing plants: providing just the right amount of water at just the right times, and otherwise letting them develop on their own (not making the mistake of the man from Sòng) (7A40)

There is nothing in the genetic "nature" of a tree or other plant that might cause it to wither and die or be pulled up, chopped down, nibbled at by cows, or frozen; plants grow differently in different conditions. As Behuniak (2005, p. xvi) notes, "In classical China, everything that grows does so in the environment that will 'have' it. Everything that grows is *located*." The environment in which the seedlings grow in 2A2 includes an orchard-owner who believes plants will grow faster if they are pulled at; the environment around Ox Mountain contains wood-choppers and nibbling cattle. As Mencius notes in 2A1, quoting a saying from the people of Qí: "One might be clever, but it's better to make use of propensity [*shì* 勢]. One might have a garden hoe, but it is better to wait for the season to arrive" (ibid., p. 5; bracketed interpolation Behuniak's). Stretching seedlings to make them grow faster may seem clever to some; most people know what horticulturists teach, that it's best to let trees indulge their "propensity" to grow, not to help them grow (*wù zhù zhǎng* 勿助長, 2A2) but merely to make their environment (soil, water, sun) as conducive as possible to that propensity. Hoeing, too, is really only useful just before and during the growing season; it doesn't really matter how well one loosens the earth during the time of the year when nothing grows.

In fact *wù zhù zhǎng* 勿助長 "don't help grow" (see, e.g., Shun, 1997, pp. 154–55) would appear to be one version Mencius offers (another, according to Sun Shi [孫奭, 962–1033], being *tiān* 天[12]—for a discussion of which see §4.5) of the Daoist principle of *wúwéi* 無爲, which is sometimes translated "do not act" or "the principle of inaction," but which actually means a kind of solicitous and "interattentive" (ecotic) participation in natural actions or events. Indeed the growing of a tree is often cited as an example of *wúwéi* 無爲: the tree does not act in growing; nor does the horticulturalist act in "growing" the tree. The tree just *grows*. (Another Daoist expression of the same idea is *wéiwúwéi* 爲無爲, acting without acting, doing without doing, effort without effort: the tree does *something* in growing, obviously, but it's not the forceful imposition of the will on the world that we normally mean by "doing.") Mencius offers his version of this principle in the context of explaining what he means by the "flood-like *qì*" (*hàorán zhī qì* 浩然之氣—see §3.1 for discussion), which, he says, is "a *qì* that fits rightness together with the Way [*dào* 道]" (*qí wéi qì yě, pèi yì yǔ dào* 其爲氣也, 配義與道). According to Mencius, the trick is to participate feelingly-becoming-thinkingly (*xīn wù wàng* 心勿忘 [2A2], lit.

"heart-becoming-mind-without-forgetting") in the situationally appropriate "action" or "doing" of *qì* 氣 without forcing it.

This botanical conceit obviously adumbrates a biological ecology in which plants grow and die in complex interactive response to/with bio-environmental conditions. I am most interested here in the tenor of these biological metaphors, the human social ecology in which people grow (or sicken and even die) morally in complex interactive response to socio-environmental conditions; but note that Mencius does not identify two separate ecologies, a biological and a social/moral, the former serving as a convenient metaphor for the latter. For Mencius each flows into and out of the other, circularly, like the *yīnyáng* 陰陽 (☯). When he discusses water flow in 6A2, he is primarily interested in its moral implications for human action; when he discusses water flow in 6B11, he is primarily interested in water management as an engineering problem, but also draws the connection with morality: poor water management leads to flooding, a disastrous result of ecologically unsound engineering that people of fellow-feeling hate, presumably because the fellow-feeling in which they participate extends not only to the people adversely affected by the flood but the other living things and creatures as well. Birdwhistell (2007, p. 121) draws our attention to the gender metaphorics of floods—"Vast, overflowing, flooding waters are associated with disorder, the lack of boundaries, danger, shame, and females"—but just as flooding brings nutrients to the soil, so too does the flood-like *qì* 氣 bring the affective nutrients of compassionate identification and understanding. For both Mencius and Aristotle, the vital life-force powering both ecologies is energy—*qì* 氣 for Mencius, *energeia* for Aristotle, the topic of chapter 3—and while that energy takes different forms in the two ecologies, being channeled in the biosphere through wind and water (*fēng shuǐ* 風水) and other material elements, in the sociosphere through affect-becoming-conation-becoming-cognition (*xīn* 心), for Mencius both ecologies are ultimately one.

2.8 Dai Zhen on Mencius and Nelson on Aristotle: Blood-*qì* (*xuèqì* 血氣) and *thumos* as "Valor"

In fact one form *qì* 氣 takes in Confucian thought—in Confucius (cf. *Analects* 16.7) and later Confucians, if not in Mencius—is the "blood *qì*" (*xuèqì* 血氣), which can mean "bloodline" in the sense of one's parentage, but was also used to mean "valor" or "courage" (see Shun, 2002, p. 219). This is a physiological energy, understood by Chinese medicine as actual blood flowing through the body, that is also a moral force with significant socioemotional consequences. As Van Norden (2008, p. 19) notes, when Mencius says to King Xuan, "I ask Your Majesty to not be fond of small courage. Wielding a sword, angrily staring, and saying, 'How dare he face me?!'—this is the courage of a common fellow. It is for opposing a single person. I ask Your Majesty to enlarge it" (1B3), Zhu Xi associates that "small courage" with "blood *qi*" (*xuèqì* 血氣). This is worth mentioning here not only because, as we will see, Dai Zhen 戴震, widely regarded in China as the scholar who established the correct reading of Mencius for the modern age, makes the "passions of the blood-*qi*" the fountain out of which virtuous behavior flows, but also because it is remarkably close semantically to the ancient Greek notion of *thumos*, around which Aristotle builds his key rhetorical coinage *enthumēma* "enthymeme."

Thumos literally means "anger," but as Cooper (1984, p. 12) notes, Homer frequently used it to mean "valor"—the kind of valor shown by soldiers in battle. The term was brought into philosophical use by Plato, who in the *Republic* (435c–441c) made it the third part of his tripartite conception of the soul. The first part is reason, which performs calculations and governs the soul; the second is the appetitive part, which is governed by the body's need for simple physiological survival and so is not susceptible to reason. The third part, then, Plato calls *thumos*, usually translated as "the spirited part," with "spirit" pointing us not to a disembodied spirituality but to what are often known as "animal spirits," or "high spirits," a kind of emotionally charged (high-arousal) body state that for Plato stands between and can in some sense mediate between reason and the appetites. Reason can calm and otherwise oppose *thumos*; *thumos* can stifle or otherwise oppose the appetites.

According to Plato, the correlative of reason in the animal world is the human, in society the ruler, and in governmental structure aristocracy. The correlative of appetite in the animal world is the wild beast, in society the worker, and in governmental structure democracy, oligarchy, and tyranny. The correlative of *thumos* in the animal world is the lion, in society the soldier, and in governmental structure timocracy. Each also has its own desire: reason for wisdom, appetite for profit, *thumos* for honor (Greek *timē*, the organizing principle of timocracy). As some scholars have noted (see Renault 2010), *thumos* is the soul's channel of social regulation:

> *Thumos* must then be defined as a powerful tool in the education of the character, because it links the individual with his/her community. *Thumos* might be a "weak point" of the analogy in

a sense, but it also helps to explain how the analogy can never be taken as a mere isomorphism.

Without reason, *thumos* acts according to a frame of values which the community values, and does not question them as such: *thumos* "adheres" to them. If the worst comes to the worst, *thumos* transforms the individual into a man who makes of *honour* a mere object of value.

Soldiers, Plato (375ab) insists, must be like watchdogs: full of physical vigor, which gives them strength, speed, and the courage to face enemies on the battlefield. Not only must they not fear danger; they must be energized by it, inspired by it to heroic deeds, noble sacrifices. These are the attributes that Plato calls thumotic. When Leontius feels a desire to gaze upon corpses, he is filled with disgust, shame, indignant scorn for his own surrender to a base appetite (439e–440c): this moral indignation too is *thumos*.

As Nelson (1985) notes, one of the key distinguishing features scholars (see Cooper, 1984, p. 16; Annas, 1981, p. 128) have assigned to *thumos* is a grounding in the attribution of social value—especially the value of honor. Specifically that means that *thumos* is concerned not only with *being* honorable but with being *perceived* as honorable. Honor, reputation, integrity, face are not so much *intrinsic* as they are *perceived* attributes of the individual, which is to say that they exist not so much in the individual as in collective acts of attributing them to individuals. Group attributions are not only *felt* by the individual but internalized and turned on the self by the individual, leading to self-esteem (internalized honor, reputation, face) and shame (internalized dishonor, disgrace, loss of face). This is the topic of chapter 4; we will see there that what is at work in this social phenomenon is not just judgment or evaluation but the social *circulation* of value: the individual who has internalized these group values also applies them to the other members of the group, enforces their general (group-wide) validity by participating in group judgments of the self and others.

Nelson (1985) argues persuasively that *thumos* for the ancient Greeks is fundamentally a *manly* virtue, embodying physical and emotional strength, valor in battle, and the vigorous pursuit of manly aims in general. A closely related term is *andreia*, derived from *andros* "man," sometimes translated "bravery" or "courage," but as Gosling (1973, p. 77) argues,

> This word is better translated "manliness" than "courage." For though courage is a conspicuous element in andreia, the word

conceals the connection with the word for "man," and it is clear from a number of passages (c.f. *Gorgias* 491–2, 512e, *Republic* 359b, 544–50) that it covers a wider range than "courage." Further Plato uses "anandros" (unmanly) as well as "deilos" (cowardly) as the opposite of "andreios," and in contexts that clearly involve a general appeal to lack of prowess. In fact commonly "andreia" connotes the characteristics of the admirable, successful man usually connoted by "arête" (excellence) prior to Plato, and often by Socrates' interlocutors in the dialogues.

In addition, Annas (1981, p. 127) notes the importance for Plato (and apparently for ancient Greek culture) of thumotic *training*: *thumos* can exist in a "raw" or untrained state, in small children, say, or animals, but there is what Aristotle will call an entelechy to *thumos*, a directionality of self-realization that drives the thumotic part of the soul to grow both stronger and more focused, better controlled by "reason"—specifically by what Aristotle will call practical reason, which is the "common" (collective) sense of the better parts of society. To the extent that *thumos* is a Greek virtue, it can only crudely and simplemindedly be reduced to a tidy dualism like virtue versus vice, or "a real man" versus "a coward" (wimp, pansy, etc.—the patriarchal dualizing of men as *thumotic* and women as *athumotic*). It is, rather, an *emergent* virtue, one that grows with interactive self-realization. As Nelson (1985, np) sums up the scholarly consensus:

> Thumos is then to be understand as *admiration for an ideal type of manliness*: (a) *ideal* because it is centered in certain values; (b) *manliness*, because the values are predominantly concerned with the way a real man should live; (c) a *type*, because there is no fixed notion of manliness, rather it is a bundle of concepts, not necessarily perfectly coordinated or harmonized, which various particular actions and motivations approximate; (d) and *admiration*, because it involves a personal drive to live up to the ideal type, to participate in it, and to advocate and defend it.

The "valor" (blood-*qì* or *xuèqì* 血氣) of which Dai Zhen writes in his commentary on *MZ* 7A4[13] is not nearly as bellicose a virtue as the *thumos* that Plato and Aristotle take over from Homer, but it is equally passionate (*yù* 欲), and equally grounded in the circulation of social value (see chapter 4):

聖人順其血氣之欲，則為相生養之道，於是視人猶己，則忠；
以己推之，則恕；憂樂於人，則仁；出於正，不出於邪，則義；
恭敬不侮慢，則禮；無差謬之失，則智；曰忠恕，曰仁義禮
智，豈有他哉？

The sage follow[ing] his blood-*qi*'s passions [*yù* 欲] [is the right] way [*dào* 道] to make[/provide] reciprocal [*xiāng* 相] birth/life and nourishment/sustenance/care [*shēng yǎng* 生養]:

[a] [if you] regard [another] person as [your own] self, then [you will experience] loyalty [*zhōng* 忠];

[b] [if you] use self to push [into] that [other person's feelings], then [you will experience] the Golden Rule [*shù* 恕];

[c] [if you let flow into you] sorrow [and] happiness from [that other] person, then [you will experience] fellow-feeling [*rén* 仁];

[d] [if you let your words, behaviors and attitudes] emerge [*chū* 出] out of uprightness [*zhèng* 正] and not evil [*xié* 邪 "demonic," the evil influences that cause disease], then [you will experience] rightness [*yì* 義];

[e] [if you] honor [others] and [do] not humiliate [them], then [you will experience] ritual propriety [*lǐ* 禮];

[f] [if] no divagation[,] no deigning to cheat, then [you will experience] wisdom [*zhì* 智].

Say loyalty [and] forgiveness, say fellow-feeling [and] rightness [and] propriety [and] wisdom, [wouldn't you say that from all that sufficient] joy exists? (Dai, 1777/1995, p. 34; my literal translation)[14]

This is a list of the "passions" (*yù* 欲 can also be translated "desires, appetites, lusts") of the sage's blood-*qi* and the reciprocities to which they lead. Dai Zhen tropes those reciprocities as child-birth (*shēng* 生) and child-rearing (*yǎng* 養), or as animal husbandry, or as life (*shēng* 生) and the fostering of life (*yǎng* 養), with the twist that the birthing and raising of the metaphorical child or animal are not hierarchical (parent to child, human to pet) but reciprocal or mutual (*xiāng* 相) activities, so that each participant in the exchange births and raises important inclinations and orientations in the other. Or, in the other construction of *shēng yǎng* 生養 as living and fostering or nourishing life, the kind of life that is fostered is reciprocal because the fostering itself is reciprocal.

Thus, for example, (a) regarding another person as oneself leads to loyalty, but loyalty specifically as a circulatory and mutually reinforcing *group* commitment. This is not, in other words, the kind of unilateral loyalty in which a long-suffering wife is faithful to a heartlessly womanizing husband, or in which a loyal employee is treated capriciously by a tyrannical boss; it is a mutual or reciprocal loyalty in which each party inspires and fosters loyalty in the other, and becomes progressively better at both inspiring and showing loyalty.

(b) *shù* 恕, Dai's central term, is tricky.[15] In contemporary Chinese it means "to forgive, to excuse, to show mercy," but in older usage it seems to have been considerably more complicated. Some dictionaries of traditional Chinese make it synonymous with (c) *rén* 仁; others differentiate the two, making *rén* 仁 a group-centered feeling of connectedness (the group heart) and *shù* 恕 a self-centered feeling of connectedness, the use of one's own feelings and desires to guess at what others are feeling or might want. Following this latter path—as do Shun (2002, p. 220) and Chin and Freeman (1990, 100), who call it "reciprocity," and Tiwald (2010), who calls it "sympathy" and "perspective-taking"—leads me to translate *shù* 恕 as the Golden Rule (see Nivison, 1996, ch. 5)—a narrower and more focused interpretation, obviously, than either "reciprocity" or "sympathy." So constructed, *shù* 恕 is the practice of not doing or giving to others anything that one would not want done or given to oneself. Remember from §2.4 that Chan (1963, p. 16) translated *rén* 仁 in the *Analects* as "the golden rule": Chinese scholars claim that Mencius uses *shù* 恕 to mean what Confucius meant by *rén* 仁, and expands *rén* 仁 significantly. It is clear how some would take *shù* 恕 to be synonymous with *rén* 仁; if the group heart-becoming-mind is a circulation of feelings, then feelings are constantly cycling through all the individual members of a group, and *rén* 仁 and *shù* 恕 would be slightly but significantly different phenomenological constructions or "perspective-takings" (Tiwald, 2010, p. 146) of that circulation. Namely, *shù* 恕 would be the self-to-other flow, the feeling the individual has of externalizing personal feelings, and *rén* 仁 would be the other-to-self flow, the feeling the individual has of internalizing group feelings—feeling other people's sorrow and happiness, as Dai says here. (It is also clear how contemporary Chinese might have narrowed *shù* 恕 into forgiveness or mercy: using one's own feelings or motivations as a touchstone for others' feelings or motivations would tend to make one understanding and therefore forgiving.) In any case it is unmistakable that both *rén* 仁 and *shù* 恕 depend on the *sharing* of affective orientations—including, notably, happiness (*lè* 樂), which, like Aristotle, Dai understands as essentially transpersonal in nature.

(d) Showing honor and deference to others rather than humiliating and bullying them seems unilateral, but as I began to suggest above, and as we'll see more fully in chapter 4, honor is a collective rather than individual trait. Individuals don't possess honor: they are honored or constructed as honorable by others;[16] and the desired result of honoring others is precisely reciprocity, a *mutual* or mirroring observance of proper behavior (*lǐ* 禮, for which see §3.9).

And (e) the *uprightness* (*zhèng* 正) out of which something, anything, any sort of behavior or attitude—Dai Zhen's Chinese is strategically vague on this count—emerges (*chū* 出) sounds in English like a morphological anticipation of the *rightness* [*yì* 義] that results. But in fact even in English the two words trace divergent metaphorical trajectories, the "right" in *uprightness* troping the right angle as a vertical posture (a right angle with the ground) as honesty and integrity, the "right" in *rightness* troping the right angle as the horizontally correct choice (a right angle with the wrong path) as situational appropriateness. An upright posture is a physical fact that can be displayed by an individual; the metaphorical uprightness-as-integrity that Dai Zhen means is a social construct like honor or face, *attributed* to the individual by the group. If the sage has a *passion* for participating in that group attribution of uprightness, the result is a sensitive attention to and alignment with the behavior that is *right* for the group in any given situation—with the added complication that the alignment with the current group is also subtly but powerfully guided by a higher alignment with the group of sages or exemplary persons.

Finally, (f) the sage's *wúchā* 無差 or *chā*-lessness is not so much an "avoidance of mistakes" (Chin and Freeman have "by avoiding mistakes, one achieves wisdom," which sounds like a prescription more for bureaucratic caution than for wisdom) as it is a steadfast *nondeviation from* the group determination of the best path, an adherence not to some stable abstract mistake-free perfection but to group guidance.

Because the products of these passions are not sex but communal reciprocities, the "valorous" passions that give rise to those products cannot be the carnal lusts implied by Chin and Freeman's "physical desires" (in contemporary Chinese the phrase *xuèqìfānggāng* 血氣方剛, lit. "blood gas square rigid," is used to describe teenagers' hormonal lusts). Still, it is clear that blood-*qì* is a physically or physiologically (corporeally) transmitted force that is experienced as desire.

The only way to regard others as one's own self, or to infer others' feelings from how one feels, is truly to *share* the grief and joy and other feelings of other people. One must *feel* those feelings, as if they were one's own. As Dai Zhen reads him, this is the truly radical notion for which Mencius argues.

2.9 Mencius: *rén* 仁 as Group *xīn* 心

To sum up the findings of the last four sections, then, *rén* 仁 is "benevolence" or "humaneness" in the specific dispositional (*xìng* 性) context of feeling that one is unable to bear (*bùrěn* 不忍) other people's suffering. The *rén* 仁 person is "benevolent" only secondarily because s/he is nice; s/he is nice primarily because s/he feels what other people feel. This participation in shared affect makes it painful not only to *cause* others pain but to be around others when they are in pain caused by someone else. Very much like *philia* and *to philein* for Aristotle, *rén* 仁 for Mencius is not an individualistic concept, but an immersion in felt community, in connectedness, in relationality.

It seems clear, then, that "benevolent/-ce" is not really an adequate translation of *rén* 仁:

[a] it is too narrow a term to cover the full range of moral inclinations that Mencius incorporates into *rén* 仁;

[b] it is far too weak a moral virtue to make its absence a dangerous moral flaw; and

[c] some of the most obvious moral outliers not covered by "benevolent/-ce" seem to be relational or "circulatory" states rather than individualistic dispositions.

As we saw in §2.4, therefore, there has been a growing trend since the early 1960s to shift from the "benevolence" translation favored by the tradition running from Collie (1828) through Legge (1861/1970) to Lau (1970/2003) (and all the way up to Van Norden 2008) to "humanity" and "humaneness," from Chan Wing-tsit (1963) and W. A. C. H. Dobson (1963) to David Hinton (1998) and Irene Bloom (2009). This newer translation tradition would indeed solve (ab), above, but these translators still tend to make "humane/humanity" the quality of a single individual and so fail to address (c). Tang (1962, p. 36) offers "human-heartedness," which expands the semantics of *rén* 人 "humanity" (signaled in the 亻 "human" radical of *rén* 仁) to include *xīn* 心 "heart," certainly a key component in the Confucian thinking behind *rén* 仁; but to have a human heart would not on the face of it seem to entail that one is even humane. And, like "humanity" and "humaneness," Tang's translation does not hint at the connectivity in (c).

Richie (2003/2005) gives us one useful expansion of the later translation tradition by translating *rén* 仁 as "co-humanity"; Behuniak (2005) gives us another, using the quasi-Fourierist term "associated humanity."[17] As translations of *rén* 仁, both Behuniak's Fourierist "associated humanity" and Ritchie's semantically similar "co-humanity" have the salutary and rather rare effect of capturing (c) the connectivity implicit in the Chinese term, and even seem to represent the two parts of the character: the 亻 "person, human" radical and the character for two 二, as in two linked or associated people. As Behuniak (90–91) writes: "Associated humanity grows initially from the family. To lose family feeling, and by extension one's associated humanity, amounts to forfeiting participation in the novel construction of an emergent human world. Outside the circle of associated humanity lies the perverse world of the animal; within the circle of associated humanity reside the emergent standards of human morality and feeling."

To the extent that we take *rén* 仁 to be a form of *humanity*, then, either Ritchie's "co-humanity" or Behuniak's "associated humanity" is an excellent English translation. And since *rén* 仁 is a derivative of *rén* 人 "person, human," and as we will see in a moment Mencius specifically defines the *rén*-ist 仁也者 phonologically as *rén* 人 or human (7B16), there are plenty of good reasons to choose one or the other of these renditions. The only problem with those translations is that, to the extent that we think of *rén* 仁 in terms of the interactive phenomenology fleshed forth by Dai Zhen and his many followers, "co-humanity" and "associated humanity" may come to seem rather abstract, insufficiently *felt*.

Specifically, as we saw in §2.8, the Confucian tradition emerging out of Dai's reading of Mencius would make *rén* 仁 the ability to feel other people's feelings—indeed to *share* other people's feelings, to participate affectively in the becoming-communal of ecosis, through the group *xīn* 心, the group heart-becoming-mind. (See also Nivison, 1996, p. 70 on the Song philosopher Cheng Hao 程顥, who noted that in medical usage, *bùrén* 不仁 means "numb, having no feeling." "Just so," Nivison adds, "one may be said to be 'not *ren*' if one is morally 'unfeeling,' insensitive to the feelings and sufferings of others.") For Mencius the ability to feel (*xīn* 心), and specifically to let our thinking emerge out of our feeling, makes us higher primates potentially human, in the sense of being potentially moral; the most perfect fulfillment of that potential is the ability to *feel together*, to participate in a *feelingly* (and thus morally) associated co-humanity. It's not just that we are "associated," in other words, or that we "share humanity," as Ritchie's translation would suggest; it's that our shared humanity is transmitted through feelings, and that it is this affective channel of ecotic circulation that makes becoming-moral and thus becoming-human possible. The lack of that channel makes us not just not very nice, and not just inhumane, but *inhuman*. As Mencius says explicitly in the Child at the Well section (2A6), "whoever is devoid of the heart of compassion is not human." In modern parlance, it makes us sociopaths—unfeeling monsters.

In this light, in fact, I would suggest that Behuniak (2005, p. 105) missed a significant opportunity in translating *dào èr: rén yŭ bùrén éryĭ yĭ* 道二: 仁與不仁而已矣 (4A2) as "there are only these two ways: associated humanity and coercion." Why not "there are only these two ways: associated humanity and dissociated inhumanity"? Dissociation, after all, usually as a result of severe childhood trauma, is generally thought to be the primary trigger of sociopathology—the strongest form of inhumanity, of *bùrén* 不仁, that we know.

As Mencius says explicitly in 7B16, explaining *rén* phonologically as both 人 "person, human" and its emotionally-becoming-morally "associative" derivative 仁, the *rén*-ist (仁也者) is *rén* (人也). Only the person who pursues or partakes in *rén* 仁 is human. He adds: *hé ér yán zhī, dào yĕ* 合而言之, 道也, lit. "join [these two] words, [this is] also the Way." The whole line is rendered into English by our various translators:

> Mencius said, to be benevolent is man. When man and benevolence are united, they are called Taou. (Collie, 1828, p. 178)

> Mencius said, "Benevolence is *the distinguishing characteristic of* man. As embodied in man's conduct, it is called the path *of duty*." (Legge, 1861/1970, p. 485)

> Mencius said, " 'Benevolence' means 'man.' When these two are conjoined, the result is 'the Way.' " (Lau, 1970/2003, p. 317)

> Mencius said, "Benevolence means man. The correct way is benevolence and man combined." (Zhao et al., 1993, p. 533)

Mencius said, "Humanity is the human. Put them together and you have the Way." (Hinton, 1998, p. 262)

Mencius said, "Humaneness is to be human. Spoken of collectively, it is the Way." (Bloom, 2009, p. 159)

Note there first of all that Mencius specifically defines *rén* 人 "the human being, human/ity" phonologically not as *rén* 仁 but as *rén yě zhě* 仁也者 "the *rén*-ist"—which is to say, not as an abstract character trait like "benevolence" or "humaneness," but as a person who is somehow integrally involved with that phenomenology. Collie's infinitive verb phrase "to be benevolent" arguably comes closer to that sense than the abstract nouns used by the others. But then of course "to be benevolent is man" is awkward almost to the point of incomprehensibility; "to be benevolent is to be human" would have been much clearer, and closer to the poetic economy of Mencius's original Chinese phrasing. Most of the other translators have similar problems: Lau's (and Zhao et al.'s) " 'Benevolence' means 'man' " only improves slightly on Collie's syntactic stumble, and Bloom's "Humaneness is to be human" feels like a step backward. Why not "To be humane is to be human"? Hinton, too, striving valiantly for the verbal economy of Mencius's phonological explanation, ends up giving us a tautology. Humanity is the quality of being both humane and human, to be sure, and he wants the former; but the latter is the more insistent connotation, so that he ends up implying not *to be humane is to be human* but *to be human is to be human*. A similar tautology would result from Tang's "human-heartedness": to have a human heart is to be human, or perhaps human-heartedness is humanness.

The deeper question these translations raise, of course, is the matter of what *rén* 仁 *is*, and how it relates to being human. By sticking with Collie's "benevolence," obviously, Legge, Zhao et al., and Lau all give up on Mencius's phonological definition of *rén* 仁 as derived from its etymon/homonym *rén* 人; but then, given the divergent etymologies behind *rén* 人/仁 and "human/e/ness/ity," this is not a crushing argument against the "benevolence" translation tradition. Translators often have to make do with less than adequate equivalents. Nor, for that matter, is it a crushing argument against the newer tradition of rendering *rén* 仁 as "humane" or "humanity" that it captures something of the phonological and semantic parallels *rén yě zhě, rén yě* 仁也者, 人也 ("the humane-ist is human") but does not hint at the affective connectivity in *rén* 仁: some semantic loss or shift is inevitable.

Still, Ritchie's "co-humanity" and Behuniak's "associated humanity" do more effectively capture the connectivity of *rén* 仁; as Behuniak puts it explicitly, "Hence, for Mencius, the Confucian way (*dao* 道) amounts to 'associated humanity coming together [*he* 合] in what is human [*ren* 人]'" (2005, p. 91; Behuniak's interpolations). A more aphoristic (and thus more Mencian) rendering might be "Co-humanity is true humanity" (Ritchie) or "Associated humanity is true humanity" (Behuniak).

I would, however, like to point us down a different terminological avenue—one that will significantly converge with Aristotle on *philia* "friendship" and *to philein* "friendly feeling." As we saw in §2.8, for Dai Zhen *rén* 仁 is a phenomenology of shared affect, or "feeling together," and that latter is obviously a collocation with a history in Western languages. The Greek roots for "feeling together" give us the English word "sympathy"; the Latin translation of those roots gives us the term Lau used for *cèyǐn* 惻隱, "compassion"; the etymological trajectory from Greek *empatheia* "in-feeling" to Rudolph Lotze's 1858 German coinage *Einfühlung* gives us "empathy."[18] Each of these has unfortunate connotations, sympathy and compassion with pity or condescension (projecting some small part of one's feeling onto the less fortunate so as to mitigate one's own sense of privilege and entitlement), empathy with a very specific literary/aesthetic history (see Robinson, 2008, ch. 5); but any one of them, it seems to me, would arguably capture more of the collectivist phenomenology that Dai Zhen fleshes out than the individualistic terms "benevolence" or "humaneness."

The descriptive translation I offer in my section heading—"*rén* 仁 as group *xīn* 心—would require us to jettison the Mencian phonological explanation *rén yě zhě, rén yě* 仁也者, 人也: neither "the group heart is humanity" nor "group feeling is humanity" brings us anywhere near the phonological equation of that definition. It would, however, allow us to get closer to a related explanation in 6A11 than any of Mencius's other English translators: *rén, rénxīn yě* 仁, 人心也 would be "group feeling is human feeling," or "the group heart-becoming-mind is the human heart-becoming-mind" (cf. Aristotle's insistence that we are social animals, and live affectively through connection to others).

If on the other hand we wanted to push this phenomenological translation a few steps closer to the phonology of the *rén* 仁 = *rén* 人 explanation, while still avoiding the historical connotations of sympathy, compassion, empathy, and so on, an alternative Anglo-Saxon translation of *rén* 仁 might be "fellow-feeling," in which one feels whatever one's fellow-humans (*rénrén* 人人) are feeling. I find the first instance of this translation in a brilliant book on Sun Yat-sen from the thirties, Paul Linebarger (1937/1973, p. 14):

> The Chinese term 仁 *ren* is frequently rendered "benevolence," a Western word which, while at times an appropriate equivalent, fails to carry the full burden of meaning. Sun [Yat-sen] speaks

of an interpretation of history antagonistic to dialectical materialism—the interpretation of history by 仁 *ren*. A "benevolent" interpretation of history means nothing whatever to a Westerner. If 仁 *ren* is translated into a different configuration of words, and given as "group-consciousness" or "social fellow-feeling," the result, while still not an exact equivalent of the Chinese, is distinctly more intelligible.[19] (Wade-Giles romanization replaced with Chinese character and pinyin)

A translation of *rén yě zhě, rén yě* 仁也者，人也 using "fellow-feeling," for example, might be *the fellow-feeling fellow feels human*; or, more expansively, *to feel one's fellow-humans' feelings is to feel completely human*.

The radically phenomenological orientation in that translation—*to feel completely human*—may seem insufficiently ontological to some readers, for whom *rén yě zhě, rén yě* 仁也者，人也 is about not just *feeling* human but *being* human. For the Confucian tradition coming out of Dai Zhen's Mencian commentary, however, the flow of the blood-*qi*'s passions (*xuèqì zhī yù* 血氣之欲) into community, into felt connectivity, is primary, and serves as an organizing standard for the virtuous reciprocities that later, emergingly, give us a sense that *rén yě zhě, rén yě* 仁也者，人也. An uneasiness with the primacy of that phenomenology may reflect a conditioned preference for the ontological tradition that flows out of the ancient Greeks (Parmenides, Plato, and Aristotle) and dominates Western philosophy; what people tend to mean when they say that "there is no Chinese philosophy" or "Mencius was not a philosopher" is that there is no stable ontology in Mencius, or in many other Chinese thinkers.

Or try "fellow-feeling" in another context (2A7), where, quoting the *Analects* 4.1, Mencius writes:

孔子曰：『里仁為美；擇不處仁，焉得智？』夫仁，天之尊爵也，人之安宅也，莫之禦而不仁，是不智也。不仁不智，無禮無義，人役也。

Confucius says: "[A] neighborhood/hometown [full of] fellow-feeling is beautiful; [if you] choose not to reside [in] fellow-feeling, how [are you to] obtain wisdom?" Human fellow-feeling [is] heaven's noble honor [and] a person's still/safe/peaceful residence. [If there is] nothing to resist/oppose [your feeling other people's feelings] and yet [you have] no fellow-feeling, [there will] be [in you] no wisdom. [If there is in some person] no fellow-feeling

[and] no wisdom, [if s/he] lacks ritual propriety [and] lacks righteousness, [that] person [is a] slave. (my literal translation)

Fellow-feeling, this makes clear, is more than a feeling; it is a *shared* feeling. And it is more than a momentary shared feeling, more than a "state-feeling"; it is a trait-feeling, a group feeling-becoming-disposition, an ecotic (becoming-communal) affective connectivity, which Mencius tellingly tropes sequentially as a living space of varying size: *lǐ* 里 "neighborhood, hometown" and *zhái* 宅 "residence." There are obviously forces that might reasonably make one shy away from living in that space; one would not want to share feelings communally with a group that was wicked or dissolute, for example. (In this light one might suggest that the best English translation of *rényì* 仁義, and thus—perhaps radically—of Mencian morality in general, would be *a fitting fellow-feeling*, or, more expansively, *a fellow-feeling that best fits the occasion*. This highly situational conception of morality seems radical in the West, where morality is expected to have and impose stable contours; but it is a good fit with Mencian ecotic or becoming-communal thinking about morality.) If no such forces are present, if the people around one are good, honest, hard-working, caring, and so on, there is absolutely no reason not to let the communal feelings flow; and to refuse that opportunity would be to foreclose on wisdom. (See §4.5–6 for discussion of *tiān zhī zūn* 天之尊 "heaven's honor.")

And since fellow-feeling and wisdom are two of the four shoots of virtue, it is clear that Mencius is envisioning a kind of deprivatory domino effect that metaphorically enslaves the *bùrén*-ist or non-fellow-feeling-ist (不仁者: 4A8, 7A24, 7B1), traps him or her in a dispositional deadend. Without fellow-feeling (*rén* 仁) there is no wisdom (*zhì* 智); without wisdom there is no situationally fitting behavior (*yì* 義); without fitting behavior there is no ritual propriety (*lǐ* 禮). In some sense *rényì* 仁義, which Lau fittingly translates in 3B9 as "the path of morality," is shorthand for the full path of morality, which moves through all four shoots: *rén yì lǐ zhì* 仁義禮智. Or, as Mencius puts it in the passage we considered just above, the human heart is a group heart (*rén, rén xīn yě* 仁, 人心也: 6A11), and lives in that group heart as its home or neighborhood (2A7); fitting behavior is the road on which the heart sets out (*yì, rén lù yě* 義, 人路也: 5B7, 6A11), and ritual propriety is the door through which the heart passes at the end of its journey (*lǐ, mén yě* 禮, 門也: 5B7), or, for that matter, at the beginning of the journey, since the exemplary person can go in *and* out through the door. Mencius does not specifically identify the metaphorical value of wisdom (*zhì* 智) on this road, but it might not be pushing the metaphor too far to suggest that wisdom is at once the vehicle that the heart drives down the road and the destination toward which it drives—what lies just through the door of *lǐ* 禮. The wisdom-vehicle might also be imagined as powered by the endlessly replenishable fuel of *qì* 氣 as a situated configuration of *tiān* 天 ("forces": see §4.5), and steered by the four shoots or virtuous dispositions themselves, as they emerge and take shape out of the traveling.

6A11 specifically imagines the heart straying off the road (and therefore implicitly not going in through the door); a person whose heart has strayed is urged to go after it, to bring it back to the road. Even worse than straying off the road, however, is not setting out on the road at all, because one lacks the fellow-feeling that is the becoming-communal heart-as-traveler. This inability or refusal to travel down the path of morality is the slavery of which Mencius speaks. Metaphorically it is a slavery to place—what we would refer to colloquially in English these days as "being in a bad place" spiritually or emotionally—and it is specifically an entrapment in the solitude of the individual skin, in feeling that is not group feeling and so is not human feeling. That this trap or slavery is not irreversible is clear from that first passage I mentioned above where Lau found himself unable to stick to "benevolence": "After three years, Tài Jiǎ repented and reproached himself, and, while in Tóng, reformed and became a good and dutiful man" (5A6, Lau, 1970/2003, p. 209; names pinyinized). His "reform" was a crossing over from slavery into freedom, from the "bad place" in which he was trapped over into the reproachful self-scrutiny that made it possible for him to head off down the road of morality.

2.10 Mencius: *rén zhèng* 仁政 as Government as Persuasion

Now it is time to return to the question of *rén zhèng* 仁政—what Collie, Legge, Zhao et al., Lau, and Van Norden translate as "benevolent government." *Pace* Zhang (2010), who is quite eloquent on the disastrous consequences of this dominant Confucian misinterpretation of *rén zhèng* 仁政 in China right up to our own day, Mencius does not mean by this (just) what we mean by benevolent dictatorship, where the dictator uses his power to help and protect the otherwise helpless and defenseless people. He also means that the ruler enters into fellow-feeling with his subjects, feels what they feel, and so not only knows when a given policy would be good or bad for them but is able to teach them, help them grow, by getting them to participate communally in *his* feelings. As we saw in §2.3, he "governs" reciprocally *with* them. Whatever Mencius means by *zhì* 治—not exactly "govern," though that is the traditional translation; perhaps a better translation would be something like "exert a guiding influence on"—the sagacious ruler and the people do it to each other.

This is the sense in which *rén zhèng* 仁政 is *persuasive* government, rule by rhetorical pressure circulated through the group heart-becoming-mind rather than by commandment or coercion. The absence of fellow-feeling (*bùrén* 不仁) that Lau variously translates as "cruelty" (2A4, 4A1–3, 4A8, 6A18) and "ruthlessness" (7B1, 7B13) and Behuniak (2005, p. 105) translates as "coercion" is primarily for Mencius not a desire to *inflict* pain and suffering on others, but an inability or refusal to *feel* other people's pain and suffering. It may only secondarily make the non-fellow-feeling-ist either indifferent to other people's pain and suffering, and thus casually willing to inflict it in the pursuit of his or her goals, or morbidly fascinated by other people's pain and suffering, precisely because s/he doesn't feel it, and thus *eager* to inflict it, so as to learn more about it. The problem with *bùrén zhèng* 不仁政 "non-fellow-feeling government" (the opposite of *bùrěnrén zhī zhèng* 不忍人之政 "can't-bear[-other-people's-suffering] person's government") is not just that it is channeled through coercion rather than persuasion, through cruelty rather than compassion; it is that a lack of fellow-feeling makes it impossible for the ruler to feel what the people need and desire, turning them into inert objects, numbers, demographics, or at best infants on the verge of wells and oxen being led to slaughter. This leaves him emotionally blind and deaf, without bearings in a world that is organized and steered morally by *xīn* 心 "feeling-becoming-thinking," and so also, obviously, without any sense of where the pressure points and handles and channels are that will enable him to participate meaningfully (persuasively) in the moral organization and steering of that world. It is not just that not knowing what the people need makes it impossible for the ruler to give it to them; it is that not participating in the group heart-becoming-mind gives him no way to give them something slightly different from what they want, and give it in a way that will nudge them to grow (like the horticulturist watering plants, 7A40), a way that will persuade them that this X is better for them in the long run than what they thought they wanted would have been for them in the short run. If he can't feel their feelings, he can't *know* what is needed; but even more important, he can't *guide* them to what is needed.

As a fellow-feeling *persuader*, in other words, the *rén* 仁 ruler is also a fellow-feeling *teacher* (7A40; see also Birdwhistell, 2007, p. 107). He teaches the people through persuasion; and he persuades through participation in fellow-feeling. When Mencius says in 2A2 that *xué bù yàn, zhī yě, jiāo bù juàn, rén yě* 學不厭, 智也, 教不倦, 仁也, which Lau (1970/2003, p. 65) translates as "not to tire of learning is wisdom; not to weary of teaching is benevolence," he does not mean that teaching is a form of charity or philanthropy in which the teacher gives unstintingly and unwearyingly of himself or herself. Rather, he means that good teaching—the kind that the teacher does not weary of, or burn out on—is channeled through fellow-feeling (see Robinson, 2012).

Note also that the specific phrase Mencius uses in 4A8 for what Lau (1970/2003, p. 157) translates as "listen to reason" is literally "participate in words": "How can one get the cruel man to listen to reason [*bùrénzhě kě yú yán zāi* 不仁者可與言哉]? He dwells happily in danger, looks upon disaster as profitable and delights in what will lead him to perdition. If the cruel man listened to reason, there would be no annihilated states or ruined families." That first question, repeated conditionally in the first clause of the third sentence, is literally "the no-fellow-feeling-ist can how participate in words?" For the person who does not participate in communal fellow-feeling (the *bùrén*-ist) words become empty shells that are bandied about cynically in order to achieve one's purpose; the end of this *in a ruler*, Mencius is implicitly warning here (this is one of the *MZ* 4 decontextualizations), is the loss of nations and families/homes, and ultimately disaster and perdition for himself as well. Legge and Zhao et al. here follow the original Chinese more closely:

> Mencius said, "How is it possible to speak with those *princes* who are not benevolent? Their perils they count safety, their calamities they count profitable, and they have pleasure in the things by which they perish. If it were possible to talk with them who so violate benevolence, how could we have such destruction of States and ruin of Families!" (Legge, 1861/1970, p. 298; emphasis Legge's, signaling his interpolation)

> Mencius said, "How can we speak up with an unbenevolent man? He considers his danger as his safety and his calamity as his profit; and finds pleasure in what will cause his destruction. If we could speak up with an unbenevolent man, there would be no lost states or ruined families." (Zhao et al., 1993, p. 267)

By translating *yú yán* 與言 as "speak (up) with" and "talk with," these translators imply that the non-fellow-feeling rulers in question have isolated themselves from participation in communal discourse, in conversation. This does in fact mean, as Lau implies, that they are thus unable to "listen to reason"; but reason is not all they are unable to listen to, and the implication of the Chinese is that the saving force is not reason but heartfelt verbal community. Lau's translation makes it sound as if the optimal goal for the advisors of this sort of ruler is to make him understand, rationally, the catastrophic consequences of his cruelty, for once he understands—once he has "listened to reason"—he may desist. What Mencius is explicitly asking instead is how the advisors can get the ruler to *participate* in their verbal advice, to play a role in it, feel a part of it; implicit in his formulation is the possibility that participation in *words* can then model and even induce a participation in shared feelings.

It should be clear, here, that *bùrénzhě kě yú yán zāi* 不仁者可與言哉 "how can one get the non-fellow-feeling ruler to participate in words?" contains an implicit theory of rhetoric. It implicitly equates *rén* 仁 "fellow-feeling" or "the group heart-becoming-mind" with *yú yán* 與言 "participate in words" as a collectivist model not just for communication but for *persuasive* communication—at the highest levels of government, here specifically, in high officials' attempts to steer the ruler's attempts to steer the people, but more broadly also, I'm suggesting, in anyone's attempt through fellow-feeling to guide a group's feeling-becoming-(disposition-becoming-)thinking-becoming-action. Ruling a group through persuasion is difficult; ruling a group through nonverbal persuasion would appear to be more difficult still. According to Mencius, however, this participatory persuasion through shared feeling is the only way governmental rule can actually *steer* or *lead* the people. Forcing them to obey laws or decrees upon punishment of prison or death may be a more effective way to achieve compliance in the short run; but superficial outward compliance is *all* it achieves. It is not actual guidance, and therefore not actual rule.

This is why Mencius says that only fellow-feeling-ists should occupy "high seats" or leadership roles (*shì yǐ wéi rén zhě, yí zài gāo wèi* 是以惟仁者, 宜在高位: 4A1): as he explicitly goes on in that section to warn, the inhuman(e) dispositions that arise out of a lack of fellow-feeling are themselves contagious, and when they emerge in people occupying "high seats" they are "scattered" or "broadcast" *ecotically* (by group ethical contagion) to the multitudes (*bùrén ér zài gāowèi, shì bō qí è yú zhòng yě* 不仁而在高位, 是播其惡於眾也). The ruler whose participation in the group heart-becoming-mind has shaped his or her disposition virtuously spreads that virtue contagiously to and through the people; the inability or refusal to feel other people's feelings shapes one's disposition in vicious ways that also spread, a kind of runaway nightmare ecosis which in fact was pandemic in Warring States China.

This is the process he is describing in 4A9:

> Mencius said, "It was through losing the people that Jie and Zhou lost the Empire, and through losing the people's hearts that they lost the people. There is a way to win the empire; win the people and you will win the Empire. There is a way to win the people; win their hearts and you will win the people. There is a way to win their hearts; amass what they want for them; do not impose what they dislike on them. That is all. The people turn to the benevolent as water flows downwards or as animals head for the wilds. Thus the otter drives the fish to the deep; thus the hawk drives birds to the bushes; and thus Jie and Zhou drove the people to Tang and King Wu. Now if a ruler in the Empire is drawn to benevolence, all the feudal lords will drive the people to him." (Lau, 1979/2003, p. 159; names pinyinized)

Fellow-feeling has *attractive* powers. People feel drawn to it, pulled into its orbit, as water does to lowlands, and as animals do to the wild. Group feeling-becoming-thinking for Mencius is where human beings most naturally and abundantly live; as such it is both a powerful ground for moral growth and the most moral ground for the growth of power.[20] He is, obviously, seeking rhetorically here to *tempt* the ruler into fellow-feeling by appealing to his lust for power—convincing him that ruling through fellow-feeling is the surest way to amass and safeguard power—but his belief that fellow-feeling will transform the ruler's power for good makes this more than just a cynical ploy.

2.11 Aristotle on the Available Persuasivity (*to endekhomenon pithanon*)

The remaining question to ask about the collective subject or agent of *pistis* and *zhi* 治 is: what are the audience members doing *in being persuaded* and the people doing *in being governed*? I have been arguing for a shift in the philosophical center of gravity in the study of rhetoric from the rhetor to the collective subject that includes both the rhetor and the audience; but a glance back through the sections of chapter 2 will give the impression that neither Aristotle nor Mencius devoted many column inches to an investigation of the audience's contribution to the success of that group subject.

And I think that such an impression would not be entirely inaccurate. While Aristotle in particular theorized the emotions and the dispositions at considerable length in *TR* 2 precisely in order to subjectify the audience, to give it a collection of faces and bodies and dress styles and so on, so that the rhetor could read it as guidance to the construction of effective arguments, and while *TR* 2 has been lauded as the first psychology textbook in Western thought, most scholarly readers also recognize a significant failure of the imagination in Aristotle's treatment of the emotions and dispositions. Above all, Aristotle gives his students only the most rudimentary and superficial indications of how they should be taken as guides to audience response, based on readings of audience members' visual signs (emotional displays on the stage of the body and the age, class, gender, and other outward signs of disposition). As a consequence, some scholars (see Kennedy, 1991, p. 113) have read them as written separately and then inserted into the middle of the treatise without proper editing or rethinking.

While it's true that *TR* 2 provides only very rudimentary and superficial instructions as to the use of the chapters on the emotions and the dispositions, it's not true that Aristotle fails entirely to integrate them. In *TR* 1.2, after all, he provides a list of the things that the rhetor should *find* and *see* (*theorein*) around him or her and draw on in building an effective argument, and in 1.2.5 he does specifically mention the audience's emotions:

1.2.2: the "atechnic arguments" to be found in people's conversations, confessions, contracts, testimonials, and the like

1.2.4: people's tendency to believe or trust or allow themselves to be persuaded by certain kinds of socially accepted speakers

1.2.5: the emotions (*pathē*) felt by an audience

1.2.7: specialized real-world knowledge

1.2.8–10: enthymemes and examples

1.2.11, 13: people's opinions

1.2.12: the kinds of things people tend to debate

1.2.14–18: signs and probabilities

The items in this list are dispersed among, and include, the three channels of persuasion, *logos, ēthos,* and *pathos* (*TR* 1.2.3–6); Aristotle gives us the audience's side of *ēthos* in 1.2.4 and the audience's side of *pathos* in 1.2.5. Arguably, too, the real-world knowledge in section 7 and the opinions in 1.2.11 and 13 could be vague allusions to the dispositions. So while he could have rewritten *TR* 2 more dynamically and interactively, so as to underscore the complex ways in which the audience's body states both condition and regulate the rhetor's argumentative success, and thus (as I'm arguing) participate in an icotic group subject that persuades-and-believes, he has left *some* trace of his intention for *TR* 2, here in *TR* 1.2.

In some sense the "title" of this list in the first line of *TR* 1.2 is Aristotle's first definition of rhetoric, as the *dunamis peri hekaston tou theōrēsai to endekhomenon pithanon* (1.2.1, 1357b26): "the ability in each case to see/observe the available persuasivity" (my literal translation). What he is saying there, I suggest, is that rhetoric as strategic persuasion depends on the rhetor's ability to see, read, engage, understand, participate in, and so exploit *the deep social ecology of rhetoric*. What the rhetor sees or observes in this titular definition is indeed the "available *means* of persuasion," as *to endekhomenon pithanon* is traditionally translated; what that translation often conditions readers to miss, however, is that they are the *socioemotionally* (affectively-becoming-conatively and ecotically-becoming-icotically) available means of persuasion, which is to say, what the culture offers in any given case as support for persuasion. The reason this translation causes the deep ecology of rhetoric to drop out of the definition, I suggest, is that "means of persuasion" is primarily used in English translations of the *TR* to render *pisteis*, persuasive strategies and structures marshaled rationally in the rhetor's head and then expressed in speech—what reductive rationalist readings of the treatise have long (at least since the Roman tradition from Cicero to Quintilian) taken to be the truest focus of the book. Translating *to endekhomenon pithanon* as "the available means of persuasion" tends to assimilate it to that interpretive juggernaut, so that even here in *TR* 1.2, when he is sketchily but unmistakably listing the impulses and inclinations that *the audience and their culture* contribute to persuading-and-believing, Aristotle's readers have tended to focus their attention on what the rhetor does argumentatively. Both "means of persuasion," obviously, are essential for rhetoric to work: without strategic organization in the rhetor's head, speech would potentially not be persuasive at all, and thus would not qualify as rhetoric; but without the felt connections or collectivizations or identifications that circulate through groups, without what Susan Miller (2008, pp. 51, x) calls the "interactive phenomenology" of the "cultural work" done by rhetoric, without audience emotions, dispositions, opinions, ways of speaking, factual knowledge, and so on, even the best-formed *pisteis* would not persuade.

Another indication that he is talking about something other than persuasive strategies in *TR* 1.2 is that there is really nothing about persuasive strategies that is "seeable" or "observable." The rhetor *knows* them: s/he doesn't have to *see* them. *Pisteis* are to be mastered, internalized, produced; what is to be seen *peri hekaston,* observed in each specific rhetorical situation, is something else, something external enough to be studied from across a room.

What, though, does Aristotle mean by *seeing* or *observing* the available persuasivity? To put that question more theoretically, how would he theorize *to theōrēsai* in *dunamis peri hekaston tou theōrēsai to endekhomenon pithanon*? If *to theōrēsai* is visual observation, what exactly is the rhetor looking at? If it is mainly body language, as I'll be suggesting in chapter 3, how does the rhetor *know* what it is s/he's seeing? Or does s/he even need to know this? Or are there several different levels of knowing? The ability to see becoming-persuasivity on the stage of people's bodies may for many rhetors be preconscious and preanalytical, a "knack" by which they "instinctively" orient themselves to the best way to persuade their audience, as Socrates snidely says to Gorgias: "The orator need have no knowledge of the truth about things; it is enough for him to have discovered a knack of convincing the ignorant that he knows more than the experts" (459c, quoted in Lindsay, 1998, p. 7). Stan Lindsay (ibid.) calls this knack "implicit rhetoric," and suggests that it points to the possibility that "factors exist implicitly (often preconsciously) which allow an orator, for example, to convince 'the ignorant that he knows more than the experts.'" A knack for reading the audience body language that is one of the key resources of the socioaffective ecology of rhetoric is itself one of those resources, and as such is affectively prestructured by the group, so that the prospective rhetor *feels* his or her way to it—but it is the entelechial beginning of knowledge, a knack-becoming-notice, a feeling-becoming-seeing. Knowing what we know about Aristotle on *hupokrisis* "acting," which is usually translated "delivery" but is essentially body language (see §3.6), can we imagine him agreeing with this take on *to theōrēsai* as a feeling-becoming-seeing, a knack-becoming-notice?

Note that *to theōrēsai* appears twice more in TR 1.2, in 1.2.7 and 1.2.11, and in each case seems to refer to the ability to see visible signs (*sēmeia* and *tekmēria* [1.2.16–18, 1357b1–22]) as the invisible things to which the signs point (see also Miller, 2008, pp. 66–71). Since Aristotle also tells us there that "enthymemes are derived from probabilities [*ex eikotōn]* and signs [*ek sēmeiōn*]" (1.2.14, 1357a33; Kennedy, 1991/2007, p. 42), and *ta sēmeia* are arguably *visible*-becoming-invisible and *ta eikota* are visible-becoming-*invisible, to theōrēsai* is presumably the seeing-becoming-understanding of the visible-becoming-invisible as well. In section 7, for example, Aristotle tells us that because people believe or are persuaded through speech, through what appears true through speech, the rhetor must not only be able to "syllogize" (*sullogisasthai*) but also *tou theōrēsai peri ta ēthē kai peri tas aretas kai triton tou peri ta pathē* (1.2.7, 1356b23), to be observant "about" (*peri*) characters (*ta ēthē*), virtues (*tas aretas*), and emotions (*ta pathē*). All three of those things that must be "seen" or "observed," clearly, are visible-becoming-invisible, things that perhaps may first be "seen" or "observed" visibly in people's behavior and body language, but then, as *peri* "about" suggests, must be dynamically (re)construed (and perhaps then "studied," as Freese [1926, p. 17] translates *to theōrēsai* there) as the *teloi* of those visible signs in invisible characters, virtues, and emotions. And in section 11 he insists, puzzlingly—since he has been concerned with the rhetor's attention to the resources for persuasion *peri hekaston* throughout the chapter—that *oude hē rhētorikē to kath' hekaston endoxon theōrēsei* (1.2.11, 1356b33), literally "rhetoric doesn't see/observe according to every opinion." The only way this makes sense is if *to theōrēsai* has now been "purified" or "perfected" in the entelechial sense as studying or theorizing—and indeed W. Rhys Roberts (1941/1984, p. 2156) translates that phrase as "the theory of rhetoric is concerned not with what seems reputable to a given individual," George Kennedy (1991/2007, p. 41) as "neither does rhetoric theorize about each opinion." There is, we might say, an entelechy of *to theōrēsai*, moving from the actual physical *observation* of visual signs in specific rhetorical situations, through *study* of the more general invisibles to which those signs point in those specific cases (dispositions and emotions), to *theorizing* about persuasivity in general.

3

Energy Channeled through Body Language

3.0 Introduction

My focus in chapter 2 was *rén* 仁, which I linked to Aristotle's collectivistic *to philein* "friendly feeling" and tentatively translated as "fellow-feeling," and theorized as the collective agent that is the subject both of *pistis* as persuading-and-believing and of *zhì* 治 as governing-and-being-governed, and so also the reticulatory medium of *to endekhomenon pithanon* "the available persuasivity." *to philein* and *rén* 仁, then, would be early Greek and early Chinese anticipations of what Kenneth Burke and Arne Naess would later call "identification," and thus the deep-ecological core of the rhetorical views of both Aristotle and Mencius.

We also saw that *to philein* and *rén* 仁 are forms of collective feeling-becoming-thinking, a group heart-becoming-mind, a transpersonal *xīn* 心 or *shēn xīn* 身心 that Mencius qualifies as the *cèyǐn zhī xīn* 惻隱之心 "secret sorrow's heart" (translated by Lau as the "heart of compassion") and the *bùrěnrén zhī xīn* 不忍人之心 "can't bear [other people's suffering] person's heart" (translated by Lau as "heart sensitive to the suffering of others," or "sensitive heart" for short). The interactive group phenomenologies that we've seen contributing to *to philein* and *rén* 仁 along the way include friendship (*philia*), love (*ài* 愛), faithfulness or trust (*xìn* 信), loyalty (*zhōng* 忠), happiness (*eudaimonia*, *lè* 樂), and an inclination to implement the Golden Rule (*shù* 恕), as well as the other virtuous dispositions or "shoots" through and to which the heart-becoming-mind travels: behavior that fits the situation and the group (*yì* 義), ritual propriety (*lǐ* 禮), and wisdom (*zhì* 智).

And as the growth metaphor in "shoots" implies, Mencius also understands the "virtuous" group body-becoming-mind of *rén* 仁 that ecologically regulates power and persuasion in social life as *emerging* organically out of deeper forces or propensities (*shì* 勢), and only gradually becoming more stably, but never rigidly, organized (*dìng* 定) as dispositions. In a sense the emergence is itself a disposition-to-emerge (an entelechy, as Aristotle would say), but there is also a disposition-to-let-things-emerge (the *wù zhù zhǎng* 勿助長 or "don't help grow" disposition) that should be developed to shield/facilitate the emergence.

The emerging force or forceful emergence on which I propose to focus here in chapter 3 is *qì* 氣, sometimes translated as "energy" or "configurative energies"—but energy specifically as channeled through the *social human body*, the body as an interactive stage for the performance of communicative events. At the end of §2.2 I noted that the affective self or *shēn xīn* 身心 may in some cases withdraw into the mind and view the organic body or *shēn tǐ* 身體 as its big dumb ride; the important point to add to that comparatively is that this would be the Cartesian view, the most radical version of Western rationalist dualism, and that in early Chinese philosophy *tǐ* 體, despite its *gǔ* 骨 "bone" radical, is never a "big dumb ride" or mindless *res extensa*. Sinologists since Boodberg (1953, pp. 326–27; see also Hall & Ames, 1987, pp. 87–89; Ames, 1993, pp. 152–53) have also noted that *tǐ* shares the "vase" phonetic with *lǐ* 禮 "ritual form": "Both are 'container' notions, and as such, both are 'shapes' that configure qualitative energies" (Behuniak, 2005, p. 116). As Behuniak translates Mencius, "The will [*zhì* 志] commands the configurative energies [*qì* 氣], and the configurative energies fill the body [*tǐ* 體]" (*MZ* 2A2). "Ritual forms," Behuniak adds, "are an embodiment of patterns generated out of environments in which productive integration is sought"—and specifically an "embodiment" in the literal sense in which these environmental integrations are "patterned" through the training of the body, the ritual habitualization of movement to signal and in some sense to store the memories of the group body-becoming-mind. The ritual training of the body that Mencius calls *lǐ* 禮 is one of the "four shoots" that are rooted in feeling-becoming-thinking and trained into a disposition, which in turn trains the body for both fleeting emotional body language (facial expression, gesture, posture) and more lasting dispositional body shape (for discussion see §3.9, below).

Also to be found in 2A2 is one of the most famous passages in the *MZ* dealing with *qì* 氣; there Mencius is asked what he is good at, and says he *knows speech*[1] (*zhī yán* 知言) and is *good at nourishing his flood-like qi* (*shàn yǎng wú hàorán zhī qì* 善養吾浩然之氣). Because "knowing speech" is patently relevant to a rhetoric, this passage bears close examination in a discussion of the *MZ* as a rhetorical treatise; but the passage is complex enough that I propose to devote the bulk of the chapter to an unpacking of the key concepts that contribute to a full understanding of it, and to return to "knowing speech" (*zhī yán* 知言) only at the end, in §3.8. As we'll see in §3.1, the English term *energy* derives from the Aristotelian coinage *energeia*, which means not the modern scientific sense of energy but "working within" and is generally considered to be synonymous with the *entelekheia* or entelechy; throughout this chapter (and book) it is important to remember that I am using "energy" in a very broad sense, to cover all the concepts loosely associated with *energeia*, *qì* 氣, and, in Kennedy and Perelman, "rhetoric." Energy in this purview is *not* the quantifiable and transferrable "property of objects" that modern science understands it to be; just what it is, I propose to develop slowly, over the course of the chapter. In §3.2–3.5 we take a look at the connections between Aristotelian *energeia* and rhetoric, first through the striking thesis offered by one of the most influential recent translators of and commentators on Aristotle's *Rhetoric*, George Kennedy, to the effect that rhetoric *is* energy (§3.2); after an excursus on vitalism (§3.3) we look at two other takes on rhetoric and energy, Susan Miller's notion of the "charismatic signifiers" that drive and guide persuasion (§3.4) and Jeffrey Walker's suggestion that for Aristotle persuasion is directed or channeled most powerfully through the *energeia* activated in the audience by the speaker's *hupokrisis*, "delivery" or "acting" (body language) (§3.5). This will lead us in §3.6 and §3.7 to a rethinking of body language and shared affect in Aristotle, and finally, in §3.8, back to Mencius on "knowing (embodied) speech"—and specifically, to whether there is a connection between *zhī yán* 知言 "knowing speech" and *yǎng qì* 養氣 "cultivating energy." Is it possible that for Mencius the cultivation of energy facilitates knowledge of speech? I close the chapter, then, with a consideration of *lǐ* 禮 "ritual propriety" as group memory embodied in trained collective dispositions (§3.9).

3.1 Aristotle: Energy and Entelechy

First, then, what *is* that energy that is "cultivated" or "nourished" in *yǎng qì* 養氣? The English word "energy," which seems to be the closest English equivalent to *qì* 氣, derives from the Greek word *energeia*, almost certainly an Aristotelian coinage, from the roots *en* "in" + *ergon* "work." For Aristotle, certainly—leaving open the question of whether he borrowed or coined the term—*energeia* is whatever is currently "in work" or "at work" (or "in action") in a process or event. As Aristotle uses it, *energeia* becomes virtually synonymous with *entelekheia* "entelechy," a term that he did unquestionably coin, from similar roots (*en* "in" + *telos* "end" + *ekhein* "to have," thus "having an end within"); the two are often translated "actuality," as in *Metaphysics* 1047a30–36:

> The word "actuality" [*energeia*], which we connect with "complete reality" [*entelekheia*], has, in the main, been extended from movements [*ek tōn kinēseōn*] to other things; for actuality [*energeia*] in the strict sense is thought to be identical with movement [*kinēsis*]. And so people do not assign movement to non-existent things, though they do assign some other predicates. E.g. they say that non-existent things are objects of thought and desire, but not that they are moved [*kinoumena*]; and this because, while *ex hypothesi* they do not actually exist [*ouk onta energeia*], they would have to exist actually [*esontai energeia*] if they were moved. (Ross, 1941/2001, p. 823)

This is a view of "reality" or "actuality" as a kind of work-flow or movement toward the end or "completeness" that is within. Aristotle's entelechial vision does not mean, however, that reality is somehow end-*driven*, or teleological—that everything that exists is merely a pale imperfect copy of some transcendental end or perfection that moves it infinitesimally toward itself, as it has often been replatonized by Christian and post-Christian thinkers since Thomas Aquinas. It means rather that the end or perfection or completeness is constantly *emerging from within*, and specifically emerging out of work, out of a generative energetic working-through. It is, in other words, a radically ecological concept that is far closer to Mencian concepts of the condition-dependent emergence of dispositions than has generally been recognized.

The coinage *entelekheia* is also a pun on the word *endelekheia* "persistence"; the two terms share the stability of *ekhein* "to have," which is related morphologically to *hexis* "disposition," a being a certain way through holding on, holding steady in a given state or condition. For Aristotle all things that exist have a disposition to be in a certain kind of work or motion, to act or orient themselves in a certain way or direction; so powerful is this tendency or persistence, this disposition, that to lack it is not to exist, not to be actual. In some sense the *telos* that is "had within," the new concept that Aristotle smuggled into the very morphological core of *endelekheia*, is that disposition, that innate inclination to persist in a certain kind of working; but it is also the (principle that animates the) becoming that emerges out of that working, which semantically charges "persistence" with change as emergence, as flow.

This notion is also, obviously, highly reminiscent of Mencius's notion that persisting in certain ways of feeling-becoming-thinking creates moral dispositions, which in turn lend the body a postural disposition (§3.8); and the idea that this Aristotelian "being-at-work-staying-itself" (Sachs, 1995, p. 74 and *passim*) *is* energy/*energeia* is even more obviously congruent with Mencian thought. *qì* 氣 is many things in Chinese thought, from spirit to a fluid-like physical energy that circulates through the body like or as blood; but one thing it never is for Mencius is supernatural, an otherworldly force that comes from somewhere else and "energizes" sublunary life. The Aristotelian notion that energy is the at-work-ness of things, as a kind of transindividual *byproduct* of working, acting, moving through the world, an at-work-ness that involves both becoming and staying the same, may not be expressly formulated in precisely those terms in Mencius, but it is quite easy to imagine him accepting Aristotle's definition as a workable paraphrase of his own.

Note also that for Aristotle happiness (*eudaimonia*) is simply the *energeia* of human life, and specifically, as we saw in §1.1, a group phenomenology that is energized (worked or activated inwardly) through interactions with friends (see Schankula, 1971). One might even suggest that for Aristotle *philia* "friendship" is the *dunamis* or potential of collective life that is activated/energized by or through *to philein* "friendly feeling" as the *energeia*/*entelekheia* "actuality" of happiness. The only significant way this Aristotelian social ecology differs from Mencius's conception of *rén* 仁 is that, because Mencius is mostly addressing rulers and their advisors, he structures ecosis or "becoming-good" primarily around good government rather than the good life, and thus takes as his greatest good not happiness but peaceful and prosperous rule and a sage's reputation. The people's earthly happiness is important in the *MZ* mainly as an indicator of good government (e.g., 1B10, 5A5–6).

It should be obvious, however, that there is a high degree of scalable congruity between the two ecologies. When Mencius is read as addressing ordinary people rather than rulers and their advisors, in fact, the "goods" that he holds out as carrots to people striving to cultivate *rén* 仁 and *qì* 氣 are typically taken to be remarkably close to what Aristotle calls *eudaimonia* or happiness. Confucius, it should also be noted, ranked worldly happiness with friends very high (*Analects* 5.26, 11.26), and Mencius hints at the same in passing (especially in 4A12), and generally, as we saw in §2.3, places a high value on friendship as well.

3.2 Kennedy on Aristotle: Rhetoric as Energy

In the introduction to the first edition of his translation of Aristotle's *TR*, Kennedy (1991, p. 7) strikingly suggests that rhetoric is "the energy inherent in emotion and thought, transmitted through a system of signs, including language, to others to influence their decisions or actions." Note the word order there: rhetoric is not the *transmission* of that energy through a system of signs to influence others; it is the *energy* that is so transmitted. When the rhetor observes *to endekhomenon pithanon*, s/he "sees" or "observes"—feels, experiences, is jolted by—energy. When s/he marshals *to pithanon* or persuasivity to influence others, s/he summons and rechannels that energy through various semiotic systems, including (as we'll see) both verbal and body language.

Out of context, this formulation is admittedly a bit sketchy.[2] A fuller context would be:

> Both animals and human beings have a natural instinct to preserve and defend themselves, their territory, and their group and families. They do this by physical acts and by the use of signs, including utterances such as howls, cries, and human speech. *Rhetoric*, in the most general sense, is the energy inherent in emotion and thought, transmitted through a system of signs, including language, to others to influence their decisions or actions. In developed human societies, such as ancient Greece, social and political contexts emerge that mold speech into certain conventional forms shaped by the psychology and expectation of audiences. Both literature and public address develop in this way. (Kennedy, 1991, p. 7)

Note there that Kennedy first posits a general life-organizing force, a "natural instinct," a drive or impulse of some sort, that causes "animals and human beings . . . to preserve and defend themselves, their territory, and their group and families," and a set of means (various communicative signs and "physical acts") by which that force can be actualized (*energeia/entelekheia*). Then he defines rhetoric as the energy that drives the latter part of the equation, the actualization of the force through sign systems. It's possible to imagine that, without this rhetorical energy, sign systems might be powerless to channel the "natural instinct" for self-preservation and self-defense into actual social regulation designed to effect that self-preservation and that self-defense—like an artificial language that nobody bothers to learn, say, and that therefore remains a kind of clever invention or lovely filigree that may be admirable without being efficacious.

But then this energy or actual-working goes underground, as it were, at least rhetorically in Kennedy's paragraph: we tacitly jump hundreds of thousands of years, from some sort of rhetorical primal scene up into "developed human societies," societies presumably developed through precisely the kinds of regulatory strategies mobilized by the life-organizing force, powered by the rhetorical energy that inheres in emotions and thoughts, and transmitted through sign systems. This is, one assumes, though Kennedy does not say so explicitly, how societies develop. This is the regulatory moment out of which "social and political contexts emerge that mold speech into certain conventional forms shaped by the psychology and expectation of audiences." There is:

[a] the-life-organizing force

[b] the rhetorical energy that powers that force, channeled through the medium of emotions and thoughts

[c] the sign systems that transmit that energy from body to body

[d] the organization of that bodily contagion into "the psychology and expectation of audiences"

[e] the conventional rhetorical forms molded out of speech (and presumably other sign systems) by reference to audience psychology and expectations

[f] persuasion, rhetorical influence over others

Traditional quickie definitions of rhetoric focus on (f); the classical study of rhetoric is generally thought to formalize (e). What goes before (ef), namely (abcd), constitutes something like the vitalistic underbelly of rhetorical study, the part that isn't usually talked about, even though it's all there in Plato and especially Aristotle.

Let us postpone a discussion of (a) vitalism to §3.3. The interesting questions about (bcd) for my purposes are:

[Q1] What kind of energy is it?

[Q2] Where does it come from?

[Q3] How does it "inhere" in emotion and thought?

[Q4] How is it "transmitted through a system of signs"?

[Q5] How is it organized into what Aristotle calls *to endekhomenon pithanon* "the available persuasivity"?

(Q1–2) Does Kennedy mean by (b) rhetoric-as-energy a modern physiological energy, something biochemical? Or does he mean something like the Freudian libido, a bodily energy that is generated and structured and channeled more by social impulses than by our DNA? Or does he mean Aristotle's *energeia*, action or actuality as the state of being "in work" or "at work," so that (Q3) "the energy inherent in emotion and thought" would be something like the working-out or working-through of the actuality of emotion's and thought's potentiality? (Q3–4) What is the contagiousness of rhetorical energy, and (Q4–5) how can (c) sign systems serve as its carrier from speaker to listener, from writer to reader?

Kennedy (1992, p. 2) offers a not entirely satisfactory answer to these questions:

> "The window is shut" is a communication. Its rhetorical quality is dependent on its context. It might, for example, be a mild reassurance to a recipient concerned about rain blowing into a room, or an exclamation of frustration by a thief who had planned to climb in. "Shut the window," even without knowing its context, seems inherently more rhetorically intense. The speaker is expressing an order or wish. The statement carries some authority to make the particular request. The recipient's responses are limited to executing the order, refusing to execute the order and thus denying the authority of the speaker, or demanding some equality in negotiating the situation. The recipient might say "Shut it yourself." Or "Why? It's stuffy in here." If the first speaker adds a reason, and thus creates an enthymeme ("Shut the window because the wind is blowing the papers off the desk"), the rhetorical energy is somewhat reduced. Authority is less obvious, appeal to the judgment of the recipient is implied. There is recognition of the possibility for deliberation. I would provisionally describe the rhetoric of these sentences as a matter of their energy level. It is easy to see that they might be expressed in different degrees of shrillness or calmness of voice. Thus they also involve different degrees

of expenditure of physical energy in their utterance. Rhetoric in the most general sense may perhaps be identified with the energy inherent in communication: the emotional energy that impels the speaker to speak, the physical energy expended in the utterance, the energy level coded in the message, and the energy experienced by the recipient in decoding the message. In theory, one might even seek to identify some quantitative unit of rhetorical energy—call it the "rheme"—analogous to an erg or volt, by which rhetorical energy could be measured. I leave that to the experimentalists.

This gives us a list of the types of energy he means: emotional, physical, and "the energy level coded in the message, and the energy experienced by the recipient in decoding the message." This is useful detail. But (Q1–2) what is the relationship among those different forms or levels or quanta of energy? Do they connect up? (Q4) If the author or speaker "codes" some energy or energy level "in" the message, does the recipient in decoding it get *that* level of energy? (Q4) If "in metaphor, energy is expended by the author in defamiliarizing the language and by the reader in mentally experiencing the presence of a force affecting the meaning" (ibid., p. 3), does the author expend energy "into" the text, where it becomes a "force affecting the meaning" that is experienced as energy by the reader? And (Q1) is it the same quantum or level of energy? Or (Q2) is energy everywhere, lying in wait for energy sources not so much to "create it" as to ruffle or churn it up, vector new rhetorical forces through it? "Rhetorical assertion conveys energy," he writes, "and can spark reaction in another energy source" (ibid.): (Q1) what is that "spark," exactly? Metaphorically the energy is volatile, like an electromagnetic field that changes as a moving charge is run through it; but (Q1) what is the tenor of the metaphor? Either Kennedy has not expended enough energy in "defamiliarizing the language" here or I'm not expending enough energy in "mentally experiencing the presence of a force affecting the meaning." Presumably the "energy sources" of Kennedy's description are animate beings—primarily humans, but other animals as well, any living creature capable of wanting something. They possess energy in a physical sense, obviously, but the energy that Kennedy refers to does not seem to be the kind of biochemical energy measurable in a skin-conductance test; it has a figurative element to it that seems somehow vaguely phenomenological, referring to perceived intensity—but (Q3) what? The fact that he wants to imagine "some quantitative unit of rhetorical energy—call it the 'rheme'" (ibid.)—suggests the extent to which this energy is phenomenological rather than strictly physical. If it were a purely physical energy—kinetic, potential, thermal, gravitational, electromagnetic, elastic, nuclear, chemical, etc.—it would be measured in joules, not rhemes. "Rhetoric is least effective," he says, "when either speaker or audience is tired, for the physical energy required on both sides is lacking" (ibid.): rhetoric requires some sort of (Q3) intensification of the attention we devote to communication, and that does expend physical energy, and becomes more difficult to summon up when we're tired. But rhetoric for Kennedy is *not* that physical energy; it is that physical energy plus something else, something unnamed.

Kennedy (1991, p. 7) called rhetoric "the energy inherent in emotion and thought, transmitted through a system of signs, including language, to others to influence their decisions or actions"; here (1992, p. 2) he notes (providing a fuller answer to Q3) that "rhetorical energy is not found only in language. It is present also in physical actions, facial expressions, gestures, and signs generally." But (again Q3) what does "present in" mean, exactly? Some of these features, especially the facial expressions and gestures, are the body language that Aristotle calls *hupokrisis* "acting," or what is usually translated as "delivery" (see §3.6). To the extent that physical actions are performed by animate creatures with more or less specific intentions, the "energy" in them can be imagined as carrying or intensifying (or, we will see Jeffrey Walker suggesting in §3.5, directing the audience's attention to) intentionality; signs too, in the broadest semiotic sense of anything that is taken to be meaningful by an interpreter, can be imagined as invested with that same energy as a vehicle of intentionality. But does "present in" imply that the energy *dwells* or *is stored* there? Or is the imagination of a stop sign as invested with rhetoric-as-energy merely a human phenomenology?

This all is by way of introduction to Kennedy (1992), the body of which is devoted to the enumeration and explication of eight theses:

[1] "Rhetoric is prior to speech" (p. 4)

[2] "The receiver's interpretation of a communication is prior to the speaker's intent in determining the meaning" (p. 7)

[3] "Rhetoric is prior to intentionality or to any belief on the part of a speaker about the meaning of a sign or its effect on others" (p. 9)

[4] "The function of rhetoric is the survival of the fittest" (p. 10)

[5] "The rhetorical code evolves by selective variation" (p. 10)

[6] "Among the traditional parts of rhetoric (invention, arrangement, style, memory, and delivery), delivery is prior to the others" (p. 12)

[7] "Writing is prior to speech but not prior to rhetoric" (p. 13)

[8] "Rhetorical invention, arrangement, style, memory, and delivery are phenomena of nature and prior to speech" (p. 14)

All but the two Darwinian theses there (4 and 5) are about priority: rhetoric is prior to speech (1, 8), writing (7), and intentionality and beliefs about meaning and audience impact (3); interpretation is prior to intention (2); and delivery (acting) is prior to invention, arrangement, style, and memory (6). Rhetoric, clearly, *comes first*—presumably because it is a "phenomenon of nature."

Now clearly Kennedy is right that *something* here is a phenomenon of nature. Something like the collective phenomenon he describes, some group pressure exerted on individuals to conform to shared norms, does exist in and among social animals, and does preexist verbal(izable) intentionality, speech, writing, and other specific communicative acts. Since rhetoric is usually defined as the human verbal *marshaling* of that pressure for specific persuasive purposes, Kennedy's thesis seems counterintuitive, and perhaps a bit extreme; but I propose that we can obviate the counterintuitivity in his thesis by recognizing the "phenomenon of nature" Kennedy identifies not as rhetoric *in toto* but as *part* of rhetoric, a part that is both pre-communicative (in Kennedy's sense of priority) and peri-communicative (in the sense that it always *accompanies* any specific attempt to communicate). In Aristotle's terms from chapter 1, I suggest that (ef) *pistis* as persuading-and-believing, as any given act of group communication, is always preceded/accompanied by (bcd) *to endekhomenon pithanon* "the available persuasivity," the general communicative conditions for rhetorical persuasion, the rhetorical biosphere or social energy field in which persuasion becomes possible. This latter, then, would be Kennedy's "energy." As Susan Miller (2008, p. 8) puts it, "persuasion is always a matter of trust that precedes any form of its expression": Kennedy would say "energy" rather than "trust," but both energy and trust (and especially energized trust) are preexisting resources for persuasion that the rhetor *draws on*, from the social ecology of affective value that organizes becoming-communal meaning, significance, weight, and so on. The dominance-and-submission patterns that Kennedy traces in several different human cultures and several species of "lower" animals, the symbolic replacement of physical conflict with various kinds of semiotic displays (shouting, roaring)—all these are the interactive conditions that support persuasion.

The question remains, however: (Q1) What *is* this (b) rhetorical energy that is prior to speech, writing, and intentionality? It is "a force affecting the meaning"; but what kind of force? The fact that Kennedy echoes the language of Darwinian evolution might suggest that he believes in the *random* "selective variation" of rhetorical evolution, and thus would distance himself from (a) Aristotelian (or Lamarckian) vitalism; but in fact he never quite says this. The selective variation of rhetorical evolution may not be random; it may have a vitalistic selector. Kennedy (1992, p. 10; emphasis added) glosses his Darwinian theses (4 and 5) by saying that "rhetoric acts as a *mechanism* for survival by facilitating successful adaptation of an organism to environmental change"; and while that word "mechanism" would seem to be at war with vitalistic principles, we note that Deleuze and Guattari (1972/1984) call the vitalistic forces in *Anti-Oedipus* "desiring-machines." "Mechanism" may in fact be shorthand for something like "the interactive functioning of all the guided and guiding organismic and populational impulses that together facilitate adaptation to environmental change." His one reference to a vitalistic life force seems to deny that that is what he is talking about: "In speaking of rhetoric, I have defined it as an energy existing in life. But energy exists apart from living organisms and the energy of the life force, and thus rhetoric is perhaps a special case of the energy of all physics as known from subatomic particles" (p. 13). Rhetorical energy is a *physical* energy, nothing vitalistic; and yet it is also a guiding and organizing force that clearly exceeds the kind of "energy of all physics as known from subatomic particles" that he wants it to be.

Frankly, I don't think Kennedy knows precisely what he means by rhetorical energy. He has a series of analogues for it, which he uses metaphorically or through negation to hint at what he is groping toward—a vitalistic life force, a physical (electromagnetic? biochemical?) energy, a mechanism, a volatile force field or vector field in which chain reactions are somehow "sparked"—but these are all ways of talking around what he means, and thus of avoiding theorizing what is not fundamentally understood.

I want to take two more passes through this "energetic" reading of rhetoric, offered by Susan Miller (§3.4) and Jeffrey Walker (§3.5); first, however, let us make a quick *excursus* into the issue of vitalism raised two paragraphs ago.

3.3 *Excursus:* Vitalism in Mencius and Aristotle

It is generally agreed that Chinese philosophy during the Warring States period was *qì*-based and therefore fundamentally vitalist; what that means, however, as Mencius admits when asked to define the "flood-like *qì* 氣," is difficult to describe. For the Daoists, *qì* 氣 often seems to be a mystical, supernatural force; for the Confucians, it more typically seems to be an inexplicable force arising out of, and as an inexplicable byproduct of and steering function for, the normal mundane functioning of humans, other living things, and other natural processes. Indeed while one possible translation of *qì* 氣 is "vital force," another might be "inexplicable force": in Chinese the term is often used to refer casually to forces we don't understand (another Confucian term for which is *tiān* 天 "heaven": see §4.5).

Not only is Aristotle philosophically very close to Mencius and his fellow Warring States Confucians on this secular vitalism; he also articulates its functionality far more attentively than they. Richard Hughes (1965, p. 157) made the case several decades ago that the unique quality of Aristotle's theory of rhetoric "springs from three sources: from Aristotle's *vitalism,* from his concept of *argument,* and from his concept of the *topics.*" He added:

> The first, the vitalism, is the most important, for this is the root and cause of argument and topic. By *vitalism* I mean that assumption, ubiquitous in Aristotle's writings, springing from his concern for entelechy, that all the arts are generative. His biological studies predisposed him to see reality as the end product of form evolving into its ideally realized material structure. As there is an embryo, an evolution and finally a status in the biological kingdom, so too in the intellectual kingdom. The literal *life-ness* of the arts, and particularly the language arts, is at the heart of Aristotle's rhetoric. Realities, verities, concepts, attitudes are not thought of as static but as dynamic, as continually evolving to a point of status. There are many generative instruments to aid this evolution: music, drama, poetry . . . and rhetoric. Rhetoric is one art of moving an idea from embryo to reality. It is, consequently, an art which rests not at the end of the intellectual process, but an art which is *within* the process. There is no hyperbole, but only a sound literalism, in calling Aristotle's rhetoric a *creative* rhetoric. (Hughes, 1965, p. 157)

"All the arts are generative," obviously, means that the entelechy of *tekhnē*, of art, of all human artistic and intellectual creation, is constitutive: it is a constant bringing-into-being of "realities, verities, concepts, attitudes." Rhetoric for Aristotle is "one art of moving an idea from embryo to reality," not only in the sense that the idea is always in the process of becoming a real idea, but also in the sense that it is (constantly re)shaping the human, social, symbolic, dramatistic reality (to put it in Kenneth Burke's 1945/1962 terms) in which we live. Arne Naess would expand that shaping ecotically to encompass the entire biological reality in which we live—and in that expansion would stand closer to both Aristotle and Mencius.

Note also Hughes's insistence there that the entelechy of rhetoric "rests not at the end of the intellectual process, but . . . *within* the process": there has been a very strong inclination among readers of Aristotle in the West to binarize the entelechy into two radically different stages, the middle and the end, the current actuality and the future perfection toward which it strives, and to subordinate the former to the latter. This is the misreading of Aristotle that we found Behuniak (2005, p. xii) inheriting from his predecessors in §1.4: Benjamin Schwartz taking *xìng* 性 to be "'an innate tendency toward growth or development in a given, predetermined direction,'" A. C. Graham reading *xìng* 性 "'on lines rather suggestive of Aristotelian teleology,'" leading Behuniak to conclude that, "throughout the secondary literature, the default understanding of *xing* is 'nature' with a predetermined end." As Hughes reminds us, the *telos* that is "had within" the entelechy is a potential perfection that is every moment emerging from the at-work-ness of the current actuality. The ecological conditions (*ming* 命) or circumstances (*kath' hekaston*) on whose shaping influence Behuniak rightly insists—not only the rain and the dew on Ox Mountain but the woodchoppers and the grazing cows (§2.7)—are part of that at-work-ness, part of the vital configurative energy that for Aristotle as well as Mencius shapes the emergence of the "end."

Hughes also insists that the entelechial shaping tool employed by the rhetor is always *argument*, whether that takes the form of narrative, exposition, or description. "By argument," Hughes (1965, p. 158) insists,

> Aristotle means *discovered judgment*. Men may make assertions of incontrovertible fact, or men may make statements of mere opinion: neither kind of statement is the concern of rhetoric. Rhetoric is concerned with the spacious middle ground between fact and opinion, with the area of probabilities. A *probable* area is one where separate items of experience have not yet evolved

into a reality. Like the "unlick't bear whelp," such an area of experience is still a protoplasm, not yet a shape. Aristotelian argument means the generative power of the rhetorical process producing a judgment from just such an area.

Again, there, we find the constitutive power of rhetoric, of argument: it doesn't just produce a judgment from the unformed protoplasms of pre-icotic human experience; it produces a judgment that evolves a "reality." We will see in chapter 4, though, that "mere opinion" (*doxa*) is *part* of the vital entelechy that evolves icotically into "plausibilities" (*ta eikota*), which are collectively naturalized as the "reality" on which "judgments" can be based; and we will see later in this chapter (§3.5–6) that opinions enter into that entelechial icosis precisely by being "energized"—presenced as affect-becoming-conation—through body language.

Just what sort of vitalistic force drives this rhetorical project, though, Hughes doesn't stop to ask. In his summary, it seems as if the rhetor does it all, in his (not yet her) head: discovers an area of preicotic protoplasm, an "area of experience" that is "not yet a shape," and then individualistically discovers, evolves, and disseminates a judgment about it, giving it form, like a dim analogue of Creation. "The rhetorician," Hughes writes, "is primarily the man who discovers a judgment in an area where experience is still flexible enough to take many shapes. He is, secondly, the man who shares that judgment with other men" (1965, p. 158). But Hughes doesn't specifically theorize the individualism on which his formulations implicitly rest, or even insist on it much; in fact, his summary of this notion in the very next paragraph shifts into a depersonalized syntax that might be read as suggesting a collective agent at work: "Argument, then, is a generative process. It is the evolution of a judgment and then the projection of that judgment in such a way that the process will be duplicated in the intellect and imagination of the audience" (ibid.). The two-stage formulation of that process—first "the evolution of a judgment," then the "projection of that judgment" so that the audience is infected with it as well—suggests that Hughes is still thinking mostly individualistically, the judgment first evolved in a single head, then sent out into the world; but that same two-stage formulation, that description of argument as a generative process involving both speaker and listener, suggests that the audience is somehow actively involved in the generative process as well.

The term "vitalism" has come to be somewhat fraught in Western thought, because it seems to suggest a mystical or magical force that wields natural becomings from the outside, from some supernatural realm. The dualizing supernaturalism of the monotheistic tradition issuing out of Zoroastrianism into Platonism and on into Hellenized Judaism, and the latter's most influential heresy, Christianity, tends to make Western interpreters of vitalist thinking imagine a vital force that is both in control and made up of a substance that is dualistically opposite to what it controls: spirit rather than flesh, mind rather than matter, immortal rather than mortal, etc. As Byron Hawk (2007, pp. 4–5) notes, however, this is a narrow and misleading conception of vitalism:

> While vitalism has romantic variations, at its roots it is theoretically and historically distinct. The fundamental question that cuts across all vitalisms is "What is life?" Each episteme, period, or paradigm answers the question of life differently according to its own situation and within its own discourse, but they are all trying to come to grips with what drives self-organization and development in the world. Historically, the general answers have ranged from an animistic, abstract, or mystical power that exists outside of and operates on the world, to an evolutionary and physio-chemical process that operates in the world, to a complex combination of material, biological, historical, social, linguistic, and ultimately technological processes that produce emergence. Life is situated in the relationships among these bodies and their forces. Rather than seeing life as an autonomous force, or as caused by physico-chemical or purely biological processes, this latter view [complex vitalism] situates life within complex, ecological interactions. I see in each of these answers two key assumptions: that life is fundamentally complex (and that complexity must be accounted for or addressed) and that life is fundamentally generative (force, energy, will, power, or desire is central to this complexity).

I would add a third assumption: that the need to explain the complexity of life tends to lead to the positing of generativity, or else that the discovery of generativity tends to lead to an appreciation and an understanding of the complexity of life. In other words, the two assumptions that Hawk adduces are not isolated but intertwined.

The explanatory difficulty faced by a complex secular (post-mystical) vitalism—such as in fact Confucius and Mencius and their followers developed—is the need to account for the emergence out of social and sociobiological processes not only order and organization but the generative "force, energy, will, power, or desire" to *create* order and organization. Darwin's theory of natural selection explains the emergence of order out of natural processes, but—and this makes it by default nonvitalistic—it does not posit a generative *will* or *desire* to create order out of natural processes. Darwin insists on *random* selection. It is, in fact, this leap from the random to the desired that makes even a secular vitalism difficult for many contemporary intellectuals to swallow. The positing of some complex vitalistic agent or agency that *wants* to bring order to natural processes seems to many hopelessly outdated, inextricably lodged in the history of religion. There are spirits, there is a Creator, there is a Life Force, there is Love . . . and where there is Love . . .

Thinking again of Hughes's reading of Aristotle's conception of rhetoric as vitalistic, we note that several key Kennedyan factors seem to be missing from it: (a) the life-organizing force, (b) the rhetorical energy, and (c) the transmission of that energy from body to body. All this is adumbrated in Hughes only (if at all) by his polemics in favor of Aristotelian rhetoric as a *generative* art. If rhetoric has the power to *generate* or *constitute* symbolic or dramatistic realities, surely that requires a collective agent? Surely that power or "energy" must be channeled through, and perhaps even generated or created or constituted out of, what Hughes calls the "duplication" of the process in the audience's intellect and imagination, or what Kennedy calls the "transmission" of that energy from body to body?

The interesting question for a vitalist reading of Aristotle is: if the entelechy is the *having* of an end within, who or what is the subject of the verb *ekhein*? Who or what *has* the end in the entelechy? The vitalism that Richard Hughes stresses as primary in Aristotle's thinking but does not linger long over would suggest that the haver is the vitalistic power that drives the entelechy, the supraentelechial force that *desires* the movement from potential to actuality. But what is that? "By *vitalism*," Hughes writes, "I mean that assumption, ubiquitous in Aristotle's writings, springing from his concern for entelechy, that all the arts are generative": right, but what does the generating? "The arts" "themselves"? The artists?

And if we follow most Aristotle scholars and take *energeia* as more or less synonymous with *entelekheia*, then the *energeia* of the *entelekheia* would be a working through (toward) the actualization of potential—not just a becoming, but an active becoming, a striving, an actualization of some overriding vitalistic *desire* to create philosophical order out of a "formidably unstable object of inquiry." Just what vital force desires that creation of order out of instability will take us some time to work out, and the main interpretive work to be done on that head will be done in chapter 4; in brief, however, I want to argue that in both Aristotle and Mencius it is the culture, the group. To the extent that the aim of philosophy is to work through *doxa* "opinion" to *epistēmē* (organized and habituated knowing), I take Aristotle to be saying that that philosophical project is conducted not by the philosopher alone, but by the culture, which "(self-)chooses" the philosopher as its spokesperson, its articulatory channel. If the entelechy is not the *telos* but the whole process, not the end of the process but the having of an end within, what we find in Aristotle's epistemic purification of public opinion is not pure logic liberated from public opinion, not systematic philosophy liberated from the sloppy groupthink of the agora, not truth liberated from appearances, but the culture's collective *doxa*-becoming-*epistēmē*, embodied group opinion striving icotically to become a clearly demarcated understanding.

3.4 Miller on Kennedy on Aristotle: Energy as Charisma

In §3.2 we saw Susan Miller offering an alternative construction of the "available persuasivity" as *trust* rather than energy; let us now take a closer look at her specific reading of Kennedy on Aristotelian rhetoric as energy, which she takes to be a salutary reframing of the whole field of rhetoric, long confined as it was to a collection of rationalist structures for "persuasive" speech or writing.

Miller's own rethinking of these issues leads her to suggest something apparently similar to Kennedy's energy: "accounts of persuasion need to consider the emotional effects of charisma. A later doctor in an expensive suit whose educated speech is familiar to us projects a whole range of charismatic signifiers that makes some of us think she will be a trustworthy clinician" (2008, p. 31). "Charismatic signifiers," obviously, are more socially organized than Kennedy's energy; but the "emotional effects of charisma" do seem to partake of something like Kennedy's (b) energy, (c) transmitted from body to body in (d) collectively guided ways that regulate signification.

Note that charisma derives from *kharis* "grace, favor," and *kharizō* "to grant a favor or request, to gratify a passion, to give freely of something"; in (Attic) Greek *kharisma* is the gift or favor itself, later (in Koine Greek) becoming a divine gift like glossolalia. Specifically, *kharis* is grace or favor in the ecotic circulation of affect between the giver and receiver of a gift, the doer and recipient of a favor. When it is felt by the giver of something or the doer of a favor, it is usually translated "grace, graciousness, kindness, goodwill"; when it is felt by the receiver of a gift or a kindness, it is usually translated "thankfulness, gratitude." This complex obviously returns us to the philosophical realm of *rén* 仁 explored in chapter 2: the emotion Aristotle studies in *TR* 2.7 is usually identified as *kharis* and translated "kindliness" or "benevolence." But as David Konstan (2007, pp. 158–68) points out, Aristotle is listing and analyzing *emotions*, and "kindliness" and "benevolence" are not emotions—they are dispositions. And the emotion Aristotle theorizes in that chapter is not *kharis* but rather *ekhō kharin*, lit. "to have favor," which Attic Greek uses to mean the "inward" or "toward-me" kind of favor that one feels in receiving a gift, suggesting that the emotion Aristotle is interested in there is actually *gratitude*. If he were theorizing kindliness or benevolence, the *kharis* felt while giving a gift, he would have written *ferō kharin* lit. "to bring/carry favor" or *tithēmi kharin* lit. "to put/place favor." And in any case, as we've just seen, *kharis* itself is not a property or trait or state possessed by an individual but an ecosis, a becoming-communal phenomenology of which individuals passingly *partake*, either "having" it (*ekhō kharin* "feel gratitude") or "carrying" it (*ferō kharin* "feel benevolence").

Konstan's reading of *kharis* in *TR* 2.7 as "gratitude" works far better than "benevolence" in a rhetorical situation, too, since "rarely would one try to induce in an audience a sudden impulse to bestow a favour," but "litigants often emphasize the benefactions they have bestowed on their fellow citizens of the city in an effort to elicit the jurors' gratitude" (2007, p. 161). Konstan (ibid., p. 164) notes further that gratitude "was also vital to a society predicated on competition and reciprocity, where maintaining one's status in the forum of public esteem required continual effort and wariness."

Nivison (1996, pp. 24–33), in fact, traces the etymological origins of *dé* 德 "virtue" to precisely this "feeling of a debt of gratitude for a kindness or gift or service" as intensified in ancient Chinese society into "an ambient psychological force" (ibid., p. 25), a "moral force" (ibid., p. 32) thought to inhere in and radiate from the king:

> The *de* of the king thus automatically produces a complementary response within his field of "moral force." To the extent that his character, his *de* such as it is, has the quality of good order, this *de* will affect those around him, in such a way that their behavior will be smoothly and functionally related to his, effortlessly and naturally on both sides. This character and its producing of effects are his *de*-as-king. (ibid.)

This description is in every way resonant with both Mencius on the contagiousness of *rén* 仁 (§2.4 and §2.9–12) and Miller on Kennedy's "rhetorical energy" as "charismatic signifiers" that ferry the affectively charged social value attached specifically to gifts and favors and the debts they incur through the community, through what I theorize in chapter 4 as a doxicotic economy. As her reference to "Max Weber's claim that Athenian leadership was 'charismatic,' thus based on emotional appeals" (ibid., p. 48) suggests, Miller seems to be using the adjective "charismatic" in the general sense of "affective" or "somatic," and only obliquely and "secularizingly" alluding to Weber's theory of charismatic authority "resting on devotion to the exceptional sanctity, heroism or exemplary character of an individual person, and of the normative patterns or order revealed or ordained by him" (Weber, 1922/1947, p. 328). Miller's reading of Weber's definition would almost certainly focus on the words "devotion" (collectively organized and intensified trust) and "normative patterns or order" and downplay the mystical attributes usually ascribed to the charismatic leader as "endowed," as Weber writes, "with supernatural, superhuman, or at least specifically exceptional powers or qualities" (ibid., p. 358); but clearly the superhuman/supernatural energies Weber detects in charisma resonate with Nivison's remarks about ancient Chinese conceptions of the "*de*-as-king."

What Miller offers us, then, is a sociology of rhetoric-as-energy based on the social organization of energy into signs that map patterns and pathways of normative (collectively prescribed and policed) response to and within an affective ecology of value. In Kennedy's conception rhetoric-as-energy is a force of nature; in Miller's revision it becomes not just social structure but social pressure, intensified affect not just disseminated virally through a population but organized as becoming-communal conation.

3.5 Walker on Aristotle: Rhetoric as Driven by Feeling-Activating-Energy (or Energy-Activating-Feeling)

Ecotic conation or conative ecosis is, however, mostly implicit in Miller's reading of Kennedy on Aristotle. Jeffrey Walker (2008, p. 81) offers a more explicit energy-based interpretation of Aristotelian feeling as the action-potential of all politics, poetics, and rhetoric, suggesting that for Aristotle, *pathos* is "a physically embodied, psychologically compulsive will-to-act" that has a tendency to "warp" the mind and thus to "strongly determine how it perceives and interprets any 'premises' presented to it, which it attends to, which it allows to count most powerfully, and which it ignores," but that can also, sometimes, at least in theory, be productively *channeled*.

Walker (2008, pp. 78–79) makes this case first through a close look at Aristotle's two mentions of *katharsis*, in *Politics* 1341b38 and *Poetics* 1449b28, exploring the analogical relationship between the *pharmakon* that "causes the secretion of 'juices' from the body, resulting in a pleasurable feeling of well-being," in the case of medical *katharsis*, and the *tekhnē* (a rhythm, a melodic mode, or a persuasive argument) that "in the case of *logos* or music . . . causes the soul of the hearer to be 'put into a state' (both Aristotle and Gorgias use the verb *kathistanai*) or to have its 'disposition' (*taxis*) rearranged according to the 'disposition' (*taxis* again) of the *pharmakon* or *technē* applied." This "state" that the poetic, musical, or rhetorical *tekhnē* puts the hearer's soul into is in fact a specific *pathos* or bodily (affective) state: "The expressed *pathos* is caused to 'come out of' the soul by the *pharmakon/ technē*, just as 'juices' are caused to come out of the body. But the different *pathē* that *logos* or music may draw from the soul are not necessarily bad or harmful 'juices,' for the listeners may be 'put into a state' of courage or delight, as well as any other mood, and the *katharsis* of a *pathos* from the soul does not involve its being 'purged away' but rather its becoming manifest." This cathartic making-manifest, he suggests, in fact involves the *directionalizing* and *intentionalizing* of diffuse body states that are unpleasant because they cannot issue into action, and so manifest themselves as random deadend distress: "Blood boiling around the heart without any accompanying perception of 'insult' is not yet 'anger' but only a diffuse state, a choleric temper perhaps, a readiness to be provoked to anger by the first plausible (or even implausible) provocation that comes along." This diffuse state is fairly common in our ordinary lives, but can also be artistically aroused, through the application of the *tekhnai* of music or rhetoric—especially when, say, the music or the argumentation is "wrong" or inappropriate for one's current emotional state, so that it mostly jars or jostles without framing the resulting body state becoming-cognitively. "*Katharsis* of a specific emotion," Walker argues, "requires both physical arousal and the active presence within the soul of an appropriate conceptual frame. . . . For Aristotle, an emotion is a will-to-act in a specific way—a mode of intentionality—which is prompted, quasi-syllogistically, by sensations and perceptions that are mediated by cognition or (in humans) by *logos*."

The "implications" of this reading that Walker mentions in his subtitle are three in number. The first is that "*all* intentional or attitudinal states, including the states of *believing* and *doubting*, or of the moods of rational assent and dissent, are types of *pathē* and emerge from within existing affects" (ibid., p. 83). Because, as the Greek etymology suggests, the *pathē* are not willed but "suffered," believing and doubting "are not consciously willed attitudes but are experienced as *pathē* that arise from the affective/appetitive psyche's powers of interpretation and response" (ibid,. p. 84). Believing and doubting can again to some extent be *channeled* cognitively, but they cannot be "commanded" by reason.

Walker's (ibid., pp. 84–85) second implication moves us specifically into the *tekhnai* of rhetoric. Let me quote at some length:

> A second implication, closely related to the first, is that Aristotle's account of emotional psychology provides a basic model of "practical reasoning" generally, and—since that is the very realm with which rhetoric is concerned, as Aristotle conceives it (*Rhetoric* 1.2.12)—one may argue too that the process by which emotion/intentionality and willed action (*pathos* and *praxis*) arise as the "conclusion" from a conjunction of heterogeneous "premises" is also the process on which enthymematic argument (and rhetorical persuasion generally) depends. It is indeed its rootedness in *thumos* and the *pathē* that gives an *enthumēma,* or indeed any argument whatsoever, its value and its relevance for the audience the rhetor wishes to persuade; and it is the enthymeme's simultaneous embodiment of a heterogeneous set of *pisteis,* combining the "assurances" of *logos* (as apodictic propositional reasoning) with those of *pathos* and *ēthos,* that makes it a powerful "encouragement" to belief and action. "Encouragement" may actually be the best translation of *enthumēma,* insofar as *thumos* means "heart" as the seat of affect. In such a view, it begins to appear that all enthymemes are enthymemes of *pathos* and that if we grant as well the Aristotelian view of enthymematic skill as the heart of skill in rhetoric, the art of rhetoric is at heart a *technē/pharmakon* for the *katharsis* by means of *logos,* discourse, of the *pathē* involved in practical judgment, choice and action. This comes close to saying, with Socrates in the *Phaedrus,* that rhetoric is a *technē psuchagōgia,* an "art of guiding the soul" by means of words (261a).

The psychagogic art of rhetoric, in other words—rhetoric as transpersonal conation—is channeled primarily through enthymemes, which Aristotle calls the "body of persuading-becoming-believing" (*sōma tēs pisteōs*: 1.1.3, 1354a15) because the "heart" of the enthymeme is *thumos,* that passionate spiritedness that for Aristotle was what Walker calls the "seat of affect." This is the sense in which rhetorical persuasion is affective-becoming-conative-becoming-cognitive. Note, though, that as Walker reads Aristotle rhetoric is *always* affect-becoming-conation—*thumos/pathos* that is by definition channeled/experienced as normative/conformative group pressure—but doesn't always become cognitive; subliminal advertising, for example, is designed to stop short of arousing a cognitive response, and the kinds of habitualized pressures one finds in families work in very similar ways.

Or perhaps we could say that rhetorical persuasion is always affect that is *actually* becoming-conative and *potentially* becoming-cognitive. The cognitive tip of that ecotic iceberg is, of course, the potentiality—verbalized persuasion or *logos*—that has traditionally been taken to be the exclusive focus of the *TR*, and by extension of all rhetoric.

We have already considered the semantics of *thumos*, in §2.8, in connection with Dai Zhen's conception of the passions of the blood-*qì xuèqì* 血氣 or valor; in that light, we might now venture to "translate" (or loosely paraphrase) Aristotle's suggestion that the enthymeme is the *sōma tēs pisteōs* by saying that the enthymeme is the body of the group speech act by which persuasion becomes belief. But of course as Aristotle's own list in *TR* 1.2 (see §2.11, above) makes clear, the available persuasivity on which the rhetor draws is more than just enthymemes; as chapter 2 suggests, in the aggregate it is the body-becoming-mind of the community of language-users that makes enthymemes seem to them meaningful summations of this or that aspect of experience. People *feel* the meanings of enthymemes, and are able to use them and recognize them with the deep and undeniable feeling that the good ones do refer to reality and the bad ones don't, because the linguistic and cultural values that structure their world—structure "truth" and "reality" and "identity" for them—are circulated icotically through the group in the form of persuasive-becoming-believing feeling-becoming-thinking-becoming-knowing-becoming-truth (what I will be theorizing in §4.15 as *doxicosis*). Anything that we currently believe—including things like "2 + 2 = 4" and " 'to persuade' is a verb meaning 'to change someone's belief so as to conform to your own' " and "it's important to be fair" and "the sun rises every morning" and "the sun doesn't so much 'rise' as emerge into view as the earth rotates in space" and "my family loves me" and so on—was once something that we had to be persuaded of; but because the persuasion wasn't necessarily always propositional, we may think of many beliefs as "natural," as things we have somehow simply registered objectively as facts. Somatic theory says that we were persuaded in those cases too—it's just that the persuasion happened on a "lower" level of the body-becoming-mind. We were persuaded affectively-becoming-conatively, through ideosomatic (collective affective-becoming-conative) pressures placed on us to conform to group assumptions and norms. The body of persuading-becoming-believing in those cases is so bodily that we hardly even notice it happening; but it is still an event in an entelechial body-becoming-mind that *can* be articulated in propositional form.

The third implication Walker adduces is the connection with energy, namely, that the success of these enthymematic *tekhnai* depends on the *tekhnai* of acting, *hupokrisis*, also translated into English as "delivery." As Walker (2008, p. 85) writes, this is also "what Chaim Perelman has called 'techniques of presence,' that is, techniques of emphasis that lend psychological prominence and memorability—or what Aristotle calls *energeia*—to particular sets of 'premises' while shifting others into the background or margins of attention."[3] In the complex enthymeme Walker himself constructs to undermine purely rationalistic readings of Aristotle's logic,

- Since rhetorical enthymemes are designed to shape the audience's *pathē*, and:

- Since the *pathē* are themselves structured enthymematically, and:

- Since "the *pathē* rise from cognitive frameworks that typically (and in a debate necessarily) will include *competing premises*," therefore:

> it will never be sufficient for the rhetor merely to declare the "premises" that should conduce to one or another mode of emotion-intention-judgment-action in the practical reasoning of an audience. It will always be the cognitive frames endowed with greatest "presence" or *energeia* in the audience's psyche that determine *which enthymemes* most effectively, persuasively guide its practical reasoning toward a specific *pathos/praxis*, or indeed which enthymemes are even perceived as enthymemes. And thus it will always be techniques of presence that largely condition, or determine, which enthymemes an audience attends to and responds to in its heartfelt thought. (Walker, ibid., p. 85)

Walker is arguing, then, that by building a theory of *pathos* into the *TR*, and especially by coining a thumotic (passionate) term for the basic unit of practical reasoning, Aristotle is tacitly—and perhaps grudgingly, or even unknowingly—admitting that practical reasoning is powerfully and perhaps even primarily guided by *pathos*. If practical reasoning thus becomes "a psychagogic art or *pharmakon* for emotional *catharsis*" (Walker, ibid., p. 91), clearly what Perelman calls "techniques of presence"—the speaker's body language, or what Aristotle calls *hupokrisis* "acting"—will play an overwhelmingly significant psychagogic role in guiding and directing persuasivity.

3.6 Aristotle: *hupokrisis* as Body Language

Let us turn our attention, then, to *hupokrisis,* the "acting" or body language whose principles Aristotle outlines in *TR* 3.1:

> The first thing to be examined was naturally that which came first by nature, the facts [*pragmata*] from which a speech has persuasive effect [*to pithanon*]; second is how to compose this in language [*tēi lexei diathesthai*]; and this is something that has the greatest force but has not yet been taken in hand, the matter of the delivery [*peri tēn hupokrisin*]. . . . It is a matter of how the voice should be used in expressing each emotion [*pros hekaston pathos*], sometimes loud and sometimes soft or intermediate, and how the pitch accents should be entoned [*pōs tois tonois*], whether as acute, grave, or circumflex, and what rhythms should be expressed in each case; for [those who study delivery] consider three things, and these are volume, change of pitch, and rhythm [*megethos harmonia rhuthmos*]. Those [performers who give careful attention to these] are generally the ones who win poetic contests; and just as actors are more important than poets now in the poetic contests, so it is in political contests because of the sad state of governments. (3.1.3–4, 1403b18–21 and 26–34; Kennedy, 1991/2007, p. 195)

Volume, tonalization, and rhythm, then, are the "presencing" or "energizing" strategies the rhetor-as-actor uses to maximize *to pithanon,* the persuasivity of his or her speeches. Aristotle adds his antidemocratic jab at the end, his lament that this "hypocritical" approach to persuasion is made necessary by "the sad state of governments," *dia tēn mokhthērian tōn politōn*: as Walker (2008, p. 75) notes, *mokhthēria* "badness, wickedness, depravity" comes from *mokhtheō,* " 'to labor' or 'to be weary with toil,' and suggests a vulgar sensibility blunted by hard work and limited education." Kennedy (1991/2007, p. 195n7) explains that this "seems to reflect the Platonic view (e.g., *Gorgias* 463a-b) that political oratory under democracy had become a form of flattery and that it offered entertainment to the mob." And in fact Aristotle can't just leave it there, but must clarify:

> An *Art* concerned with [the delivery of oratory] has not yet been composed, since even consideration of *lexis* was late in developing, and delivery seems [*dokei*: see §4.13–15] a vulgar matter when rightly understood. But since the whole business of rhetoric is with opinion [*pros doxan*: see §4.1–2], one should pay attention to delivery, not because it is right but because it is necessary, since true justice seeks nothing more in a speech than neither to offend nor to entertain [*mēte lupein mēt' euphrainein*]; for to contend by means of the facts themselves is just [*dikaion gar autois agōnizesthai tois pragmasin*], with the result that everything except demonstration is incidental [*exō tou apodeixai perierga estin*]; but, nevertheless, [delivery] has great power [*mega dunatai*], as has been said, because of the corruption of the audience [*dia tēn tou akroatou mokhthērian*]. (3.1.5, 1403b35–1404a9; Kennedy, 1991/2007, pp. 195–96)

This is, obviously, more kneejerk Platonism, not only in the repetition of the antidemocratic slur *dia tēn tou akroatou mokhthērian* but in the antiemotional assumption that any attempt to make the audience feel pain or pleasure (*mēte lupein mēt' euphrainein*, lit. "neither to pain nor to delight") constitutes a perversion of justice. Since Aristotle has defined emotion as judgment saturated with pain or pleasure, his wistful utopian stricture here against mobilizing either pain or pleasure for rhetorical purposes means that for him in an ideal world—presumably Plato's Republic—all decisions, or perhaps only legislative and judicial ones, would be made by cold reason alone, with no interference from feelings. As many commentators have noted, this Platonic utopianism harks back to the sentiments of *TR* 1.1.

And yet, disapprove as he might, Aristotle still insistently invokes communal norms rather than abstract truth as the key to persuasion:

> Emotion is expressed [*pathētikē de*] if the style, in the case of insolence, is that of an angry man; in the case of impious and shameful things if it is that of one who is indignant and reluctant even to say the words; in the case of admirable things, [if they are spoken] in a submissive manner; and similarly in other cases. The proper *lexis* also makes the matter credible [*pithanoi de to pragma kai hē oikeia lexis*]: the mind [of listeners] draws a

false inference of the truth of what a speaker says because they feel the same about such things, so they think the facts to be so, even if they are not as the speaker represents them; and the hearer suffers along with the pathetic speaker [*sunomopathei ho akouōn aei tōi pathētikōs legonti*], even if what he says amounts to nothing. As a result, many overwhelm their hearers by making noise. (3.7.3–5, 1408a16–26, Kennedy, 1991/2007, p. 210)

Here is the "hypocritical" advice to the rhetor-as-actor: match your voice to the emotion you want to convey to your hearers. Aristotle's word for "proper" in "the proper *lexis*" is *oikeia*, "fitting" or "proper" or "natural" in the sense of "local" (not alien, not foreign), related to *oikos* "community" and *oikeō* "to inhabit, settle, colonize (a place)": as we'll see in greater detail in chapter 4, in connection with another adjective associated with *oikos*, *eikos* "probable/plausible," it is the community's "ecotic/icotic" organization of verbal and nonverbal communication that makes certain ways of speaking "credible" (*pithanos*). What you match your voice to, in fact, is not just "the emotion you want to convey to your hearers" but the community's icotic construction of both verbal language and body language and their relation to emotion. By doing so you not only "express emotion," as Kennedy somewhat problematically renders *pathētikē de* "now [it is] pathetic/emotional," but actually *transfer* that emotion to your hearers, so that they suffer along with you. (The repetition of *pathos* in *sunomo**pathei** ho akouōn aei tōi **pathētikōs** legonti* suggests that a possible loose translation of that might be "the hearer feels what the speaker feels." This is (c) the transmission of energy from body to body of which Kennedy wrote: §3.2.) It's not that you can *be* emotionally persuasive by acting in this way, but that this *is* emotional: Aristotle's impersonal description *pathētikē de* suggests that the emotion or emotionality is not so much felt by one person as it is shared inter- or transsubjectively. Presumably what Aristotle means by "many overwhelm their hearers by making noise" is that many strike down or disable their hearers' *rational resistance* (reason as the true self) with the body language of volume, tonalization, and rhythm (verbal and nonverbal communication as "meaning" and "noise," respectively).

3.7 Aristotle on Shared Affect

For Aristotle all this pathetic noise-making is made necessary by democracy: only the workers, those whose moral sensibilities have been dulled by physical labor, function in this way. But note that his objections to *hupokrisis* or body language are specifically directed to its *icotic* use: toward the role played by embodied "hypocrisy" in persuasivity. In a more generally ecotic context, where our interactions with others are directed not to legislative or juridical decision-making but to the becoming-good or becoming-normal (becoming-communal) of social interaction, Aristotle actually insists that our emotions—especially as displayed on the stage of our bodies—must be conducive to virtuous social behavior, which he defines precisely in terms of appropriate affect (*NE* 1109a23). As Sherman (1989, p. 49) points out, this is especially true of *philia* or friendship: "we do not fulfil the role of a true friend if we fail to respond with proper feeling to another's anguish or joy" (see *EE* 1240a36–39, 1244b18–23). The circulation of appropriate affect (*to philein*) through the group is the very definition of *philia*. But for Aristotle the same is true of all social interaction, which depends for its collective coherence not just on my appropriate affective responses to you and yours to me but to what Sherman (ibid.) calls "the *direct communication* of emotion and bodily response" (emphasis added; see *NE* 4.6, 1126b28–33). "Others," Sherman adds, "must directly *feel* our presence" (emphasis added).

The past few decades have seen a return to the explanatory power of Aristotle's thinking on this score. The regulatory power of body language in groups has been studied by sociologists, nonverbal communication researchers, and social neurophysiologists for several decades now; what they have found is that the body language of approval and disapproval (and other regulatory impulses, but mainly those two) is *mimicked* by others in the group, and through that mimicry, the body states of those other people are actually simulated by each member of the group in her or his own body.

This research—which begins to address the transmission of energy from body to body, as posited but not explained by Kennedy (§3.2)—began with William B. Carpenter's (1874) discovery that we unconsciously tend to mimic other people's body language in our own bodies, a phenomenon that came to be called the Carpenter Effect and has since been confirmed many times by later researchers. Howard Friedman's nonverbal communication team (Friedman et al., 1979, 1981) picked the Carpenter Effect up in the late seventies and early eighties as the channel for the interpersonal transmission of emotional states (see also Hatfield et al., 1994), but the neurological mechanism by which emotional states are "transferred" from body to body was not identified in the laboratory until the 1990s, when Antonio Damasio's neurological research team at the University of Iowa linked it with their somatic theory. Ralph Adolphs headed up a smaller group that began to investigate it, and, beginning in 1994, to publish papers that addressed subjects' ability to recognize somatic states in other people's faces (Adolphs et al., 1994, 1998, 2000). None of the group's publications in the late nineties, however, addressed the question of an actual transfer or transmission of evaluative/regulatory social feelings from one person to another; it was not until Adolphs (2002, p. 171) that the subgroup offered a very sketchy neurophysiological model for the process, suggesting in a scant eight lines that "knowledge of other people's emotions may rely on simulating the observed emotion." But the very next year, Damasio (2003, pp. 116–17) summarizes that study and expands significantly on Adolph's team's hints; let me quote at some length:

> A recent study from Ralph Adolphs speaks directly to the issue of simulated body states. The study was aimed at investigating the underpinnings of empathy and involved more than 100 patients with neurological lesions located at varied sites of their cerebral cortex. They were asked to participate in a task that called for the sort of process needed for empathy responses. Each subject was shown photographs of an unknown person exhibiting some emotional expression and the task consisted of indicating what the unknown person was feeling.
>
> Researchers asked each subject to place himself or herself in the person's shoes to guess the person's state of mind. The hypothesis being tested was that patients with damage to body-sensing regions of the cerebral cortex would not be capable of performing the task normally.
>
> Most patients performed this task easily, precisely as healthy subjects do, except for two specific groups of patients whose performance was impaired. The first group of impaired patients was quite predictable. It was made up of patients with damage to visual association cortices, especially the right visual cortices of the ventral occipito-temporal region. This sector of the brain is critical for the appreciation of visual configurations. Without its integrity, the facial expressions in the photographs cannot be perceived as a whole, even if the photos can be seen in the general sense of the term.
>
> The other group of patients was the most telling: It consisted of subjects with damage located in the overall region of the *right* somatosensory cortices, namely, in the insula, SII and SI regions of the right cerebral hemisphere. This is the set of regions in which the brain accomplishes the highest level of

integrated mapping of body state. In the absence of this region, it is not possible for the brain to simulate other body states effectively. The brain lacks the playground where variations on the body-state theme can be played.

It is of great physiological significance that the comparable region of the left cerebral hemisphere does not have the same function: Patients with damage to the left somatosensory complex perform the "empathy" task normally. This is one more finding that suggests that the right somatosensory cortices are "dominant" with regard to integrated body mapping. This is also the reason why damage to this region has been consistently associated with defects in emotion and feeling, and with conditions such as anosognosia and neglect, whose basis is a defective idea of the current body state. The right versus left asymmetry in the function of the human somatosensory cortices probably is due to a committed participation of the left somatosensory cortices in language and speech.

This is what I have elsewhere (see Robinson, 2008, pp. 20–23, 30–32; 2012, pp. 33–38; 2013b, pp. 150–54; 2013c, p. 357) called the somatic transfer: a somatic orientation in one body is transferred to another body.[4] Based on sensory evidence, typically visual or aural observation of another person's body (but also *imagined* sensory evidence, as when reading a novel), the recipient of the "infection" comes to feel more or less what the other is feeling. The classic case of this infection is the contagious yawn: when someone else yawns, it requires enormous effort not to start yawning oneself. I call this almost instantaneous mimicking of another person's body states in your own, which serves to "infect" you with the other person's feeling, "somatic mimeticism" or "somatomimesis." (Note that the feeling itself does not "leap" across the gap between bodies; it, or something very like it, is recreated mimetically in the target body.) Some people are more susceptible to this infection than others: many men, for example, scoff at such observations, insist that it never happens to them, and attribute it to weak-mindedness or overemotionalism: the hypersensitive woman who cries at strangers' funerals or is wracked with anguish at the suffering of a character on a soap opera. But in fact it functions at some level in almost everyone, even the scoffers; if it didn't, they would find it virtually impossible to get along with other people—to stay in a relationship or a job, for example, for more than a day or two.

Aristotle may disapprove of all this, but in his chapters on the emotions he also gives numerous quite undisapproving—even in places laudatory—examples of its functioning. The *locus classicus* is again *to philein* "friendly feeling," which as we've seen is very close to what Mencius calls *rén* 仁:

> We may describe friendly feeling towards anyone as wishing for him what you believe to be good things, not for your own sake but for his, and being inclined, so far as you can, to bring these things about. A friend is one who feels thus and excites these feelings in return. Those who think they feel thus towards each other think themselves friends. This being assumed, it follows that your friend is the sort of man who shares your pleasure in what is good and your pain in what is unpleasant, for your sake and for no other reason. This pleasure and pain of his will be the token of his good wishes for you, since we all feel glad at getting what we wish for, and pained at getting what we do not. (2.4.2-3, 1380b36-1381a8; Roberts, 1941/1984, p. 2200)

You feel pleasure, and because I feel friendly toward you, your pleasure is contagious, so I feel it too; your pain similarly awakens a sympathetic pain in me.

But this is mere observation, not analysis; Aristotle nowhere asks how this transfer of emotion from body to body is possible, though some such somatic transfer would seem to be crucial to his theory of rhetorical persuasion. On occasion he seems to be on the verge of exploring the mechanism of transfer, as when he discusses the interrelated emotions of pity, indignation, and envy:

> Let pity then be a kind of pain excited by the sight of evil [*lupē tis epi phainomenōi kakōi phthartikōi*], deadly or painful, which befalls one who does not deserve it; an evil which one might expect to come upon himself or one of his friends, and when it seems near. (2.8.1, 1385b13-15; Freese, 1926, p. 225)

> For if indignation is being pained at the sight of good fortune that is apparently undeserved [*lupeisthai epi tōi phainomenōi anaxiōs eupragein*] . . . (2.9.7, 1387a9; Freese, ibid., p. 233)

> It is equally clear for what reason, and of whom, and in what frame of mind, men are envious, if envy is a kind of pain at the sight of good fortune [*lupē tis epi eupragiai phainomenēi tōn eirēmenōn agathōn*] in regard to the goods mentioned; in the

case of those like themselves; and not for the sake of a man getting anything, but because of others possessing it. (2.10.1, 1387b22-24; Freese, ibid., p. 239)

Each of these emotions is defined as a pain at the *appearance* (*phainomenon*) of something, its emergence into our visual field—as an unpleasant reaction to a visual stimulus. Aristotelian philosophy begins with the *phainomena* (how things *look*) and the *endoxa* (how things *seem*) and begins to seek out explanations that make sense of them; in this case we might argue that the *phainomena/endoxa* include not only the visual impressions but the somatic ones as well, in each case the pain-becoming-emotion-becoming-judgment with which the definition begins. If in pity we *see* the other person's suffering and *feel* his or her pain, what we see and feel are both *phainomena*, appearances, visual and somatic simulacra of the actual suffering that *we* generate mimetically. Aristotle insists, in fact, on the slight but significant distancing involved in pity: "Amasis . . . did not weep when his son was led off to death but did for a friend reduced to begging; for the latter was pitiable, the former dreadful; for the dreadful is something different from the pitiable and capable of expelling pity and often useful to the opponent; for people no longer pity when something dreadful is near themselves" (2.8.12–13, 1386a19–24; Kennedy, 1991/2007, pp. 140–41). If we feel the other person's suffering too strongly, the resulting pain is not pity but something much stronger, like dread. But it is also important that the pitiable objects not be *too* distant:

> One should grasp here, too, that people pity things happening to others insofar as they fear for themselves. And since sufferings are pitiable when they appear near at hand [*epei d' engus phainomena ta pathē*] and since people do not feel pity, or not in the same way, about things ten thousand years in the past or future, neither anticipating nor remembering them, necessarily those are more pitiable who contribute to the effect by gestures and cries and display of feelings and generally in their acting [*kai holōs hupokrisei*]; for they make the evil seem near by making it appear before the eyes [*poiousi phainesthai to kakon*] either as something about to happen or as something that has happened, and things are more pitiable when just having happened or going to happen in a short time. (2.8.13–15, 1386a27–35; Kennedy, 1991/2007, p. 141)

The fact that "acting"—the body language now not just of vocal volume, tonalization, and rhythm but of "gestures and cries and display of feelings"—brings the evil closer and thus makes pity possible also makes it possible for us to pity people who suffered ten thousand years ago, if someone acts out their suffering for us: a rhetor, say, or an actor on the stage. This is effectively the theory behind what Perelman calls "presencing": body language makes an event viscerally *present* to onlookers, so that they feel it as if it were happening to them, that instant.

And note that Aristotle is essentially describing (though again not theorizing) two different somatic transfers: one from the suffering person to the observer, generating what we might call primary pity, the other from the actor to the observer, reenacting the original sufferer's suffering and so generating what we might call secondary pity. To the extent that the primary/secondary hierarchy suggests—in Platonic copy theory, which is still with us today—that secondary pity is going to be inevitably *weaker* than primary pity, however, it is misleading, as the pity awakened by actors (or rhetors) is often stronger than the pity awakened by an actual suffering person. This is not merely because the acting "brings the evil closer," as Aristotle suggests, but also because it mediates (or cathartically "purifies") the cognitive or evaluative moment for us, gives us the raw emotion without requiring that we undertake the complex evaluative calculations needed to decide whether this person is close enough to us to warrant our pity but also far enough to awaken pity rather than dread, etc. Hence the "ironic" fact that it is often easier to feel a deep, intense, unabashed pity for a character in a play or a movie than it is for a close family member with whom our relationship is emotionally more complex (more historically striated).

It's also possible, of course, that Aristotle does not mean "sight" literally—does not mean seeing someone else's body language of suffering or smug delight—but is using sight metaphorically to mean largely nonvisual interior "sight," a *mental* image, perhaps largely abstract, of the other person's good or bad fortune. If this is the case, it might explain why it never occurs to him to reflect on the strange body-to-body coincidence or disincidence of pain or pleasure in these emotional responses—the fact, say, that pity is pain at someone else's pain but indignation is pain at someone else's pleasure. If emotion for him is physical pain or pleasure caused by a mental image, and if the mental image is of the abstract *idea* of someone else's fortune—if we don't actually see someone else suffering or gloating—then it might be argued that no body-to-body somatic transfer takes place. But remember his remark in *On the Soul* (431b23) that so powerfully inspired Hegel, according to which *epistēmē* is the *epistēta* (understanding is the things understood) and *aisthēsis* is the *aisthēta* (perception is the things perceived): ultimately it doesn't matter whether we perceive a *hupokrisis* that exists outside of us physically or merely imagine or remember it. Our perceptual experience of an imagined or remembered *hupokrisis* will generate a somatic state that is difficult to distinguish from one based mimetically on physical sight. Phenomenologically, the "appearance" (*phainomenon*) in the perceiver's head *is* the thing perceived.

In one significant case, however, that of the social emotion of shame, Aristotle does clearly seem to be talking about emotional responses to the actual physical sight of other people's body language, and thus of the regulatory social phenomenon we have come to call "face" (more on this in chapter 4):

> Since shame is imagination [*phantasia*] about a loss of reputation and for its own sake, not for its results, and since no one cares about reputation [in the abstract] but on account of those who hold an opinion of him, necessarily a person feels shame toward those whose opinion he takes account of. He takes account of those who admire him and whom he admires and by whom he wishes to be admired and those to whose rank he aspires and those whose opinions he does not despise. Now people want to be admired by those and admire those who have something good in the way of honors or from whom they happen to be greatly in need of something those people have in their control, as lovers [want love or sexual favors]; but they aspire to the rank of those [they regard as] like themselves, and they take account of prudent people as telling the truth, and their elders and educated people are of such a sort. And they feel more shame at things done before these people's eyes and in the open; hence, too, the proverb "Shame is in the eyes." For this reason people feel more shame before those who are going to be with them and those watching them, because in both cases they are "in" their eyes. (2.6.14–18, 1384a22–38; Kennedy, 1991/2007, p. 134)

Here at first Aristotle wants to map physical vision into the realm of postvisual representations, *peri adoxias phantasia* "a mental image of disgrace," and then to subsume it into the feeling-based realm of *doxa* "opinion/reputation," admiration, and *timē* "honor" that we'll be concerned with in chapter 4 ("no one cares about reputation [*doxēs*] but on account of those who hold an opinion of him [*dia tous doxazontas*]"); but he returns to the specifically visual channel of somatomimesis when he gets to the eyes, which—though he only implies this here, and does not work it out—are the channels both of other people's disapproving body language and of our perception of that body language. "Shame dwells in the eyes" both of the people whose visible bodily disapproval we thematize as "disgrace" (or, in the later more bodily terminology, a loss of face) and of our own visual apparatus, which may seem to us to "burn" with the condemnatory emotional freight it is carrying.

This body-to-body contagion of somatic states should be crucial not only to Aristotle's theory of emotion, but to his overall conception of rhetorical *ēthos* and *pathos* as well, the manipulation of emotion to make listeners feel that the speaker's character is just and the speaker's emotion is justified. How, but for this somatic contagion or mimeticism, could the speaker, using only embodied speech acts, make listeners feel the appropriate things? How, if it were not for somatic mimeticism, could a series of speech acts (embodied performatives) instill in listeners the feeling that the speaker is someone like them, someone who feels like them, someone who feels what they feel, someone they should therefore feel friendly toward? It should be obvious that it will not be enough for the speaker merely to internalize some abstract mental conception of his or her listeners' characters, and seek to organize his or her speech acts around that image; the speaker will need to *mimic* the listeners' body language, set up a mimetic exchange of friendly gestures, postures, facial expressions, and vocalizations with them, so that the somatics (or what George Kennedy calls energy) of friendly identification flows back and forth between them.

3.8 Mencius on (the Body Language of) Speaking and the Flood-like *qì*

Now let us return to Mencius, and the question we left open in §3.0 regarding whether there is any significant connection between "knowing speech" (*zhī yán* 知言) and "cultivating *qì*" (*yǎng qì* 養氣).[5] When asked what he means by "knowing speech" (*zhī yán* 知言), Mencius replies that he can detect the impairment of vision (*bì* 蔽) in half-truths or flatteries (*bì* 詖), the impairment of mobility (*xiàn* 陷) in obscenities and lewd remarks (*yín* 淫), the impairment of right orientation (*lí* 離) in profanity (*xié* 邪), and the impairment of strength (*qióng* 窮) in prevarications (*dùn* 遁). How does he know these things? What guides his interpretations?

What Mencius presumably finds problematic in the "spoken half-truths, biased words, flatteries" (*bì* 詖, with the *yán* 言 "speech" radical) is that they persuade by expressing only one aspect or part of the truth, typically the "better" or eulogistic part, hence "flattery"; as a verb *bì* 蔽, with the *cǎo* ⺿ "grass" radical, means to conceal, to screen, to shield, or to cover. Lau (1970/2003, p. 63) and Behuniak (2005, p. 37) translate *bì* 蔽 as "blindness," Hinton (1998, p. 49) as "what lies hidden": what is screened or hidden from the viewer is the part of the truth that doesn't fit a narrow or impaired vision.

yín 淫 is associated not only with excess and a lack of control but all manner of sexual immorality; what Mencius claims to see in or behind it or its verbal forms is *xiàn* 陷, a becoming trapped or stuck in a pitfall or sinkhole. The problem with this type of speech is not simply that the pit or hole that traps the speaker is a trope for sexual matters; it is also that the speaker is *trapped* there, cannot move, cannot extricate himself from the trap. In a philosophical tradition that values movement, growth, emergence, flows, the impairment of movement is at least as damning as where the speaker happens to be stuck.

In Chinese medicine, *xié* 邪 are unhealthy influences that cause disease; in religion, they are demonic, nefarious, iniquitous influences, evil pressures or inclinations; in speech, therefore, they are profanities, impieties, curses, sacrilegious remarks, which are to be shunned not just because they are against religion but, more important, because the kind of casual angry/dismissive profanity that is bandied about in everyday life has an infectious impact on the people who hear it. The general tendency of the term is to pull the speaker and everyone within earshot away from health, off the right path, in a *wrong direction,* which is *lí* 離 "to leave, to part from."

dùn 遁 is literally to evade, flee, escape, and thus here to use words to evade probing into uncomfortable truths, to sidestep delicate questions, to avoid revealing embarrassing or compromising past actions, current beliefs or feelings, or future intentions. Mencius claims that such evasions reflect *qióng* 窮 "exhaustion, poverty," specifically an impoverishment here not of financial resources but of physical or (here especially) moral strength. It requires moral strength to face up to uncomfortable truths; an impairment of that strength drives the speaker to equivocate, prevaricate.

The interesting question for a *rhetorical* reading of this passage is: what exactly is Mencius "reading" when he claims to "know words" (*zhī yán* 知言)? Translating *yán* 言 here as "words" is perhaps misleading, as it might suggest to English readers that what Mencius is reading is the semantics of specific verbal units. Pictographically 言 actually suggests a downward view from the forehead, watching as sound waves are emitted forward (visually upward on the page) out of the mouth (*kǒu* 口)—and thus speaking as a corporeal event. In that sense *zhī yán* 知言 would be a knowledge of the *body language* of speech.

A significant parallel with this reading might be found in *MZ* 7A21, a passage to which we will be returning in §4.3, in connection with the concept of *xìng* 性; what interests me here is how the exemplary person "roots" (*gēn* 根) the four shoots (*sì duān* 四端 [2A6]: fellow-feeling, rightness, ritual propriety, and wisdom) in feeling-becoming-thinking (*xīn* 心), so that they put out "new growth" (*shēng* 生) as body-language-becoming-physical-disposition: "a clarity [*suì* 睟: literally bright eye] in the face [*miàn* 面] and a fullness [*àng* 盎: like a bowl full of rice] in the back and shoulders [*bèi* 背: literally the way this person carries burdens], and on into the four limbs [*sì tǐ* 四體], so that they communicate clearly even though they cannot speak [*bù yán* 不言]."

The botanical metaphor Mencius uses throughout (§2.7) here suggests that the rooting of the four shoots in feeling-becoming-thinking *trains* the body, like a vine or the branches of a decorative tree, into specific physical inclinations in the face, the back, and four limbs. The horticulturalist training a vine or a tree at first constrains its growth, limits it, gives it the desired directionality by tying the new shoots to support structures; but gradually the shoots learn that directionality, internalize it, make it their own, and so no longer need the constraint. In the shape of the mature tree one can clearly see the guiding hand of the horticulturalist; but the tree is not the mere inert clay that the horticulturalist has shaped, but rather learns to participate in the shaping, learns to interact productively with the guiding hand. The question we will be returning to this passage to ask in §4.3 is: who or what is the horticulturalist in the etheecotic growth of the human individual? Who wields the shaping influence over his or her growth? The individual him- or herself? The culture? Biology? God?

Shun (1997, p. 159) notes that Chinese commentators have tended to take the four limbs there as signifying *conduct*;[6] but surely what Mencius is referring to here is not conduct in general but specifically *posture* as a corporeal display of the virtue or vice that has shaped or trained them. In addition to dispositional or trait posture (revealing long-term ethical attributes), there is also emotional or state posture (revealing fleeting ethical attitudes), which might be understood broadly to include gestures: *caring* is typically displayed by leaning forward and reaching out to touch a hand, an arm, a shoulder, a knee, or, in more intimate relationships, a cheek, the lips; hugging is certainly performed not just with the arms but with all four limbs (the legs must be positioned for a hug), and indeed with the four limbs as an emblem of the whole body. The adjective "upright" in both English and Chinese tends to be used metaphorically to signify not so much virtuous conduct as virtuous dispositions in general; as we've seen (§2.3, §2.8), *zhèng* 正 "upright" also means "just" and "correct" (of behavior, see 4A18), and the various other Chinese words for an upright posture have similar metaphorical uses, *jiǎng* 顈 meaning "honest," *zhí* 直 "frank, forthright," and so on. And don't English-speakers also assume that a virtuous person will tend to stand tall—and indeed that standing tall, with a straight back (not slouching), will tend to make growing children virtuous? When in "The Second Coming" W. B. Yeats makes his rough beast *slouch* toward Bethlehem to be born, surely the beast's posture expresses its moral disposition without speaking?

In fact Mencius elsewhere links *zhèng* 正—postural uprightness in the metaphorical sense of a virtuous disposition—explicitly to facial expression, specifically the expressivity of the pupils, and spoken words:

> Mencius said: "There is in man nothing more ingenuous than the pupils [*móu* 眸] of his eyes. They cannot conceal his wickedness. When he is upright [*zhèng* 正] within his breast, a man's pupils are clear and bright; when he is not, they are clouded and murky. How can a man conceal his true character if you listen to his words [*tīng qí yán yě* 聽其言也] and observe the pupils of his eyes?" (4A15; Lau, 1970/2003, p. 163)

Note there: *listen* (*tīng*) to his words. This is not a purely intellectual response, based on abstract semantic understanding; it is first and foremost an *auditory* response, an embodied reaction to an embodied signal. In 7A21 the exemplary person embodies (*xìng* 性) the "four shoots" as a collection of physical expressions or displays that begin as fleeting body-language *states* but are gradually transformed—trained—into more lasting (dispositional) bodily *traits*: a clarity of the eye, a squareness of the back and shoulders, a general uprightness of the four limbs. In 4A15 the upright person reveals his or her uprightness through the same clarity of eye, and the morally questionable person reveals that moral failing in a cloudiness of eye. The implication is that if one dispositionally embodies virtue in such a way as to *shape* or *train* these bodily forms, they become visual fields in which the dispositions that shaped them can be read. Or, more broadly, they become visual and auditory fields: as Mencius writes in 6B15, "It is only when his intentions become visible on his countenance and audible in his tone of voice that others can understand him" (Lau, ibid., p. 285). Here what is expressed as body language is not moral inclinations but semantic intentions, and expressed specifically as situational states rather than lasting dispositional traits; but Mencius would no doubt want to say that the *ability* or *tendency* to convey one's semantic intentionality through facial expression and tone of voice is itself a learned dispositional trait.

And obviously Mencius's knowledge of "words" or speech (*zhī yán* 知言) in 2A2 would have to involve the same kind of observation and interpretation of the visual and auditory body language of speech as in 6B15, the reading and understanding of facial expression, gesture, and posture as well as intonation, pitch, timbre, and other vocal features. Surely it is not a stretch to imagine *dùn* 遁 "evasive speech" broadly enough to encompass not merely evasive semantics but shifty eyes and tone of voice as well as a deflected posture? Or to imagine *xié* 邪 "profanity" broadly enough to encompass not merely words marked "profane" in the dictionary but aggressive or dismissive facial expressions, tonalizations, and gestures? Or to imagine *yín* 淫 broadly enough to encompass not merely inappropriate sexual semantics but leering eyes and tone of voice and lascivious gestures and postures?

What makes it possible for Mencius to track other people's *yán* 言 "speech as a corporeal event" back to the configurative orientations that shape it, then, may be most proximately his knowledge of how dispositions shape the body, and how (fellow-)feeling-becoming-thinking shapes dispositions. The specific "psychological" impairments that he says he can see in various kinds of speech are obstructions or impoverishments or redirectionings of feeling-becoming-thinking (*xīn* 心), which at best (*rén* 仁) harmoniously conditions and is conditioned by the group, but in less ideal situations leads to people feeling unable or unwilling to look at the full complexity of a thing (*bì* 蔽 > *bì* 詖, *qióng* 窮 > *dùn* 遁), feeling sexually frustrated (*xiàn* 陷 > *yín* 淫), or feeling pulled in irreligious directions (*lí* 離 > *xié* 邪). The becoming he is reading, then, is actually feeling-becoming-thinking-becoming-disposition-becoming-speaking; and the rhetoric he is adumbrating is actually a social psychology of rhetoric.

But then it is important to remember that for Mencius feeling-becoming-thinking itself flows out of *qì* 氣—and perhaps it is not too great a leap from his two-pronged reply to the question of what he is good at that his prowess at one conditions his prowess at the other: that his ability to nourish his flood-like *qì* (*hàorán zhī qì* 浩然之氣) is precisely what makes it possible for him to know spoken words in the deeper sense. Just what the flood-like *qì* is remains a bit mysterious, as does the foreclosed feminine sexuality with which, as Birdwhistell (2007, p. 121) reminds us, patriarchal metaphorics associate it;[7] but if it is some intense phenomenological state of arousal that *feels* like being flooded, and we take that state to have a guiding effect on knowledge (of words as of other human actions and states, and perhaps nonhuman ones as well), then we might speculate that the flood-like *qì* is a flooding of phenomenal being with what Manfred Porkert (1974, p. 167) translates as "configurative energy." For Mencius that energy arises out of worldly activity, and specifically out of worldly *interactivity*—out of collective action, as a kind of transpersonal byproduct of beings/doings interacting in relationship. This speculative reading of the passage would ultimately suggest that what makes it possible for Mencius to understand spoken words is his skill at flooding not just his own being but the group *shēn xīn* 身心 or *rén* 仁 (what Aristotle would call the *ēthos*-plus-*pathos* that serves as the group subject of *pistis*) that he and the speakers of those words collectively occupy with the energy (*qì* 氣) that vitally configures them.

3.9 Mencius on *lǐ* 禮 "Ritual Propriety"

Given the Confucian (and especially Mencian) notion that everything flows out of everything else—that everything that is exists not in stable ontological boxes but in ecologies of interactive emergence—I would like to conclude this chapter by suggesting that in the *MZ* the emergence of energy as feeling, of feeling as disposition, of disposition as body shape and body language, and of body language as speech is organized by what the Confucian tradition calls *lǐ* 禮. Mencius does not expatiate at length on *lǐ* 禮, variously translated as "the rites," "ritual," "ritual form," "ritual observances," and "ritual propriety," and it is easy to read the few chapters that do deal with it explicitly in negative terms, as a series of avoidances:

- When handing an object to a woman, a man must not touch her hand (4A17)

- At court it is not proper to cross the room to approach or to chat with a person of higher status (4B27)

- It is not proper to marry without informing one's parents first (5A2)

- It does not matter how well the giving of a gift accords with the Way; if the giver is a highway robber, it is never proper to accept it (5B4)

- It is not proper for a ruler to support an exemplary person financially without hiring him to do a job (this is like feeding a dog, disrespectful to the person thus supported) (5B6)

- A gift given without the proper decorum is not a gift at all, and does not need to be acknowledged (6B5)

A list like this makes *lĭ* 禮 look like a simple mechanical obedience to rules, and specifically to rules as prohibitions. And in an important sense it doesn't change that impression significantly to note that Mencius often urges flexibility, situational judgment, "discretion" (*quán* 權, lit. "weighing"), as in 4A17, when he specifically says that if a man's sister-in-law is drowning it is permitted to touch her hand to save her life, or in 5A2, when he says that Shun 舜 did right in not informing his parents before marrying because his parents would not have allowed him to marry, and marriage is one of the greatest of human relationships (because it produces heirs). If we understand *lĭ* 禮 in terms of prohibitions and prescriptions and occasional situational exceptions to those ordinances, it is difficult to understand it as part of the deep ecology of social value, to which we turn in chapter 4.

There is, however, another way of reading these passages that does ground *lĭ* 禮 in a social ecology. The first thing to note is that for Mencius rites and rituals are born out of feeling (*xīn* 心), which, as the *Book of Rites* tells us, comes not from outside (*wài* 外) but is "focused in the person [*zizhong* 自重]" (quoted in Behuniak, 2005, p. 114; Behuniak's interpolation). The first people to decide to bury their dead parents, Mencius mythologizes, spontaneously and naturally *felt* that this was the best thing to do with the dead (3A5). It is also important to remember that this feeling out of which ritual propriety emerges is not private or idiosyncratic but *integrated* (*chéng* 誠). This is the same character that some translate as "integrity" and take to mean an inner coherence or organization of ethical being, and there is a sense in which that depiction is accurate; but in Confucianism *chéng* 誠 is primarily a *communal* integratedness, an experience of being part of the larger community, and thus an ethecosis rather than an individualized ethics. The integrity that may be experienced as a personal quality or possession is produced through the integration of personal feeling into collective feeling, or, perhaps, the circulation or reticulation of collective feeling through the individual. This collective feeling is regulatory, of course, but the Confucian idea is not that the individual is a dangerous wayward being that needs to be hemmed in by rules; rather, the individual is empowered, even energized, by integrated participation in ritual propriety. As Behuniak (2005, p. 115) puts it, "ritual form is a pattern or configuration that enables the optimal expression of qualitative energies (*qi* 氣) by fitting human experiences and actions productively into the patterns and dispositions of the environing world. Ritual propriety is itself a 'disposition' that facilitates the discharge of qualitative energies and emotions" (Behuniak's interpolation).

That collectively organized and channeled disposition is also, Behuniak adds, the shape of humanity: the coherent ways in which we are trained to express our sociality through specifically *human* social practices. We share a great deal with the other social animals—the persuasive/expressive *energy*, for example, that we've seen George Kennedy calling rhetoric (§3.2)—but we are not birds, or lower mammals. "Ritual," as Behuniak (ibid., p. 120) puts it, "makes humans by shaping their dispositions." It's not just that birds don't bury or otherwise honor their dead, or marry, or sacrifice; it's that they don't *heighten* or *intensify* (in the term from the *Book of Rites*, "get the most" [*jin* 盡] out of) their experience through human rituals (quoted in ibid., pp. 114, 120). They may have rituals of their own, and those rituals may heighten their experience as well; but they aren't *human* rituals. *li* 禮 is the shaping of the ecology of affect as the specifically human ecology of social value.

It may in fact be useful to reframe Confucian *li* 禮 in terms of what Paul Connerton (1989) calls the creation of a "social memory" through ritual. Following Oakeshott (1962), Connerton distinguishes between morality as the conscious following of a rule and the kind of morality that arises out of collective habit-memory, learned by "living with people who habitually behave in a certain manner" (quoted in Connerton, ibid., p. 30). That latter is an *affective-becoming-conative* morality that according to Connerton tends to take social shape through the trained synchronization of bodily movement. The most obvious examples of this, Connerton insists, are found in the kinesthetic communication one finds in religious and patriotic ceremonies, in which the group repetition of simplified and organized gestures, postures, and movements (as well as words) serves to reenact and thus retain in collective memory events that are significant for group identity. These ritual commemorations often arise without conscious, analytical planning or codification; they emerge out of group interactions, "living with people who habitually behave in a certain manner." They can at any stage be codified, written down, pre-scribed (though a better term for this belated codification might be "post-scribed"), and often are; but their commemorative power never depends on such codifications, and codification may be resisted or even rejected by the participants in such commemorations as entirely lacking in the kind of deep preconscious affective-becoming-conative communication that is the actual channel of commemorative power.

One of the salient points Connerton (1989, p. 44) makes about ritual is that it restricts participants' actional options: rites are "expressive acts only by virtue of their conspicuous regularity. They are formalized acts, and tend to be stylized, stereotyped and repetitive. Because they are deliberately stylized, they are not subject to spontaneous variation, or at least are susceptible of variation only within strict limits." Or, as he puts these limits in kinesthetic terms, "Performatives are encoded also in set postures, gestures and movements" (ibid., p. 59). In religious and political rituals, "The body is held braced and attentive in standing; the hands are folded and placed as though bound in praying; persons bow down and express their impotence by kneeling; or they may completely abandon the upright posture in the abasement of bodily prostration" (ibid.).

What makes the application of Connerton's theory of ritual as group memory to Mencius difficult, of course, is that *lǐ* 禮 only tends to come up in the *MZ* in "problem" cases, cases in which the participants' actional options cannot or should not be ritually restricted as strictly as *lǐ* 禮 would seem to prescribe. Mencius seems especially inclined to invoke "discretion" (*quán* 權) when *lǐ* 禮 is at odds with one of the four hearts (§4.4): with the heart of compassion (*cèyǐn* zhī xīn 惻隱之心), for example, in the case of the drowning sister-in-law (4A17), or, in several other cases (not crossing a room to chat with a person of higher status, 4B27; not accepting patronage from a ruler without being hired, 5B6; not acknowledging a gift given without the proper decorum, 6B5), with the heart of deference (*gōngjìng zhī xīn* 恭敬之心). The heart of deference also governs both the all-important virtue of filial piety (*xiào* 孝) and its extension to the five relationships (*wǔlún* 五倫, 3A4): son with father (*fùzǐ* 父子: the primary one), minister with ruler (*jūnchén* 君臣), wife with husband (*fūfù* 夫婦), younger with older (*zhǎngyòu* 長幼), and friend with friend (*péngyou* 朋友). And yet it is clear not only that there can be conflicting pulls among these various relationships, but that in certain cases a "lower" relationship can be given precedence over the highest of all, filial piety, as when Mencius argues that it was acceptable for Shun 舜 to marry without telling his parents, because his parents would have prevented the marriage, and marriage is a great social good (5A2). There are also cases in which the conflicting prescriptions occur not between *lǐ* 禮 and the four hearts or the five relationships but within *lǐ* 禮 itself, as when the giver is right but the way of giving is wrong, or the way of giving is right but the giver is wrong (5B4). As presented in the *MZ*, the patent complexity of human social interaction seems to riddle Confucian *lǐ* 禮 with loopholes and escape clauses and exceptions. As a result, even though Mencius repeatedly defends the most conservative Confucian conceptions of *lǐ* 禮, and his own actions as justified by those conservative conceptions, it is not particularly surprising to us as modern readers that Mencius's detractors in his own day accused him of being a *lǐ* 禮 opportunist, a casuist in the worst sense of the word (see Eno, 2002), someone who invokes *lǐ* 禮 mainly to protect and mystify his own (or Shun's 舜) sense of sagely entitlement. In very many of the specific passages that invoke *lǐ* 禮 in the *MZ*, in fact, Mencius seems to stand far closer to "us," to our modern sense of the casual unstructured informalities of everyday social interaction, than he does to Confucius.

Assuming that such is not actually the case, I suggest that the interesting question is how we are to explain the strong *appearance* that it is. How do we reconcile Mencius's rhetoric of strict compliance with what seemed to many of his contemporaries, as it does to superficial readings of the *MZ* today, to be the behavioral "reality" of his opportunistic and even insouciant violations of *lǐ* 禮?

One well-trodden path leads through dualism, of the sort that tends to fuel East-West civilizational oppositions: Mencius is either [a] a radical iconoclast (perhaps even a proto-modernizing proto-Westernizer) who is only pretending to adhere to the old outdated rules of *lǐ* 禮 or [b] a devout conservative Confucian whose first and deepest loyalties are always to the universally valid rules of *lǐ* 禮. If he is (b), then [a1] his detractors in the *MZ* who are always trying to catch him out are simply wrong about him, and [a2] Western individualistic notions of total freedom, spontaneity, and creativity are profoundly suspect; if he is (a), then [b1] ritual is a reactionary straitjacket that Mencius is attempting to shed and [b2] the rule-bound rigidity with which Confucianism is often associated is actually a cultural fossil that has nothing to do with Mencius (or even possibly Confucius).

I suggest three deep-ecological moves past this dualistic distortion.

1. The first is to recognize the extent to which (a2) and (b2) not only overlap quite extensively but stand in fairly close proximity on the same scale. So far from marking off the extremes of radical iconoclasm and the hive mind, freedom without restriction and restriction without freedom, (a2) and (b2) in fact map different degrees of social organization and regulation. While it is obviously true that conversational and other impromptu social exchanges are not what Connerton calls "expressive acts only by virtue of their conspicuous regularity"—their participants are expected to contribute surprise, innovation, creativity, novelty to them, and a certain apparently

spontaneous unstructuredness is therefore at the core of our most basic understanding of them—it is equally true that they do also restrict actors' options. If they didn't do so, in fact, no one's behavior would ever be comprehensible to others. Their socially imposed regularity is an essential ingredient of their power to guide and shape the interpretive uptake of their expressivity.

To appreciate this regularity we need only think of an experience we may have had with a disruptive participant in an informal impromptu conversation: a "crazy" or "out-of-control" person who wouldn't let anyone else talk, or who interrupted others mercilessly, constantly, and randomly (who broke the unspoken "rule" making turn-taking, or the equitable allotment of speaking turns, an ecotic group decision rather than a unilateral one); who repeatedly said nonsensical things with no relevance to what had gone before (broke the ecotic "rule" requiring conversational participants to work together to construct a meaningful interaction); whose body language was completely inappropriate for the things s/he said—turned-away posture and no eye contact for semantically engaged speech, fully person-focused posture and eye contact for the nonsensical irrelevancies—(broke the "rule" requiring conversational participants to use body language meaningfully not only to signal intentions but to perform becoming-communal "conversation-structuring acts"), and so on. The importance of social stabilization in apparently unstructured and therefore highly labile exchanges is most evident when it is fractured, undermined, rendered problematic. The work done on the ethnomethodology of speech by Harold Garfinkel (1969) and on conversational frames by Erving Goffman (1974), as well as other "performative" (see Robinson, 2006) approaches to speech communication, are relevant here.

The ecotic scalability of social stabilization (group homeostasis) in (a2) and (b2) might be likened to what Derrida (1971/1988) calls the "iterability" of a communicative act, namely its repeatability-with-a-twist, which is to say, the destabilizing power of the stabilizing effect it has on communication. Iterability, to put that differently, is all about maintaining stability through regulated repetition, but the repetitions undertaken to maintain that stability also destabilize the precarious social order thus regulated. Stepping up the stabilizing regime moves one (the collectivized "one") in the direction of (b2) collectivism, the becoming-communal and becoming-normal organization of group behavior; the further one moves in that direction, however, the more vulnerable one's exchanges become to deviations, and the more disruptive (becoming-individualistic or b > a) the effect of any such deviation will be. Backing off the stabilizing regime moves one in the direction of (a2) individualism, individual freedom, and thus spontaneity and unpredictable innovation; but as the ethnographers, sociologists, and ethnomethodologists of speech have shown, even the most apparently "spontaneous" and "free" social interaction is organized/organizing, stabilized/stabilizing, becoming-communal (a > b), in the interest of rendering each participant's contribution to the interaction meaningful (interpretable).[8]

I have elsewhere (Robinson, 1991, pp. 10ff) identified these two impulses as (b) *ideosomatic* (the circulation of somatic pressures through a group for purposes of social regulation) and (a) *idiosomatic* (the slight deflections or redirectionings introduced by individual group members as they circulate or "reiterate" ideosomatic impulses). In the terms I have been developing here out of Aristotle, ecosis/icosis would be the ideosomatic exchange (see §4.12); the idiosomatic counterpressures, at least when they are slight individual twists on the regulatory (eth)ecotic movement of becoming-communal or the regulatory (dox)icotic movement of becoming-persuasive, might be termed "iterecotic" or "itericotic." The many idiosyncratic innovations that Mencius introduced into the Confucian tradition would be idiosomatic/iterecotic/itericotic in this sense. (The idiosomatics of full-on counterideosomatic resistance lies beyond the scope of this book, though we return to it briefly in §4.11, in the context of shamelessness.)

2. But this reciprocal scalability as a theoretical intermeshing of dualistic extremes is only the (a2-b2) background to the key (a1-b1) issue of how Mencius suggests we adapt our actions to *lǐ* 禮. The second deep-ecological move past the dualistic distortion is to remember that the highest priority for Mencius is *rén zhèng* 仁政 "fellow-feeling government," which as I argued in chapter 2 is *persuasive* government, government grounded in the circulation of persuasivity through both ruler and ruled, and thus what I will be theorizing in chapter 4 as *doxicotic* government. To the end of spreading doxicosis throughout the population, the second-highest priority for Mencius is *ethecotic* growth, becoming-communal/becoming-normal ecotic growth in the ruler and his advisors, and ultimately in the common people as well. To the extent that *lǐ* 禮 is a codification of the group norms around which ecosis is organized—Connerton's kinesthetic as well as the more obvious moral norms, and the epistemic (icotic) as well as conversational and other interactive norms—it is an important engine of ethecotic growth. Learning first to avoid breaking the rules, and then gradually to assimilate oneself so thoroughly to the rules that they become second nature, is the secret to all moral improvement; the main difference between Confucian/Mencian moral improvement and what Sunday School teachers teach little

Western Christians about moral improvement is that for Confucius and Mencius, as for Oakeshott and Connerton, the most important form of moral improvement proceeds not through obeying a checklist of rules but through "living with people who habitually behave in a certain manner."

3. The third and final move is to invoke group dynamics. If Mencius occasionally seems almost cavalier about *lǐ* 禮, if his quickness to invoke "discretion" (*quán* 權) gives his critics ample ammunition against him, that may be because he is so highly attuned to the complex overlaps among group normativities, to what might be called cultural differences—the different ethecotic effects different groups have on their members—that he is unwilling to reduce all ecosis to a single set of behavioral rules such as his society has inherited as Confucian *lǐ* 禮. (He also seems to be unwilling to rethink and reframe Confucian *lǐ* 禮 in any kind of radical way, which contributes to the slippery impression he sometimes gives, as he weasels out of an accusation—as if possessed of a "larger" or "broader" or "higher" exemplary conception of *lǐ* 禮 that he was hesitant to disseminate.) He remains committed to the ethecotic effects of *lǐ* 禮, the power of group conformity to transform the individual in salutary ways; but he also insists that the main thing is to *feel* (*xīn* 心) one's way through the collective pressures to belong, to serve others through fellow-feeling (*rén* 仁), to love (*ài* 愛) and be loyal (*zhōng* 忠), and thus to grow ethecotically. The Confucian Way for Mencius is neither (b) a collectivistic straitjacket nor (a) an individualistic *carte blanche* but a complex ethecosis or becoming-communal to which individuals with their stray impulses and their conformist desires *all* contribute. As we will see in §4.5, there are collective social "forces" (*tiān* 天) that shape our feeling-becoming-thinking (*xīn* 心), but that does not mean that our response to that shaping must be passive; *pace* Bryan Van Norden (2008, p. xxvii; see §4.3), Mencius tropes human ethecosis not simply as the growth of a pear tree but also as the interactive work of the horticulturist "growing" the pear tree (i.e., the individual is metaphorically at once the gardener and the tree and the transitive-becoming-intransitive growing that joins them).[9] *tiān* 天 is literally "heaven" or "the sky," and many of our English translators render it "Heaven"; a Christian interpretation would be that we should let Heaven (Providence, God, etc.) make the decisions, and conform ourselves as submissively as possible to those decisions coming from on high. But it is not only Christian interpreters of the *MZ* that make this mistake; conservative Confucian scholars do as well. Van Norden, after all, gets his radically passivizing understanding of the *MZ* not from the Bible but from the twelfth-century Chinese neo-Confucian scholar Zhu Xi. Confucianism is of course often taken to entail a conformism that borders

on the robotic, and historically neo-Confucianism has sometimes meant a retreat from prevailing sociopolitical conflicts into a "purified" (reactionary) understanding of key Confucian concepts so as to mandate passive submission to one's "lot"; but this has never been the only current in Confucianism. Recognizing these tensions within the Confucian tradition will become especially pressing in our discussion of honor, dishonor, and shame in chapter 4, where it may begin to seem as if the ecology of social value that regulates behavior in Mencius does so in ways that allow no freedom, no creativity, and thus no change. For Mencius, however, humans are not pear trees, not role robots programmed to perform prescribed actions; they (we) are active participants in group activities, and our contributions to those activities actively shape the group. If that shaping were not possible, there would be only one group: the human race. There would be no cultural difference, no local variation, and above all for Mencius no potential for growth, no groups in which ethecosis began producing exemplary people, even sages, and thus ultimately no Confucian Way.

Mencius insists specifically (7A1) that the best way to "get the most" (*jìn* 盡) out of one's *xīn* 心 is to know and follow one's own inclinations (*xìng* 性), and that to know/follow one's own inclinations is to know/serve *tiān* 天 (see §4.5). This is not a dualistic either-or choice between submission and resistance, between (b) becoming the perfected group-controlled honeybee and (a) acting on whatever crazy random iconoclastic whim strikes one; it is an intelligent participation in the becoming-communal of ecosis. Mencius doesn't quite formulate all this quite so clearly, but implicit in his remarks is a set of assumptions about individual behavior in groups:

[1] *lǐ* 禮 is the ideosomatic regulation of individuals' behavior by *groups*, and groups differ one from another (cf. the five relationships).

[2] Different individuals at their various stages of moral development need different ideosomatic pressures in order to continue to grow, and ideally (in accordance with 1) different groups will provide those different pressures.

   [a] Some "low" groups will in fact actively prevent their members from growing morally—will maintain such a low level of ethecotic stability that according to Mencius their members cannot rise even to the level of the human—but even they will shame and dishonor their members that break the rules, and that unpleasant expe-

rience (see §4.11) may well push some to leave those low groups and strive higher.

[b] The "highest" or "noblest" group is the group of exemplary persons (recorded for future readers in the *Analects*, the *MZ*, and other Confucian works), which at the pinnacle of moral development produces sages, the best rulers, and the best scholar-officials.

[3] Because each member of a group will have been shaped ideosomatically by the group (1–2), "following one's own inclinations" will to a large extent mean acting as the group has conditioned one to act.

[4] That conditioning by the group (3) will often be experienced as a surrender to *tiān* 天 "forces" and *mìng* 命 "conditions."

[5] *Submitting* to those ideosomatic pressures for the individual member of a group (3–4) also means submitting to *circulating* those pressures to others in the group, and thus to acting as ethecotic horticulturalist as well as ethecotic tree (thereby contributing unawares to (4)).

[6] Because each individual is biologically distinct from all others, experiences life in a different body, "following one's own inclinations" will also inevitably mean introducing slight but significant individual differences (iterability) into the circulation of evaluative affect (5) that is ethecosis.

While the encouragement to follow our inclinations is part of the ethecotic shaping of individual behavior in the image of the group, then, it is also (6) a potentially disruptive or redirective part, an iterecotic impulse that has the power to pull the group both downward into "animal" behavior (2a) and upward toward exemplarity (2b), toward the true Confucian Way. That Way leads through conformity, to be sure, group belonging based on fellow-feeling (*rén* 仁), a flexible and sensible adherence to ritualized group norms (*lǐ* 禮), a responsive and responsible adjustment (*yì* 義) to prevailing social and other forces (*tiān* 天) and conditions (*mìng* 命); but it is also a belonging that is predicated on growth, on iterecotic emergence, and thus on change, and the ethecotic change that Mencius envisions always engages the deepest inclinations of the individual. *yì* 義 (fitting behavior) and *lǐ* 禮 (ritual propriety) for Mencius are both "smart" trajectories steering a middle course between the dualistic extremes of complete ideosomatic conformism and the maverick idiosomatics of radical nonconformism or iconoclasm. In steering that middle course the exemplary person's feeling-becoming-thinking (*xīn* 心) both configures and is configured by the energies of *qì* 氣 along "moral" (ethecotic) lines conducive to the icosis of social value.

4

The Circulation of Social Value

4.0 Introduction

What is your reputation made out of? Obviously, out of what *people tell others* about you; out of the *opinions people spread* about you; out of what *people hear* about you. As we saw Eric Havelock noting in §1.5, the fact that Aristotle's *doxa* means both opinions (as something A possesses about B) and reputation (as something B possesses as a result of what A says) seems problematic to many English readers (and especially translators) of Aristotle; the fact that Mencius's term *wén* 聞 means both hearing about B and the reputation B accrues in the process is equally problematic, or could be, in an intellectual tradition that expected philosophical concepts to refer to one individual and his or her or its properties at a time.

Like the *pistis/zhì* 治 pair in chapter 2, in fact, I suggest that the *doxa/wén* 聞 pair can usefully stand as a jumping-off point for a discussion of a "circulatory" or "reticulatory" (ecotic/icotic) group subject like "society" or "culture" or "the people," who do not merely *have beliefs* or *have values* but mobilize and energize beliefs and values consecutively, or interconsecutively, or perhaps reciproconsecutively, by swapping them around, by internalizing other people's beliefs and values and passing them on to others, with slight itericotic shifts (§3.9), but accompanied with "presenced" or "energized" (§3.5–6) pressure to conform. Beliefs and values are often thought of as propositional structures, and typically they can be stated as propositions; but the incredible tenacity with which we cling to our beliefs and values in the face of opposition (or even just difference) suggests that they are in fact first and foremost affective impulses—that our affective adherence to a belief or a value has far more to do with our feeling of belonging to a group or of living in a universe that makes sense than it does with our ability or willingness or even inclination to defend it logically.

Theorizing this group dynamic as (dox)icosis, as becoming-persuasive, or the becoming-communal of persuasivity, is the burden of this last chapter: first, in §4.1–2, through two different explanatory models of the icotic circulation of *doxa* in Aristotle and *wén* 聞 in Mencius; then, in §4.3–5, a digression on Mencian thinking about "human nature" that begins fairly sketchily to move us in a social-constructivist direction; from there we return to Aristotle on *doxa*, specifically now in terms of the social phenomenon Erving Goffman theorizes as face-work (§4.6); then Aristotle on the rhetorical actualization of opinion (specifically a *slighting* opinion) as energized persuasion, with a brief look at Mencius on something like the same topic (§4.7); then two sections, §4.8–9, on conceptions of honor in Aristotle and Mencius, respectively, followed by another two sections, §4.10–11, on conceptions of shame in Mencius and Aristotle, respectively, with a return to Goffman on face in the latter. §4.12 is my primary theorization of ecosis/icosis as the somatic exchange; it is followed by three sections (§4.13–15) that work through Aristotle's verb form of *doxa*, *dokeō*, toward a theorization of doxicosis.

4.1 Aristotle/Mencius: *doxa*/*wén* 聞 as Opinion Circulated as Reputation

If, as Eric Havelock complains (see §1.5), *doxa* and *dokeō* are "truly baffling to modern logic in their coverage of both the subjective and objective relationship," the wild proliferation of such terms in classical Chinese makes such philosophical texts as the *MZ* and Laozi's *Dáodéjīng* (道德經 "Tao Te Ching") well-nigh untranslatable—and, from one point of view, perhaps not even deserving of the name "philosophy." Certainly the Platonic tradition in logical thinking, moving up through the centuries via Augustine, Thomas Aquinas, Descartes, Jerry Fodor, and so on, has insisted not only on establishing clear separations between object and subject, mind and body, reason and emotion, science and opinion, but on reserving the name "philosophy" for treatises that successfully establish such separations. It is difficult enough to think *doxa* or *wén* 聞 in its full circulatory complexity in English; that difficulty is rendered conceptually even more strenuous because the Platonic assault on *doxa* has been so overwhelmingly successful—at least in Western analytical philosophy.

We might begin to rethink *doxa* and *wén* 聞, then, through a rival philosophical tradition, one that is considerably more Aristotelian than Platonic in its orientation to knowledge, namely the ordinary-language philosophy developed at Cambridge and Oxford in the 1930s and 1940s. We might, for example, turn to the approach developed explicitly out of Aristotle by the Oxford ordinary-language philosopher J. L. Austin in "The Meaning of a Word" (1940/1961, p. 27). Austin there draws attention to Aristotle's tripartite division of types of meaning in *Categories* 1a1–15—synonymity, homonymity, and paronymity—and in particular to that last, wherein, "on different occasions of its use, the word may possess connotations which are *partly* identical and *partly* different." Austin then notes that the "three senses" in which "things are *productive*" in *TR* 1.6 are specifically paronymous: "some as being healthy is productive of health; some as food is productive of health; some as exercise is, in that it usually produces health" (1.6.3, 1362a32–34; Kennedy, 1991/2007, p. 62). "When we speak of a 'healthy exercise,'" Austin (ibid.) comments, "the word 'healthy' has a connotation which is only partly the same as that which it has in the phrase 'a healthy body': a healthy exercise is an exercise which produces or preserves healthiness in bodies. Hence healthiness^a, when predicated of an exercise, means 'productive or preservative of healthiness^b,' i.e. of healthiness in the sense in which it is predicated of bodies. Thus 'healthiness^b' and 'healthiness^a' have connotations which are partly identical and partly different."

Should we say, then, with Havelock, that the word "healthy" is "truly baffling to modern logic in its coverage of both static states and dynamic causation"? We would be less likely to find that "coverage" baffling, one line of argument might proceed, because as native or highly competent speakers of English we have been naturalized to it—to the point where it took a J. L. Austin reading Aristotle even to notice that there was a potential semantic problem there. What Austin suggests specifically is that "healthy" as applied to exercise is a *metaphorical extension* of "healthy" as applied to bodies—and that the term can be and is extended further: from exercise to "healthy" lifestyles, which encompass not only healthy exercise but diet and such, and "healthy" attitudes toward health, and so on (see Lakoff, 1990, pp. 19–20 for discussion).

By the same token, *doxa*-as-reputation might be read as a metaphorical extension of *doxa*-as-opinion. Reputation, after all, is an extension or reflection of opinion: if enough people are of the opinion that you are a good person, then you have a good reputation (*eudoxia*); if by your actions you destroy enough people's good opinion of you, you suffer a loss of reputation (*adoxia*). And as we move from *doxa*-as-opinion to *doxa*-as-reputation, we note the cognitive shift in the meaning of the word: an opinion held by A about B *becomes* B's reputation. If B's *doxa*-as-reputation is a character trait, a property, something she owns, it is not a property in the same sense as A's *doxa*-as-opinion is. A forms an opinion about B; it is A's opinion, not B's. As a result, B has a reputation; it is B's reputation, but it is based on, perhaps even built out of, A's opinion, not B's. This shift is neither "in the word" nor "in the world," but rather arises out of or is generated by the human cognitive (inter)activity that restlessly seeks meaning and order, and imposes them wherever possible, by whatever means available. There is no intrinsic reason why there should be a single word in Greek for both opinion and reputation; certainly no reason to expect other languages to have a single word for both. This is just the way the Attic Greeks happened to see things.

The same kind of metaphorical extension of meaning might, however, be said to be at work in Chinese *wén* 聞 as well. The character appears 87 times in the *MZ*; in 82 of those occurrences, it means "to hear," typically in the collocations "Can I hear about X?," "I have heard," and "I have never heard." In three cases (5B7, 6B13) it means something like "well-informed" or "knowledgeable"; in two cases (4A1, 6A17) it means "reputation." The character 聞 is built around the *ěr* 耳 "ear" radical (pictographically the ear is in a doorway), which explains why it is so commonly used to mean "hear"; in modern Chinese it also means "news," "to tell or make known," and "well-known," all likewise clearly related to hearing (and perhaps doorways), albeit in a rather more multifaceted circulatory sense than the one we found with *zhì* 治: it is the news itself, the hearing and the telling of the news, the well-known quality of the news, the well-informed quality of the person who hears the news, and the well-regarded quality (reputation, renown, fame) of the person *about* whom one hears the news. Oddly, at least from an English perspective, it also means "to smell" or "sniff out"—though in English we do *sniff out* the news, using a bloodhound (not an ear in a doorway) as our metaphorical vehicle.

One of the phenomena that this sort of perspective on "serial semantics" would seem to entail is an *associational contagion* to meaning. A certain strong leaning in the Western philosophical tradition has taught us to resist this contagion, to say, when confronted with the kind of semantic series to which Austin points, "No, healthy refers to bodies, and we need a different word when we refer to the quality of food or lifestyle that provides for healthy bodies, such as 'health-producing.'" But it does seem fairly common even in Western languages, and certainly common in Chinese, for the speakers of a language to ignore such strictures and let meanings leach over from one semantic function to another. When a word begins by meaning "hearing" and soon comes to mean "telling" as well, or "hearing" and "being heard," "telling" and "being told," it seems reasonable to imagine at work or in play an interactive "crowd phenomenology" in which the boundaries between speaker and listener blur together, in which your hearing contributes so intensely to my telling that it comes to seem like I am hearing you tell me in the very telling I'm doing to you. The Western (antiobjectivizing) tradition of phenomenology does in fact posit something like this intersubjective contagion, in the move from Roman Ingarden's *The Literary Work of Art* (1931) to the Constance school of *Rezeptionsästetik* (Hans Robert Jauss and Wolfgang Iser) to American reader-response theory (Norman Holland, David Bleich, Stanley Fish): the reader in this tradition is also regarded as an active producer of the text s/he reads. Dialogical addressivity in Bakhtin (see Holquist, 1990, chs. 1–2) works much the same way to infect all speaking with the addressee's hearing. But the serial semantic contagion of *wén* 聞 pushes further past the reciprocity of hearing and telling to "infect" it with the knownness of the news that is heard-and-told, the knowingness of the people who hear-and-tell it, and the knownness of the person about whom it is heard-and-told. Semantically *wén* 聞 traces a highly complex crowd phenomenology, a phenomenology of crowd wisdom or disaggregated agency (see Robinson, 2001, ch. 6).

It should go without saying, then, that the kind of hearing/telling of the news/opinion that becomes a reputation cannot involve just a single individual's "quirky" or "maverick" view. The opinion or the news has to be reported by at least several people. It has to be a consensus or group opinion that, to the extent that it seems to be A's opinion, is really only "occupying" A for a while. A reputation is created not by a single person's opinion but by group opinion. For B to "have" a reputation, the opinion about B on which it is based must really be "had" by not only A but the collective that contains A as one of its members. *Doxa* as opinion-becoming-reputation, then, like *wén* 聞 as hearing-becoming-reputation, is never one person's opinion: it is definitively the "property" of a group, circulated through that group, and taking on the form and heft of "consensus" as it circulates.

Studies of social intelligence, or "the wisdom of the crowd" (see Surowiecki, 2004)—of crowd-sourcing, wikis, Yahoo! Answers, and social news sites like Digg and Newsvine—also suggest that it functions best when the crowd at work on a problem is diverse and when the problem they are at work on has a correct answer. Crowds made up of people who share an ideology tend to create a mob that is inherently biased and therefore unlikely to work through complexity to the right answer—what we might call a "nightmare democracy," the kind of scare-tactics democracy that is typically painted in blood on the walls by antidemocrats. It is easy to argue that reputations are loose "truthy" constructs that have no connection to right answers and therefore don't need or rely on diversity; but in fact a lynch mob is by definition a form of "crowd wisdom" that a democracy will want to counteract precisely through a legal process based on the deliberations of a diverse crowd (not just a jury but a jury + judge + opposing counsels + expert witnesses) dedicated to sifting through complexity to the right answer. Aristotle and Mencius lacked the kind of long history with democracy that might have encouraged them to reflect complexly on questions of diversity within the crowd and its effect on the communal creation of truth and reality; but arguably the "populist" or "protodemocratic" utopianism that pervades the *MZ* is implicitly or anticipatorily grounded in just some such theory of crowd wisdom, and it has historically been precisely the lack of experiences with or theories of such wisdom that has made Mencius's utopian thought seem so politically dangerous in China; and we will see some of Aristotle's rudimentary attempts to work through those complexities later in the chapter (§4.13–15).

Let's begin by looking at two specific passages, the kind that do not normally set off "truly baffling"/confusing alarm bells in scholars of Aristotle or Mencius.

First, in *MZ* 4A1 Mencius speaks of unnamed rulers who *yŏu rén xīn rén wén* 有仁心仁聞, literally "have *rén* heart *rén* reputation." Lau (1970/2003, p. 149) translates that "despite their benevolent hearts and reputations," Van Norden (2008, 88) as "there are some who have benevolent hearts and benevolent reputations," both simply applying the same adjective to the sequence of nouns, even though the syntactic move from 仁心 to 仁聞 manifestly involves a significant metaphorical shift. While in 仁心 the heart is benevolent, in 仁聞 it's not that the reputation is benevolent but that the ruler has "a reputation for benevolence" (Legge, 1861/1970, p. 288), or "a reputation for humaneness" (Bloom, 2009, 73), or, as Zhao et al. have it, in the plural, "there are some who have benevolent hearts and have won renown as benevolent men." In 仁心 fellow-feeling is attributed directly to the rulers' hearts; in 仁聞 we "hear" (as it were) *other people* attributing fellow-feeling to the rulers' hearts, and Mencius reporting on that "heard" attribution. Hearing has become news and finally well-known enough to become a reputation; but the reputation, now at two or three removes, is still described with the adjective initially used to describe the rulers (and their hearts).

Or consider a slightly more complicated case from *TR* 1.10. This is a chapter that George Kennedy titles "Topics About Wrongdoing for Use in Judicial Rhetoric," but the passage I want to look at anticipates Aristotle's discussion of "ethical" dispositions in *TR* 2.12–17: having noted that people do things either "not on their initiative or on their own initiative," and that the former includes things done by chance or by necessity, and that those done by necessity are either coerced or caused by nature, he tells us that "whatever they do on their own initiative and of which they are the causes, these things are done by habit [*di' ethos*] or by desire [*di' orexin*]" (1.10.7, 1368b33–1369a1; Kennedy, 1991/2007, pp. 84–85). He goes on to list the seven causes of action (1.10.8, 1369a5): chance (*dia tukhēn*), nature (*dia phusin*), force (*dia bian*), character (*di' ethos*), reason (*dia logismon*), passion (*dia thumon*), and appetite (*di' epithumian*). *Thumos*, you'll recall from §2.8, was originally anger, then valor, then (for Plato) the "spirited" constituent of the soul; *epithumia*, derived from *thumos*, is the lowest constituent of Plato's soul, the appetites. Freese (1926, p. 109) translates those last two "anger" and "desire," Cooper (1932, p. 57) as "passion" and "desire," Roberts (1941/1984, p. 2179) as "anger" and "appetite," and Kennedy (1991/2007, p. 85) as "anger" and "longing." Then the passage with *doxa* in it (1.10.9–10, 1369a15–23):

> And similarly, both the just and the unjust (and others said to act by their habitual character [*kata tas hexeis prattein*]) will do things either through reason or through emotion [*ē gar dia logismon ē dia pathos*]; but the former will do good things by character or emotion [*dia ēthē kai pathē*], the latter the opposite. Yet there surely are consequences of having specific characters or emotions [*hexesi*]; for good reputations [*doxai*] and sentiments [*epithumiai*] in regard to his pleasures follow immediately and equally for the temperate person from his temperance, and to the intemperate person the opposites [follow] in regard to the same things. (Kennedy, 1991/2007, p. 85)

> Similarly, with just men, and unjust men, and all others who are said to act in accordance with their states [*kata tas hexeis prattein*], their actions will really be due to one of the causes mentioned—either reasoning or emotion [*ē gar dia logismon ē dia pathos*]: due, indeed, sometimes to good dispositions and good emotions [*dia ēthē kai pathē*], and sometimes to bad; but that good qualities should be followed by good emotions [*hexesi*], and bad by bad, is merely an accessory fact—it is no doubt true that the temperate man, for instance, because he is temperate, *is* always and at once attended by healthy opinions [*doxai*] and appetites

[*epithumiai*] in regard to pleasant things, and the intemperate man by unhealthy ones. (Roberts, 1941/1984, p. 2179)

There, clearly, Kennedy has interpreted *doxai* and *epithumiai* as attitudes and orientations coming from *outside* the *sōphron* (person of sound mind) or *akolastos* (licentious person), as other people's reactions to the person's behavior, while Roberts (following Freese and Cooper) takes them to be attitudes and orientations coming from *within* the *sōphron* or *akolastos*. For Kennedy, the person acts temperately or intemperately and others react with their opinions and sentiments, which become the person's reputation; for Roberts, a temperate or intemperate character or disposition will naturally lead to (be attended by) "healthy opinions and appetites." For Kennedy, the "following" in "follow immediately and equally" (*epakolouthousi*) occurs in relationship between the actor and the social group, and so is *inter*active; for Roberts, that verb becomes not a "following" but an "attending" that occurs in relationship between the actor's inclinations and actions, and so is what we might call *intra*-active. When Kennedy takes *epithumiai* to be the individual's inward orientations, he translates them as "longings"—longings in this case specifically for "pleasures" (*ta hēdea*) rather than for people—but, ignoring that lexical habit (*hexis*) here, he gives us the semantically questionable "sentiments" instead.

Note too that neither translator seems to know what to do with *hexis*: Kennedy translates *tēs hexeis* first as "habitual character," but then, apparently taking that phrase to be (at least in this context) synonymous with *ēthē kai pathē*, renders *hexesi* "character and emotion"; Roberts renders it first "states," presumably meaning body states, since *hexeis* are embodied dispositions or habits, but then he too shifts to rendering it "emotions." *Hexis* was translated into Latin by Cassidorus as *habitus,* and Pierre Bourdieu's (1979/1984) theory of *habitus* would suggest that it circulates ecotically through populations much as I suggest *rén* 仁 does: one (radically post-Aristotelian but in a sense quite Mencian) solution to the problem we find in the comparison of Kennedy's and Roberts's translations might be to associate the hexitic force that shapes both *doxai* and *epithumiai* with the crowd, the mass, the community, the group, with ecosis/icosis, so that what we find at work here is not only the definition of certain people as "temperate" and others as "intemperate" but the circulation through various groups of icotic approval-impulses for temperance and icotic disapproval-impulses for intemperance, in an attempt to *organize* opinions, attitudes, inclinations, habits, emotions, motivations, and appetites in socially acceptable ways.

4.2 Aristotle/Mencius: *doxa*/*wén* 聞 as Feeling-Becoming-Thinking

If we can provisionally agree, then, that *doxa*/*wén* 聞 is a kind of collective/circulatory hearing-the-news/opinion-becoming-reputation entelechy—members of Group A circulating (telling/hearing) opinions of Individual B until they begin to emerge icotically (becoming-persuasively) as Individual B's reputation—what *is* it? Is it a belief or belief system that is exclusively, primarily, typically, or conceivably expressed verbally as a proposition or series of propositions? If so, what is the difference between a belief that *is typically* expressed as a proposition and a belief that only *might be* expressed as a proposition? For surely there is a difference? Just how propositional is an opinion that exists mainly as a vague inclination that might, in the right hands, be *converted* into a proposition? This is an important question, it seems to me, precisely because vague inclinations would seem to be more susceptible to the kind of collective "occupation" of a group mind than conscious propositional beliefs.

Try this: imagine a friend, an actual friend of yours. Now imagine how you feel about him or her, and how the other members of your group feel about him or her. What differences are there in the opinion-becoming-reputation kind of feelings you and your friends harbor about this person? Or, to run that the other way, what level of dispositional or inclinational generality would you need to move to in order to iron out all the differences in how people in your group feel about this friend? For example, isn't it more likely for everyone in the group to agree that s/he is a "good" person than that s/he is a "trustworthy" person, and more likely for them to agree, further, that s/he is a "trustworthy" person than, say, that s/he is the best person to have with you in a family crisis? The more propositional specificity you want to add to the shared opinion-becoming-reputation type of feeling about your friend, I suggest, the harder it is going to be to get everyone in the group to agree. And, conversely, the longer the opinion-becoming-reputation orientations remain unstated, unspecified, at the level of inchoate affective/evaluative "up or down" inclinations—good or bad, positive or negative, smiles or frowns, hugs or cold shoulders—the more likely they are to be shared by the whole group. Just try and get your friends together to write down a list of characteristics of this person that everyone can agree on. Articulation of group opinions inevitably breeds disagreement. Better to leave the list unspecified, preconscious, felt.

Or take fame, another common translation of both *doxa* and *wén* 聞. What is the propositional content of fame? There isn't one. The opinions that constitute reputation can be reduced to propositions: X is a good person, honorable, upright, reliable, etc. Reputation, we might say, is opinion-as-feeling in motion toward opinion-as-thinking. But try to reduce fame to propositions. It can't be done. We can say that Yo Yo Ma (马友友) is a brilliant cellist, but that doesn't reduce his *fame* to a proposition; it only provides a somewhat inadequate background explanation for it. His fame is born out of many people's *admiration,* which can be reduced to a proposition like "he is a brilliant cellist," or even something more inchoate like "he is wonderful," but there is still a quantum leap from admiration to fame. Is it possible to admire a cellist who isn't famous? Of course it is. All we can say about that sort of person is that s/he *should* be famous, or *could* be famous—not that fame is the inevitable *telos* of the entelechy that is my admiration. It's also possible to admire Yo Yo Ma because he's famous, even if you're tone-deaf and hate classical music and couldn't tell a cello's timbre from a bassoon's. It's possible to admire rich and famous people without knowing anything about them, without knowing how they made their money or how nice they are to old people and small children—just because they're famous. What is Paris Hilton famous for? For being famous. There is a circularity to fame that makes it a tougher nut to crack conceptually than "mere" reputation. Presumably fame too stands in some kind of integral relation to opinion; but what? The only propositional opinion that has anything to do with Paris Hilton's fame, it seems to me, is "Paris Hilton is famous." What *makes* her famous is something else altogether, something preconscious and prepropositional—a kind of excitement, perhaps, a bodily arousal that is partly but not primarily sexual, a body state that cycles constantly in and out of her fame, so that her fame excites us and our excitement makes her famous. Think of the hysteria over the Beatles, when they came to the United States in 1964. Think of the hysteria over Hitler in Germany in the thirties. The *doxa/wén* 聞 that made them famous (and rich, and powerful, and admired, even worshipped) was not particularly mental, logical, analytical, conscious, propositional.

A tentative formulation, then: *doxa* and *wén* 聞 are more feeling than thinking. Or, entelechially: *doxa/wén* 聞 is feeling-becoming-thinking, body-becoming-mind. In Chinese terms, *doxa/wén* 聞 emerges out of, and is guided by, *xīn* 心.

But then that formulation opens an interpretive can of worms, especially in readings of Mencius. In *MZ* 6A4 we find Mencius in disputation with Gaozi, who argues that *rén* 仁 (fellow-feeling) is *nèi* 內 "internal" and *yì* 義 (the sense of situational rightness) is *wài* 外 "external"; commentators disagree on the precise meaning of "internal" and "external" there, but in a long and detailed philological and philosophical unpacking of both the passage itself in Chinese and the various historical interpretations of it, Shun (1997, pp. 91–112) persuasively argues that for Mencius, rather than being "external" in the sense of being rule-based and simply imposed on the individual from the outside, *yì* 義 is "internal" in the sense that "one's recognition of what is *yì* 義 derives from certain features of the heart/mind [*xīn* 心]" (ibid., pp. 103–104; Wade-Giles romanization pinyinized and Chinese characters added).

The question that remains, however, is: what is the *source* of the "internality" of *xīn* 心? Clearly it is "internal" to the individual body, therefore also to the phenomenology of life as experienced by the individual; but how does it get there? Or does its internality mean that it is simply a private, idiosyncratic, purely subjective orientation to ethics, developed internally through idiosyncratic experience, as most Western and some Chinese thinkers would normatively assume about an ethics based on a motto like "do whatever feels right"? Clearly not, for Mencius. As Shun (1997, p. 139) adds, *yì* 義 derives from *xīn* 心, and, "more specifically, from shared predispositions that already point in the direction of the ethical ideal." Does this then mean that *xīn* 心 is a "natural" or "native" predisposition to an ethical sense that is innate to the human animal? Not only have many, perhaps most, of Mencius's commentators made this assumption (see especially Bloom, 1994, 1997, 2002); it seems difficult to imagine what else it could be. If all humans have what Mencius calls the "four hearts" (to which we turn in §4.4), surely they must be *born* with those hearts? In 6A15, the passage that we discussed at length in §2.6 and I ended up translating as "The heart is a feeling-becoming-thinking organ: when feeling becomes thinking, it engages; when it fails to become thinking, it does not engage" continues *cǐ tiān zhī suǒ yǔ wǒ zhě* 此天之所與我者, which Lau (1970/2003, p. 131) translates "This is what Heaven has given me." And *tiān* 天 is indeed normally translated "heaven" or "Heaven," suggesting to the Christian missionaries among Mencius's translators that *xīn* 心 is "given" or created by a personal God, and at the very least, even to the most secular of Mencius's readers, that it is something that we're born with.

To unpack this complex cluster of ideas, at which Mencius only hints, I propose to make another Mencian digression—on whether *xìng* 性 is an innate nature or a learned disposition in §4.3, the four hearts in §4.4, and the "external" forces (*tiān* 天) and conditions (*mìng* 命) over which we have no control in §4.5—before returning to Aristotle on *doxa* in §4.6.

4.3 Mencius on the Dispositional Embodiment (xìng 性) of Virtue

The most obvious place to look in Mencius for answers to questions about the sources of xīn 心 is his concept of xìng 性, or rén xìng 人性, traditionally translated "human nature" and taken to be a stable property of the human animal. xìng 性 is derived pictographically from shēng 生 "life, birth" (the 忄 "heart" radical + shēng 生), and is often used synonymously with shēng 生 in early Chinese histories like the Gúoyǔ (國語, fifth to late fourth century BCE) and the Zuǒ Zhuàn (左傳, before 389 BCE) (Shun, 1997, pp. 37–38); as it can also be translated "sex" and "sexuality," the temptation is strong to associate it with biology and inbornness. And as we'll see, an interpretive tradition emerging out of Zhu Xi in the twelfth century and continuing well into the twentieth century has indeed associated xìng 性 with inborn human nature.

Behuniak (2005) argues persuasively that this biologizing tendency has most decisively been dislodged by the Guōdiàn findings in 1993, especially the *Dispositions Arise from Conditions* (xingzimingchū 性自命出). Since the Guōdiàn Chǔ bamboo strips (郭店楚簡) are Confucian texts that fill in much of the century-long gap between Confucius and Mencius, and so give us a much clearer understanding of the tradition in which Mencius was working, the impact of this find on Mencius scholarship has been transformative; Chinese scholars are now suggesting that the *MZ* is a late instance of the Sī Mèng scholarly tradition (思孟学派) at the *Jìxià* Academy (稷下學宮), according to which xìng 性 is not human nature but, in Behuniak's (2005, p. xvi) words, a " 'disposition' that arises in the process of transaction within a set of localized conditions, and this process results in the formation of something aesthetically distinct." As Pang Pu 龐朴 (1999, p. 32) puts it, xìng 性 in these pre-Mencian texts is "like a locomotive without the tracks," picking its way across a changing human social landscape in interactive response to local conditions.

Let us take another look at the passage from 7A21 that we considered in §3.8 in terms of the ethecotic training of the body (posture as a trained sign of moral dispositions); there the open question remained whether the metaphorical "horticulturalist" that trains the body ethecotically is the individual, the culture, biology, or God. The key phrase that Mencius repeats three times in quick succession in the passage is *jūnzǐ suǒ xìng* 君子所性, or literally "that which [*suǒ* 所] the exemplary person xìng 性," where *suǒ xìng* 所性 is an active (transitive) *doing something to something* (see also 7A30 and 7B33).[1] Mencius offers a series of the exemplary person's "satisfactions" (7A19) and "joys" (7A20–21) in order in each case to insist that these are *not* the things that an exemplary person will *xìng* 性, and then in the passage we'll be examining gives us a list of what the exemplary person does *xìng* 性.

In the context of an interpretive tradition that wants to translate *xìng* 性 as inborn nature, this passage poses interesting problems. How do you turn the English noun "nature" into a transitive verb? Most of our translators have fudged the obvious transitivity of the verb as it appears in 7A21, assimilating it to more static conceptions of nature by rendering it copulatively, or, more recently (beginning with Hinton in 1998), using quasitransitive (cryptocopulative) verb phrases like "knows that it is X."

Collie (1828, p. 168) gives us this (with the verb phrases he uses to represent *xìng* 性 bolded and numbered):

> To stand in the middle of the Empire, and give peace and tranquility to all the people within the four seas, is what the superior man delights in, but [1] **his heaven-derived nature rests** not in these. The [2] **nature** of the superior man **is such**, that although in a high and prosperous situation it adds nothing to his virtue, and although in low and distressed circumstances it impairs it in nothing. The superior man's [3] **nature consists** in this, that benevolence, justice, propriety, and wisdom have their root in his heart . . .

Obviously, none of Collie's verbs for *xìng* 性 points to a transitive *doing something to something*: (1) "rests" (which is actually a translation of Mencius's verb *cún* 存 "to survive, to exist, to lie somewhere"), (2) "is," and (3) "consists in" are all intransitive/copulative rather than transitive, implying a simple description of what *xìng* 性 *is* rather than what it *does*.

Note also that, as a Christian missionary, Collie wants to make *xìng* 性 "heaven-derived nature"—though there is nothing in the Chinese that would warrant such a transcendental modifier. Mencius's term for "the Empire" is the conventionalized phrase *tiān xià* 天下, literally "heaven down" or "sky down," in the sense of "the land under (the) heaven(s)" or "the land under the sky," meaning imperial China (or the world); since the Chinese think of their country as the "middle kingdom," too—*zhōngguó* 中国—the first three characters of that passage, *zhōng tiān xià* 中天下, which Collie translates as "in the middle of the Empire," carry a hint of China as well. But there is no "heaven-derivation" in that phrase, and no heaven at all modifying *xìng* 性. (We will return to look more closely at *tiān* 天 in §4.5.)

Collie served from 1824 till his death in 1828 as the third headmaster of the Ying Wa College (英華書院), the world's first Anglo-Chinese college;

the college was founded in 1818 in Malacca, Malaysia, by the London Missionary Society, and Collie's English translation of the Confucian Four Books was published posthumously there the year of his death. The next translation was done in the 1850s (published in 1861) by the seventh headmaster of the same college, James Legge (1815–1897). Legge served in that office from 1839 to 1856, but, when Hong Kong was ceded to the British three years into his tenure, moved the YWC there; it remains there today, though it has since moved from Hong Kong Island to Kowloon. Both men undertook their translations of the Chinese classics during their headmasterships, working collaboratively with Chinese converts; Legge's work on the Chinese classics continued for three decades after his 1867 return to England. Here is Legge's (1861/1970, pp. 459–60) version of the same passage, again with his renditions of *xìng* 性 bolded and numbered:

> 2. 'To stand in the centre of the kingdom, and tranquillize the people within the four seas;—the superior man delights in this, but [1] **the highest enjoyment of his nature is** not here.
>
> 3. '[2] **What belongs by his nature** to the superior man cannot be increased by the largeness of his sphere of action, nor diminished by his dwelling in poverty and retirement;—for this reason that it is determinately apportioned to him *by Heaven* [Legge's italics].
>
> 4. '[3] **What belongs by his nature** to the superior man are benevolence, righteousness, propriety, and knowledge.'

Legge is more forthright than Collie about his insertion of a capitalized Heaven into the passage, marking it as an interpolation with italics; but his understanding of the noun behind *xìng* 性 is essentially the same as Collie's, a static heaven-given nature. Syntactically his rendering of the verb is slightly more complex than Collie's, especially in (2) and (3), where "nature" is inserted into an adverbial phrase modifying "belongs"; (1) avoids the simple equation Collie builds ("his nature is") by adding "the highest enjoyment of," a nominalization of the transitive verb "enjoys." But the meaning of "belongs by his nature" remains copulative, indicating what the superior man's nature *is*.

One might assume from these first two versions that the inclination to render *xìng* 性 copulatively as referring to a static "human nature" reflects not only a Christian but a missionary worldview; but the same inclination to translate the verb as a static copulative verb phrase containing "nature" appears in a version published in 1998 by David Hinton (p. 242), whose stated loyalties are not to Christianity but to poetry and the contours of the original Confucian philosophy:[2]

> "To stand at the center of all beneath Heaven and bring contentment to people everywhere within the four seas—that's what fills the noble-minded with joy. But it isn't [1] **what answers to their nature**. Their [2a1] **nature gains nothing** if they manage the great affairs of state, and it [2a2] **loses nothing** if they live in destitute obscurity. This is because the noble-minded [2b] **know their given nature to be** complete in itself.
>
> "Humanity, Duty, Ritual, wisdom—[3] **such aspects of their nature take** root in mind, flourish in appearance." (bolding and bracketed numbers added)

Hinton has here succeeded in finding superficially transitive verbs (answer, gain, lose, know, take) that function copulatively to *recognize* a static state of affairs: (1) "answers to" is a copula that is semantically only slightly more complex than "is"; (2a) "gains" and "loses" in this context are semantically intransitive (cf. "grows and shrinks," "increases and decreases"), and still function as descriptions of the nature of "nature"; (2b) "know . . . to be" is again copulative in function; and the verb in (3) is actually not "take" but "take root," a rendering of *gēn* 根 "root," leaving Hinton's rendering of *xìng* 性 there effectively verbless.

Note also that the Chinese character that Hinton translates as "given" and "complete in itself" is *dìng* 定, meaning "decided, ordered, determined, organized." It can be construed as "unchanging," but its resistance to change is not necessarily something given; it is simply the result of some sort of organizing or ordering activity. If the "organizer" is "heaven" or "Heaven," as it is for Collie and Legge, or biology, as it seems to be for Hinton, then it is given, static, immutable; if the organizer is the exemplary person himself, it is simply a robust *resistance* to every passing influence from external forces, like success or failure, poverty or wealth.

One last translation organized or ordered around this static copulative sense of *xìng* 性 would be Van Norden's Zhu Xi–influenced rendition:

> A gentleman takes joy in taking his place in the middle of the world and making all the people within the Four Seas settled.

> But that is not [1] **what he regards as his nature**. It does not [2a1] **add to a gentleman's nature** if he puts great things into effect, nor does it [2a2] **subtract from his nature** if he lives in poverty. This is because [2b] **what belongs to him is already settled**. A gentleman [3] **regards** the benevolence, righteousness, propriety, and wisdom that are based in his heart **as his nature**. (Van Norden, 2008, p. 176)

Like Hinton, Van Norden structures the passage around transitive verbs (especially "regards") that function copulatively to recognize a static state of affairs: (1/3) "regards as his nature" is effectively the same complex copulative syntax as Hinton's (2b) "know their given nature to be"; (2a) for both translators ("gains/loses," "adds to/subtracts from") is also syntactically parallel. Van Norden's (2b) "belongs to him" would appear to be Legge's (2/3) "belongs by his nature to the superior man," with "by his nature" left implicit. There is, in other words, syntactically nothing new here. Van Norden's treatment of *dìng* 定 as "already settled," however, because the time frame of the "settling" is unstated (whether before or after birth), is more open to a sociocultural understanding of "nature" than Collie's "heaven-derived," Legge's "apportioned by Heaven," or Hinton's "given" and "complete in itself." "Nature" still seems to point to something innate, but in his introduction Van Norden (2008, p. xxvii) complicates that pointing:

> As you can see, "nature," *xìng* 性, is etymologically related to the word *shēng* 生, whose senses include "to be born," to grow," and "to live." Some thinkers emphasize the first sense. So for Mengzi's later Confucian critic Xunzi, "that which is so by birth is called 'human nature.'" However, Mengzi thinks of the nature of something as the manner in which it will live, grow, and develop if given a healthy environment for the kind of thing it is. For example, it is the nature of a pear tree to bear fruit, but the sprout of a pear tree will not yet be able to do so. Indeed, most pear tree sprouts never mature into full-grown trees, because they get insufficient soil, water, and light. But it is still their "nature" to produce pears.

This suggests that Van Norden is at least partly thinking Mencius through Aristotle—and, as we'll see, not without reason, as Mencius does seem to be very close to Aristotelian thinking here. Another English translation of Van Norden's understanding of *xìng* 性 here might in fact be "entelechy": "the manner in which it will live, grow, and develop if given a healthy environment for the kind of thing it is" is precisely how Aristotle understands the entelechial nature of things as well. As we began to see in §3.9, however, while Van Norden's formulation seems an entirely accurate and adequate account for pear trees, it works less well as a metaphor for human ethical growth and maturation: an organism's passive dependence on sufficient environmental support seems an inadequate foundation for the *MZ*'s *transitive* conception of *xìng* 性 as an actual transformative doing. Van Norden's use of a cryptocopulative (faux-transitive) syntax for the verb remains entirely congruent with the pear tree's passivity.

Shun (1997, p. 181) notes that historically in China interpretations of this passage fall into three phases; the four translations we've looked at so far reflect the first, according to which "the superior person has the ethical attributes by birth." In this reading, represented historically in Shun's account by Zhu Xi (朱熹, 1130–1200) and his almost exact contemporary Zhang Shi (张栻, 1133–1181), relative wealth and power have no effect on *xìng* 性, obviously, because *xìng* 性 is innate and therefore in no way contingent on experience. Collie's "heaven-derived" and Legge's italicized interpolation in "apportioned to him *by Heaven*" introduce a quasi-Christian providentiality that is alien to the secular thought of the *MZ*; but Hinton's more secular reading of that line, "the noble-minded know their given nature to be complete in itself," imposes a structurally similar kind of rigidity on Mencius's thought.[3] According to Van Norden's entelechial reading, "what belongs to him [that] is already settled" is his nature, and is "already settled" at birth; but it is an innate potentiality that may never be actualized.

In the second phase of the interpretive history of this passage in China, Shun (1997, p. 181) tells us, "to *xìng* 性 something is for the person to regard the thing as *xìng* 性 and hence to follow and nourish it" (Wade-Giles romanization pinyinized, Chinese character added). In this twentieth-century interpretation, advanced by A. C. Graham in 1967 and Mou Zongsan (牟宗三, 1909–1995) in 1985, the circumstances of one's life have no effect on *xìng* 性 because one's ethical response to those circumstances is within one's control. This interpretation is adumbrated in Hinton (2b) and Van Norden (1/3), though neither makes explicit the implication that "to *regard* the thing as *xìng* 性" is also "to follow and nourish it"; the second interpretation's full semantics appear in the English translation that most scholars tend to quote (and that Van Norden identifies as the "faulty" version that he sets out to correct), D. C. Lau's (1970/2003, p. 295; bolding added):

> To stand in the centre of the Empire and bring peace to the people within the Four Seas is what a gentleman delights in, but that which **he follows as his nature** lies elsewhere. That

> which a gentleman **follows as his nature** is not added to when he holds sway over the Empire, nor is it detracted from when he is reduced to straitened circumstances. This is because he knows his allotted station. That which a gentleman **follows as his nature**, that is to say, benevolence, rightness, the rites and wisdom, is rooted in his heart . . .

As Shun's tracing of this interpretive history suggests, what is notable about Lau's translation is that the relationship between the noun "nature" and the verb "follows" is rather more complex than the copulative relationship in the first phase: rather than simply *being* this or that, being something "given" or "settled," as it was for Collie, Legge, Hinton, and Van Norden, human nature for Lau is a channel of guidance that gives shape and direction to action. Still, Lau is even more rigidly deterministic than the others in his rendition of *fēn dìng gù yě* 分定故也 as "he knows his allotted station"—an interpretation that is very much in line with the quietism and passive acceptance of one's "lot" counseled by Zhu Xi's Mencius.

Shun (1997, pp. 182–83) contests both of these first two interpretative phases:

- *The first ("innate nature") interpretation*: Mencius himself refutes this view in several passages (4B28, 4B32, 6A7), arguing explicitly that we are all the same at birth and develop very different *dispositions* (*xìng* 性) through moral growth.

- *The second ("channel of guidance") interpretation* would require syntactic contortions that do not sit comfortably with Mencius's Chinese.

- *The third interpretation*: in this approach, the most recent one, "to *xìng* 性 something is to cultivate oneself so that the thing truly becomes part of oneself" (Shun, p. 181). This interpretation is first offered by Ames (1991), who argues, controversially (for the backlash against Ames, see Bloom, 1994, 1997, 2002), that *xìng* 性 is actually a cultural achievement; indeed Ames (p. 153) himself translates *jūnzǐ suǒ xìng* 君子所性 as "what the (superior) person cultivates as 性."

"Here," Shun (1997, p. 181) adds, meaning the third interpretation, "the reference to not being affected by circumstances amounts to the claim that one has cultivated the ethical attributes in oneself with such firmness that one cannot be swayed by circumstances, whether favorable or unfavorable"—the resistance to external influences indicated in Mencius's Chinese by *ding* 定. In this reading *xìng* 性 is not only transitive, but a transitive verb that incorporates what it acts upon into the subject, and so is actually transitive-becoming-copulative; Shun's own suggested translation, "to embody" (p. 183), meets this requirement perfectly. What Mencius's exemplary person *xìng* 性 "embodies" is the four virtuous states of the body-becoming-morality-becoming-mind; to embody them is not just to *cultivate* them but to internalize them, and to be transformed inwardly by them. Specifically, the virtuous body states are not stable states but tendencies, inclinations, attitudinal and behavioral proclivities that seek so insistently and so repeatedly to shape and guide action that eventually they pervade the body-becoming-mind and become second nature—so that they are often mistaken for "first" (biological) nature.

So if we take this latest construction of the impact Mencius intended to have on his source readers—based on recent archeological discoveries that give us a fuller understanding of the Confucian ideas in the air during Mencius's own time—as a guide to "the response . . . of the original receptors," what would the translation look like? Perhaps something like this (filling out the translation with the end material from our discussion in §3.9):

> To stand in the center of the Empire, to bring an orderly life to the people within the four seas: this gives the exemplary person pleasure, but s/he does not embody that pleasure as a propensity toward virtue. The exemplary person embodies virtue so robustly that, no matter how great or straitened the conditions in which s/he lives, s/he is not buffeted by external circumstance. S/he embodies fellow-feeling, rightness, ritual propriety, and wisdom by rooting them deeply in feeling-becoming-thinking, so that they put out new growth as a clarity in the face and a fullness in the back and shoulders, and on into the four limbs, so that they communicate clearly even though they cannot speak.

4.4 Mencius: The Four Hearts

What the exemplary person is rooting the four shoots in, and so embodying them, obviously, is *xīn* 心, which I suggested in §2.6 might usefully be translated "feeling-becoming-thinking." The "rooting" of *xìng* 性 in *xīn* 心 is at the core of Mencius's conception of "human nature" (in the loose sense of "what human beings are like"), and will bear more unpacking, both here and in §4.5 on *tiān* 天 and *mìng* 命.

In 2A6 and 6A6 Mencius provides overlapping lists of the "four hearts" and their desired growth into the "four shoots." In 6A6 he simply says of each heart that a person always has it (*rén jiē yǒu zhī* 人皆有之); in 2A6 he says more radically that without each heart one is not human (*fēirén yě* 非人也). The two lists differ only in their identification of the heart that puts out the shoot of *lǐ* 禮 "ritual propriety":

cèyǐn zhī xīn 惻隱之心 heart of compassion	—	*rén* 仁 fellow-feeling
xiūwù zhī xīn 羞惡之心 heart of shame	—	*yì* 義 rightness
círàng zhī xīn 辭讓之心 (2A6) heart of modest compliance *gōngjìng zhī xīn* 恭敬之心 (6A6) heart of deference	>	*lǐ* 禮 ritual propriety
shìfēi zhī xīn 是非之心 heart of approval and disapproval	—	*zhì* 智 wisdom

As we saw in §2.6, the translation of *xīn* 心 is problematic. Since the character 心 is pictographically a representation of the cardiac muscle, these two lists are generally referred to as "the four hearts"; but of our various translators[4] in these passages, only Collie, Lau, and Hinton render *xīn* 心 as "heart." Van Norden gives us "feeling," and the others hint at the complexity of the term by using more than one term, Dobson and Zhao et al. giving us both "sense" and "feeling," Legge both "mind" and "feeling," and Bloom "a mind that *feels* pity and compassion" (2009, p. 35; emphasis added).

I argued in §2.6 that, to the extent that the "hearts" are feelings, they are complex social feelings(-becoming-thinkings) that involve an affective-becoming-cognitive assessment of other people's social status, attitude, and physical situation or activity. At the very simplest level of social functioning:

- one's heart goes out to the child in danger of falling into a well (2A6) *because* one determines that the child is in danger and helpless before the danger;

- one feels deferential or modestly compliant toward a person *because* one determines that s/he is of higher status;

- one feels shame *because* one determines that others either do already or will or may soon disapprove of something one has done; and

- our sense of right and wrong is saturated in the approval and disapproval of others (hence James Legge's and Bryan W.

Van Norden's translation of *shìfēi* 是非 "right and wrong" as "approval and disapproval," and cf. Shun [1997, p. 71; Wade-Giles romanizations pinyinized]: "*shì* and *fēi* are more than just knowing what is proper or improper; they also involve approving of what is proper and disapproving of what is improper").

The cognitive processes involved in deciding that the child is in danger—too close to the edge of the well for safety, too young and inexperienced to appreciate the danger, too uncoordinated to move safely away from the edge—are fast, of course, almost instantaneous, which might make one want to conclude that they aren't cognitive at all, that they are "instinctual" (whatever that might mean). All the rapidity of that reaction means, however, is that the cognitive processes have been habitualized, automatized, and so pushed down into the "unconscious," or what Freud would call the "preconscious," but might in this case also be called the "postconscious." Mencius specifically rules out other kinds of cost-benefit analysis: we do not react instantaneously ("instinctually") to save the child because we hope to benefit from the parents' gratitude, or because we want to be praised for our heroism, or because the child's cries are unpleasant; we simply *read* the child's inability to save itself, *feel* its imminent jeopardy, and so feel an inclination to rush to save it as if we ourselves were the ones in danger. But still, that impulse has to be based on a cognitive assessment at least of the child's helplessness and vulnerability, and possibly also of the "wrongness" (contrary-to-the-natural-order-of-things-ness) of a child's accidental death. It is, we might say, a cognitive-becoming-affective-becoming-conative-becoming-kinesthetic impulse: the habitualized and automatized cognitive assessment of the situation activates the (affective) heart of compassion, which (conatively) launches us into (kinesthetic) action, either in the physical world (we rush to save the child) or in our imaginations (we simply feel the impulse to save the child but for whatever reason are unable to act on it).

Similarly, the Western conception of deference, reverence, respectful behavior, modesty, compliance, etc.—the various renditions of *círàng zhī xīn* 辭讓之心 and *gōngjìng zhī xīn* 恭敬之心—as purely cognitive, based on status differentials (I am of lower status than that person, so I should act deferentially, reverently, respectfully, modestly, etc. around him or her), may in many cases set us at odds with social practice. Certainly with people we know well—our family members, neighbors, coworkers—our deferential behavior tends to be less a conscious decision based on a cognitive analysis of the relationship and more like the instantaneous heartfelt response that

Mencius describes in the person who sees a small child crawling toward the edge of a well. We don't consciously adjust our attitudes, speech, and other behavior when we enter the presence of a parent or other older relative or neighbor, or our boss at work: we just adjust. But again, that simply suggests that the cognitive assessment has "gone underground," into affectivized habit: we *feel* the changed relationship context rather than analyzing and appraising it consciously, and respond to it in the way that feels right. As Mencius says (7A1), we follow our inclinations. That feeling of situational/relational "rightness" is in fact more or less what Mencius and the Confucian tradition call *yì* 義—though that is technically not the "shoot" that grows out of the heart of deference (see §3.9), and though there are some important nuances that we will need to account for below (§4.5). In particular, there is the fact that the *yì* 義 feeling of rightness that guides the exemplary person to adjust "properly" or "appropriately" to situations and relationships is conditioned not by *mìng* 命 "conditions" in general, nor by (merely) the haecceity of any given situation or relationship of which the subject happens to be a part, but by the special exemplary *mìng* 命 "conditions" that condition the Confucian Way, and condition also the exemplary person who pursues it.

Linking the *shìfēi zhī xīn* 是非之心, which most translators (Collie, Dobson, Lau, Zhao et al., Hinton, Bloom) render "the heart (feeling/sense/mind) of right and wrong," with the heart of shame is even more telling in an East-West contrastive light: right and wrong in the West tend to be checklisted items, codified instructions for behavior, including thought and speech; for Mencius the difference is something one *feels*, and feels specifically, in Legge's and Van Norden's translations, as the approval or disapproval of others, which are then internalized as the feelings of self-approval/self-esteem and shame/self-reproach (for discussion, see §4.10). But again, the largely affective nature of this response does not mean that it is some kind of atavistic "instinct" or random subjective feeling; it is an affectivized habit originally derived from a cognitive learning process, and thus in a sense a thinking-becoming-feeling impulse (which can also be *brought* into consciousness, making it thinking-becoming-feeling-becoming-thinking).[5] Shame is a formative social feeling in the Confucian tradition; in the *Zhongyong* 中庸 20 Confucius famously says that *zhī chǐ jìnhū yǒng* 知恥近乎勇, to know shame is to be close to bravery, and clearly Mencius confirms that linkage by making the heart of shame the key to *yì* 義 "rightness."

The observation that shame is a *social* feeling reminds us that in fact none of the four hearts is primarily individualized. All four are relational, social in the most insistent sense, collectivized affective-becoming-conative-becoming-cognitive pressures or inclinations that may be found at any given moment in this or that individual only because they are constantly cycling *through* the individual members of any group. The most striking example of this is *shìfēi zhī xīn* 是非之心, which is literally "the heart of is/isn't" but is translated by Lau as "the heart of right and wrong" and by Legge and Van Norden as "the feeling of approval and disapproval": it is the circulatory or reticulatory "heart" of social regulation, experienced affectively-becoming-conatively as a pressure to conform to group norms, morally as a behavioral code, ontologically as reality versus unreality. The agent or grammatical subject of this moral construction of reality, as Martin Heidegger (1927/2001) would say, is "one," *das Man*, in the collectivized sense of "what one does" and "what one does not do": "one knows" what "one does" and either does act that way or deviates from it with a great deal of uneasiness before and during, and a feeling of shame (or uneasy resistance to shame) after, because "one" is the collectivized self, the group as it is experienced phenomenologically by each member. Shame is this collectivized *one's* self-punishment for deviation from group norms, and as such an extremely powerful reminder of the need to be aware of, and ideally to submit to, group guidance.

In that sense, obviously, the heart of deference is the group heart that regulates social behavior across status differentials, making deference simply *what one does* around people of higher social status. If one doesn't, again, one activates the group heart of shame, which is to say, feels shame, feels ashamed. That feeling serves as a collectivized reminder to behave more normatively (deferentially) next time.

The circulatory collectivization of the four hearts certainly means that they are not private, subjective fantasies or idiosyncrasies; but does that collectivization, especially in the light of Mencius's claim that without the heart of compassion one is not human (2A6), rule out the possibility that we are born with them? If the four hearts are *shared* by a culture, does that mean they are necessarily *created* by that culture?

The second passage in which Mencius lists the four hearts (6A6) is also the passage in which he makes his clearest pronouncement on the source of human inclinations toward the ethical life: the discussion of Gaozi's argument that people are not *born* good or evil but can be *made* good or evil (6A6). There Gongduzi reports what Gaozi says, and Mencius replies, in a literal translation at first, with the problematic terms left untranslated: "Thus if one's *qíng* 情, then can do good, this is called good. If one does not-good, not the fault of *cái* 才."

cái 才, to begin with the easy one, is "ability," "talent," but also "situation." *qíng* 情 is more complex, and Shun (1997, pp. 183–87, 212–16) devotes several pages to an exploration of its shifting semantic linkages with *xing* 性: while both refer to "what a thing or person is like" as well as sex and sexuality (especially the biological differences, which are not clearly demarcated even in modern Chinese from the cultural gender differences), and in fact seem to be used almost interchangeably by Mencius and other early Confucian writers, each has slightly divergent connotations.

qing 4情	*xing* 性
characteristic tendencies that are hard to change	characteristic tendencies that are vulnerable to environmental influences (can be improved or damaged)
the facts of a situation, what is genuinely true, as opposed to the gossip; but also something that can be passed around verbally or concealed	no connection with the distinction between "facts/authenticity" and gossip
typically true of a class or type because true of each member of that class	may vary in individual members of the same class or type
the emotions and desires, such as the love of life and fear of death	no connection with the emotions

The key point to note there is that nothing in the semantics of either term makes the "characteristic tendencies" *innate*. This fact is in sharp contradistinction with the majority of both Chinese commentators and English translators, who have tended to understand this passage, and Mencius's ethics in general, as organized around characteristic tendencies that humans are born with (all numbering and bolding added):

> Mencius replied, if you observe the [1a] **natural dispositions**, you may see that they are virtuous: hence, I say, that [1b] **nature** is virtuous. If men practise vice, it is not the fault of their [2] **natural powers**. (Collie, 1828, p. 144)

> 5. Mencius said, 'From the [1a] **feelings proper to it, it is constituted** for the practice of what is good. This is what I mean in saying that [1b] ***the nature*** is good.

6. 'If men do what is not good, the blame cannot be imputed to their [2] **natural powers**.' (Legge, 1861/1970, p. 402; italics Legge's)

Mencius said, "It is of the [1] **essence of man's nature** that he do good. That is what I mean by good. If a man does what is evil he is guilty of the sin of denying his [2] **natural endowment**." (Dobson, 1963, p. 113)

Mencius said, "Man is in his [1a] **essence** capable of becoming good. That is why I say [1b] **human nature** is good. That man should become evil is not a question of his [2] **essence**." (Zhao et al., 1993, p. 415)

"As far as [1] **what is genuinely in him** is concerned, a man is capable of becoming good," said Mencius. "That is what I mean by good. As for his becoming bad, that is not the fault of his [2] **native endowment**." (Lau, 1970/2003, p. 247)

"We are, [1] **by constitution**, capable of being good," replied Mencius. "That's what I mean by good. If someone's evil, it can't be blamed on [2] **inborn capacities**." (Hinton, 1998, p. 202)

Mencius responded, "Our [1a] **natural tendency** is to do good. This is what I mean by its [i.e., [1b] **the nature's**] being good. Doing what is not good is not the fault of our [2] **natural disposition**." (Gardner, 2007, p. 88)

Mengzi said, "As for [1a] **what they are inherently**, they can become good. This is what I mean by calling their [1b] **natures** good. [*Many interpreters follow Zhu Xi in translating the first part of this verse, "Their innate emotions can only be good." Zhu Xi means the "hearts" referred to later in the chapter.*] As for their becoming not good, this is not the fault of their [2] **potential**." (Van Norden, 2008, p. 149; gloss and italics Van Norden's)

Mencius said, "One's [1a] **natural tendencies** enable one to do good; this is what I mean by [1b] **human nature** being good. When one does what is not good, it is not the fault of one's [2] **native capacities**." (Bloom, 2009, p. 124)

The only translator in that group to build the *feelings* associated with *qíng* 情 into his translation, obviously, is Legge; Van Norden quotes/translates Zhu Xi's gloss of *qíng* 情 as "*innate emotions*," with its typical Zhuian insistence on the innateness of the emotional "nature" Mencius is talking about, but then neglects to build those emotions into his translation of *qíng* 情. That translation, "what they are inherently," like Lau's "what is genuinely in him" and Legge's "the feelings *proper* to it," seems to be an attempt to get at the "genuine state of affairs" associated in Chinese with *qíng* 情, without necessarily taking a stand on the innate or learned origins of that state; indeed Van Norden here again hints strongly at an Aristotelian entelechial construction of "human nature" by rendering *cái* 才 as "potential." And certainly the "tendencies" that appear in Gardner and Bloom would seem to adumbrate both the core semantics of *qíng* 情 and the entelechial thinking that Van Norden hears behind *cái* 才.

The most insistently repeated term in those translations, however, is "nature," both in its substantive ("essence of man's nature" in Dobson and "the nature's" in Gardner's interpolated gloss) and adjectival forms ("natural dispositions" as both 1 in Collie and 2 in Gardner, "natural powers," "natural tendencies," and "natural endowment"). We also have "native," which I take to be roughly synonymous with "innate" (and etymologically tied to "nature"), in our "native endowment" in Lau and "native capacities" in Bloom. And it is striking that in 1b, just in case we didn't understand in 1a that Mencius is talking about **human nature**, Collie, Legge, Zhao et al., Gardner, Van Norden, and Bloom all add "nature" to *suǒwèi shàn yě* 所謂善也 "this is called good."

Now the English noun "nature" can be used loosely to mean "the way a thing is," whether that way is a collection of conditioned or innate characteristics or some mixture of the two. But the adjectives "natural" and "native" would appear to entail what "innate" and "inborn" make explicit: that the person with those "dispositions," "powers," "tendencies," "capacities," or "endowments" was born with them, and that they are therefore immutable. And "human nature" in English does seem to entail some form of biological essentialism. It does, therefore, seem a bit excessive that where Mencius uses terms that could be read as indicating the way humans are due either to biological hardwiring or to social conditioning, his translators mostly attempt to foreclose on a sociocultural etiology for "human nature."

The difficulty these translators have in rendering the subtlety of Mencius's claims here, I suggest, is not simply a matter of their feeling an ideological pressure to essentialize human nature as a stable inborn given.[6] It is also that Mencius is mapping out a tricky middle ground between

Gaozi's "it's all nurture" and the obvious binary opposite to that notion, "it's all nature." If Mencius believes that Gaozi is wrong about people being born *without* any innate goodness or evil, surely that means that Mencius believes that people are born *with* innate goodness? It doesn't, necessarily; other indications in the *MZ* suggest that the Mencian truth lies somewhere in between those two dualized extremes. Just what that between is, however, is hard to say—partly because Mencius himself doesn't spell it out.

One workable middle-ground solution, obviously, would be the Aristotelian one Van Norden hints at: treat goodness not as a *trait* or *endowment* that humans are born with, but as a *potential*. If humans are born with anything genuinely or inherently related to goodness, in other words, it is not a positive *thing* so much as it is an entelechy, a likely (but idealized) trajectory for future development. Because for Aristotle things and creatures do not necessarily actualize their potentials, and because nothing is actual until it is actualized, goodness could only be considered an "essence" (Dobson, Zhao et al.) in a radically antiessentializing (perhaps existentialist) sense: as something that is achieved, if ever, only well after birth. By the same token, "Our natural *tendency* is to do good" (Gardner, Bloom) could be construed as a restatement of "Our entelechy is to do good" only if we treat "natural" not as biological but as something like "part of what it means to be human" and "tendency" as the entelechy itself—a tendency that is actualized, if at all, over the course of a lifetime, and not every time we make a decision. "Powers," too (Collie, Legge), might be read etymologically as referring to potentials (the word is after all derived from the Latin for "power") rather than positive characteristics. "Capacities" (Hinton, Bloom), a translation of *kěyǐ* 可以 "can, is able to," could be read the same way, as referring to an anticipatory framing of what we *should in theory someday* be able to do, rather than, once again, as positive characteristics.

Recalling that *cái* 才 "ability" can also be a situation, we might want to suggest that in speaking of *qíng* 情 "the emotional facts" and *cái* 才 "ability" Mencius *situates* the ability to do good (*wéi shàn* 為善) in emotional maturity, emotional moral readiness—what he calls the four hearts—and that those interactive group affects work so effectively to "humanize" group members (subjectify them as fully enculturated ethical human beings) that their functioning comes to seem like "human nature." But that still doesn't answer the question of how that situatedness emerges out of *xīn* 心, and what the status of *xīn* 心 is at birth. How is it, exactly, that all humans have the four hearts? Shun (1997, p. 213) also notes that there is a problem with Mencius's formulation, in that if he means only the *ability* to be good, there is no reason to suspect that that ability would exclude the ability to be bad, and thus that there is no real difference between his position and Gaozi's (告子) argument that no one is born good or bad but can be made good or bad. Presumably for Mencius the emergence of *cái* 才 out of *xīn* 心 would have to be *guided* in some way for this key point in his philosophy to work; but guided how? To begin to answer that, we need to take a closer look at *tiān* 天 and *mìng* 命.

4.5 Mencius: "External" Forces (*tiān* 天) and Conditions (*mìng* 命)

In Chinese-English dictionaries, *tiān* 天 is translated as "heaven" or "the sky"; *mìng* 命 in some contexts is "fate" or "destiny," in other contexts "decree" or "order" or "command." The Daoist and Confucian traditions have tended to use the two terms rather differently, the Daoist usage leaning more toward the supernatural, the Confucian more toward the secular; hence the problems inherent in translating *tiān* 天 in a Confucian text even as "heaven," let alone as "Heaven." As Shun (1997, p. 78) points out, Mencius tends to use *tiān* 天 much as Confucius does in the *Analects*, to account for "things which one regards as important but over which one has little control, and hence things with regard to which one feels a sense of dependence on some higher authority." Mencius uses *mìng* 命 in very similar ways, in fact; the difference between them, Shun (ibid., p. 76) notes, is "probably that the former emphasizes the source of such things and the latter the outcome." Hence Behuniak's (2005, p. 111) suggestion that *tiān* 天 be translated as "forces" and *mìng* 命 as "conditions": "Judging by the *Dispositions Arise from Conditions* document, 'conditions' denote any phenomena encountered in the course of emerging in formative transaction with the world—a broad notion, indeed. Confucians defer to the causal efficacy of the innumerable formative conditions that shape experience." Or, for that matter, to "the causal efficacy of the innumerable *forces* that shape experience": in Confucian thinking, the two concepts are closely related, specifically as "external" influences on human behavior, forces and conditions that shape experience from outside the nexus of desire, will, intention, planning, and so on that the individual may identify phenomenologically as her or his own.

Now, as Behuniak notes, this concept of "externality" obviously covers a lot of territory:

- It could mean something like what we would call "biology," or what Mencius is sometimes taken to mean by *shēng* 生 ("life," "birth," "to be born," "to give birth").

- It could mean something not only transhuman but transnatural, like "Heaven" (as Collie and Legge translate *tiān* 天), or just "God," or, as *mìng* 命 is sometimes translated, "fate" (one of the Greek Moirai).

- It could cover entirely random accidents, and be translated "chance" (the Greek goddess Tukhē).

- Or—and this is the direction I will be pursuing—*tiān* 天 and *mìng* 命 could, as Behuniak (ibid.) insists, could be taken to "retain the transactional aspect of the 'social' across the range of their extended meanings."

It is presumably in this last sense, in fact, the social, that Mencius refers to *tiān zhī dào* 天之道 (4A12, 7B24), literally "the Way of *tiān*." The Confucian Way, the collection of ethical practices that organize the good life, could not possibly be shaped by *tiān* 天 as a supernatural force (there is none such in Confucian thought), or as a purely nonvitalistic biological force (for how could blind mechanical biology in the Western sense generate an ethical Way?), let alone as chance or accident; the only kind of transindividual force that could conceivably shape an ethical pathway or ideal would have to be a social force. It is presumably also in this social sense that Mencius describes *rén* 仁 (fellow-feeling) as *tiān zhī zūn* 天之尊 (2A7, 6A16), literally "*tiān*'s honors" or "*tiān*'s ranks," usually interpreted to mean "the ethical attributes" (Shun, 1997, p. 169). And it seems beyond question that it is the social organization of *tiān* 天 that Mencius means in saying that *tiān* 天 shapes *xīn* 心 (6A15) and its "abilities" (*cái* 才, 6A7), and that the best way to "get the most" (*jìn* 盡) out of one's *xīn* 心 is to know/follow one's own inclinations (*xìng* 性), and to know/follow one's own inclinations is to know/serve *tiān* 天 (see Shun, ibid., p. 78).

In other words, *tiān* 天 is the word Mencius uses to describe the sociocultural forces that shape:

[a] each individual's feeling-becoming-thinking (*xīn* 心);

[b] that feeling-becoming-thinking's inclinations or predispositions (*xìng* 性) and abilities (*cái* 才);

[c] the individual's willingness to follow those inclinations and cultivate those abilities; and

[d] the ethical Way (*dào* 道) constituted by the willingness of large numbers of such individuals to follow their *tiān*-derived inclinations and cultivate their *tiān*-derived abilities.

If those forces are indeed sociocultural, obviously, the (a-d) things shaped by them cannot possibly be innate. Mencius never *says* they are sociocultural forces; they are just *tiān* 天. But if they are neither supernatural nor biological, and cannot possibly be random, sociocultural is really all they *can* be.

The difficulty commentators run into when they apply this exclusionary logic, however, is that Mencius also seems to set the ethical Way (*dào* 道) up as somehow transsocial, larger or greater than just some set of group norms—indeed perhaps even universal. As Shun (1997, p. 85) notes, "Since *yì* 義 is determined by standards that do not necessarily coincide with ordinary social standards, *yì* 義 does not originate in prevailing social opinion[; rather,] there is evidence that Mencius regarded *yì* 義 as in some sense deriving from the heart/mind (*xīn* 心)" (all quotations from Shun in this paragraph have replaced his Wade-Giles romanizations with pinyin and Chinese characters). This contrast obviously makes it seem as if *xīn* 心 is somehow *not* shaped by sociocultural forces. Or again: "Passages 7A:1 and 7A:2 concern one's cultivating oneself so that one follows what is proper and willingly accepts unfavorable conditions of life that are not within one's control or are of such a nature that altering them requires improper conduct. This implies that one should devote effort to ethical pursuits and not worry about external conditions of life" (ibid., p. 83)—but it would seem that the *xīn* 心 that teaches one to pursue ethical ends (and thus the Way (*dào* 道)) and the unfavorable external conditions (*mìng* 命) that often thwart those ends are both from *tiān* 天. And again: "Passage 7A:9 enjoins one to be contented 'whether appreciated by others or not' and 'not to abandon *yì* 義 in adversity or to depart from the Way in success'" (ibid., p. 76). Adversity and success (and "whether appreciated by others or not" as signs of success and adversity, respectively) are those same external conditions, which means that Mencius is adjoining people to follow their *tiān*-derived inclinations and cultivate their *tiān*-derived abilities (viz., the Confucian Way) regardless of *tiān*-derived conditions (*mìng* 命).

Given these tensions or flatout contradictions between or among impulses attributed to *tiān* 天, therefore, it would seem essential not to take those forces as in any way monotheistically or otherwise uniformly willed, "providentially" directed: the concept simply means *whatever* forces one senses or projects that are beyond one's control, including for early Chinese thinkers the supernatural, the biological, the social, and the random, and for Confucian thinkers those minus the supernatural. For that matter, the biological and the social forces that impinge on one's activities may themselves seem either organized or random; either way, they are still *tiān* 天. Hence the possibility that *tiān* 天 is the source both of [1] ecological conditions (*mìng* 命) like the seasons, other climate and weather patterns, the proximity of a large city with wood-choppers and cows, and so on (to use the Ox Mountain example from 6A8), or people's appreciation for or indifference or hostility to one's actions, *and* of [2] (a) one's feeling-becoming-thinking, (b) the ethical inclinations and abilities arising out of (a), (c) one's inclination to pursue (b), and (d) the Confucian Way arising out of (c). As Shun makes clear, Mencius enjoins us to cling to (2) in the face of (1)—even though *tiān* 天 is manifestly the source of both, which is to say, both (1) and (2) are beyond one's control.

Does this mean that one's *decision* or *determination* to pursue the Way is beyond one's control? Or that one's *ability* to pursue the Way is beyond one's control? In a sense, yes. Just as (c) the inclination to pursue the Way is from *tiān* 天, so too is the consolidation of that inclination into a decision or determination or ability from *tiān* 天. All one can do is *cultivate* that inclination, as a gardener cultivates a plant: not by *making* it grow, not by stretching it like the man from Song (2A2), but by "not helping it grow" (*wù zhù zhǎng* 勿助長), which is to say, by interacting with it encouragingly, creating conducive conditions for its growth. Human beings may be *mostly* passive before *tiān* 天 and *mìng* 命, but in a Mencian purview never entirely.

Implicit in this formulation is also a potential-but-essential distinction within *tiān* 天 between [a] what Shun calls "ordinary social standards" or "prevailing social opinion" ("Since *yì* 義 is determined by standards that do not necessarily coincide with ordinary social standards, *yì* 義 does not originate in prevailing social opinion") and [b] the sociocultural forces that condition human feeling-becoming-thinking to grow toward the pursuit of ethical ends. The fact that both are "social" should not mislead us into concluding either that (a = b) or, since (a) and (b) are obviously at loggerheads, that the sociality of (a) somehow precludes the sociality of (b). The key difference between the two is that (a) is organized specifically around "*ordinary* social standards" and "*prevailing* social opinion," while (b) is organized around *extraordinary* or *exemplary* social standards, around social opinion that prevails only among exemplary persons. Both (a) and (b) seem phenomenologically to be beyond one's control, and are therefore *tiān* 天 (forces) and *mìng* 命 (conditions); but the forces and conditions in each are organized by different social groups, by ordinary people in (a) and extraordinary/exemplary people in (b). As Mencius says in 7A42: "When the world is on the way [*dào* 道], that course inspires the person [*shēn* 身 'body, person, morality']; when the world is off the way [*wúdào* 無道 'without *dào*'], the person [*shēn* 身] aspires for that course. I have never heard of a course inspired by what people [*rén* 人] just happen to be" (translated/quoted by Behuniak, 2005, p. 126).

Let us pause here to note, too, that "I have never heard" in that passage is *wèi wén* 未聞—one of the 82 cases in which Mencius uses the literal ear-based "hearing" sense of *wén* 聞. This explicitly grounds the "truth" Mencius pronounces on the relationship between sociocultural forces and individual inspiration/aspiration in things he has heard, and implicitly also in telling-becoming-hearing-becoming-reputation, which is to say, in icosis: the becoming-persuasive of hearing-and-telling. And as usual, the individual as an ethical entity is indicated with *shēn* 身 "body": a social actor wrapped in skin, or what Kenneth Burke refers to as our biological "apartness." The larger collective social actor that "just happen[s] to be" is *rén* 人, source of *rén* 仁 "fellow-feeling"—and while in this chapter Mencius might be read as suggesting that the *rén* 人 that "just happens to be" is *not* the source of *rén* 仁, a more accurate reading would be that that "ordinary" *rén* 人 is the source of an ordinary *rén* 仁 out of which the Confucian Way calls people to aspire upward toward an exemplary *rén* 仁.

As Shun (1997, p. 147) unpacks the thinking behind 7A15, you're born into a family and grow up loving your parents; gradually you learn to conceptualize that love, and later to extend it to and through other groups and relationships as *rén* 仁. That's all culture, obviously, all nurture, and presumably it's the origin of the compassion that makes you feel distress for the child at the well (2A6), and, in Mencius's myth from 3A5, the disgust you feel at wild animals gnawing at your dead parents that you've tossed in a ditch instead of burying. (If that heart of compassion isn't a cultural achievement, if it's inborn, why was there ever a time when people *didn't* bury their parents?) Mencius does not theorize the opposite of this process of enculturation into "associated humanity" (*rén* 仁), but as we saw in §2.10, severely abusive families may traumatize their children into "dissociated inhumanity" (*bùrén* 不仁), so that they become unfeeling monsters. Because these socialization or enculturation processes occur in early childhood, however, before the child possesses language or the kind of linguistically organized analytical consciousness that could track the historicity of the transformation, the resulting "hearts" and "dispositions" do tend to feel like innate human "nature."

There remains, however, the question of the Aristotelian entelechy: is there nevertheless some *potential* for good that all humans are born with, though many of us, shaped by "ordinary social standards" or "prevailing social opinion," never actualize that potential? Mencius does indeed seem to think so—though again he never quite theorizes it. (I will be postponing a solution to this problem until §4.12.)

4.6 Aristotle: *doxa* as Face

What I'm looking for here in Mencius's terms, then, is an account of how *tiān* 天 and *mìng* 命 work ecotically (as a deep social ecology) to shape the icosis of persuasivity, or becoming-persuasive—and Mencius will not get us there. He seems to assume some such social ecology, even founds his conception of becoming-human on it, but he does not theorize it. Aristotle doesn't exactly theorize it either, in fact; but he uses *doxa* and its derivatives, along with *pistis* and *eikos* and their derivatives, so complexly that the resulting semantic web lends itself to theorization as (dox)icosis. The next step toward that theorization involves a rethinking of *doxa* (and the *mìng* 命 of "whether [one is] appreciated by others or not") as icotic *work*, as a becoming-persuasive social "energizing" (*ergon*) of opinion, or what Erving Goffman (1955/1967) calls "face-work."[7]

Goffman (p. 5) defines face as "the positive social value a person effectively claims for himself by the line others assume he has taken during a particular contact." If *doxa* is face as a positive social *value*, which may be "effectively" (behaviorally) claimed by the social actor or assigned by the others in the group, surely there is no logical fusion or confusion of subject and object—any more than there is logical fusion or confusion when the value of monetary currency is determined collectively. Goffman's primary metaphor for face is in fact economic: to "gain face" is to raise the value of the line or character or personality-image one has been projecting, so that one's "stock goes up"; to "lose face" is to experience a drop in the value of that line, so that one's "stock goes down."

"Loss of face," in fact, works as an approximate translation of Aristotle's *adoxia* "ill-repute, disgrace," which Kennedy translates as "loss of reputation." David Konstan (2007, p. 87) seems to translate *adoxia* precisely thus in "If anger was a response to a loss of face or *doxa* as the result of an affront, then *praotēs* [which he translates as 'satisfaction'] as an emotion was elicited by behaviour that enhanced public respect and esteem"—there "face" and "public respect and esteem" are both translations of *doxa*, and it is at least arguable that by "loss of face" Konstan means *adoxia*. It is only an approximate translation, however: *adoxia* is typically thought of as more static than the dynamic (kinetic) "loss of face," which may be ephemeral, situational, something that will have no lasting deleterious effect on the social actor's reputation. The relationship between face and reputation will vary culturally, of course, some cultures being notoriously absolute about face—lose it once in passing and your reputation is destroyed forever, or for a very long period of time—while others are more forgiving, allowing social actors to lose face briefly without suffering a more lasting loss of reputation. In any case, thinking *doxa* as face encourages us to explore the social dynamism of Aristotle's conception (and by extension Mencius's *wén* 聞 as well), the ways in which reputation does not so much exist in some sort of pure ontological state but rather is formed and transformed through circulatory affective judgments in changing social situations. (By the same token, "gain of face" might serve as a more dynamic or kinetic English translation of *eudoxia* than the standard "good reputation.")

The "line" by reference to which the social actor gains or loses face is for Goffman (1955/1967, p. 5) "a pattern of verbal and nonverbal acts by which he expresses his view of the situation and through this his evaluation of the participants, especially himself." A line might be defined in redynamized Aristotelian terms as situational *ēthos* or character: a more or less stable, but only situationally or contextually and therefore temporarily stabilized, presentation of self that serves as a kind of baseline reference point for the group in assigning relative social value to the actor's performance. If the line or situational *ēthos* one is projecting in a given encounter is solemn, for example, as at a funeral, it will be important not to let one's outward presentation of that character shift even momentarily into mirth. A single mirthful gesture or facial expression or phrase would break the character's "line" in that encounter—would be "out of character."

Goffman situates face-as-value, in other words, in a kind of social exchange where all social actors, like economic agents in a currency exchange, are constantly both monitoring the value of their own and others' face *and* raising or lowering other actors' face-value with respect to their own. An individual's own face, in other words, isn't something s/he can control; it is neither "subject" nor "object"; it is circulated through the entire social economy. As the dynamic social environment in which we all live, it is *míng* 命; as an active social force regulating our behavior, it is *tiān* 天. As Goffman (1955/1967, p. 10) puts it, "while [an actor's] social face can be his most personal possession and the center of his security and pleasure, it is only on loan to him from society; it will be withdrawn unless he conducts himself in a way that is worthy of it." If the culture values altruism, for example, it becomes virtually impossible to gain face through the loss of another person's face; indeed, one gains face by "giving" others face.

The consequences of understanding *doxa* as face can be illustrated in this passage from *TR* 1.7:

> And things related to truth [*ta pros alētheian*] [are greater] than things related to opinion [*tōn pros doxan*]. The definition of *related to opinion* is what a person would not choose if he were going to escape notice [*ho lanthanein*]. As a result, to get a benefit [*eu paskhein*] would seem [*doxeien*] to be more [often] chosen than to do good; for a person will cho[o]se the former even if it escapes [others'] notice [*lanthanei*], but it is not the general view [*ou dokei*] that one would choose to do good secretly [*lanthanōn*]." (1.7.36, 1365a39–1365b1; Kennedy, 1991/2007, p. 74)

The obvious Platonic/philosophical preference for truth over opinion that Aristotle expresses here has fed tidy moral binarizations of his take on the two: truth/*alētheia* good, opinion/*doxa* bad. But note that *doxa* functions in that passage as both the lowly "things related to opinion" (*tōn pros doxan*) that are of less value than "things related to truth" (*ta pros alētheian*) and as the optative "seeming" (*doxeien*) that Aristotle theorizes here *as* truth. In fact, the two appearances in the passage of the verb *dokeō* (to think, suppose, imagine, expect, but in the impersonal third-person *dokei* usually translated as "to seem")—*ou dokei* ("not the general view," lit. "not seems") and *doxeien* ("would seem" or "might seem")—would seem to represent a sliding from seeming-as-opinion in the direction of seeming-as-truth. Both seemings, to be sure, are Aristotle's philosophical summaries of how people act, both what they do (they want to "suffer good," have good things come to them, more than to do good) and what they say or believe (they don't believe that anyone does good in secret). But George Kennedy hears in *ou dokei* the connotations of "public opinion" or "the general view," how most people see things; in "to get a benefit would seem to be more chosen than to do good," the seeming quietly sets up Aristotle's own pronouncement of a general truth. Could it be that *dokei* (positive seeming) is how things seem to the philosopher, while *ou dokei* (negative seeming) is how things (don't) seem to the masses?

If we read *dokeō* as the verb form of *doxa*-as-face, *doxa*-as-social-value, then the seemings become valuings, and what Aristotle is theorizing is not a set of opinions but an economy of social value. In that light, his opening salvo, "*kai ta pros alētheian tōn pros doxan*"—truthy things are better than opiniony things—should be read not as an atavistic binarizing Platonism, but rather as an attention to the entelechy, an entelechial sliding from opinion-as-value to truth-as-value. (More on *dokeō* in §4.13, where we'll also be considering more closely the possibility that the entelechial movement from *tōn pros doxan* to *ta pros alētheian* is not Aristotle's own but the Greek community's.)[8]

Perhaps, then, *ta pros doxan* are to be valued less highly than *ta pros alētheian* because *ta pros doxan* are the vague quasi-bodily and therefore largely unconscious *feelings* of the masses; but as Aristotle himself, the philosopher, picks up that seeming and theorizes it, he maps analytical reason onto it, gives it new cognitive definition, so that what seems likely *to him* looks increasingly like truth. But this also suggests that *doxa* does not lie around passively waiting to be picked up and thought about by the philosopher, but rather, as I suggested in §4.2, itself moves entelechially from feeling toward thinking—or rather "we," the group, the crowd, the culture, tend to push *doxa* from inchoate and inarticulate felt orientations toward greater conscious understanding. As *doxa*-as-feeling becomes *doxa*-as-thinking, we begin to push it—or, since we are not aware of doing so, it as *tiān* 天 begins to push us—vitalistically toward a philosophical perception or construction of truth.

4.7 Aristotle/Mencius: The *energeia doxēs* and the *oligōria doxēs, qīng* 輕 and *zūn* 尊

Thinking about *doxa/dokeō* as face, as a circulatory social value, as the circulation of a felt-becoming-thought judgment, also casts a new light on Aristotle's phrase *energeia doxēs* (*TR* 2.2.3., 1378b10–13): "Belittling [*oligōria*] is an actualization of opinion [*energeia doxēs*] about what seems worthless (we think both good and bad things worth serious attention, also things that contributed to them [*kai ta sunteinonta pros auta*], but whatever amounts to little or nothing we suppose worthless)" (Kennedy, 1991/2007, p. 116). We see there the entelechial *mìng* 命 "conditions" (*ta sunteinonta*) that we tend to organize axiomatically, or value, in this case by assigning a low value to them; we see also the "seeming" (here not *dokeō* but *phainomenon*) and the "supposing" (*oiō*) that contribute icotically to the persuasivity of a valuing. But what is an "actualization of opinion," exactly?

One well-established interpretive strategy makes the actualization of opinion no more mysterious than its verbal or behavioral *expression*. Lane Cooper (1932, p. 93), for example, has "an active display of opinion": if *doxa* is opinion, and opinion is propositional belief, then the *energeia doxēs* is simply the uttering of the opinion aloud. And if we take *energeia* and *entelekheia* to be roughly synonymous, this would imply that the verbal utterance or behavioral enactment of an opinion is the actualization of that opinion's potential. As George Kennedy puts it in a footnote: "That is, by word or deed one person 'puts down' another as of no account, and what was only a possible opinion is given actual expression" (1991/2007, p. 116n9). So also Cope (1877, 2, p. 15): "The mere opinion of the worthlessness of so and so, has now . . . assumed the form of an active or actual expression of the contempt by the outward token of 'slight regard.'" And why not? This is, after all, more or less the dumbed-down Cartesian model of communication that we find in, say, middle-school English classes: the spoken or written sentence (the *res extensa*) as the expression of a thought (born in, and reigning emblem of, the *res cogitans*). What else could there be to it?

One fairly obvious *energeia* or "at-work energy" that we might want to add to a communicative model of this sort in a study of rhetoric, in fact, might be persuasion—the *rhetorical* actualization of an opinion that is not yet being used to persuade anyone of anything. But if the actualization of opinion is not merely expression or display but persuasion, what exactly is being actualized? What is the power or potential lying dormant in derogatory opinions that is actualized in *oligōria*? What, to put it etymologically, is the in-work or at-work that has to be done in order to bring that power or potential to persuasive actuality?

If *doxa* is not opinion-as-propositional-thought but face, social value assigned collectively to situated behavior, the in-work that is done in energizing it is *valuing* (evaluating, valencing, assessing, judging)—as in fact the English translations "slighting" and "belittling" suggest. Assigning someone a lower (or for that matter higher) value than s/he expects is work, in-working, *energeia*, a critical social working whose product is face. It is work that circulates through a group, often preconsciously, affectively; and as it circulates, it tends to bring increased order, increased structure, to the group's understandings. Aristotle calls this entelechial process *ta sunteinonta*, things that are "stretching together" or "drawing tight" or "bracing up"; J. H. Freese translates the movement implied in the plural noun as "or tend to become so" (1926, p. 175), suggesting the "natural tendencies" we found earlier in English translators' conception of *qíng* 情 (§4.4). Because we are typically not aware of participating in this entelechial process, and no individual can control it, *ta sunteinonta* seem like the social conditions (*mìng* 命) of our living-together, or like the social force (*tiān* 天) regulating those conditions; but they are also an interactivity in which we play an active if mostly preconscious part.

As the group works to enact (energize) the stretching-together of things, a consensus or collective judgment takes shape and imposes meaning and structure on the world: this is worthwhile, that is worthless; this is good, that is bad. If the *energeia doxēs* is also the *entelekheia doxēs*, that actualization is not so much the simple verbal or behavioral expression of opinion as its energization/organization as binary social valuations, good versus bad, praise versus blame, enlargement versus disparagement. (Does Kennedy, with his theory of rhetoric as energy [see §3.2], really not want to recognize in the *energeia doxēs* the hint of energy being expended, the sense that work is being done and some form of group energy is being channeled into collective speech acts like *oligōria*? Is belittling really for him just the giving to "a possible opinion" an "actual expression"?)

Another passage that explicitly links *doxa* with *oligōria* describes a person who is "shameless through contempt of public opinion [*ho d' anaiskhuntos di' oligōrian doxēs*]" (*TR* 1.10.4., 1368b23; Kennedy, 1991/2007, p. 88). The interesting question there is, if *oligōria* is small concern and *doxa* is propositional belief—if they are both more or less abstract mental constructs—what power could they possibly have over an emotion like shame, or over a maverick resistance to socio-emotional (shaming) group pressure like shamelessness? George Kennedy hears more than a mere paucity of concern in *oligōria* here, and renders it "contempt," itself an emotion, though not one that Aristotle theorizes as a separate emotion; it appears in his discussion of anger in *TR* 2.2 as one of the three classes of *oligōria*: "and there are three species of belittling: contempt [*kataphronēsis*], spite [*epēreasmos*], and insult [*hubris*]; for one who shows contempt belittles [*ho te gar kataphronōn oligōrei*] (people have contempt for those things that they think are of no account, and they belittle things of no account)" (2.2.3–4, 1378b13; Kennedy, ibid., pp. 116–17). In translating *oligōria* as "contempt" in *TR* 1.10, then, Kennedy is reducing it to one of its component cases. But note that *kataphroneō* is to *show* contempt, to behave contemptuously, to express the emotion of contempt outwardly; *kataphronēsis* is not so much the emotion itself as its outward expression. (*Phroneō* is "to have an attitude"; *kataphroneō* is morphologically "to have an attitude downward," suggesting the emotion or attitude itself, or at least the having of it. Attic Greek usage, though, tends to associate the verb and the noun with outward behavior, not necessarily spoken.) If cataphronetic *oligōria* is the *energeia doxēs* about what seems worthless, and finding a thing worthless is contempt, then contempt *is* the *doxa* that is reworked or actualized as (this particular form of) *oligōria*.

Unsurprisingly, given the importance in most cultures of honoring and dishonoring, valuing and devaluing, praising and slighting, Mencius too writes of a similar tension (3B4):

How is it that you give honour [*zūn* 尊] to the carpenter and carriage-wright, and slight [*qīng* 輕] him who practises benevolence and righteousness? (Legge, 1861/1970, p. 270)

How is it that you respect [*zūn* 尊] carpenters and wheelwrights, yet regard lightly [*qīng* 輕] those who practice benevolence and righteousness? (Van Norden, 2008, p. 80)

Why is it that you will honor [*zūn* 尊] the woodworker and the carriage maker and disparage [*qīng* 輕] one who practices humaneness and rightness? (Bloom, 2009, p. 64)[9]

We have seen *zūn* 尊 before, in §4.5, where Mencius described *rén* 仁 as *tiān zhī zūn* 天之尊 (2A7, 6A16), literally "*tiān*'s honor"; the idea is that human honor consists of praise and flattery and gives the honoree a pleasant but ultimately empty feeling, but "heaven's" honor consists of fellow-feeling, a true affective reward that also perpetuates itself in positive (in fact utopian) ways. Mencius's inclination to associate this latter (obviously equally social) honor with the vague forces he calls *tiān* 天, without theorizing the icotic gradations by which human honor is escalated to "heavenly" honor, is perhaps the strongest reason for his decreasing usefulness as we move toward a theorization of doxicosis. To put that differently: in the terms I am developing here, both *tiān zhī zūn* 天之尊 "heaven's honor" and *rén zhī zūn* 人之尊 "people's honor" are social ecologies, ecoses-becoming-icoses, and specifically becoming-icoses that are themselves interrelated icotically in an ordinary-becoming-exemplary ecology, an intensification or escalation of ethecosis from ordinary valuing to extraordinary valuing; but Mencius wants to dualize them, to imagine a vast differential gulf between them, creating conditions within which it comes to seem natural to his English translators to treat "heaven's honors" as somehow akin to the shinier crowns the blessed will wear in a Christian heaven.

qīng 輕, which appears 13 times in the *MZ*, adjectivally can mean "unimportant" or "frivolous" or "small in number"—very close to the "small stuff" etymology of *oligōria*—but also "unstressed" or "neutral," an "unmarked" middle ground between praise and blame, enlargement and belittling. As Van Norden's translation suggests, it is also used as various opposites of "strong," like "gentle," "soft," and "light" (a gentle or soft or light touch or caress, a soft or quiet tone of voice, mild symptoms); a tendency to trust easily (be gullible or naïve: *qīngxìn* 輕信) or enter easily into dangerous or foolish courses of action (be rash or hasty: *qīngshuài* 輕率). In modern Chinese the transitive verbal usage we find in the *MZ* as *qīng* 輕—"despise, scorn, show contempt for"—tends to be specified as *qīngshì* 輕視, literally "to regard as *qīng* 輕."

It is possible, of course, to conceive "finding a thing worthless" in purely abstract mental terms, as a propositional belief: one calmly, rationally, analytically says or thinks, "that thing is worth nothing." It could even be reduced to an arithmetic formula like "value of x = 0," or perhaps to the kind of Zenonic infinitesimal logic (*qīng* 輕 as *vanishingly* small in number) that approaches zero without ever quite reaching it. We note that the opposite movement in Mencius, *zūn* 尊 as honoring, can also be traced back to math: with a *cùn* 寸 "inch" radical, *zūn* 尊 also means "old, senior, ancient," which is to say, *large* in number. Aristotle's discussion of the *energeia doxēs* as an entelechial movement from the emotion or attitude of contempt to its actualization as belittling, however, suggests that it would be reductive here to ignore the body-becoming-mind process involved in *oligōria*. And our discussion of *doxa*-as-face suggests that there may be more emotion involved in even an arithmetic determination of value than the equation above might otherwise suggest.

Nor does the entelechial movement stop at the verbal or other behavioral expression of a felt contempt; as Konstan (2007, p. 47) writes:

> The sharp distinction that Aristotle draws between anger and hatred or enmity may seem surprising, but it follows from his understanding of the nature of the two emotions. Enmity, according to Aristotle, is the opposite of friendship or affection; whereas friends desire the good of the other, the object of hatred is to inflict harm (2.4, 1382a8). The object of anger, however, is to cause pain to the other. A slight makes one feel small, and the only way to get even is to induce a similar feeling in the other. It follows that, for an angry person to get revenge, the original offender must be aware of it (*aisthesthai*), since there is no such thing as unperceived pain (hence the stipulation in the definition of anger that the revenge, like the slight itself, must be perceived), whereas to one who hates it is a matter of indifference whether an enemy is aware or not of the damage done to him. That is why we may wish that people whom we hate should die, but when we are angry, what we desire is that the other person feel in return (*antipathein*) the kind of diminishment that provoked our anger in the first place. (2.4, 1382a14–15)

The whole point for Aristotle is that *oligōria* circulates: it doesn't just express a slight; it inflicts a wound, causes pain, "makes one feel small," and because "dishonor [*atimia*] is a feature of insult, and one who dishonors belittles [*ho d' atimazōn oligōrei*]; for what is worthless has no repute [*oudemian ekhei timēn*], neither for good no[r] evil" (2.2.6, 1378b23; Kennedy, 1991/2007, p. 117), it engenders anger, a pain that wants "to induce a similar feeling in the other." "The cause of pleasure to those who give insult," Aristotle writes, "is that they think they themselves become more superior by ill-treating others. That is why the young and the rich are given to insults; for by insulting they think they are superior" (2.2.6, 1378b28–29; Kennedy, ibid.). There is a whole social affective-becoming-cognitive-becoming-conative economy to belittling, a circulation of negative judgment: to feel better about yourself, and to make others think/feel/see your superiority, you belittle others; your belittling deprives those others of the feeling of honor or worth that you are trying to aggrandize for yourself, generating anger, which makes them want to inflict the same pain on you that you have inflicted on them.

I want to return to the *oligōria doxēs* in "shameless through contempt of public opinion" (1.10.4., 1368b23; Kennedy, 1991/2007, p. 88), but we have been seeing references to "honor" (*zūn* 尊 and *timē*) in passing, along with "dishonor" (*rŭ* 辱 and *atimia*) and the connection between slighting/belittling and dishonoring in "one who dishonors belittles [*ho d' atimazōn oligōrei*]," and I propose now to make a three-section digression to explore it: Aristotle's conception of honor not as a possession but as a social value or valuing like face in §4.8; another term Mencius uses for honor (*róng* 榮) in §4.9; and then, by way of segueing back to Aristotle on being "shameless through contempt of public opinion" in §4.11, Mencius on shame in §4.10.

4.8 Aristotle: *timē* as Value

If belittling circulates, and belittling causes dishonor, then dishonor circulates too; and it's time to determine just what that means. Is dishonor (*atimia*) the same thing as disgrace/face-loss (*adoxia*)? Are *timē* (honor) and *eudoxia* (a good reputation) synonyms?

Eugene Garver (2008) has argued that honor is no longer all that relevant to what he calls "modern man"; indeed, he says, the ancient Greeks' all-pervasive obsession with honor makes Aristotle's emotion-based practical reason alien and irrelevant to us. "Aristotelian practical reason and emotion make sense for people whose primary external good is honor," he writes;

"Humean practical reason and emotion are appropriate when the central external good is money" (p. 59). Garver's notion is that because we are Humeans whose "central external good is money," there is no easy road back to Aristotle for us.

I suggest that Garver is wrong on two counts. One is that it now seems strange, in the light of chapter 2's discussion of group feeling-becoming-thinking and chapter 3's discussion of energized body language, to call honor an "external good"—or, for that matter, even to externalize the "good" that is money. We *feel* honor, inwardly; and what we feel is not just personal pride, or personal dismay at a loss of honor, but a group affect that coaches us on the social significance of honor or dishonor for our identity, our sense of self in the larger social context of which we are a part. And we feel that group affect through the mirroring of energized body language that we see and hear in and on the bodies around us. Bodies affect us. Honor is a warm, admiring group affect that charges our own bodies with self-esteem; dishonor is a cold, condemnatory group affect that charges our bodies with self-criticism, even self-loathing. (And is "money" really all that different? Doesn't "being rich" or "being poor" assume social meaning for us not just through buying power or its lack but through the way other people treat us, respond to us, honor or dishonor us?)

The second count on which I think Garver is off-base is that the part of "honor" that seems old-fashioned and not particularly relevant or interesting to us is not the *feeling* of honor (or dishonor) but merely, I suggest, the *name* of honor—the sound of the word. We tend to associate the *word* honor with "old" "traditional" societies that we see in movies about the Sicilian Mafia; we tend to think that honor means living according to a rigid code, and that dishonor is worse than death.[10] If that is the case, Garver's complaint about the irrelevance of Aristotle's concept of honor to us today may simply be a translation problem: when we recall that *timē* can also be translated as "value," and that socially circulated value is Erving Goffman's definition of "face," perhaps we will not find Aristotle's ancient Greek psychology utterly alien. (I realize that some Westerners still today associate "face" exclusively with Asian cultures, especially China and Japan. This is a stereotype that is similar to the exclusive association of "honor" with traditional warrior cultures—and one that I assume Goffman's essay will have helped to dispel.) The quotation about *timē* that prompted this section, which Kennedy translated "because dishonor [*atimia*] is a feature of insult, and one who dishonors belittles [*ho d' atimazōn oligōrei*]; for what is worthless has no repute [*oudemian ekhei timēn*], neither for good no[r] evil" (2.2.6, 1378b23; Kennedy, 1991/2007, p. 117), might also be translated:

"devaluation *[atimia]*[11] is a feature of arrogant abuse *[hubreōs]*, and one who devalues belittles *[ho d' atimazōn oligōrei]*; for what is good for nothing has no value *[oudemian ekhei timēn]*." Does this sound impossibly distant from our own assumptions?

Aristotle's English translators in fact often find themselves rendering *timē* as value, whenever it veers into the semantic territory of assigning a high worth to *things* rather than people: *duo tōn tois pollois timiōtatōn* (1.6.10, 1362b18), for example, can be rendered "two things most *honored* by most people" (Kennedy, 1991/2007, p. 62), but, since it seems a bit strange in English to honor things, also finds its way into English as "two things which the generality of men most *value*" (Cooper, 1932, p. 31) and "two things which the majority of men *prize* most highly" (Freese, 1926, 63; cf. also Roberts, 1941/1984, p. 2166; emphasis added to all three quotations). If "honor" is no mystical state of pure integrity but simply a form of social currency or value, a channel of collective judgment, a measure of what we take to be most important, surely we are just as concerned about it today as Aristotle's Greeks were in his day.

Garver's inclination to binarize those who love money (*hoi philokhrēmatoi*) and those who love honor (*hoi philotimoi, TR* 1.5.9, 1361b3), or things that "bring honor rather than money *[timē mallon ē khrēmata]*" (1.9.16, 1366b37; Kennedy, 1991/2007, p. 77), does in fact have textual warrant in Aristotle; but that warrant is not exclusive. In *TR* 2.16, for example, Aristotle writes that *ho de ploutos hoion timē tis tēs axias tōn allōn*, "for wealth is a kind of standard of value *[timē]* of other things" (2.16.1, 1391a1; Kennedy, ibid., p. 154), suggesting that *timē* covers a kind of blurring of societal value and monetary value, or the bleeding of monetary value into societal value. Similarly, in *TR* 1.7, where the *timē*-words include not only the base noun *timē* but *atimia* "disgrace" and *hai timai* "rewards," he writes of "things of which the rewards [are greater]; for reward is a kind of evaluation *[hē gar timē hōsper axia tis estin]*" (1.7.30, 1365a9; Kennedy, ibid., p. 70).[12] In 1.8 *timēmatōn* is the "property qualification" for full participation in oligarchic rule (1.8.4, 1365b33): the monetary-becoming-societal valuation of one's assets. And in 1.14, finally, *timeō* is another kind of assessment, namely the act of establishing the "punishment value" of a certain crime: gravely insulted, Euctemon has committed suicide, and Sophocles—probably not the playwright—argues in court *ou timēsein ephē elattonos ē ho pathōn heautōi etimēsen* (1.14.3, 1375a1), literally "he was not going to value, he declared, less than the sufferer for his own self had valued," or, as Kennedy (ibid., p. 101) translates that, "said he would not fix the penalty as less than the victim had assessed it for himself."

Nor does Aristotle's term that morphologically translates as "those who love honor," *hoi philotimoi,* necessarily connote honorable behavior or adherence to a code of honor. The standard dictionary translation of *hoi philotimoi* is "the ambitious," and Aristotle insists that "the ambitious man does wrong for the sake of honour [*ho de philotimos dia timēn*]" (1.10.4, 1368b20; Roberts, 1941/1984, p. 2178). *Philotimountai* means "they are ambitious," and, in *kai pros hous philotimountai, ē huph' hōn zēlousthai boulontai kai mē phthoneisthai* (2.4.24, 1381b22–23), for example, in the syntactic context of *pros* + accusative, "they are competitive with/emulous of," which is to say, they are ambitious to achieve the same rank or prestige or other sign of social value others hold or desire. (Kennedy [1991/2007, p. 126] translates the phrase "and [they are friendly] toward those whose prestige they would like to attain and [those] by whom they wish to be emulated and not envied.")[13] *Timē* is not so much a stable psychological possession that indicates virtue, clearly, as it is a marker or unit of currency in social scorekeeping.

Perhaps the most interesting passage on *hoi philotimoi,* however, also mentions *hoi philodoxoi* and *hoi doxosophoi*:

> *kai hoi timōmenoi epi tini diapherontōs, kai malista epi sophiai ē eudaimoniai. kai hoi philotimoi phthonerōteroi tōn aphilotimōn. kai hoi doxosophoi: philotimoi gar epi sophiai. kai holōs hoi philodoxoi peri ti phthoneroi peri touto.* (2.10.3, 1387b30–34)

> And those [are envious] who are exceptionally honored for something, and especially for wisdom or happiness. And the ambitious are more envious than the unambitious. And those [are envious] who are wise in their own conceit; for they are ambitious for wisdom. And on the whole, those fond of fame in some way are envious in that regard. (Kennedy, 1991/2007, p. 145)

> Also if we are exceptionally distinguished for some particular thing, and especially if that thing is wisdom or good fortune. Ambitious men are more envious than those who are not. So also those who profess wisdom; they are ambitious to be thought wise. Indeed, generally, those who aim at a reputation for anything are envious on this particular point. (Roberts, 1941/1984, p 2211)

> And those who are honoured for some special reason, especially for wisdom or happiness. And the ambitious are more envious

than the unambitious. And those who are wise in their own conceit, for they are ambitious of a reputation for wisdom; and, in general, those who wish to be distinguished in anything are envious in regard to it. (Freese, 1926, p. 239)

It is felt by those who are pre-eminent in their reputation for a given thing—above all, if they are thus noted for wisdom or good fortune. And the ambitious are more envious than the unambitious. Pretenders to wisdom are given to envy, since they are ambitious to be thought learned. So all, generally, who aim at a reputation for anything are envious in regard to that particular thing. (Cooper, 1932, p. 127)

Note how the *timē*-words and the *doxa*-words there blend and merge: *hoi timomenoi* become not only "those who are honoured" but, in Cooper's translation (following Cope, 1877),[14] "those who are pre-eminent in their *reputation* for a given thing," a semantic expansion of the Greek that pushes *timē* into the realm of *doxa*; and in rendering *philotimoi gar epi sophiai*, Freese hints at *doxa* in "ambitious of a *reputation* for wisdom" and Roberts and Cooper similarly give us "ambitious to be *thought* wise." In summing up his remarks of the previous sentences in *kai holōs hoi philodoxoi peri ti phthoneroi peri touto*, too, Aristotle shifts from *hoi philotimoi*, the adjectival noun he has been using thus far, to *hoi philodoxoi*, as if they referred to the same character traits in the same people. Clearly, here, *doxa* and *timē* are either synonymous or partly overlapping terms for the positive social value or valuation that people tend to love; and to the extent that their love for that value prompts them to strive for it, to attempt to win more of it for themselves, they become ambitious. What they are striving for, obviously, is *face*—the circulation of felt approval through the group.[15]

The most interesting term in that passage, though, is one we haven't looked at yet: *hoi doxosophoi*, who Aristotle says are *philotimoi gar epi sophiai*, literally "ambitious in respect to wisdom." Freese and Kennedy follow Liddell-Scott in rendering *hoi doxosophoi* as "those who are wise in their conceit," Cooper follows Cope (1877, 2, p. 125) in making them "pretenders to wisdom," and Roberts has "those who profess wisdom." Kennedy sticks closely to Aristotle's Greek in describing these people as "ambitious for wisdom," which remains as problematic in English as it is in the original text: if in their own conceit they are already wise, why should they strive for wisdom? The key to the crossover from *kai hoi doxosophoi* to *philotimoi gar epi sophiai* is that the *doxa* in *doxosophoi* and the *timē* in *philotimoi* are, in the end, more or less synonymous: they are the high social value assigned to wise people, not the wisdom itself. That is what these people love and strive to attain: the reputation for, or positive social value attached to, being wise. Thus Freese translates the phrase more loosely as "ambitious of a *reputation* for wisdom"; Roberts and Cooper describe *hoi doxosophoi* as "ambitious to be *thought* wise."

In numerous other places as well, in fact, Aristotle uses *timē*-words in ways that seem synonymous or overlap with, or emerge ecotically out of, his *doxa*-words. In *TR* 1.5, for example, he makes *timē* the outward sign of an inwardly felt or experienced *doxa*—"Honor [*timē*] is a sign [*sēmeion*] of a reputation for doing good [*euergetikēs eudoxias*]" (1.5.9, 1361a28; Kennedy, 1991/2007, p. 59)—so that it seems that *timē* and *doxa* are simply different stages in the circulation of approval through the group. *Timē* is also equated with two different doxotic "approval-plus" body states (interactive feelings and/or energized body language): admiration (*kai to thaumazesthai hēdu dia auto tōi timasthai*, "And to be admired is pleasurable because it is the same as being honored" [*TR* 1.11.18, 1371a22; Kennedy, ibid., p. 90]) and respect (*kai tois eithismenois timan ē phrontizein*, "those who have been accustomed to honor and respect them" [2.2.16, 1379b4; Kennedy, ibid., p. 119]).

On the philosophical surface, Aristotle's emotion chapters (*TR* 2.2–11) are not about the circulation of social value, or the becoming-communal of persuasivity; as has often been noted, they create the first psychological textbook in Western thought by applying a series of fairly "cold" or reductive analytical categories to emotional states:

- *A dual definition of two opposed emotions* (anger = desire for retaliation over an unjustified slight; calm = the quieting down of anger)

- *A specification of accompanying body states* (anger is accompanied by distress; fear is accompanied by pain and agitation)

- *A specification of what kind of person, or a person in what kind of situation, is likely to feel the emotion* (people who are not getting what they want out of life tend to be more inclined to anger than people who are more satisfied)

- *A specification of what is imagined* (loss of reputation in shame, a near-future disaster in fear)

- *A specification of the kinds of people one typically feels this emotion toward* (friends for *to philein* or a *rén* 仁-like fellow-feeling, those who treat one badly in anger)

- *Specification of the rhetorical uses to which knowledge of this emotion might be put:*

> At one and the same time, then, the persons at whom anger is directed and the dispositions of those angry and the kinds of causes have been stated; and it is clear that it might be needful in a speech to put [the audience] in the state of mind of those who are inclined to anger and to show one's opponents as responsible for those things that are the causes of anger and that they are the sort of people against whom anger is directed. (1379b39–1380a4; Kennedy, 1991/2007, p. 120)

Subtextually, however, these chapters flesh forth a whole vision of Greek society as organized by and through the circulation of social value, which Aristotle calls *timē* and *doxa*; and my reading suggests that it is actually this vision of the social ecology or ecosis (becoming-communal) of value that makes those chapters relevant to a discussion of persuasion. It's not just, in other words, that the rhetor needs to know some psychology in order to be able to persuade people effectively, though that is how Aristotle himself typically justifies these chapters; it's also that the social ecology of affective value provides the context and the condition of possibility for all social action, including icosis or becoming-persuasive as one of the pressures that are circulated through that ecology.

4.9 Mencius: *róng* 榮 as an Outgrowth of as *rén* 仁

As we've seen, one term Mencius uses for "honor" is *zūn* 尊, with the inch radical; another is *róng* 榮, which in modern Chinese becomes *róngyù* 榮譽. On its own *yù* 譽, with the *yán* 言 "speech" radical, means "reputation," again extended metaphorically from "to regard as" (cf. Mencius's *wén* 聞 [§4.0–4.2] and *shì* 視 [in modern Chinese *qīngshì* 輕視 "to scorn, to slight," literally "to regard as *qīng* 輕" (§4.4)]). The etymology of *róng* 榮 is somewhat different: with a *mù* 木 "tree" radical, it also means "to flourish" and "to prosper," and so has to do with growth, specifically with the ecosis that "grows" honor by circulating social value.

For example, in 2A4 Mencius says that honor (*róng* 榮) follows (*zé* 則) from fellow-feeling (*rén* 仁) and *rǔ* 辱 "disgrace" follows (*zé* 則) from no fellow-feeling (*bùrén* 不仁).[16] It is tempting to read that to mean that a person is honored *because* s/he shares fellow-feeling with others, as if *rewarded* for virtuous behavior; one might imagine a recognition ceremony in which the fellow-feeling-ist is "honored" with speeches, a plaque, etc. But Mencius hints that honor actually *grows out of* fellow-feeling: *zé* 則 is an *imitative* following, a modeling of X on Y, and thus also a standard or norm or rule as a pattern or regularity that emerges out of guided and increasingly regulatory imitation. Honor (*róng* 榮) should thus be thought of as of the same substance as fellow-feeling (*rén* 仁), a gradual accretive escalation (outgrowth) of the more positive fellow-feelings that the honoree is circulating. By the same token, if the absence of fellow-feeling (*bùrén* 不仁) becomes an affective negativity that is circulated through the group, disgrace (*rǔ* 辱) is a gradual accretive escalation of that negativity. It's not even that others react *against* the *bùrén*ist's negativity with a condemnatory negativity of their own; *rǔ* 辱 is part of (emerges out of) the same "insult" circulated by the *bùrén*ist.[17]

4.10 Mencius on the Heart of Shame:
xiūwù zhī xīn 羞惡之心

Now let us return to Mencius on the "heart of shame." While Confucius tended to use the character *chǐ* 恥 for "shame," Mencius mostly prefers *xiū* 羞. He uses it eight times, four of those on its own in contexts (2A9, 3B1, 4B33, 5B1) where it obviously means "shame, shameful, ashamed," the other four, as we've seen (§4.4), in his parallel descriptions (2A6/6A6) of the "four hearts," in the compound *xiūwù* 羞惡:

> *xiūwù* 羞惡
> Collie: "shame and hatred"
> Legge: "shame and dislike"
> Dobson: "shame and disgrace" (2A6), "shame" (6A6)
> Lau: "shame"
> Zhao et al.: "shame"
> Hinton: "conscience"
> Van Norden: "disdain"
> Bloom: "shame and aversion" (2A6), "shame and dislike" (6A6)

Now, as I understand the morphology of *xiūwù* 羞惡, the two characters together do not form a single word; rather, they are to be read as separate semantic items. I have seen four interpretations of those items:

Interpretation	Character	Part of Speech	English Word Definitions	Composite English Translation
1	xiū 羞	adj.	ugly	NA
	wù 惡	adj.	bad	
2	xiū 羞	adj.	ashamed	shame (Lau, Zhao et al.)
	wù 惡	adj.	ashamed	
3	xiū 羞	adj.	ashamed	shame and hatred/dislike
	wù 惡	verb	detest, dislike, disdain	aversion (Collie, Legge, Bloom)
4	xiū 羞	verb	detest, dislike, disdain	disdain (Van Norden)
	wù 惡	verb	detest, dislike, disdain	

I am told that classical Chinese has a strong preference for parallel structure, making (3) a relatively unattractive reading: the fact that it reads the two characters as an adjective and a verb would, at least according to one school of thought, make it unlikely as an English unpacking of the Chinese. Still, three of our translators, including Collie and Legge, who worked on their translations with Chinese converts, did opt for it. Since (1) is semantically peripheral to the "heart" Mencius is discussing, setting (3) to one side would leave as our two primary rival translations (2) and (4).[18] Shun (1997, p. 59) comes down strongly in favor of (4), translating not only xiū 羞 and wù 惡 but Confucius's chǐ 恥 (which also appears 19 times in the MZ) as "disdain" or "regard as below oneself": "Whereas wù 惡 focuses on the occurrence as something that one dislikes, chǐ 恥 focuses on it as something that is beneath oneself or lowers one's standing. Also, chǐ 恥 often involves a resolution to remedy the situation . . ." (Wade-Giles romanizations replaced with pinyin and Chinese characters). And about xiū 羞 Shun (pp. 59–60) writes:

> xiū 羞, on the other hand, is focused more on the badness or the low standing of oneself as reflected in, or as likely to ensue from, the thing that occasions xiū 羞. In the Mèngzǐ 孟子

[*MZ*], we find such examples as the charioteer who *xiū* 羞 teaming up with an archer who can catch birds only if the charioteer breaks the rules for proper driving (3B:1), or the Qí 齊 man's wife and concubine who *xiū* 羞 when they discover that their husband feeds himself by begging for food used in sacrifices to the dead (4B:33). In each example, a past or (as in the case of the charioteer) contemplated action by oneself or (as in the example of the Qí 齊 man) by someone to whom one is intimately related occasions *xiū* 羞 because the occurrence is regarded as beneath oneself. The focus is the effect on the self rather than the thing that occasions *xiū* 羞. This is unlike *chǐ* 恥, whose focus is the thing that occasions *chǐ* 恥 even though the thing is still seen as something beneath oneself. (Wade-Giles romanizations replaced with pinyin and Chinese characters)

I have quoted Shun at length because his descriptions of *xiū* 羞 actually seem to pull us in different directions. The Qí 齊 man's wife and concubine may indeed feel disdain—an angry contempt from a position of moral superiority—for their husband, but in addition would be very likely to feel shame—a self-loathing grounded in a strong sense of moral inferiority or deficiency or fault—before the rest of society. More than that, their disdain for their husband would likely be conditioned by the shame they feel at his behavior, by the way they take his behavior to shame them in the eyes of society. The social ideal would be, as in Aristotle, that contempt (*kataphronēsis*) or slighting (*oligōria*) circulates through its targets as shame (*aiskhunē*): society's public contempt for the Qí 齊 man's behavior shames his wife and concubine into showing private contempt for it (and him), which may shame him into mending his ways; if he continues to resist this public and private shaming, he will be branded "shameless through contempt of public opinion [*ho d' anaiskhuntos di' oligōrian doxēs*]" (*TR* 1.10.4., 1368b23; Kennedy, 1991/2007, p. 88). We might, therefore, translate *xiū* 羞 in 4B33 as neither shame nor as disdain but shame-becoming-disdain, with perhaps a somewhat stronger emphasis on shame, since as women in a traditional culture the two of them are socially relatively powerless: there is very little they can do about the shame except vent it on their husband in the form of disdain, and hope that it shames him into behaving better.

The charioteer's reaction in 3B1 seems closer to pure disdain—indeed we could paraphrase Shun's line about him as "the charioteer who disdains teaming up with an archer who can catch birds only if the charioteer breaks the rules for proper driving"—but clearly there is an implicit nod toward shame in his disdain as well, in that he is unwilling to team up with the cheating archer for fear of being shamed (in his own eyes and/or the eyes of others) by the cheating. Implicit in the charioteer's *xiū* 羞, I suggest, is a becoming-disdain as a *learning* from shame: having felt shame in the past, and disliked (*wù* 惡) it, the charioteer has learned to abjure or renounce or shun (or disdain) the kind of behavior that is likely to make him feel it again. If the man's wife and concubine feel *shame*-becoming-disdain, then, perhaps what the charioteer feels is shame-becoming-*disdain*.

Birdwhistell (2007, p. 113) has a different take on this, suggesting that Mencius, along with traditional Chinese culture in general, associates shame with women and other social inferiors, who "lack sufficient self-control and so are likely to behave in a wild manner. . . . Men who value a more martial and aggressive type of masculinity do not want their behavior to be seen as similar to that of women, and they feel shame if it is. They see shame, like compassion, as female gendered behavior." Thus when Mencius attempts to shame rulers into ruling compassionately, he is quite riskily encouraging them to act like "women"—or, as Mencius puts it, to rule (literally act) as the people's fathers-*and*-mothers (*wéi mín fùmǔ* 為民父母, 1A4, 1B7, 3A3; *fùmǔ* 父母, 2A5).

Note also, however, that Birdwhistell (ibid.) also follows Legge in translating *xiūwù* 羞惡 as "shame and dislike (of shameful behavior)": one possible gendered reading of the concept in Mencius might understand *xiū* 羞 "shame" as normatively gendered "feminine" and *wù* 惡 "dislike/disdain" as normatively gendered "masculine," so that in 4B33 (which Birdwhistell does not discuss) the Qí 齊 man's behavior would be shameful and therefore "womanish," and his wife and concubine might be taken to be attempting to shame him into feeling masculine dislike or disdain for shameful behavior—into "being a man." This would in turn suggest that in *disliking* or *disdaining* his shameful behavior, the wife and concubine are provisionally and temporarily (punitively) occupying a subject-position normatively associated with men, and that, if they are successful in their project and their husband comes to disdain his former shameful behavior, they will drop back into their default (normative "feminine") submissiveness. The upshot of this reading would be, obviously, that the ethecotic movement implied in shame-becoming-disdain would also be implicitly gendered as woman-becoming-man, submissive-becoming-dominant, prenormative-becoming-normative, wild-becoming-controlled, etc., and that the fear of sliding back in the counterethecotic direction (man-becoming-woman, etc.) would intensify dislike into disdain, positive ethical growth into negative moralism, and so on.

The socioaffective dynamic at work here is reminiscent of Judith Butler's (1991) notion of "panicked heterosexuality," a phenomenological critique of heterosexism that demystifies the calm sense of occupying a normative ground that heterosexuals are normally taken to feel by looking at the fear that they often experience that they might *become* gay, or that their clothing or behavior might make others *perceive* them as gay. In the model I've been developing here, heterosexism would be an ecotic (becoming-normative) construct that is maintained *as* the communal norm through shame-becoming-disdain, and the resulting (mostly suppressed) panic built into disdain that some momentary slip or inattentiveness might expose the social actor to the disapproval or even disgrace that generates shame.

I agree with Birdwhistell that Mencius is appropriating for an expanded patriarchal masculinity something like the compassionate heart traditionally attributed to mothers; but I don't mean to imply by this invocation of Butler that Mencius is engaged in any way with the heteronormative policing of sexual identities. I only mean that the "disdain" Shun and Van Norden hear in *xiūwù* 羞惡 seems steeped in what Butler identifies as the moralistic suppression of shame-related panic that often polices social norms. Van Norden not only translates *xiūwù zhī xīn* 羞惡之心 as "the feeling of disdain" but notes in his Introduction (2008, p. xxx) that "this second passage [6A10] argues that all humans disdain to do certain shameful things that would otherwise benefit them, and this 'heart' is the basis of righteousness." The phrase "disdain to do certain shameful things" itself implies what I'm calling shame-becoming-disdain; and indeed elsewhere Van Norden finds himself translating *xiū* 羞 as "shame," as in 7A7, where he also inserts an odd-sounding translation of Zhu Xi's relevant commentary:

> Mencius said, "Shame is indeed important for people! *[Zhu Xi comments, "'Shame' is the feeling of disdain that we have inherently" (2A6, 6A6).]* Those who are crafty in their contrivances and schemes have no use for shame. If one is not ashamed of not being as good as others, how will one ever be as good as others?" (Ibid., p. 173; italicized interpolation Van Norden's)[19]

The claim that shame *is* disdain jars in English; as my definitions on the fly five paragraphs ago suggest, shame is "a self-loathing grounded in a strong sense of moral inferiority or deficiency or fault" and disdain is "an angry contempt from a position of moral superiority"—very different emotions, obviously. But if we read *xiū* 羞 as neither shame alone nor disdain alone but shame-becoming-disdain, it becomes clear how even an English translator strongly committed to one or the other might be pulled in different directions in different contexts, and how a Chinese commentator like Zhu Xi might feel able to equate the two.

We might want to unpack the emotional complex at work in Mencius here along something like these lines. We are so dependent on other people's good opinion (*róng* 榮 or *zūn* 尊 or *timē* or *eudoxia* as upward valuing) for our sense of self, and especially our sense of self-worth and self-esteem, that:

[a] other people's disapproval (*qīng* 輕 or *kataphronēsis* or *oligōria*) is profoundly disturbing, and disgrace (*rǔ* 辱 or *atimia* or *adoxia*) is devastating;

[b] the devastating emotion that we feel at disgrace, and that disturbs us in others' disapproval, is precisely shame;

[c] it is important for us to feel that shame, because it teaches us to shy away from behavior that disgraces and shames us;

[d] once we have been shamed enough times to avoid doing specific disgraceful or shameful things, we begin to feel disdain for those behaviors, and for the individuals and groups that commit them, and may even promote them.

The word "disdain" in English remains a bit problematic for me, due to the strong connotations it carries of easy kneejerk *class* contempt, a conditioned disgust at the lower orders; but I suggest that it does hint admirably at what Judith Butler calls the suppressed *panic* a moralist feels at the possibility that s/he might accidentally backslide into the kind of behavior that leads to disapproval or even disgrace. If the ecosis in shame-becoming-disdain is precarious enough to police normative behavior (and attitudes, etc.) by constantly threatening norm-followers with its collapse or reversal (disdain-becoming-shame) at the tiniest deviation from the norm, then perhaps "disdain" is indeed the right English term for "regarding a behavior as below one." This kind of neo-Freudian queer-theoretical extremism doesn't sound particularly Mencian, perhaps; but it would be arguably implicit in the term on which Shun and Van Norden insist.

Van Norden (2008, p. xxxii) in fact makes a vivid case for disdain as a Mencian virtue, primarily by defining *yì* 義 "rightness" as fundamentally negative, and thus morality as a form of panicked moralism: for him *yì* 義 "emphasizes *prohibitions* against our performance of certain actions" (emphasis Van Norden's), based on our *disdain* for them, which he thematizes as "integrity." "Righteousness (*yi*)," he continues, "is the integrity of a person who disdains to demean himself by doing what is base or shameful, even if doing so would reap benefits. So, for example, a righteous person will not accept a gift given with contempt (6A10), beg in order to obtain luxuries (4B33), or cheat at a game (3B1)" (ibid.). And it does seem that the exemplary person's refusal to do those things could plausibly be construed as a moralistic self-policing, a negative action based on prohibitions and disdain—and thus, in Butler's terms, on the suppression of shame-related panic. It's just that that negativity does not seem to reflect a particularly high level of ethical growth. Surely the next step beyond such negativity would be a *positive* orientation to action in the world that seeks out the best people and best choices, and is constantly constructing out of social and political situations something better than existed before? This latter construction of *yì* 義 seems to me much more Mencian—much more richly steeped in ethecotic exemplarity—than the kind of panicky moralistic prohibitions and disdain for shameful behavior around which Van Norden builds his translation.

But then perhaps the best way to understand *xiūwù* 羞惡 is as a transitional heart, something all humans have that leads them *onto* the ethecotic path of emotional maturation but not very far up it. The heart of shame might then be understood as leading social actors up out of shame at disapproval (*qīng* 輕) or dishonor/disgrace (*rǔ* 辱) into the socioemotionally precarious realm of moralism—as a gradual "perfection" of self-policing through the habitualization of fear-based prohibitions, combined with a progressive suppression of the shame-based panic that attends the behavioral and attitudinal vigilance required to sustain norm-conformity—which is to say, as a movement from human disgrace in the *direction* of human honor that cannot even hope to lead us from human honor toward "heavenly honor" (*tiān zhī zūn* 天之尊: §4.5, §4.15). If we understand *xiūwù zhī xīn* 羞惡之心 as operating at this low "introductory" level of ethecotic growth, it would perhaps be sufficient to translate it as "the heart of shame-becoming-disdain."

In fact, if Birdwhistell is right (and I think she is) that Mencius is cagily advocating (at least in the ruler) a counternormative movement from woman-versus-man to something like woman-plus-man—a kind of pangender ethecotic ideal—this would militate both against Shun's and Van Norden's reading of *xiū wù* 羞惡 as (just) disdain and against a patriarchal construction of *xiū wù* 羞惡 as (just) woman-becoming-man. What Birdwhistell calls Mencius's "transgender ideal" would also attempt to persuade the ruler (and implicitly perhaps others as well) to transcend the heart of shame-becoming-disdain into the fatherly/motherly heart of compassion.

4.11 Aristotle (and Goffman) on Shame: *hē aiskhunē*

Now let us return to the *oligōria doxēs* in "shameless through contempt of public opinion [*ho d' anaiskhuntos di' oligōrian doxēs*]" (1.10.4., 1368b23; Kennedy, 1991/2007, p. 88) from which we digressed in §4.7, and ask: what is it about the belittling of opinion that makes a person shameless? And what exactly is that "opinion"? Kennedy renders *doxa* there as "public opinion," and it should be clear by now that what is being belittled in that phrase is not a single person's opinion but the opinion(s) of a group; belittling a single person's opinion would be arrogance (*hubris*, which Kennedy has been translating as "insult"), leading to anger in the victim, not shamelessness in the perpetrator. What causes shame is the imagination of group disapproval; what causes shamelessness, clearly, is not just contempt for group disapproval but a contemptuous or dismissive refusal to *yield* to group pressures to conform to social norms. What causes shamelessness, to put it in terms of face, is a refusal to yield to the social ecology that controls face, the ecosis that assigns face-gain or face-loss to specific behaviors. That ecosis is so powerful because it is grounded in communal affect, in the power of shared evaluative affect to inflict regulatory pain and pleasure; it requires a supreme effort to resist that pressure precisely because the felt rewards for compliance and punishments for noncompliance are somatically intense. The shameless person is in effect mustering an individualistic counterideosomatic regime, a resomatization of group disapproval for the individual as individual contempt for the group.

Aristotle writes: "Since shame is imagination about a loss of reputation [*peri adoxias*] and for its own sake, not for its results, and since no one cares about reputation [*doxēs*] [in the abstract] but on account of those who hold an opinion of him [*dia tous doxazontas*], necessarily a person feels shame toward those whose opinion he takes account of [*anankē toutous aiskhunesthai hōn logon ekhei*]" (2.6.14., 1384a22–27; Kennedy, 1991/2007, p. 134). I would venture first a slight correction, there: I don't think Aristotle really means that shame *is* the imagination of a loss of face (*peri adoxias phantasia* **estin** *hē aiskhunē*); I think he means that fantasizing or imagining (also remembering) a loss of face *triggers* shame. He has, after all, defined shame as "pain or confusion [*lupē tis ē tarachē*] about what seems to cause a loss of face [*peri ta eis adoxian phainomena pherein*]" (2.6.2., 1383b13; my translation), and there is no reason to assume that the *peri adoxias phantasia* or the *peri ta eis adoxian phainomena pherein* itself *is* a pain or a confusion.

Compare now Erving Goffman's (1955/1967, p. 8) description of the genesis of shame:

> When a person is in wrong face or out of face, expressive events are being contributed to the encounter which cannot be readily woven into the expressive fabric of the occasion. Should he sense that he is in wrong face or out of face, he is likely to feel ashamed and inferior because of what has happened to the activity on his account and because of what may happen to his reputation as a participant. Further, he may feel bad because he had relied upon the encounter to support an image of self to which he has become emotionally attached and which he now finds threatened. Felt lack of judgmental support from the encounter may take him aback, confuse him, and momentarily incapacitate him as an interactant. His manner and bearing may falter, collapse, and crumble. He may become embarrassed and chagrined; he may become shamefaced.

This is very close to Aristotle's definition: "Should he sense that he is in wrong face or out of face [*peri adoxias phantasia*], he is likely to feel ashamed and inferior [*lupē tis ē tarachē*] because of what has happened to the activity on his account and because of what may happen to his reputation as a participant [*anankē toutous aiskhunesthai hōn logon ekhei*]." For both Aristotle and Goffman it is the social actor's *sense* (*phantasia*) that s/he is "in wrong face or out of face" (*peri adoxias*) that causes the somatic (affective-becoming-conative-becoming-cognitive) reaction that we call shame. What Goffman adds to Aristotle—but entirely in the spirit of Aristotle's discussion, it seems to me—is the notion that the actor becomes "emotionally attached" to "an image of self" (a "line," or what I called above a situational *ēthos*), and the sense of being "in wrong face or out of face" is actually born out of a felt clash or conflict between the desired (positively somatized) *ēthos* and the feared (negatively somatized) *ēthos*. As Goffman puts that: "Further, he may feel bad because he had relied upon the encounter to support an image of self to which he has become emotionally attached and which he now finds threatened."

What Goffman also seems to be adding to his own and Aristotle's discussions here is a new conception of face-as-emotion, face as the outward motion of the body, or body language: "Felt lack of judgmental support from the encounter may take him aback, confuse him, and momentarily incapacitate him as an interactant. His manner and bearing may falter, collapse, and crumble. He may become embarrassed and chagrined; he may become shamefaced." Face-as-value may be felt, but it is also somewhat abstract, in the sense that it must be *mapped* mentally as real; face-as-emotion is corporeally immediate, both viscerally felt in one's own body and unmistakably visible or audible on or in someone else's.

It is likely that the term "face" as an English translation of Chinese *miànzi* 面子 initially reflects this corporeal immediacy, the display of emotion(al response to something unseen) on the faces of others physically present; the movement Goffman theorizes in shame from the sense of loss of face-as-value to loss of face-as-emotion would thus be a reconstructed invisible-becoming-visible chronology based on the reading of bodily (facial) *sēmeia* as caused by suspected invisible triggers of those signs. For Goffman the actor's perception of being "in wrong face or out of face" generates fears of a loss of face-as-value, which produce bad social feelings that cause the loss of face-as-emotion:

[1a] the actor deviates from the line s/he is attempting to maintain (s/he "is in wrong face or out of face");

[1b] the activity in which s/he is participating is disrupted in some crucial way;

[1c] s/he senses this;

[1d] s/he imagines future damage to her or his reputation as a result (imagined loss of face-as-value);

[1e] her or his emotionally invested sense of self is threatened (threatened loss of face-as-self-esteem);

[1f] s/he feels a "lack of judgmental support," presumably from the other members of the group;

[1g] s/he loses face-as-emotion.

But Goffman's account seems incomplete. First off, in (1f), what *is* that "lack of judgmental support"? Is it a somatic response from the other members of the group? If so, what sort of response is a "lack"? Is it really just a lack of support, or is it active disapproval, a negative judgment? And what is the relationship between that response and the disruption of the activity in (1b)? Is it possible that the group's somatic response to the actor's deviation from the line s/he is maintaining *is* the disruption? If we imagine the actor giggling at a funeral, say, or hooting sarcastically at a wedding, what else could the disruption be besides the somatic signals of disapproval from the others present? In Goffman's account those other bodies-becoming-minds involved in face-work—or what we might call here "shame-work"—are only shadowy, barely imagined presences. But surely shame-work is always a *collective* action, a group ecosis? Surely the actor always produces and experiences shame with or through the people who, as Aristotle says, "hold an opinion of him" (*dia tous doxazontas*, 1384a24)? A literal translation of *oudeis de tēs doxēs phrontizei all' ē dia tous doxazontas* might be "no one cares about reputation other than on account of the reputers"—where are those *doxazontas* or "reputers" in Goffman's account? (Even if we imagine the social actor sitting alone in a room in the evening and feeling intense shame over something that happened during the day, or thirty years ago, isn't s/he still experiencing that shame in felt relationship with the people who observed his or her loss of face?)

And second, as Aristotle reminds us with *peri adoxias phantasia*, what about cases where no one present notices what Brown and Levinson (1987) call the "face-threatening event" (FTE), and shame is generated not by actual social disapproval but the *imagination* of social disapproval? For example, while conversing in the present, the actor remembers an FTE from the past, especially one whose general valuation somehow contradicts or undermines the line s/he is attempting to maintain in the present. Refeeling the recalled feeling of shame associated with that old FTE regenerates the shameful images and the emotions that go with it, and those emotions start moving toward open display on the body's theatrical stage, putting the actor at least potentially "in wrong face" or "out of face." As this new FTE arises from within, the actor begins not only to imagine future damage to her or his reputation (imagined loss of face-as-value) if s/he is unable to suppress the unruly emotions, but to feel anxiety about her or his ability to accomplish that suppression—and that anxiety may make it even more difficult to suppress them. Both feelings, of shame and anxiety, are marked somatically with emotional responses—constriction of the throat or chest, increased heart rate, increased flow of blood to the face—which in turn threaten to "go public" (display themselves on the body's stage as blushing, fidgeting, darting eyes, etc.) and thus to precipitate the very shameful discovery and resulting loss of face that the anxiety fears. The fear that these emotional signals of anxiety and shame might lead to that discovery reinforces the anxiety response at the same time as the speaker is trying to clamp down on it and prevent its public display as body language. To lose control over the public display of emotion would be to lose face; fear of losing face intensifies the somatic response and makes it more likely that it will in fact surface as emotion and disrupt the management of "line," of situational *ēthos*, and face will be lost.

Or, schematically:

[2a] the actor remembers or imagines a deviation from the line s/he was attempting to maintain in some past activity, or remembers a fact about her or his past that, if the people now present knew about it, would cause her or him to lose face-as-value;

[2b] s/he imagines the body language of disapproval that the others would display as an expression of that loss of face-as-value;

[2c] her or his emotionally invested sense of self is threatened (threatened loss of face-as-self-esteem);

[2d] s/he feels the uprising of shame-emotions;

[2e] s/he feels an anxiety that the loss of face-as-emotion will reveal her or his shame and cause the loss of face-as-value;

[2f] the anxiety s/he feels at the possibility that her or his body will reveal the rising shame makes it even more difficult to suppress the outward display of face-threatening body states.

In other words, it may well be—as Aristotle seems to suggest, as if "correcting" Goffman—that the imagination of *adoxia* is primary and the *adoxia* itself is secondary. Both the *peri adoxias phantasia* ("mental image of a loss of face") and the *lupē tis ē tarachē peri ta eis adoxian phainomena pherein* ("pain or confusion over what seems to cause a loss of face") seem to be (inter)subjectively constitutive of *adoxia,* so that the objective existence of *adoxia* out in the world, in society, in the bodies-becoming-minds of the rest of the group—if such a thing could even be objectively established—is not absolutely essential to the painful or confusing imagination that is shame.

4.12 The Somatic Exchange

The interesting question for me there is: what does it mean for the imagination of disgrace or loss of face to be "(inter)subjectively constitutive of *adoxia*"? That parenthetical "(inter)" suggests that the subjective constitution of *doxa*-as-face (including both *eudoxia* or face-gain and *adoxia* or face-loss) tends to be collective—the *group* doxotic imagination gives or withholds face—but that group imagination may be energetically at work on *doxa* (the *energeia doxēs*) in the situated/embodied imagination of a single social actor as well. Even in cases where no one saw the embarrassing incident, and even if no one may ever find out about it, in other words, we have to imagine the ashamed social actor as still *circulating* the imagined loss of face as shame.

What is at work in this circulation, I suggest, is the reticulatory transfer of body states through a group, via the somatic mimesis of body language—a kind of collectivized or generalized somatomimetic transfer that I have elsewhere (Robinson, 2008, pp. 30–32; 2011, pp. 168–73; 2012, ch. 4; 2013a, pp. 21–24, 35–40, 44–47; 2013c, p. 358) called the *somatic exchange*. For example:

(2a) In remembering a past or imagining a future deviation from the line I was attempting to maintain in a past activity or am attempting to maintain now, I will not just rationally *know* that such a deviation might mean trouble: I will *feel* it. I have through the somatic transfer (§3.7) empathetically experienced and mimetically internalized other people's emotional displays of disapproval for hypocrisy and other social sins in the past, and so now have developed in my autonomic nervous system a kind of collectivized stockpile of negative somatic markers (§2.6) ready to warn against hypocrisy; and those markers are activated now to mark my still-private hypocrisy as socially wrong. My autonomic nervous system marks the imagined or remembered FTE inwardly as dangerous, as to be avoided. Those earlier displays of social disapproval were enactively provoked on the (public) stages of the other bodies by their (private) negative somatic marking of some of my own or someone else's behavior that failed to conform to social standards; as those feelings activated various facial muscles, tightening lips, narrowing eyes, I mimetically re- or transiterated those emotional responses in my own body, made them my own, so that increasingly my own social failings triggered the same emotional displays on the outside as well as negative somatic markers on the inside.

(2b) Now, under pressure from my own autonomic nervous system, I imagine the body language of disapproval that the others would display if they knew of this still-private (imagined or remembered) FTE. In (2a), other people's disapproving body language (in the past) is transferred inward, internalized as my own somatic markers; now those somatic markers are transferred outward again (in the present), projected onto the imagined future faces of other people—whether those people are physically present with me now or I only imagine their presence as well.

(2c) Because my sense of self or identity is a social entity, created and maintained in relationship with other people, any felt or imagined disruption in the smooth flow of group approval for that self or identity poses a significant threat to it. It's not just, as Goffman says, that I feel an "emotional attachment" to that sense of self; it is that the self is an ideosomatic construct, created and maintained by the somatic exchange, and therefore easily threatened by the somatic exchange as well. We also develop individualistic defenses against such collective threats—we whisper to ourselves, "Who cares what they think? It's what I think that matters"—but even such defiant individualisms are powerfully tinged with the felt collectivism against which they defend.

(2d) The autonomic nervous system, designed to warn us against dangers we've encountered before, now begins to flood me with such warnings, specifically with inward somatic markers that I feel proprioceptively (increased heart rate, a prickliness in my extremities, a constriction in my throat or chest, a rush of blood to my face, etc.) or enteroceptively (butterflies or an ominous rumbling or a sharp pain in my stomach) but that may also be displayed outwardly as body language, for others to see.

(2e) Again, we have developed individualistic defenses against such warnings—we have some degree of control over our mapping of body states as feelings (our inward felt awareness of uprising shame, say), and even more control over what body states will be displayed outwardly on the body's theater—but we know from painful past experience that our control of such things is never perfect. This knowledge comes to us as the body-becoming-mind movement of somatic markers being mapped as anxious feelings, and then (though not inevitably) as thoughts, leading in me now to an increasingly conscious concern that an outward display of shameful body states will reveal my out-of-face condition.

(2f) The somatic markers of anxiety in (2e) combine with the somatic markers of shame in (2d), and together make it all the more difficult for me to keep my inward body state private. Having internalized social disapproval in the past, and reexternalized it in the present in imagined form—projected it onto the imagined bodies of those present or absent—I now struggle not to externalize it visibly onto the theater of my own body; but the pressures of the somatic exchange are powerful, and visible externalization of internal body states is difficult to resist. The "natural" or "default" or "entelechial" tendency of body states is to circulate mimetically (*fǎn* 反, §2.3) through the group; blocking that circulation is socially "abnormal" or "unnatural," opposed to the entelechy of the somatic exchange that has made us what we are, and therefore exceedingly hard to pull off.

Remember that I asked in §3.3: "If the entelechy is the *having* of an end within, who or what is the subject of the verb *ekhein*? Who or what *has* the end in the entelechy?" Mencius calls that collective subject *tiān* 天 "forces"; I'm suggesting now that, when those forces are specifically social, we identify it as the somatic exchange, a transpersonal self-guiding or self-organizing agency that is born out of individuals interacting but feels like something more than the group, something coming from outside the group, something transhuman, even transcendent, and therefore universal—as Mencius in some moods seems to assume *tiān* 天 is, and as many of his English translators (not just the Christian missionaries) seem to assume it is as well.

But note that there is not just a single somatic exchange, any more than there is a single monotheistic or providential *tiān* 天. Just as we attribute the many different and often conflicting "forces" that "condition" a situation as *tiān* 天 and *mìng* 命, so too are there as many somatic exchanges as there are social groups to which we belong: the family we live with, the family that raised us, the extended family that we see only on holidays, our various circles of friends, our various neighbors, our various work relationships, and so on. I suggest, in fact, that what Mencius means by the *tiān* 天 that guides and regulates our ethical strivings—the *tiān zhī dào* 天之道 (4A12, 7B24) or "the Way of *tiān*," *rén* 仁 (fellow-feeling) as *tiān zhī zūn* 天之尊 (2A7, 6A16) or "*tiān*'s honor," the *tiān* 天 that shapes *xīn* 心 (6A15) and its "abilities" (*cái* 才, 6A7), and so shapes us that the best way to "get the most" (*jìn* 盡) out of one's *xīn* 心 is to follow one's own inclinations (*xìng* 性), and to follow one's own inclinations is to serve *tiān* 天 (7A1)—is a certain diffuse but loosely organized collection or series of somatic exchanges with exemplary persons, especially sages like Confucius and Mencius themselves. (The *Analects* and the *MZ* are quasi-fictionalized written versions of earlier such sagely somatic exchanges, often in dialogue form, which we read imaginatively—through identification, projection, transference—as including us as fully embodied participants.) Each such somatic exchange is what we might call becoming-exemplary, a circulation of fractal or metonymic exemplary impulses toward self-improvement or self-realization through the group, so that the becoming-exemplary person (including ourselves as the readers of these texts) never exactly crosses over from "human (dis)honor" to some dualistic opposite like "heavenly honor," but is always en route, always becoming. Along the way, the human dishonor that generates shame is gradually transformed into human honor and what feels like an increasingly "natural" (sublimated, becoming-unconscious) "shunning" or disdaining of lower pleasures (the shame-becoming-disdaining that we explored in §4.10), which in turn are gradually transformed into becoming-enhanced approximations of a higher form of honor that Mencius calls *tiān zhī zūn* 天之尊 "*tiān*'s honor."

Let us also revisit the question (§4.4) about what Van Norden calls the "potentiality" of our *cái* 才 "ability" or *kěyǐ* 可以 "capacity" to be good, and Shun's (1997, p. 213) observation that the ability or potential to be good would not necessarily exclude the ability to be bad. To solve this problem, Shun (ibid., pp. 216–20) builds a somewhat tenuous web of textual parallels (*kěyǐ* 可以 "can, capacity" is used interchangeably with *néng* 能 "ability" in the *Xúnzǐ* 荀子 and *MZ* 1A7 and 6B2, and *néng* 能 entails ethical predispositions in the *Mòzǐ* 墨子) that allow him to conclude that Mencius is actually saying that we are born with an *ethical predisposition* to be good. Even apart from the shakiness of his inferences, however, it's not quite clear what an ethical predisposition to be good would even mean, or how positing such a predisposition differs from the simplistic belief (from which Shun convincingly distances Mencius) that "human nature is good."

What my model of the somatic exchange would offer by way of clarification here would be a conception of innate ("hardwired") mammalian brain structures that, while not exactly guaranteeing or even giving promise of goodness, nevertheless can and regularly do produce something like the ethecotic effects of which Mencius speaks. Namely, the somatic exchange works to regulate mammalian behavior because, at least according to the (still controversial) laboratory findings of the Damasio team, the autonomic nervous system in the mammalian brain is hardwired to store the lessons of experiential learning and "mark" decision-making processes with them somatically (the somatic-marker hypothesis, §2.6), and to build, with the help of the mirror-neuron system, simulations of other people's body states, so that the body states of everyone present tend to be brought into rough conformity (the somatic transfer, §3.7). (This, I suggest, is the neurophysiological realm in which Irene Bloom (1994, 1997, 2002) is right to insist on *some* biological substratum for the Mencian conception of "human nature.") While this hardwiring does not reliably produce "goodness" in any absolute sense (if any such thing even exists), it enables groups to exert fairly concerted and surprisingly effective pressures on their members to conform to group norms, which define the *group's* conception of goodness, so that conforming to group norms—becoming-normal—by definition means being good.

One might argue that the relativism that this group orientation necessarily entails would have been alien to Mencius—the Maasai of East Africa, for example, leave their dead out for predators to eat, a practice that Mencius would obviously find barbaric—but I would argue that the distinction Mencius himself draws between cultures that are and cultures that are not organized around the Confucian Way (7A42) indicates an openness in his thinking to cultural relativism (see §4.5 for discussion). Not that he would ever countenance moral *parity*, which is to say an easy pluralism, between two such cultures: the culture organized around the Confucian Way would always take precedence in his eyes. But he does recognize that cultural differences exist, and that "the good" may be defined differently in different cultures. Indeed his remark that "I have never heard of a course [*dào* 道] inspired by what people just happen to be" (quoted/translated by Behuniak, 2005, p. 126) might well be read as implicitly departicularizing *dào* 道 as *any* cultural "course" or "way," any organized form of social regulation, and thus as an attempt to distinguish the regulatory *dào* 道 that we associate with any culture from random "pre-societal" ("savage" or "state-of-nature") human behavior—"what people just happen to be."[20]

If we take the three principles of somatic theory (somatic markers, the somatic transfer, the somatic exchange) to be the hardwired "abilities" or "capacities" that, barring birth defects, all humans are born with, the whole superstructure of Mencian ethecosis can plausibly be built on that base: all cultures seek to shape their members into followers of their norms for goodness; those norms for goodness tend to be organized culturally into the specific areas that Mencius calls the four hearts, of compassion, shame, deference, and approval and disapproval (though the specific forms those hearts take may vary from culture to culture); all human beings, again barring the *mìng* 命 of birth defects and severe childhood trauma, are capable of developing ethically/emotionally into sages; the Confucian Way, distilled out of somatic exchanges with a few sages, like Confucius and Mencius themselves, and recorded for posterity in the *Analects* and the *MZ*, provides an excellent (though far from foolproof) guide to that development.

The somatic exchange, then, I suggest, is the engine that drives ecosis, and the ecotic organization of communication as persuasivity that I am calling icosis, as described (though she calls it "rhetoric") by Susan Miller (2008, pp. 1–2):

> My use of the word *rhetoric* thus understands it as a plurality—multiple metadiscourses derived from ritual, imaginative, and affiliative discursive practices that we trust for their well-supported and reasoned statements, but also because they participate in infrastructures of trustworthiness we are schooled to recognize, sometimes by lessons and habits we cannot name. Those infrastructures vary according to the time when a specialized plane of understanding and its consequences emerges in specific cultures—political, religious, social, technological, even meteorological impact on what we know and how we can know it. But the purpose of these prescriptive networks remains constant:

to endow a discursive practice with precedent trustworthiness. These rhetorics organize our emotional receptivity to statements on which we can depend for answers to speculative questions. They thereby guide us to choices that may not produce the best outcome but that we trust to be the "right thing," not in a shallow morality but because we are persuaded of their source's share in our best interests.

Miller's suggestion that "these rhetorics organize our emotional receptivity to statements on which we can depend for answers to speculative questions" refers, I believe, to the somatic entelechy of persuading-becoming-believing-becoming-valuing-becoming-knowing, or what I theorize more fully in §4.15 as doxicosis: the group somatization of opinion as truth(iness), as what "seems" to the group to be true, or as what Miller calls "trustworthiness."[21]

This model, in other words, explains what I referred to in §3.2 as "(d) the organization of that bodily contagion into 'the psychology and expectation of audiences.'" In Miller's terms, we are "schooled" normatively "by lessons and habits we cannot name" to develop certain dispositions and channel them somatically into communicative behavior, and to respond with certain emotions and their entelechial mappings as feelings and thoughts to certain rhetorical situations. An individual who "graduates" from this "school"—who learns to behave in accordance with group norms—is supported ideosomatically, given approval and acceptance and other forms of high social value: "Honor [*timē*] is a sign [*sēmeion*] of a reputation for doing good [*euergetikēs eudoxias*]," and as Mencius suggests, there are forms and channels of honor that outstrip even what existing societies can bestow. An individual who resists this ideosomatic regulation, who refuses or fails to conform, is subjected to fierce somatic pressures until s/he either conforms or is expelled from the group.

Before we can develop this model of the somatic exchange into a deep ecology of rhetoric—a doxicosis—however, we will need to take one more pass through the subtextual semantics of Greek *doxa*, this time specifically its verb form, *dokeō*.

4.13 Aristotle: *dokeō* as Seeming

Interesting as the noun *doxa* is in the *TR*, in many ways it pales before *dokeō*, which appears 76 times in the *TR*. Like *doxa*, *dokeō* cycles through both opinion and reputation, which is to say, in the verb form, from "I think" to "I seem." What I think of you fades imperceptibly into what you seem to me to be, and perhaps even into what you seem to yourself to be. These two apparently opposed usages resemble the results of what in other Greek verbs would be the active and passive voices—"I think" as active, "I seem" as passive—but in *dokeō* both are, rather unusually, active in form, so that they are morphologically indistinguishable from each other. In fact, it's even more complicated than that. Not only can what you think of me become what I seem to be without giving grammatical notice; I can even surreptitiously *shape* what you think of me, and thus what I seem to be, without changing verbs or verb forms: *dokeō* can mean "I think," "I seem," or "I pretend or feign." If "I think" is the obvious and presumably original "active" meaning of the verb, and "I seem" is the secondary or displaced "passive" meaning, "I pretend" would involve a double displacement, so that I wield a concealed active influence over my apparently passive seeming.

The most common use of *dokeō* is in the impersonal (semantically quasipassive) third person, *dokei* "it seems" (with an implicit or explicit indirect object: "to someone"). *dokeō* would seem, in fact, to be a quasipassive seeming far more often than it is a quasiactive thinking. Kennedy, for example, renders *dokeō* with "to seem" 58 of the 76 times that the verb appears in the *TR*. The 18 other occurrences become, in Kennedy's translation, "to think" (nine times), "to regard" (twice), "opinion" (twice), "to find that" (once), "to look like" (once), "to be" (once), "under the guise of" (once), and "reputation" (once). The telling slippage between thinking and seeming, however—the circularity of opinion and reputation—is evident from the fact that many of the 18 could easily have been rendered with "to seem" as well:

- "do not look like noses at all" (1.4.12, 1360a29; Kennedy, 1991/2007, p. 55) could have been "do not seem like noses at all"

- "[should] be thought attractive as well as fear-inspiring" (1.5.11, 1361b13; Kennedy, ibid., p. 59) could have been "[should] seem attractive as well as fear-inspiring"

- "as is thought to be the case with tyranny" (1.12.9, 1372b1; Kennedy, ibid., p. 94) could have been "as seems to be the case with tyranny"

- "those experiencing, and thinking they experience, great good fortune" (2.5.14, 1383a1; Kennedy, ibid., p. 130) could have

been rendered "those actually experiencing, and those only seeming to experience, great good fortune"
- "things truly regarded [as wrong]" (2.6.23, 1384b26; Kennedy, ibid., p. 135) could have been "things that truly seem [wrong]"

In all these cases *dokeō* is a depersonalized seeming, and does not seem to require the image of a single person or a group forming or expressing an opinion; the opinion is long since formed and has been expressed so many times that it can be described impersonally, and the indirect object ("to someone") remains implicit.

In other cases *dokeō* does seem to require that image of an individual or group opining, so that if "seems" were used, it would have to be "seems to someone" (an explicit indirect object):

- "they do not say what they think" (2.1.6, 1378a12; Kennedy, 1991/2007, p. 112), for example, could have been "they do not say how things *seem to them*"
- "for no one is thought to belittle himself" (2.3.4, 1380a13; Kennedy, ibid., p. 121) could have been "for it *seems to us* that no one will belittle himself"
- "for they think they are being serious and not showing contempt" (2.3.7, 1380a26; Kennedy, ibid., p. 122) could have been "for it *seems to them* that they are being serious and not showing contempt"
- "or what they find pleasure in" (2.4.20, 1381b13; Kennedy, ibid., p. 126) could have been "what *seems pleasurable to them*"
- "one should not speak on the basis of all opinions [*tōn dokountōn*, lit. 'of the seemings/thinkings/feelings'] of those held by a defined group" (2.22.3, 1395b31; Kennedy, ibid., p. 169) could have been "on the basis of how things *seem to a defined group*"
- in "asked the god if his opinion was the same as his father's" (2.23.12, 1398b34; Kennedy, ibid., p. 178), the image of the god actually *thinking* or *having an opinion* is crucial, so that it could have been rendered "if the same things *seem* (to be true or right) *to him as to his father*"

- "things that are thought to have taken place [also *tōn dokountōn*]" (2.23.22, 1400a5; Kennedy, ibid., p. 181) could have been "things that *seem to us* to have taken place"
- "he, too, should be thought high-minded" (2.24.7, 1401b23; Kennedy, ibid., p. 187) could have been "he, too, should *seem* high-minded *to people*"

There are several cases, however, where even this slight repersonalization (explicitation of the indirect object) would prove problematic in English. In "not to tell the tale is no different from not thinking [*mē dokein*] it [a fault]" (2.6.20, 1384b6; Kennedy, 1991/2007, p. 135), for example, translating *dokein* with "to seem" would shift the emphasis from the individual thinker who does not tell the tale and therefore seems not to think it to a depersonalized group opinion. And in "they think little of their reputation" (2.13.10, 1390a3; Kennedy, ibid., p. 152), the Greek seems too depersonalized to us in English: *oligōrousi tou dokein* is literally "they slight/disparage/demean (speak/think/act disparagingly of) the seeming," as if *to dokein* were a *thing* that one could disparage. In Greek, it is; in English, we have to personalize it, make it "their reputation," something that the actors can seem to own ("they think little of *their* reputation"), or, like Roberts (1941/1984, p. 2214), make it something other people *do*: "they feel contempt for what people may think of them."

But this is the interesting thing about *dokeō*, as about *doxa* in general: because it is fundamentally group opinion that is always channeled through individuals but only occasionally perceived as localized in individuals, it is often hard to tell from the Greek where exactly Aristotle is situating it. This makes the English translation (or critical interpretation) of *dokeō* a judgment call, one with which it is relatively easy to disagree in specific cases. In some passages, for example—whenever group opinion is so widely accepted that it seems to be simply the case—*dokeō* seems to move entelechially in the direction of neutral fact or truth, as in *hē huperokhē dokei mēnuein aretēn* "superiority seems to denote excellence" (1.9.39, 1368a26; Kennedy, 1991/2007, p. 82). In other cases it moves in the opposite (Platonic) direction, toward the exposure of opinions as illusions, as mere deceptive seemings, as in *doxei te gar tois pollois, kai hama paralogistikon [ek] tēs aitias* "for this will seem true to most people and at the same time is a fallacious argument drawn from 'cause'" (1.9.29, 1367b3; Kennedy, ibid., p. 79).

This dual entelechial movement is endemic to *dokeō*, in fact, and Aristotle repeatedly runs it both ways. He uses *dokeō* for statements of apparent fact 16 times (21%),[22] and to indicate cases of false appearances eight times (10.5%).[23] But at least once (1.15.26, 1376b31) it is primarily a group opinion that tends entelechially toward false appearances, and at least six times[24] it is primarily a group opinion that tends to be taken as fact. *Dokeō* indicates unmarked group opinion 29 times (38%),[25] by far the largest group; in addition to those cases where it tends entelechially toward fact or false appearances, however, there are other cases where it seems to be actualized as individual opinion, which also appears to be the primary referent in ten cases (13%).[26] Almost all ten of those in fact represent what Giorgio Agamben (1990/1993, p. 26) calls a "whatever singularity," an "exemplary singularity or a multiple singularity," in the sense that Aristotle is talking about a category of singular individuals, each of whom forms opinions in just this way, rather than a group functioning in society as a somatic exchange; but as we'll see, in one case (2.1.4, 1377b31) the individual's opinion is specifically swayed by emotion, which Aristotle is trying to teach the orator how to manipulate; and in another (2.6.20, 1384b6) the individual opinion is explicitly described as conditioned by the group.

In twelve occurrences (15.8%),[27] *dokeō* is enlisted specifically to help Aristotle give advice to orators on how best to manipulate public opinion so as to project just the right image; but in fact in one case, *dokeō* seems to refer to just this sort of manipulation that Aristotle otherwise encourages but identifies here specifically as an example of false appearances:[28] "to seek a loan under the guise of asking a favor [*kai daneizesthai hote doxei aitein*], to ask a favor under the guise of demanding a return of something owed, to ask for the return of something under the guise of asking a favor, to praise with the apparent aim of asking a favor and, when unsuccessful, nonetheless [continuing to ask]; for all these are signs of stinginess [*panta gar aneleutherias tauta sēmeia*]" (2.6.7, 1383b27–31; Kennedy, 1991/2007, p. 133). There, interestingly, *dokeō* channels the manipulation of appearances, while *sēmeia* "signs" channels the opinion-becoming-fact that *dokeō* often represents: the semiosis by which seeming to do one thing in order to gain some furtive advantage in another is read as "signs of stinginess" is not some static factual event but precisely doxosis, the circulation of *doxa* through the group as thinking-becoming-seeming. In this case, in other words, the semiosis of stinginess involves the circulation through the group not just of signs but of interpretive/evaluative somatic orientations (affective valences-becoming-meanings that are strongly felt as true or accurate) to those signs.

The default setting for *dokeō* in the *TR* is group opinion that tends to be taken as fact—hence the overwhelming prevalence of depersonalized "seemings" as English translations for the verb: "And one should even use trite and common maxims if they are applicable, for because they are common, they seem true [*orthōs ekhein dokousin*], as though everyone agreed" (2.21.11, 1395a10–11; Kennedy, 1991/2007, p. 167). Sometimes, as we've seen—"For this will seem true to most people [*doxei te gar tois pollois*] and at the same time is a fallacious argument [*paralogistikon*] drawn from 'cause' " (1.9.29, 1367b3; Kennedy, ibid., p. 79), for example—Aristotle will want to insist, Platonically, that group opinion is *wrong*, contrary to truth; but for the most part he is more interested in the pragmatic rhetorical value of *to dokein* than in its truth-value. Thus for example in the very next section of *TR* 1.9, he advises orators to "attribute what is honored to what is honorable, since they will seem related [*dokei geitnian*]" (1.9.30, 1367b11; Kennedy, ibid., p. 80); and two sections later he encourages the orator to "take coincidences and chance happenings as due to deliberate purpose; for if many similar examples are cited, they will seem [*doxei*] to be a sign [*sēmeion*] of virtue and purpose" (1.9.32, 1367b24–26; Kennedy, ibid., p. 80). In the *to nemesan* or indignation chapter of *TR* 2, Aristotle explains how old wealth comes to seem more "naturally" or "obviously" justified than new wealth: "For the newly rich cause more annoyance than those wealthy a long time and by inheritance. . . . The reason is that the latter seem [*dokousi*] to have what belongs to them, the former not; for when something [such as inherited wealth] has always been evident [*phainomenon*] in this way it seems truly [*alēthes dokei*] to belong to those who have it, with the result that others seem to have what is not their own" (2.9.10, 1387a18–27; Kennedy, ibid., p. 143). It is significant to note that the third "seem" in that passage, "others *seem* to have what is not their own," is not Aristotle's but heard as an implicit repetition in Aristotle's Greek by Kennedy: Aristotle has *hōste hoi heteroi ou ta hautōn ekhein*, literally "so that the others might not have their own [things/riches]."[29]

4.14 Aristotle on Seeming True:
ta dokounta, ta eikota, and *to pithanon*

"Seeming" in those passages is depersonalized almost to the point of being taken for truth, but Aristotle uses *dokeō* in them to remind us that these are indeed group opinions that *seem* factual but are in actuality social constructs. Elsewhere he problematizes the seeming even more overtly, as in *TR* 2.24, in fallacious *topos* 9, where he notes that "probability is not absolute," for "some things happen contrary to probability, so what is contrary to probability is also probable," and "the improbable will [also] be probable"—but, he says, "not generally so; as in eristics, not adding the circumstances and reference and manner makes for deception, so here [in rhetoric] because the probability is not general but qualified" (2.24.10, 1402a15–17; Kennedy, 1991/2007., p. 188). For example, he says, "if a weak man were charged with assault, he should be acquitted as not being a likely suspect for the charge; for it is not probable [that a weak man would attack another]. And if he *is* a likely suspect, for example, if he is strong, [he should be acquitted]; for it is not likely [that he would start a fight] for the very reason that it was going to seem probable [*ou gar eikos, hoti eikos emelle doxein*]" (2.24.11, 1402a18–20; Kennedy, ibid., pp. 188–89). Or, as Roberts (1941/1984, p. 2235) translates that: "If the accused is not open to the charge—for instance if a weakling be tried for violent assault—the defence is that he was not likely to do such a thing. But if he *is* open to the charge—i.e. if he is a *strong* man—the defence is still that he was not likely to do such a thing, since he could be sure that people would think he *was* likely to do it."

What is probable or plausible is *ta eikota*, things that are like truth—things that are what Stephen Colbert calls "truthy" enough that we *expect* them to be true: we rely on their "truthiness," even if we know or feel (or it seems to us) that they aren't one hundred percent true. As we saw in §1.1, due to convergent pronunciations the adjective *eikos* was often associated by the ancient Greeks with *oikos* "home, household, extended family, community"—whence the terms I developed there and have been using throughout, and will be theorizing more fully in §4.15–16: ecosis (< *oikos*) and icosis (< *eikos*).

Aristotle also frequently uses a derivative of *eikos*, *epieikes*, which can be variously translated as "fair" or "fair-minded" or "virtuous" or "good," but has the morphological sense of "heightened" *eikos*, a kind of over-*eikos* or super-*eikos*. In this long passage from *TR* 1.13, for example, he invokes *to epieikes* "fairness" as a special case of *ta eikota* "probability":

> Since there are two species of just and unjust actions (some involving written, others unwritten laws), our discussion has dealt with those about which the [written] laws speak; and there remain the two species of unwritten law. These are, on the one hand, what involved an abundance of virtue and vice, for which there are reproaches and praises and dishonors and honors and rewards—for example, having gratitude to a benefactor and rewarding a benefactor in turn and being helpful to friends and other such things—and on the other hand things omitted by the specific and written law. Fairness, for example,

seems to be just [*to gar epieikes dokei dikaion einai*]; but fairness is justice that goes beyond the written law [*estin de epieikes to para ton gegrammenon nomon dikaion*]. This happens sometimes from the intent of the legislators but sometimes without their intent when something escapes their notice; and [it happens] intentionally when they cannot define [illegal actions accurately] but on the one hand must speak in general terms and on the other hand must not but are able to take account only of most possibilities; and in many cases it is not easy to define the limitless possibilities; for example, how long and what sort of weapon has to be used to constitute "wounding"; for a lifetime would not suffice to enumerate the possibilities. If, then, the action is undefinable, when a law must be framed it is necessary to speak in general terms, so that if someone wearing a ring raises his hand or strikes, by the written law he is violating the law and does wrong, when in truth he has [perhaps] not done harm [*kata de to alēthes ouk adikei*], and this [latter judgment] is fair [*kai to epieikes touto estin*].

If, then, fairness [*to epieikes*] is what has been described, it is clear what kind of actions are fair [*epieike*] and what are not fair [*ouk epieike*] and what kind of human beings are not fair [*poioi ouk epieikeis anthrōpoi*]: those actions that [another person] should pardon are fair [*epieikē*], and it is fair not to regard personal failings and mistakes as of equal seriousness with unjust actions. . . . And to be forgiving of human weakness is fair [*epieikes*]. And [it is also fair] to look not to the law but to the legislator and not to the word but to the intent of the legislator and not to the action but to the deliberate purpose and not to the part but to the whole, not [looking at] what a person is now but what he has been always or for the most part. And [it is fair] to remember the good things experienced [because of him] rather than done for him. And [it is fair] to bear up when wronged. And [it is fair] to wish for an issue to be decided by word rather than by deed. And [it is fair] to want to go into arbitration rather than to court; for the arbitrator sees what is fair [*to epieikes*], but the jury looks to the law, and for this reason arbitrators have been invented, that fairness [*to epieikes*] may prevail. (1.13.11–19, 1374a18–1374b22; Kennedy, 1991/2007, pp. 99–100)

Like most of Aristotle's detailed lists in the *TR*, this one strikes us as rich in cultural norms, and implicitly saturated as well in the acculturation process by which we come to accept and feel those norms as guiding forces in our lives. That they are specifically *sociocultural* norms seems overwhelmingly obvious to us, in fact, not just because we are post-sixties intellectuals who have traveled and lived abroad and read books and articles about such things (our *xīn* 心 has been shaped by a specific cultural *tiān* 天), but because we have such vivid memories of heated disputes in childhood over what was fair and what was unfair, and what counted as a bet, and what all was included in or required by "true friendship," and so on. Not only that: as socially competent adults we are ourselves constantly learning to (re)negotiate these unwritten laws in our own social lives—constantly being surprised, for example, that a friend has an unwritten rule that we have never heard of before, a rule that we ourselves have certainly never before felt pressure to obey, and that, frankly, we find sort of silly, and do not plan to adopt as a guide to our behavior; or being surprised on the contrary that all of our friends have an unwritten rule that we realize we really should have known and been following all along, and plan to in the future. We are ourselves, in other words, constantly being acculturated to our own community's norms—and the tiniest awareness that we aren't always quite sure what the unwritten rules of our society are serves as a nagging reminder that those rules are elusive, never quite "present" in the sense of being all that noticeable, let alone easy to pin down and articulate, let alone codify. As we move from group to group, too, the unwritten rules change; one of the curses of adolescence is that we are already expected to be adept in adjusting to these group-to-group rule-changes, and we aren't. We're just learning to be. It sometimes surprises us adults that our undergraduate students in their early twenties—even, sometimes, our grad students in their mid- to late twenties—are intimidated by the adult world, because, they say, it's full of unwritten rules that they don't yet know, and don't yet know how to get to know, and they don't know whether they even want to conform their behavior to adult rules just yet. It has been so long since we were in that same situation that their trepidation before our rules seems alien to us, as if it were governed by some strange set of unwritten rules for clueless resistance—resistance rules that are difficult and yet important for us to learn if we are to reach those students in class. Once we do know all the rules in the various groups to which we belong, we seem to be set—but that feeling, ambrosia to some (perhaps most), feels like death to others, those who crave change and upheaval and need a new job and a new city (in a new country on a new continent) to live in every few years to keep life from stagnating.

And virtually every time Aristotle uses the term *epieikes* "fair" or *epieikeia* "fairness," it seems inescapably obvious to us that the concept he is delineating is saturated in communal norms. *kai hois an ēi tou epieikous tukhein* (1.12.15, 1372b18), he writes, and his English translators render that "And those who hope to obtain indulgence" (Freese, 1926, p. 133), "Again, there are those who expect leniency" (Cooper, 1932, p. 70), "You may be able to trust other people to judge you equitably" (Roberts, 1941/1984, p. 2185), "And those [do wrong] to whom there is a chance of fair consideration" (Kennedy, 1991/2007, p. 94, who moves it to 1.12.14). The very uncertainty in those renditions, bubbling up out of the subjunctive subordinate clause *hois an ēi* "for whomever it be possible to . . ." and *tukhein* "happen or chance upon," from *tukhē* "chance," the random kind of *tiān* 天 (thus, literally: "and for whomever it [might] be possible to chance upon fairness"), reminds us powerfully that there is no solid foundation in truth here; there is only each group's regulation of behavior, which is neither universal nor locally always perfectly successful. The social structuring of *tiān* 天 within one's own group cannot be counted upon when one crosses group boundaries, enters a new group. Aristotle's English translators sometimes render *epieikes* simply "good," as in "thus emulation is a good thing [*epieikes*] and characteristic of good people [*epieikōn*], while envy is bad and characteristic of the bad" (2.11.1, 1388a35–36; Kennedy, 1991/2007, p. 146; so also Cooper, 1932, p. 129 and Roberts, 1941/1984, p. 2212). This incites in us as Aristotle's English-speaking readers the anxious desire to please, to be included in the group of "good people" seen as doing "good things," but we worry whether Aristotle—the great authority at whose feet we are sitting, but who comes from a different culture from our own—will happen or chance to consider our emulation good enough for inclusion. Or we read that "usually people do what they long to do if they can, the bad through lack of self-control, the good because they desire good things [*hoi d' epieikeis hoti tōn epieikōn epithumousin*]" (2.19.19, 1392b23; Kennedy, 1991/2007, p. 160)—Aristotle's version of the Mencian claim that when a social *tiān* 天 structures our *xīn* 心, the best way to serve *tiān* 天 is to act on our inclinations—and we nervously run our current desires through a brief inspection, hoping for the best.

When we read something like the following, then, we are inclined to be skeptical:

> Let us first speak about laws, [showing] how they can be used in exhorting and dissuading and accusing and defending; for it

is evident that if the written law is contrary to the facts, one must use common law [*tōi koinōi*] and arguments based on fairness [*tois epieikesterois*] as being more just. [One can say] that to use [the jurors'] "best understanding" is not to follow the written laws exclusively, and that fairness [*to men epieikes*] always remains and never changes nor does the common law (for it is in accordance with nature) but written laws often change. (1.15.3–6, 1375a25–33; Kennedy, 1991/2007, p. 103)

Surely Aristotle can't actually mean this, we think: surely this claim is one of his bits of cynical advice for his students, not something he himself seriously believes. Universalism of all sorts is always a safe bet with the conservatives in the audience: maybe it will work on this jury? Perhaps we should imagine Aristotle crossing his fingers here?

But that would be hasty. I hate to admit it, in fact, but I think Aristotle is inclined to believe his own universalism here—an inclination that gets him into conceptual hot water. If we look back at that passage from *TR* 2.24 that I began quoting back at the beginning of this section, for example, the trouble he gets himself into with *to eikos* once he starts contextualizing seems instructive:

Further, just as in eristics an apparent syllogism occurs in confusing what is general and what is not general but some particular (for example, in dialectic [asserting that] non-being exists [*esti to mē on on*]; for what-is-not *is* what-is-not [*esti gar to mē on mē on*]; and that the unknown is known, for it is *known* about the unknown that it is unknown [*estin gar epistēton to agnōston hoti agnōston*]), so also in rhetoric there is an apparent enthymeme in regard to what is not generally probable but probable in a particular case [*to mē haplōs eikos alla ti eikos*]. The probability is not absolute, as Agathon, too, says,

Probably one could say that this thing itself is probable. Many improbable things happen to mortals.

For some things happen contrary to probability [*gignetai gar to para to eikos*], so what is contrary to probability is also probable [*hōste eikos kai to para to eikos*]. If this is so, the improbable will be probable [*to mē eikos eikos*]. But not generally so; as in eristics, not adding the circumstances and reference and manner makes for deception, so here [in rhetoric], because the probability is not general but qualified [*kai entautha para to eikos einai mē haplōs alla ti eikos*]. (2.24.10, 1402a3–15; Kennedy, 1991/2007, p. 188)

Here he wants to refute the eristic tendency to assert paradoxes[30] like "non-being exists," and—one might be inclined to think, at first—to *parody* that tendency with mock-assertions like "what is contrary to probability is also probable" and "the improbable will be probable." Instead of dismissing these clever casuistries out of hand, however, he offers only a partial restriction on them: they are, he says, *contextually* true but "not generally so" (*all' oukh haplōs*). In specific circumstances, in other words, "what is contrary to probability *is* also probable," and "the improbable *will* be probable." At some level Aristotle must know that this is utter nonsense; he is, after all, twice on the verge of branding it eristic. But he doesn't quite know it; he hasn't quite worked it all out. When he makes the comparison that "in eristics, not adding the circumstances and reference and manner makes for deception," in fact, he has slipped off-track: the ontological paradox *to mē on on* ("what isn't is") for him is *never* true, and not, as the comparison suggests, true in a "qualified" sense, in specific circumstances. There is no specific circumstance in which "what isn't is" becomes qualifiedly true—nor should there be a specific circumstance in which "what is contrary to probability is also probable" or "the improbable will be probable." What he means, surely, as his quotation from Agathon ("Many improbable things happen to mortals") suggest, is that "what is contrary to probability may *come true*": there is a slippage between our conceptions of the world (probability) and what actually happens (fact), and sometimes that slippage hits us in the face. But pretending that the improbable then becomes *probable* is just ludicrous. It remains as improbable as ever—but, unfortunately for probability, sometimes also factual.[31]

The conceptual hot water Aristotle gets himself into here is almost certainly the result of his thinking of *ta eikota* as a quality possessed by things and events—as existing objectively in a stable nature (*xìng* 性) and never changing—so that when something improbable happens, the improbable has to be squeezed into that same nature, somehow, so that the thing or the event has to be made to appear simultaneously probable and improbable, which he suspects is wrong (eristic) but can't figure out how. But of course *ta eikota* is not a quality possessed by things; it is a way of seeing those things. It is a social(-constructivist) ecology, not an ontology. Just as the persuasive is persuasive to somebody (1.2.11, 1356b27), so too is the probable

probable to somebody—but Aristotle apparently forgets this. What makes a thing probable is not that it happens, but that the community *recognizes* its happening, names it, predicts it, expects it, evaluates it, organizes other things and events and identities in relation to it. In somatic terms, the community ideosomatizes it, circulates through the group a somatized image of it as real and true and therefore as something that may well happen, may be considered probable or likely to happen. When the expected thing does happen, then, it seems real, seems like the truth, because it is collectively expected, and therefore has been validated in advance. When something utterly unexpected happens, something that the community's worldview cannot explain, it seems unreal, untrue, like a mirage or a miracle, because the community has no way of imposing collective meaning or identity on it. That unexpected event alone does not make the improbable thing probable; at best it can instigate a collective reshaping of those ideosomatic images of probabilities and likelihoods so as to include the once-unlikely thing. Then the improbable (thing) *becomes*, over time, probable—at which point it is, obviously, no longer improbable. It is part of *ta eikota*, part of the community's normative construction of truth, or truthiness—part of the collective reality-norms that take a hit whenever something they don't predict and can't explain happens.

Though this passage (*TR* 2.24.10) might be read as in error, I prefer to read it as part of Aristotle's entelechial process of working through Plato's mystical objectivism: some Platonic atavisms inevitably remain, even as a sketchy proto-social-constructivist theory and even sketchier somatic theory begin to emerge out of the younger philosopher's commitment to ordinary-language philosophy. Like Plato, Aristotle feels impelled to move in the direction of truth; indeed like Plato he feels around him a kind of collective groundswell of movement in the direction of truth, though Plato imagines that movement as driven from above, by truth itself, by divinity, so that it is actually not so much a groundswell as it is an ideaswell or formswell, while for Aristotle the movement is driven by the community he lives in, the culture he is a part of, as it works out the patterns and implications in its own assumptions. Aristotle's epistemological problem, then, as he tentatively follows his inclination to work from below, from collective human understanding, is what truth for him will or can or should "look like"—what it can be imagined to consist of, what it might be built from or on, what its ontological status might be—and how different it might look from Plato's truth and still deserve the *name* truth.

I want to come back to the weak man and the strong man, Aristotle's *paradeigma* or example for his cryptoeristic claims that *hōste eikos kai to para to eikos* (the probable is improbable) and *to mē eikos eikos* (the improbable is probable), in a moment (§4.15). First, though, let's take a close look at another discussion of *ta eikota* and their becoming-factual or becoming-true tendencies. The passage I want to look at is *topos* 21 in *TR 23*, where Aristotle seems to be saying that wild improbability is what *makes* something true (in my literal translation):

> Another is from things that seem to happen but are incredible [*ek tōn dokountōn men gignesthai apistōn de*], because they [people] would not have thought [*edoxan*] [that they happen] had they not been or nearly been [*ei mē ēn ē engus ēn*]. And even more [or an even better reason]: for [people] accept [*hupolambanousin*] things that either are [*ta onta*] or are plausible [*ta eikota*]; if then [something is] incredible and not likely [*ei oun apiston kai mē eikos*], it would be [considered] true [*alēthes an eiē*]: for not through its likelihood or believability, at least, does it seem so [*ou gar dia ge to eikos kai pithanon dokei houtōs*]. (2.23.22, 1400a5–8)

In other words, as I read that, *topos* 21 is a strange bird in that it arises out of the doxotic circulation of opinions and beliefs (*ta dokounta*) through the group and yet fails to persuade people. What is strange about this failure is that the doxotic production of seeming (*ta dokounta*) is normally constitutive of *to pithanon* (things that seem persuasive) and *ta eikota* (things that seem plausible enough to be true), and we think that if something seems plausible it must be based in reality—must have either actually happened (*ēn, ta onta*) or must have come so close to actually happening that it might as well have (*engus ēn, ta eikota*). And indeed this is what Aristotle is urging his students to argue in court, or in any other rhetorical situation, should the need arise: what most likely happened almost certainly did happen. But then we get to the most problematic line in the passage: Aristotle suggests that his students should argue, once again apparently eristically, that what is *least* likely to be true is in fact *most* likely to be true. He doesn't quite say this, in fact; he tries to drive a wedge between what is considered *likely* to be true and what *seems* true, by associating the former with persuasivity and the latter with *ta onta* "what is"—but this is such a problematic move philosophically that we once again tend to assume that this must just be cynical advice for rhetors.

E. M. Cope (1877, 2, pp. 285–86) strives valiantly to solve Aristotle's philosophical problem, and thus to naturalize his advice:

The object of this topic is (says Brandis, u. s., p. 20) to weaken the force of arguments from probability. "In incredibilibus provocatur ad effectum, qui si conspicuus sit, resisti non potest quin, quod incredibile videbatur, iam probabile quoque esse fateamur." Schrader.

'Another (class of arguments) is derived from things which are believed to come to pass (*gignesthai*, actually to take place or happen) but (still) are beyond (ordinary) belief, (you argue, namely) that they would not have been believed at all, had they not actually been or nearly so': i. e. either *been* in existence, or come so near to it, made so near an approach to it, as to enable us by a slight stretch of imagination to realize it so as to be convinced of its existence. Any case of very close analogy, for instance, to the thing in question might produce this conviction. *ē engus* is a saving clause; 'fact or nearly so.' Rhetorical argument does not aim at absolute truth and certainty: it is content with a near approach to it within the sphere of the probable, which is enough for complete persuasion.

'Nay even more,' (we may further argue that these at first sight incredible things are even more likely to be true than those that are at first sight probable. Supply *dokounta esti* for the constr. and (*mallon*) *alēthes* or *onta esti tōn eikotōn kai pithanōn* for the sense): 'because men believe in (suppose, assume the existence of,) things either actual, real or probable: if then it (the thing in question) be incredible and not probable, it must be true; because its probability and plausibility are not the ground of our belief in it.' The argument of the last clause is an exemplification of Topic IX, § 10, *supra*, see note there. It is an inference *ek diaireseōs*, 'from division'; a *disjunctive judgment*. All belief is directed to the true or the probable: there is no other alternative. All that is believed—and *this* is believed—must therefore be either true or probable: this is not probable; therefore it must be true. *alēthes more antiquae philosophiae* identifies truth and being: *alēthes* here = *on*.

In other words, the antecedent improbability of anything may furnish a still stronger argument for its reality than its probability. Anything absolutely incredible is denied at once, unless there be some unusually strong evidence of its being a *fact*, however paradoxical. That the belief of it is actually entertained is the strongest proof that it is a fact: for since no one would have supposed it to be true without the strongest evidence, the evidence of it, of whatever kind, must be unusually strong. The instance given is an exemplification of the topic in its first and simplest form.

The scenario Aristotle is imagining is one in which there is an incredibly unlikely event in the past that the rhetor wants or needs to claim actually happened; to that end the rhetoric should invoke its very improbability (unlikelihood, incredibility) as an argument in favor of the story's accuracy, its truthiness. In Cope's gloss, the argument for the account's veracity is built not on its improbability alone but on the combination of its improbability and the fact that people have believed it (*ta dokounta*)—since people only tend to believe what is either probable or actually true. If it's not probable, and yet they believed it, it must really have happened. If it had been made-up, its sheer incredibility would have made people disbelieve it; since people did believe it, they must have had sufficient evidence to overcome their sense of its improbability. To the extent that we take this to be a cynical rhetorical strategy that Aristotle is urging on his students, I suppose it's plausible enough—plausible in its very implausibility, of course, making it an excellent example of the *topos* it's glossing—to work on a jury; but at the very least we should not build this into evidence for any epistemological optimism on Aristotle's part. He is *not* saying here that the truth will out, even in situations that seem stacked against it. Even if we accept Cope's reading, all he is saying is that a jury might fall for such an argument.

But Cope is on very shaky ground, it seems to me. The big pitfall he's treading carefully around is that he needs simultaneously to subjectify and to objectify belief: to suggest that believing is about how things *seem* to us, so that this *topos* is all about manipulating an audience, and at the same time to suggest that "the true" and "the probable" are stable objective categories of being that can be neatly and exclusively juxtaposed in a disjunctive binary. "All belief is directed to the true or the probable: there is no other alternative. All that is believed—and this is believed—must therefore be either true or probable: this is not probable; therefore it must be true." As soon as we recognize that "the probable" is something that some group of people *believes* to be probable, and add that—as Cope too points out—"the true" is in fact described by Aristotle as the *ēn ē engus ēn*, "what is or nearly is," so that "any case of very close analogy, for instance, to the thing in question might produce this conviction," the rigid binary disjunction Cope sketches between "the true" and "the probable" breaks down entirely. It's all belief. It's all *ta dokounta*, the doxotic circulation of beliefs through a group so that they become *seemings*. *ta dokounta*, *ta eikota*, and *to pithanon* are all collective constructs, all things believed by the group, so that any split between *ta dokounta* (the way things seem) on the one hand and *ta eikota* (what is believed to be truthy enough that it may as well be true) and *to pithanon* (what people are persuaded by) on the other is really just a rift in *ta dokounta*, in the seemings. More precisely, it is a rift between what the *current* audience believes, i.e., *ta eikota* and *to pithanon*, and what the rhetor claims many people *not* currently present have believed, i.e., *ta dokounta*. Aristotle is advising, then, that the rhetor use a rhetorical construction of *ta dokounta* to leverage *ta eikota* (make the story sound probable) and *to pithanon* (and thereby persuade the current audience). The *topos* would be to turn the current audience's incredulity at an implausible story against them by invoking an imaginary audience from the past or from another place who faced the same implausibility but believed anyway. There is, in other words, no philosophical rift between *what is* and *what is plausible/persuasive*; there is only a rhetorical one, in this particular *topos*. The rhetor can *seem* to create a rift between them by associating *what is* with *what seems true*, and distinguishing that odd pairing from *what seems likely* and *what is persuasive*—even though *what seems true* is in fact indistinguishable from *what seems likely*, and the attempt to persuade by making the unpersuasive seem ipso facto true (and therefore persuasive) would appear to be a rhetorical non-starter.

Aristotle's English translators since Cope have, however, followed his construction of the passage, and made it all about truth. Kennedy (1991/2007, p. 188) in particular builds Aristotle's hypothesizing of a persuasively unpersuasive and untruthlike truth into the scarlet thread running all through the passage:

> Another is derived from things that are thought to have taken place but yet are implausible, [using the argument] that they would not seem *true* unless they were facts or close to being facts. And [one can argue] that they are all the more *true* [for that reason]; for people accept facts or probabilities as *true*; if, then, something were implausible and not probable, it would be *true*; for it is not because of probability and plausibility that it seems *true*. (emphasis added; interpolations Kennedy's)

This is how a translator builds a single *alēthes*, guarded though it is in Greek by the optative mood (the "might be" or the "would be considered to be"), first into a causal inevitability, then into a virtual repetition-compulsion:

- Aristotle writes *ouk an edoxan* "[they] would not have thought," without specifying what they wouldn't have thought, and Kennedy translates "would not seem true."

- Aristotle writes *kai hoti mallon* "and because more," and Kennedy translates "And [one can argue] that they are all the more true [for that reason]" (note how he doesn't mark his interpolation "true" as an interpolation).

- Aristotle writes *ē gar ta onta ē ta eikota hupolambanousin* "for people accept things that either are or are likely," and Kennedy translates "for people accept facts or probabilities as true" (this to my mind is the most defensible of Kennedy's expansions).

- And Aristotle writes *dokei houtōs* "it seems so," and Kennedy translates "it seems true."

My reading of the passage begins with the observation that the key recurring term in it is not *alēthes* "true" but *dokeō* "to seem": the *topos* itself is from *ta dokounta* "the seemings/thinkings," and from the claim that *ouk an edoxan, ei me ēn ē engus ēn*, literally "[people] would not have thought had it not been or nearly been," and it ends on the highly problematic argument that what seems incredible and unlikely in (rhetorical) fact *might be considered true*, because its seeming-so is not grounded in its credibility or likelihood. Frustrating as it seems to us that things keep *seeming* in the passage, without seeming this or that, true or false, I think we have to resist the temptation to fill in all the seemings with the epistemologically optimistic "true." When Aristotle writes *hoti ouk an edoxan, ei mē ēn ē engus ēn* "[people] would not have thought had it not been or nearly been," it doesn't seem like a huge leap to add "people would not have thought *it true.*" *True* does seem to be implied there. But precisely because of our conditioning to *ta eikota, ta dokounta,* and *to pithanon,* to the persuasivity of group constructions of truth, the word "true" works on us like Pavlov's bell. If an authoritative speaker says or writer writes that "people think it's true," readers and listeners tend to think *well I'm people* and so hear "it's true," and start slavering for a true dinner. If it *seems* true, or people *think* it true, as Aristotle says, it might as well be. It is as good as true. But that seeming is precisely his point here: he's not making a truth-claim; he's making a persuasivity-claim. He's arguing what may *seem* true if the rhetor says X, Y, and Z, not what will seem *true.*

In *ei oun apiston kai mē eikos, alēthes an eiē: ou gar dia ge to eikos kai pithanon dokei houtōs* "if then [something is] incredible and not plausible, it might be (considered) true: for not through its likelihood or believability, at least, does it seem so," it seems inescapable that *houtōs* refers back to *alēthes*, the proadverb's immediate antecedent. By "seems so," it seems, Aristotle does this time definitely mean "seems true." That this creates problems for him, however, seems obvious from Kennedy's translation: "if, then, something were implausible and not probable, it would be true; for it is not because of probability and plausibility that it seems true." What could possibly make it *seem true* if not probability and plausibility? Cope's answer, that "all belief is directed to the true or the probable: there is no other alternative," seems predicated, Platonically, not on what *seems* true but what *is* true. That little change, in fact, would make Aristotle's sentence make good Platonic sense: "if, then, something were implausible and not probable, it would be true; for it is not because of probability and plausibility that it *is* true." But that is not what Aristotle is claiming; he is claiming that it is not because something *seems likely* or *seems persuasive* that it *seems true*. So again, what other source of that seeming is there than *ta eikota* and *to pithanon*?

One possible reading of that source might be through the Kantian *Ding-an-sich* or the Lacanian Real: that the true source of truth is whatever our communal organizations of reality around the likely and the persuasive somehow always fail to reach, fail to access, fail to organize. If what *must* be true is the uncanny event that can neither be predicted in advance nor explained after the fact because it does not fit our social constructions of reality, because it has not been and cannot be somatized and circulated through the group body-becoming-mind, then it is reality as a Kantian/Lacanian mystery.[32] And that does seem to be more or less the direction Aristotle is heading: the "truth" that must be (or might be), despite its failure to fit our cultural canons of persuasiveness.

But that reading would still not explain the *dokei houtōs* (seems so) that ends the passage. That Kantian/Lacanian mystery truth would still be something that *is* true, not something that *seems* true. Indeed the Kantian *Ding-an-sich* and the Lacanian Real are by definition precisely things that *don't* seem true, because what seems true has been organized for Kant by the human understanding, with its Aristotelian categories (quality, quantity, manner, relation), and for Lacan by the Symbolic (language and the Law of the Father)—or, for Aristotle, by *ta eikota* and *to pithanon*, which is to say, by the entelechy of *ta dokounta*.

Once again, then, I would argue that Aristotle is in process with this seeming true. He is still moving toward a full formulation (entelechial actualization) of a doxotic truth. His last sentence, I suggest—*ei oun apiston kai mē eikos, alēthes an eie: ou gar dia ge to eikos kai pithanon dokei houtōs*—is a kneejerk Platonism that he corrected at the last minute from *estin toiouton* "is so" to *dokei houtōs* "seems so," without pausing to realize that the semantic shift, demanded as it clearly is by his ordinary-language focus on *doxa*, makes hash of the whole passage.

4.15 Aristotle: Doxicosis

If the *dokeō* material from the *TR* suggests that the *telos* of communal opinion is the depersonalized feeling or seeming of truth, then, the reigning entelechy of rhetoric's deep ecology for Aristotle would be the emergent actualization of *ta eikota* out of *ta dokounta* and *to pithanon*. If we take *ta dokounta*—call it doxosis—to be the circulation of energized opinion through the group body-becoming-mind, so that things *seem to be a certain way*, and *ta eikota*—call it icosis—to be the communal construction of truth(iness) through the doxotic process, then *to pithanon* or persuasivity would be the social glue that holds the two together. People say things, tell and hear things; people express their opinions. What converts that telling and hearing of opinions into truth-seeming or truthiness, and thus into knowledge, reality, identity, truth, is the energizing of that telling/hearing with persuasivity, through the body language of "presencing" (§3.6), which I've retheorized (§4.12) as the somatic exchange. People don't just *have* opinions, or *share* opinions; they *care* about their opinions, and so communicate them emphatically, presence them with affective-becoming-conative pressure that circulates through the group. This is the viral affective ecology of which Jenny Edbauer (2005, p. 9) wrote early on (§1.1): "a rhetoric emerges already infected by the viral intensities that are circulating in the social field." It is the multiple overlapping "infrastructures of trustworthiness" of which Susan Miller (2008, pp. 1–2) wrote, which "organize our emotional receptivity to statements on which we can depend for answers to speculative questions."

The social ecology that is born of the intertwining of *ta dokounta* and *ta eikota* in the bed of *to pithanon* I call doxicosis: a becoming-persuasive that cycles collectively energized tellings and hearings of opinions about truth and fairness through the member bodies of the community. This is the theoretical terminus of our study of rhetoric: this convergence of two social ecologies (ecosis + icosis) in a doxicotic becoming-persuasive that is also a becoming-good, a becoming-normal, a becoming-human, and a becoming-communal.

If we were to imagine a *logical* opposite of doxicosis, it would be the communal construction of a seeming that is false, as in "what is not the same often seems to be the same" (*TR* 2.24.3, 1401a24; Kennedy, 1991/2007, p. 186); but since the community is the ultimate arbiter of truth, it is in practice impossible for an individual or a group to *prove* that another group's icotic claim is flatout false. All one can do is launch a countericosis, a counterideosomatic challenge to the other group's icotic claim—that which seems to one's group obviously or overwhelmingly in error.

In a sense, in fact, that is what rhetoric is: this (counter)icosis, this marshalling of a group's doxicotic resources to persuade other members of the group or members of another group that one's own (or one's group's) claims are *true*, or at least probable or plausible enough to be *like* truth, as good as true. (In a deeper sense, that is what the *TR* is: a doxicosis designed to present Aristotle's community's truth as the universal truth, the unchanging truth found in nature, so as to persuade his readers. Something like this same "natural" inclination to naturalize his own sage-culture's *dào* 道 as The Way lies behind Mencius's tendency to universalize his advice.)

The *rhetorical* opposite of the doxicotic, therefore, is not that which is false but that which is unpersuasive (*apiston, to apithanon*) and so seems to lack the icotic feeling or seeming of truth on which successful rhetoric depends. But of course, like the persuasive and the icotic, *to apithanon* too is always unpersuasive *to someone*. It may be presented rhetorically as "unpersuasive in itself," or even "untrue in itself," but persuasivity is a relational experience involved in the circulation of *doxa* through a group. The rhetorical answer to Platonic objectivist logic—Socrates' attack on rhetoric in the *Gorgias* (459c), say—is that *doxa*, finally, is all there is: that Socrates' mystical rationalism is just another rhetorical strategy, just another attempt to persuade X of Y in order to achieve Z.

What I suggest Aristotle is moving toward in the *TR*, then, is a kind of doxicotic pragmatism, a kind of interactive map of *ta eikota* and *ta dokounta* that will allow the orator who reads his handbook to sense or "see" (*theōrein*) the icosis at work pushing appearances/opinions toward justice/truth well enough to be able to jump into it, to enter it strategically, so as to be able to persuade those whom s/he needs to persuade. If—to get back to *topos* 9 of *TR* 2.24 (§4.14)—a weak man is accused of attacking a stronger man, Aristotle says, he should be acquitted, because it *does not seem plausible* that a man would risk his own neck by attacking someone who is likely to do him serious bodily harm.

The key question is: seem plausible to whom? To the jury, first of all—to the people who have to decide whether he is innocent or guilty. But that "first" is only institutionally first, pragmatically immediate, in the meeting of the people's court. There are other constituencies as well, other "reputers" (*doxazontes*), whose group orientations to this man and men like him precede and condition the seeming in the agora-as-court—generally speaking, people who have participated in the group circulation of doxicoses of relative strength and weakness and their consequences for violent behavior, and therefore think they *know* the social psychology of strong and weak men, and think they can predict their behavior in specific social circumstances. For this group such ideosomatizations may be mostly preconscious, operating at the level of a felt inclination to impose a certain structure on reality; if the body-becoming-mind of this preconscious inclination is entelechial, its *telos* may be the articulation offered by an Aristotle or other social psychologist.

Does this mean that weak men never lose their temper and let fly at strong men? No. Does it mean—and this would be the foundation of the fallacious argument Aristotle is theorizing—that what seems improbable is always untrue, or, if not, that the improbable is *always* probable and vice versa? Again, no. Improbable things happen in specific circumstances without undermining probability in general. The weak man might well have attacked the strong man, but most likely he didn't, and so should be given the benefit of the doubt and acquitted. We may well be freeing a guilty man, and so in the end serving neither truth nor justice; but so be it.

Where it gets interesting, though, is when Aristotle puts an additional twist on his example: if a strong man is accused of assault, he should be acquitted too, precisely because the man must *know* how likely it will seem that he goes around attacking people, and is therefore unlikely to do so. Aristotle only gives us a single *dokeō* here, but in fact there must be a whole series of icotic seemings, or what Stephen Toulmin calls "warrants," or what I call ideosomatizations, which to avoid controversy[33] I will avoid identifying with the universal (minor) premise that Aristotle says should usually be left out of a syllogism in creating an enthymeme because it is obvious and therefore tedious to uneducated listeners [1.2.13, 1357a18]):

- *Icotic seeming 1:* people are violent, and may assault each other out of anger or other causes

- *Icotic seeming 2:* people may indulge their violent impulses if they think no harm will come to them from that indulgence; hence, a strong man is likely to assault a weaker man

- *Icotic seeming 3*: people may curb their violent impulses out of fear for their own safety; hence, a weak man is unlikely to assault a stronger man
- *Icotic seeming 4*: people may curb their violent impulses out of fear of legal consequences
- *Icotic seeming 5*: it may seem likely to a strong man, in accordance with icotic seeming 2, that people will *expect* him to be more violent, due to his strength, and will therefore be more likely to arrest and convict him if he does indulge his violent impulses than they would a weaker man, leading him to pay particular attention to icotic seeming 4

Let's pause there a moment to note that we could build a syllogism (using Toulmin's terms) out of what we've got so far, with the defendant as rhetor: "(*claim*) I am not guilty, (*grounds*) because a strong man would have to be pretty stupid not to know that (*warrant*) people are going to assume that a strong man is likely to be violent." But that's just one point of view, drawing on the assumptions of the group but marshalling those assumptions for a single argument; to get at something like the complexity Aristotle is trying to theorize, we need at least three more icotic seemings:

- *Icotic seeming 6*: people are smart enough to pay attention to the icotic seemings governing the uptake of their behavior, and to avoid doing things that might play into existing stereotypes that may prejudice juries or other social groups against them
- *Icotic seeming 7*: it is possible (and desirable) to escalate the smart attention people pay to icotic seemings into advice for orators
- *Icotic seeming 8*: it is possible (and desirable) for orators to use that advice in ways that precondition persuasion by circulating affectively a group orientation to seeming

Icotic seeming 8 would leave us at Aristotle's *TR*, which would thus stand as the *telos* of the becoming-communal seeming-becoming-knowing (*doxa*-becoming-*epistēmē*) entelechy that structures his rhetorical theorizing—"becoming-communal" not only in the sense that Aristotle is *theorizing the community* but also in the sense that the community is *working through Aristotle*, that he is one of the theoretical channels of the doxicotic entelechy in ancient Athens (and after).

To account for what I'm doing here, then, we'd need yet one more:

- *Icotic seeming 9*: it is possible (and desirable) to escalate the smart attention Aristotle (not to mention Mencius) pays to icotic seemings into rhetorical theory for the twenty-first century

An objectivizing (Platonizing) approach to all this would need to begin with epistemology: who knows how much and how reliably?

[a] (*contra icotic seeming 5*) Did the strong man really know that people would assume that he would be inclined to violence?

[b] (*contra icotic seeming 6*) Did the strong man really know that by scrupulously avoiding reacting violently to situations he could forestall the tendency people might have to judge him in advance?

[c] (*contra icotic seeming 7*) Does every juror know that the strong man knew these things, and, if that knowledge is in principle impossible to obtain, does every juror believe the defendant when he asserts it?

[d] (*contra icotic seeming 8*) Does Aristotle know well enough what the strong man knew and what every juror knows about what the strong man knew to be able to declare that he should be acquitted?

[e] (*contra icotic seeming 9*) Do I know well enough what Aristotle means to draw adequate conclusions from the *TR*?

[f] (*etc.*) Do you know well enough what I mean to draw adequate conclusions from this book?

An objectivist would find some high degree of epistemological certainty on these questions essential for (a) the strong man's own decision-making process (*ethics*), (b) the jury's deliberations as to the strong man's guilt or innocence (*jurisprudence*), (c) the critic's deliberations on what actually happened in a specific (real or hypothetical) court case (*legal theory*), (def) the critic's deliberations on Aristotle's *TR* (*rhetorical theory*), and so on.

But Aristotle himself here takes another tack: rather than setting himself the epistemological task of determining the objective reliability of each person's or group's knowledge in this hypothetical, he pulls back to the pragmatic claim that *people will seem to know these things*, or, to run that the other way, that *it will seem to people that they know these things*, and they (and you) can and will act accordingly. The group seemings on which we base many or most or all of the tentative certainties we need for responsible and intelligent decision-making are both doxotic (presenced through the group body-becoming-mind) and icotic (constituting what the group will take as truth); and that is by and large good enough for the social animals that we are. Even if he cannot prove the truth-value of the claims he makes here, if it *feels* right to us—if it seems truthy, if it is doxicotic—we will most likely go along with it.

5

Conclusion

Aristotle and Mencius on Ecosis

The fact that this book is a study of the deep ecology of *rhetoric* places its primary focus on icosis, or doxicosis, the becoming-persuasive that is also a becoming-truthy and a becoming-real-seeming—the ways in which the deep affective ecology of social value works through the affectively-becoming-conatively valenced or energized or "persuasivized" telling-and-hearing of opinions to produce what *feels* like truth, justice, reality, and identity. But as has been clear throughout, in both Aristotle and Mencius there is no icosis without ecosis, without ethecosis, the becoming-good that is also a becoming-communal—the ways in which the deep affective ecology of social value works through the ethecotic guidance of action to produce a community that is more or less coherently organized around specific norms and values. I have noted (§1.3) that Mencius is normally read ecotically, and that my icotic reading is in many ways a reading against the grain, a teasing out of the rhetorical situations that structure the book a not always quite explicit focus on persuasivity; and that, while Aristotle's *TR* is foundational for any Western study of rhetoric-as-doxicosis, even in the *TR* it is nearly impossible to isolate his icotic concerns with persuasivity from his ecotic concerns with community, which centrally inform the ethical books. "The Mencian way is one that emerges locally through personal cultivation and individual sagacity, but the goal is communal growth and social transformation. The society that best facilitates these goals is one governed by the free intercourse of associated humanity (*ren* 仁)" (Behuniak, 2005, p. 127). "To have practical wisdom, Aristotle writes in *NE* VI. 8, is to be interested in one's own welfare as part of the common welfare: 'one's own good cannot exist without household management [*oikonomias*] or a form of government [*politeias*]' (1142a9–10)" (Sherman, 1989, p. 53).

And it is really in those two collective realms, household management and government, that doxicosis in both Mencius and Aristotle plays its most important organizing role. But it is also in those two realms in particular that Mencius insists that individual human beings are not entirely in control. *MZ* 5A, for example, constitutes a kind of Q&A biography of Mencius's great emperor-hero Shun 舜, the legendary emperor-sage from the twenty-second century BCE who best embodies the Confucian Way. Wan Zhang 萬章 and Xian-qiu Meng 咸丘蒙 ask Mencius a series of questions about Shun in the form "it is said that . . . is that true?"—the doxicotic movement from what is told-and-heard about a legendary emperor-sage to the construction of a viable truth—and Mencius corrects their misconceptions. In 5A5 Wan Zhang asks whether the Emperor Yao 堯 gave the empire to Shun instead of his own son, and Mencius replies that no man has the power to give the empire away; rather, *tiān yǔ zhī* 天與之 "heaven gave it." Wan Zhang then asks whether *zhūnzhūn rán mìng zhī hū* 諄諄然命之乎, which Lau (1970/2003, p. 203) translates "Does this mean that Heaven gave him detailed and minute instructions?"—but note that the character that Lau translates as "instructions" is *mìng* 命, which as we've seen (§4.5) can be a command or decree (or in this case instructions), but can also be life or fate or the external conditions that are beyond our control. The fact that Mencius responds by talking about heaven *not speaking*—*tiān bù yán* 天不言—but rather showing itself through its *xìng* 行 "behavior, conduct" suggests that in this context *mìng* 命 is not conditions or fate but some form of spoken order or instructions; but arguably the *xìng* 行 through which heaven shows itself *is* conditions, so the remark might also be read as Mencius's resistance to the notion of *tiān* 天 as a personalized deity with a voice by which it expresses a unified will.

In 5A6, in response to a follow-up question from Wan Zhang—specifically as an explanation for the succession of emperors after Yao and Shun, the varying characters of their sons and grandsons, and the varying success of their respective reigns—Mencius further clarifies his conception of *tiān* 天 and *mìng* 命:

> All this was due to Heaven [*tiān* 天] and could not have been brought about by man [*fēirén* 非人, lit. "not human"]. When something is brought about though there is nothing that brings it about, then it is Heaven [*tiān* 天] that does it. When something

arrives though there is nothing that makes it arrive, then it is Destiny [*mìng* 命] that does it. (Lau, 1970/2003, pp. 207, 209)

Despite the shorthand belief that early Chinese thought (and especially Confucianism) does not operate dualistically, it is pretty clear that Mencius is setting up two (or possibly three) dualisms here: [1] between the human (*rén* 人) and the transhuman (*tiān* 天/*mìng* 命), [2a] between acting (*wéi* 為) and not acting (*mò zhī wéi* 莫之為), or perhaps [2b] between a doer (*wéi zhě* 為者) and no doer (*mò zhī wéi* 莫之為). The Chinese for "When something is brought about though there is nothing that brings it about, then it is Heaven that does it" is *mò zhī wéi ér wéi zhě, tiān yě* 莫之為而為者，天也, literally "if there is no one to do it but it is done, then heaven." Implicit in these two dualisms is a definition of the human as a causal connection between a doer and doing; if that connection is broken, so that there is doing but no doer, we conclude that the (non-)doer must be that transhuman force called *tiān* 天.

Now in English, the speakers of which for well over a millennium have been predominantly Christian, it is all too easy to fill in the gaps of these dualisms by imagining that there are in fact *two* doers, one visible, the other invisible, or one embodied, the other a disembodied spirit, and so to understand Mencius to be implying by *mò zhī wéi* 莫之為 "there is no doer" simply that there is no *visible* doer, no one who acts in a human body and therefore no one who can be seen performing the action by other humans. Nor would this be only a Western/Christian/English reading of the text. After all, the very fact that *tiān* 天 is the sky or the heavens suggests the spiritualizing tendency even in the ancient Chinese conception; and various Chinese commentators have read into *tiān* 天 not just spiritualism but a "personal deity with a will" (Shun, 1997, p. 207). For example, in the *Comprehensive History of Chinese Thought* (*Zhōngguó sīxiǎng tōngshǐ* 中國思想通史), the respected Marxist historian of philosophy Hou Wailu (侯外廬, 1903–1992) reads a passage from the *Analects* (17.19) very like *MZ* 5A5 in which things grow and the seasons change without heaven *speaking* as implying that Confucius did believe *tiān* 天 was a personalized deity that could speak but simply chose not to (Hou, 1957, pp. 153–54; cited in Shun, ibid.). This reading of Confucius could of course have been ideologically motivated, aimed to discredit Confucius in the atheist People's Republic; but it does suggest that the temptation to spiritualize *tiān* 天 (and thus to dualize heaven and earth, spirit and matter, mind and body, the invisible and the visible, etc.) is not just a Western misconception of Confucian thought.

If we look more closely at the specific claims Mencius is making about Yao and Shun and their successors, however, it becomes clear that a dualizing/spiritualizing reading of the passage is problematic. A review of the "doings" that had no obvious human "doer" shows that they were all *done* by human beings—just not by any one rational agent in complete control of the process. Yao did not "give" Shun the empire; Yao died, and rather than usurp the empire from Yao's "unworthy" (*bùxiào* 不肖) son Dan Zhu 丹朱, Shun withdrew to mourn for three years, but the feudal lords and ballad singers chose Shun. Shun was chosen by people, not by a disembodied spirit. Did each feudal lord and each ballad singer choose Shun individually, rationally? Possibly, but Mencius presents it as a collective decision—made, in my terms, doxicotically. Before Yao's death, Shun served him as his chief administrator for 28 years, which, Mencius says, "is something which could not be brought about by man, but by Heaven alone" (Lau, 1970/2003, p. 205). Surely Yao and Shun played some part in bringing that about? Yes, but Mencius would insist that they could not possibly be solely responsible for it. Much had to do with Shun's administrative ability, which is an interactive skill rather than an individualistic trait; as Mencius puts it, "When he was put in charge of affairs, they were kept in order and the people were content. This showed that the people accepted him. Heaven gave it to him, and the people gave it to him" (Lau, ibid.). Shun's administrative success was clearly not something he could achieve on his own, through his own rational control of events. When Shun died, his recommendation that Yu 禹 succeed him in place of his own unworthy son was followed by the people, even though Yu withdrew just as Shun had done; when Yu died, his recommendation that he be succeeded by Yi 益 rather than his own son Qi 啟 (founder of the Xià Dynasty 夏朝, c. 2070–c. 1600 BCE) was *not* followed by the people.

The role played by *tiān* 天 in all this becomes especially interesting when we consider those "unworthy" (*bùxiào* 不肖) sons of Yao and Shun. How does the son of a revered emperor-sage grow up to be unworthy of rule? One construction of *tiān* 天 or *tiān mìng* 天命 in this case might be that some hormonal imbalance or other physiological defect or deficiency made them that way: *tiān* 天 as biology (*shēng* 生) and *mìng* 命 as the "decree" that hormones and neurotransmitters and so on give to the entire organism. But this, obviously, would not be an explanation Mencius would favor; he would use the ethecotic four shoots (*sì duān* 四端) instead. The easy modern Western pop-psychological "diagnosis" would be that Yao and Shun were "bad fathers"—that through some ethical failing these great men did not raise their sons right, and they grew up unworthy. What that pop psychology would miss, of course, would be the interactive, reciprocal, circulatory, reticulatory nature of the four shoots: *rén* 仁 is not an individualized ethical "benevolence" but an ethecotic (becoming-communal) "fellow-feeling" (§2.11); *yì* 義 is not an individualized ethical "righteousness" but an ethecotic "situational rightness" (§2.11); *lǐ* 禮 is not an individualized ethical "propriety" but an ethecotic participation in ritualized group normativity (§3.9); *zhì* 智 is not an individualized ethical (let alone epistemic) "knowledge" but an ethecotic (interactive) "wisdom." What that correction says about the relationship between child-rearing and the way children turn out is that child-rearing *is* an ethecosis: not just an ethical becoming-good or becoming-normal but an ethecotic becoming-communal. If Yao's and Shun's raising of their sons was affected by their preoccupation with matters of state—and how could it not be?—that is ethecosis. If their sons were mainly raised by servants, and the servants happened to be quite far from the kind of ethical sagacity that Mencius promotes—and how could they not be? sages are rare—that is ethecosis. For that matter, if the fathers had some ethical defect or deficiency that never showed up in their interactions with others, even in their interactions with their sons, it could still have been passed to their sons by the ethecotic contagion of shared affect—and that would have been a social-ecological (ecotic) *tiān* 天 or *tiān mìng* 天命 too. We might even paraphrase the line Mencius quotes from the *Tai Shi* 泰誓, "Heaven sees with the eyes of its people; Heaven hears with the ears of its people" (5A5; Lau, 1970/2003, pp. 205, 207), as "heaven feels with the shared affect of its people."

A corollary of this consideration of the ethecosis of child-rearing is that the succession in Yao's and Shun's cases was decided not just doxicotically by the people, through the shared affect of persuasivity, but ethecotically as well, through the shared affect of family life—the ethecotic inner sanctum for Mencius's understanding of human life. As I noted in §1.3, Mencius is usually read as primarily an ethecotic thinker, and I have set myself the task of reading him, against the grain as it were, as a doxicotic one; but there is in Mencius or Aristotle (or anyone) ultimately no doxicosis without ethecosis, because the circulation of persuasivity through a community that facilitates the social construction of "reality" is by definition a becoming-communal, an entelechial circulation of character, face, social value. The fact that, locally—as in the contagion of ethical alignments from parent to child (or anyone to anyone) without verbal communication—there can be ethecosis without doxicosis might seem to suggest that ethecosis is ecologically primary and doxicosis its secondary rhetorical "extension"; we might even be tempted to say that doxicosis as a rhetorical becoming-persuasive is the *human* extension of an ethecosis that is the fundamental channel of social regulation in all social animals. But then remember George Kennedy's suggestion that the fundamental regulatory channel in all social animals is precisely persuasion-as-energy: ultimately (eth)ecosis and (dox)icosis are names for slightly different thematizations or cultural channelings of the same social ecology.

The possibility that ecosis/icosis functions in very similar ways among nonhumans as well as humans returns us to Arne Naess and the deep ecology of Self-realization—the identificatory self-realization of the ecological self. Naess (2002, p. 2) is in fact very close to both Mencius and Aristotle here:

> Feeling at home in life is for me one of many purposes in living. . . . The important thing is that the direction I am following corresponds with that which I find significant, based on the deepest underlying principles of my life—friendship and happiness, for example. To feel at home in life requires both the willpower and the desire to participate in it actively. Woe betide him who goes round with the feeling of being a stranger, one who has landed on the wrong planet.

"Friendship and happiness" are Aristotle's *philia* and *eudaimonia*, of course, and as we've seen (§2.3), *to philein* "friendly feeling" takes us to Mencius on *rén* 仁 "fellow-feeling," arguably his central ethecotic ideal and vehicle as well as doxicotic subject as force and conditions, and friendship (*péngyou* 朋友) is the fifth of Mencius's five relationships (*wǔlún* 五倫, 3A4). Naess (pp. 2–3) goes on:

> But what does being active mean? Spinoza has taught me to take seriously in my own life an important philosophical distinction between activity and activeness. I associate the word *activity* with physical activity in the first place, but I also think of intense learning, verbal activity, and reasoning where much is evolving. For me, closeness to Nature has unveiled a marked difference between being active in Nature through play and sport on the one hand and, on the other, experiencing Nature in a way that engages us completely as human beings. The latter attitude may well be consistent with physical activity, but more characteristically it is associated with lingering in silence—perhaps without so much as moving a little finger. A word or two, perhaps even a whole stream of thought might occur to one, but it is the

pauses and the internal silence that are the hallmarks of this kind of relationship with Nature. From the outside one might not seem to be active, but as a person, one is completely absorbed. One's whole being is in reality activated in such circumstances, but outsiders do not necessarily perceive one to be in a state of activeness. The more usual state, activity, is concerned with that which is external, and we can be involved in all kinds of activity without being in a state of activeness.

I take him to mean "completely absorbed" there in some kind of quasiliteral sense, namely, that in a "state of activeness" the ecological self expands and becomes one with nature: with trees, rocks, the rough earth underneath, the breezes and sunlight and clouds above, and so on. This is, strictly speaking, a projection in the Freudian sense—what in §2.2 I called an affective self or *shēnxīn* 身心—but then the self is always a projection, always an interactive (ethecotic) phenomenology of coherence created as a fictional first-person narrative and projected onto the mind, the body, an apartment, a neighborhood, a job, a car, a city, a country, a religion, a landscape, and so on. What Ruskin derogated as the "pathetic fallacy"—the poetic ascription of feelings to nature, as in the mournful soughing of the pines, the cheerful burbling of a brook—is simply part of that phenomenology for the ecological self, "fallacious" only in a radical Cartesian purview, in which "I" am some tiny part of my brain, the pineal gland, the *res cogitans*. As Naess (2002, p. 3) puts it: "That many people do not quite grasp where I stand might stem from the fact that I feel that both I myself and life itself are a kind of current, not objects floating in a current. I do not step into the river, as the pre-Socratic Greek philosopher Heraclitus saw it. I *am* the current."

But again, this is a phenomenology, and it is specifically Naess's phenomenology: "*I* feel that both *I myself* and life itself are a kind of current." Others may feel that they and life are "objects floating in a current"; still others may despise this kind of "mystical" talk, as Murray Bookchin (1994, p. 17) does in promising to "demystify mystical and deep ecology, neo-Malthusianism, and sociobiology, all of which serve to derail serious social critique and orient it toward celebrations of 'wilderness,' the worship of nature deities, primitivism, often a hatred of technology and science as such, and a denigration of reason and the belief that progress is *possible*—especially progress cast in humanistic or human terms." As he says, programmatically: "The essays that follow emphasize that ecological degradation is, in great part, a product of the degradation of human beings by hunger, material insecurity, class rule, hierarchical domination, patriarchy, ethnic discrimination, and competition. Their focus, in short, is on the inseparability of social problems from ecological problems; hence my use of the name *social ecology*" (ibid.).

Though in rhetorical style Mencius and Aristotle are both closer to the gentle tolerance of Naess than they are to the hard angry polemics of Bookchin, as philosophers and teachers Mencius and Aristotle are ultimately more insistently concerned with the same kinds of social critique that Bookchin champions than they are with "wilderness." Aristotle's sociopolitical project in the *TR* is to train his students to "govern" a democratic Athens. As Walker (2000, p. 31) reminds us, "by the fourth century there [had] emerged a small, elite class of more or less professional *rhētores*: men who generally came from aristocratic or wealthy families, who had the requisite education and the confidence, who regularly spoke before the people in civic forums, and who were the dominant force in city politics." These were in effect the rulers of the city, and in a sense also the rulers of Athenian doxicosis, the premier regulators of the Athenian somatic exchange—which is to say, of the *demos*. In order to rule in a democracy they could not simply command but had to *persuade* people to follow their lead: they had to construct *pisteis* that would circulate influentially through the somatic exchange, and so gradually assimilate the populace to their way of thinking. As Walker (ibid., p. 13) puts it, "the ancestral/archival authority and the rhythmic/psychagogic spell of epideictic discourse are not inherently insidious forms of authoritarian mind control but suasory means—illusionistic 'witchcraft'—by which skillful speakers, chanters, and singers may promote traditional, untraditional, or even antitraditional values and beliefs." Epideictic rhetors *interact* with the doxicotic community, drawing on its power to help them make their points persuasive, but also guiding it, shaping it, directing it by what we might loosely call doxicotic remote control. It's never remote in the sense that the rhetors themselves are not part of the somatic exchange, of course: they are. The sense in which they wield remote control is that they attempt to shape the beliefs and knowledge and behavior of people they have never met, will never meet, by inserting a persuasive somatic impulse into the exchange and hoping for the best.

And if there were only a single somatic exchange in any democratic culture, that would be that. A few influential epideictic rhetors would exert the decisive guiding force over it, and effectively run everything—though of course in a sense, as we began to see in §3.9, every member of the somatic exchange would also contribute significantly by circulating the hegemonic ideological or "ideosomatic" (ethecotic/doxicotic) impulses, and even adding idiosyncratic or "idiosomatic" ("itericotic") iterations to those impulses, turning "rule" or "hegemony" into "community."

Unfortunately for the elegance of that explanation, however, there is never only one somatic exchange. There are always many—as many, in fact, as there are loose groupings of people. In the Athens of Aristotle's day the senate (*boulē*), the assembly (*ekklēsia*), and the courts of law (*dikasteria*) would all have had their separate somatic exchanges: some, those preferred by Aristotle, dominated by the "better sort of people," well-educated aristocratic men who were able to deal with the facts without being swayed by emotion; others, which Aristotle tends to discuss rather fastidiously, more emotionally turbulent. The morally questionable advice Aristotle gives his students in the *TR* is generally taken to be aimed at teaching them rhetorical prowess in those latter exchanges. But in addition to these "official" somatic exchanges there would also have been the somatic exchanges of male workers, which would not have been coterminous with the assembly in which they were all allowed and encouraged to participate, and of women, and of slaves, and of children, and of foreigners, none of whom was eligible to sit in the assembly, and of smaller groups of those classes, all the way down to individual families and friendships.

And each somatic exchange, whether it had two members or two hundred thousand, would have had its leaders, its most influential *doxazontes* or "reputers," whom the other members of the group tended to listen to and believe. This group dynamic *is* what I've been calling doxicosis. And in an important sense the rhetorical expertise of that small elite group of rhetors who in effect ruled Athens was simply a formalized version of what influential members of groups everywhere were doing—which is to say that epideictic rhetoric too was governed by the somatic "rules" (felt regularities) of doxicosis, and that its influential rhetors governed the *demos* by submitting to being self-regulated by those rules or regularities. Or, to put that differently: epideictic rhetors were taught to speak persuasively and shape the ruling somatic exchange(s) of the city not just by Isocrates, Aristotle, and the other great "sophists" of the day, but by their own friends and neighbors and family members—by their lifelong immersion in the somatics of doxicosis.

And as I argued in §1.3, Mencius's social project in the *MZ* is to convince rulers and their advisors to rule more doxicotically as well, through persuasion, through the circulation of persuasivity—and, to that end, to participate in the becoming-communal of ethecotic growth. The fellow-feeling King Xuan of Qi experiences with the ox being led to slaughter (1A7), which as I noted in §1.1 is exactly parallel with the story Arne Naess tells about experiencing fellow-feeling with a flea, is all fine and good, as

Mencius presents the case, but only as a first step toward extending that same fellow-feeling to his people, and running the kingdom so that people find it easier to earn a decent living. As has often been noted (cf. Shun, 1997, p. 164; Behuniak, 2005, p. 123), Mencius devotes considerable attention to very specific socioeconomic projects to be undertaken by the various rulers he advises: the organization of agriculture for the adequate production and distribution of food (1A3, 1A7), the regulation of land use (1B5, 3A3), the most ethical way to levy taxes (1A5, 2A5, 3B8), the organization and promotion of education (1A3, 1A7, 3A3, 7A14), and the appointing of competent and ethical officials (1B7, 2A4–5). Like Arne Naess, Mencius is philosophically interested in the self-realization (ethecosis) of the collectivized ecological self; unlike Naess, however, and more like Bookchin, he is also interested in the specific socioeconomic policies to which his ethecotic recommendations should give rise.

Democracy remains problematic for both Mencius and Aristotle, for different reasons: for Mencius because it is politically inconceivable, for Aristotle because it is politically unattractive. Still, both thinkers imagine doxicotic workarounds that strike us, more than two millennia later, with our considerable experience of a wide range of democratic political formations, as utterly practical and effective orientations to democracy. This is because their workarounds are grounded in a complex and nuanced understanding of the affective-becoming-conative-becoming-cognitive dynamics of groups in general—and democracy is simply the most widely established form of government that pares governance back as close to those group dynamics as possible. The idealization of that trend would be anarchy, which as an actual form of collective self-governance has only been tried in small radical experiments, like the nineteenth-century Fourierist Phalanxes—or "Associations," with their conception of "associative humanity"—and in some sense the utopianism of Mencius's conception of *rén* 仁 stems from its close connections with anarchy. But ultimately Mencius, like Aristotle, is no anarchist. Both thinkers valued the rule of exemplary persons—well, exemplary *men*, sages-become-rulers for Mencius, aristocrats-become-philosophers for Aristotle—who gained access to rule precisely by undergoing the process of ethecotic growth that Mencius calls the Way (*dào* 道) and Aristotle calls the entelechy by which *doxa* is collectively habitualized as *epistēmē* (see Burnyeat, 1981; Nussbaum, 1986/2001), and that I have been calling ethecosis and doxicosis, respectively.

But because the rule both Mencius and Aristotle imagined for their exemplary persuaders *was* precisely ecological, ecotic/icotic—grounded in friendship and fellow-feeling, in political extensions of family love, loyalty, and deference for Mencius and of the tendency humans in groups have to work through their opinions toward an increasingly habitualized truth for Aristotle—their rhetorical thought offers useful guides to every imaginable aspect of life in groups: workplace relationships, social networking, social work, the classroom. As we saw in §1.3, for centuries in China Mencius has almost exclusively been taken to be giving us advice for everyday living. This is completely understandable, not only because Mencius happened in the twelfth century to be canonized as the most important Confucian thinker after Confucius, but because his approach to life in groups *is* eminently useful for everyday living.

Aristotle's fate has been rather different: canonized in the thirteenth century in Europe as the great philosophical preceptor of medieval scholasticism, and a few centuries later of scientific method, he has long been the exclusive property of a few philosophers and historians of science, and widely taken to be both of not much use for everyday living and of a cast of mind radically different from—indeed opposite to—that of "Chinese philosophy." My main brief in the comparative history of philosophy part of my argument has been not only that Aristotle is much more like Mencius than we have hitherto thought, but that he is able to clarify, very much in the Mencian spirit, some points that Mencius leaves vague.

As a student of rhetoric, however, and more broadly of human communication, I take the most significant revelation arising from my comparison of Mencius with Aristotle as rhetoricians to be a complexly collectivistic understanding of persuasivity, or what I call in my title the deep ecology of rhetoric:

- the circularity of certain key concepts in both thinkers (*pistis*, *zhì* 治)
- the group heart-becoming-mind that is the collective subject of persuasion (identification, *rén* 仁)
- the secular vitalism of Mencian and Aristotelian conceptions of energy (*qì* 氣, *energeia*)
- the energization of rhetoric through contagious body language (shared affect)
- the use of energized body language to train the body-becoming-mind to dispositions
- Confucian *lǐ* 禮 "ritual propriety" as group norms, enforced and inculcated through the training of the body-becoming-mind

- the intelligent (not simply conformist) role played by the exemplary individual in adapting to the best group norms
- *xìng* 性 "human nature" as the dispositional embodiment of virtue in and through the four hearts and five relationships
- the functioning of social regulation through pressure on individual bodies-becoming-minds to conform to group norms as *tiān* 天 "forces" and *mìng* 命 "conditions"
- face as social value
- social valuing as work (energization)
- shame-becoming-disdain as the collective "heart" that propels the individual onto the Confucian Way
- the somatic exchange of persuasion as doxosis (*ta dokounta*, becoming-real-seeming), icosis (*ta eikota* and *ta pithanon*, becoming-persuasive as becoming-truthy), and doxicosis
- the somatic exchange of becoming-good, becoming-normal, and becoming-communal as ecosis

Now, obviously the implication that Mencius and Aristotle "collaborated" on the creation of this complex understanding of human communication is a theoretical artifact—one that shows, as I warned in §1.1, that the construction of such an artifact out of close comparisons of the *TR* and *MZ* is the most important task undertaken in this book, weightier by far than the exegesis of either author or either work. Indeed, as will have been noted, I do here and there push slightly past the specific formulations of both philosophers to articulate some theoretical point that neither quite managed to work out. Such rare moments, however, do not substantially change the "collaborative" nature of the theoretical framework that emerges from a fresh comparative look at both philosophers' texts and subtexts—the fact that Mencius and Aristotle demonstrably *were* working on similar problems, and coming up with strikingly similar solutions to those problems, in very much the same historical period. It is my hope that my exegetical efforts along these lines, feeble as they may be, might spark some interest in these issues among Mencius and Aristotle scholars who have dedicated their professional lives to explicating either of the two thinkers.

Notes

Chapter 1. Mencius and Aristotle as "Deep-Ecological" Theorists of Rhetoric

1. Thanks to John Schwandt for this phonology.
2. In Plato's *Laws*, for example, when Kleinias says that something is probable (*eikos*), the Athenian Stranger associates that probability with another, related to settlements, or dwellings, or habitations (*tōn oikēseōn*; 3.681a); in the *Charmides* he talks about the likelihood (*tōn eikotōn*) with which the product of two Athenian houses (*oikia*) would be handsome, noble, and best at everything (157e–158a). Early in the *Politics* Aristotle writes that the village (*hē kōmē*) is like (*eoiken*) a settlement (*apoikia*) of households (*oikias*) (1252b15); and in the *TR* he writes that if one thing has been done for another, it's probable (*eikos*) that that thing happened, for example, if a foundation, a house (*oikia*; 2.19.25, 1393a7–8). And in the *Economics* Xenophon writes that by acting in a certain way a man is *eikos ton oikon auxesthai* (likely [*eikos*] to augment his household or estate [*ton oikon*]" (11.12). I am indebted to Jonathan Fenno for these examples.
3. Here is a chapter-by-chapter breakdown of rhetorical situation in the *MZ*:

	1		2		3		4		5		6		7	
	A	B	A	B	A	B	A	B	A	B	A	B	A	B
1	ER	EA	ED	IR	ER	ED	IR	IX	ED IR	IA	EP	ED IP	IX	ED IR
2	ER	ER	ED	ED IA	ER	ED IR	IR	IR	IRA IR	ED IRAG	EP	ED	IX	IR
3	ER	ER	IR	ED IA	ER	ED IA	IX	ER	ED IR	ED IR	EP	ED	IX	IR
4	ER	ER	IR	ER	IR	ED IR	IX	ERA	ED IR	ED IRAG	EP	IA	IX	IR
5	ER	ER	IR	EAD	IP	ED IR	IX	IR	ED IR	IX	ED IP	ED IA	IX	IX

continued on next two pages

259

	1		2		3		4		5		6		7	
	A	B	A	B	A	B	A	B	A	B	A	B	A	B
6	ER	ER	IR	ED IA		EA	IR	IX	ED IR	ED IRG	ED IP	IA	IX	IR
7	ER	ER	IX	ED		ED	IX	IX	ED IR	ED IRG	IX	IR	IX	IX
8		ER	IX	EA		ER	IA	IX	ED IR	ED IG	IX	ER	IR	IX
9		ER	IX	ERA		ED	IR	IX		ER	IA	IA	EA	IX
10		ER		ER		ED	IX	IX			IX	ER	IX	IX
11		ER		EA			IX	IX			IX	ER	IX	IR
12		ER		EA			IR	IX			IX	IG	IR	IR
13		ER		ED IA			IR	IX			IX	ED IR	IR	IR
14		ER		ED IA			IA	IX			IX	ED IR	IR	IR
15		ER					IX	IX			ED IX	IR	IR	IR
16		ER					IR	IR			IX	ID	IR	IX
17							ED IA	IX			IX		IX	IX
18							ED IX	ED			IX		IX	IX
19							IX	IRAG			IX		IA	IX
20							IA	IR			IX		IR	IX
21							IX	IX					IR	ED IX
22							IA	IX					IR	ED IX
23							IX	IX					IR	ED IA
24							EA	IX					IX	IX
25							EA	IX					IX	ED IX
26							IX	IX					IX	IP
27							IX	IX					IX	IRA
28							IX	IX					IX	IR
29								IX					IX	IA

	1A	1B	2A	2B	3A	3B	4A	4B	5A	5B	6A	6B	7A	7B
30								ED IX					IR	IX
31								IX					ED IR	IG
32								ED					ED IG	IG
33								IX					ER	IG
34													IR	IA
35													ED IR	IX
36													IX	ED IX
37													IX	ED IG
38													IX	IX
39													ER	
40													IG	
41													ED IG	
42													IR	
43													ED IA	
44													IX	
45													IG	
46													IX	

Key:

E explicit address to

I implicit address to

R ruler

A advisor (high-ranking official who advises the ruler)

G gentleman

D one of Mencius's disciples

P one of Mencius's philosophical opponents

X anyone (everyman or everywoman)

4. Huang (2001, p. 22) cites statistics that "468.5 wars were fought in the 242 years of the Warring States Period, counting a big war between big states as '1,' a small battle between small states as '0.5.'"

5. This is obviously an anachronistic term for Mencius. Huang (2001, p. 80), noting the temptation to describe his political philosophy as democratic or protodemocratic, resists that temptation and calls it "populist" instead.

Chapter 2. The Group Subject of Persuasion

1. For additional cases where *pisteis* are persuasive arguments, see 1.1.9 (1354b21), 1.1.10–11 (1355a1–19), 1.2.7 (1356a22), 1.2.19 (1358a1), 1.6.30 (1363b3), 1.7.41 (1365b20), 1.8.7 (1366a19), 1.15.1 (1375a22), 1.15.33 (1377b10), 2.11.7 (1388b30), 2.18.2 (1391b24), 2.20.1 (1393a21), 3.1.1 (1403b6), 3.13.2 (1414a36), 3.13.4 (1414b8), 3.16.4 (1416b33–34), 3.17.1 (1417b21), 3.17.14 (1418b5), and 3.17.16 (1418b23).

For additional cases where *pistis* is persuasion (or *pistos* is persuasive) for some translators and belief (or believable) for others, see 1.2.6 (1356b19–20), 2.1.1 (1377b17), 2.1.2 (1377b23, 26), 2.20.9 (1394a11), and 3.17.15 (1418b20).

For additional cases where *pistis* is both a persuasive argument and something else, like belief or trust, or belief-worthiness, see 1.8.6 (1366a9), 1.9.1 (1366a25–26), 2.12.7 (1389a17), 2.14.2 (1390a32), and 2.17.6 (1391b2–3).

For additional cases where *pistis* is clearly something other than persuasion, see 1.12.19 (1372b28: translated as "trusting"), 1.15.20 (1376a33–1376b2: translated as "credible"), 1.15.26 (176b32: translated as "credibility"), 1.15.28 (1377a14), 1.15.30, and 2.23.25 (1400a35–36: translated as "trusted" or "had confidence"), 3.17.3 (1417b33–34: translated as "taken on trust"), and 3.17.7 (1418a10–11: *pistotera*, translated as "plausible" or "believable" or "obvious").

For various forms of the verb *peitho* "to persuade" (*peithein, apeithein, peithesthai, peisthenai, peisthentes, peisai, peisaimen, peithontai, peithontes, peisomenos*), see 1.1.12 (1355a26, 30, 32), 1.1.14 (1355b10), 1.2.1 (1355b28, 32), 1.7.31 (1365a12), 1.8.1–2 (1365b22, 24), 1.11.5 (1370a25–26), 1.12.22 (1372b36), 1.15.23 (1376b18), 2.5.13 (1382b29), 2.5.22 (1383b9), 2.8.6 (1385b33), 2.18.1 (1391b10–11), 2.19.9 (1391a28), 3.1.1 (1403b11), 3.11.14 (1413a17), 3.3.1 (1406a4).

For *to pithanon* "persuasivity" and its variants (*pithana, apithana, pithanoi, pithanotera, pithanotaton*), see 1.1.12 (1355a38), 1.1.14 (1355b15), 1.2.1 (1355b32), 1.2.4 (1356a12), 1.2.10 (1356b23), 1.2.11 (1356b27–28), 1.2.13 (1357a13), 1.8.6 (1366a13), 2.18.1 (1391b8), 2.20.9 (1394a13), 2.22.3 (1395b28), 2.23.1 (1396a18), 2.23.22 (1400a8, 12), 3.1.3 (1403b19), 3.2.4 (1404b19), 3.3.4 (1406b14), 3.7.4 (1408a19), 3.7.10 (1408b10), 3.8.1 (1408b22), 3.12.6 (1414a27), 3.16.10 (1417b2).

2. Mencius writes in Chinese:

孟子曰:「愛人不親反其仁, 治人不治反其智, 禮人不答反其敬。行有不得者, 皆反求諸己; 其身正, 而天下歸之。」

3. S = subject, V = verb, DO = direct object.

4. It is conceivable, of course, that Mencius intended something like the negated nominalization that Legge gives us for *bù zhì* 不治 ("his government is unsuccessful") in the other two phrases as well. Some Chinese readers have argued precisely this case with me. For example, *ài rén bù qīn* 愛人不親 lit. "love people not draw-close" could be construed as something like "if you love others and no closeness results"; but it would be difficult to construe that "closeness" or "intimacy" or "family love" as an action performed by the subject implied by the verb "to love." *qīn* 親 can be a noun like "closeness," an adjective like "close," or a verb like "draw close"; the negation of *qīn* 親 in Mencius's phrase unmistakably signals the *failure* of love to produce the desired body-becoming-mind state in others. And a Legge-like nominalization would be even more difficult to construct for *lǐ rén bù dá* 禮人不答, literally "accommodate people not respond": *dá* 答 is to reply, to respond, to echo, or to answer in kind.

5. Note in this context that the five "human relationships" (*rén lún* 人倫) of which Mencius writes in 3A4 are also—as one would expect of *relationships*—unmistakably interactive phenomenologies; but Van Norden (2008, p. 71) has found a way to individualize that notion by translating 人倫 as "human roles":

> instruct them about human roles [*rén lún* 人倫]: between father and children there is affection [*qīn* 親: also "closeness, intimacy"]; between ruler and ministers there is righteousness [*yì* 義]; between husband and wife there is distinction [*bié* 別: also "classification, separation, departure"]; between elder and younger there is precedence [*xù* 序: also "order, sequence"]; and between friends there is faithfulness [*xìn* 信: also "trust, belief, faith, confidence"].

Given that in addition to "relationship" *lún* 倫 means general states of things like "order" or "coherence" rather than individualized things like "role," and indeed that "human relationships" is the established translation of *rén lún* 人倫 here, Van Norden (ibid., p. xxv) has had to buck both the dictionary and the interpretive tradition to make the semantic change his translation represents. His gloss on this passage in his introduction is that "Mengzi advocated an educational system that instructs people in how to live up to the 'human roles,' such as being a good parent, child, ruler, minister, spouse, and friend (3A4.8)." It is possible, certainly—and in Western thought almost inevitable—to derive advice for "liv[ing] up to the 'human roles'" from descriptions of human relationships; but this specification of role requirements is not Mencius's primary concern. The claim that "between father and children there is affection" would seem to be primarily *describing* the affection arising out of that relationship, and secondarily constructing an axiomatics of the father-child relationship that *prescribes* affection, and also, perhaps, tertiarily, implying that fathers should behave affectionately with their children and that children should behave affectionately with their fathers; but note that "fathers behaving affectionately with their children" and "children behaving affectionately with their fathers" are not really descriptions of prescribed *role* behavior, in the sense of how an individual should act. This latter is how Western thought tends to reduce interactive phenomenologies, but behaving affectionately *with* someone is actually—and for Confucian thought definitively—a reciprocity, an exchange, or what I'm calling an *ecology* or ecosis.

Note also that Mencius speaks not of "father and *children*" but of "father and *son*" (*fùzǐ* 父子): Van Norden has taken the liberty of "modernizing" Mencius by implicitly including daughters among the five human relationships, even though, as Birdwhistell's (2007, ch. 6) reading would seem to suggest, this sort of inclusion makes hash of Mencius's male-centered agenda.

And for that matter, why include only daughters? Why not include mothers as well, by rendering that line "between parents and children there is affection"? Is there some consideration that makes mothers absolutely irrelevant to Mencius's concerns, but daughters significant enough that they should be included? Mencius says specifically that the ruler should be a son to his parents and a father and mother (*fùmǔ* 父母: 1A4, 1B7, 2A5, 3A3) to the people; there is no talk of daughters anywhere in the *MZ*.

6. The three translations have "benevolence [and] want of benevolence" (Collie, 1828, p. 99), "being benevolent [and] not being benevolent" (Legge, 1861/1970, p. 293), and "benevolent and unbenevolent" (Zhao et al., 1993, p. 261). Note, however, that Legge also follows Collie in rendering Confucius's pronouncement in 4A2 differently—Collie has "virtue and vice," Legge "virtue and its opposite"—and then shifting to the "benevolent and not benevolent" structure in Mencius's commentary.

7. Here Lau deviates from Collie and Legge, and Zhao et al. return to the nineteenth-century tradition:

> He repented, abhorred himself and cultivated virtue. In Tung he practiced benevolence and became just. (Collie, 1828, p. 126)

> *There* T'âi-chiâ repented of his errors, was contrite, and reformed himself. In T'ung he came to dwell in benevolence and walk in righteousness, during those three years . . . (Legge, 1861/1970, pp. 360–61)

> Three years later, Taijia repented, was remorseful, made a severe self-criticism and distinguished himself by benevolence and righteousness during his stay in Tong. (Zhao et al., 1993, p. 355)

8. In two (1A1, 2B2) of the 26 occurrences Mencius is patently treating *rén* 仁 and *yì* 義 as separate lexical items, providing a *list* of the most important virtuous dispositions, and in two other cases (6A16, 7A21) Lau takes him to be doing the same, though with only the two items in the list; in these four cases he does manage to translate the first character of *rényì* 仁義 as "benevolence." In the other 22 *rényì* 仁義 collocations, however, Lau deviates from Legge, Zhao et

al., and Hinton in reading the two characters not as two separate lexical items but as a compound noun, that larger lexical complex that Huang identifies as a key Mencian concept; in many of those cases he finds himself forced to escalate the collocation to "morality":

> If the way of Yang and Mo does not subside and the way of Confucius does not shine forth, the people will be deceived by heresies and the path of morality [*rényì* 仁義] will be blocked. When the path of morality [*rényì* 仁義] is blocked, then we show animals the way to devour men, and later it will come to men devouring men. (3B9; Lau, 1970/2003, p. 143)

> The point is that, being filled with moral virtue [*rényì* 仁義], one does not envy other people's enjoyment of fine food and, enjoying a fine and extensive reputation, one does not envy other people's fineries. (6A17; Lau, ibid., p. 261)

See also 3B4, where *rényìzhě* 仁義者 (a "*rényì*-ist") becomes "a man who practises morality" (Lau, ibid., p. 131); 6B4, where Lau renders eight consecutive mentions of *rényì* 仁義 consistently as "morality" (269); and 7A33, where the "business of a Gentleman" is "to be moral [*rényì* 仁義]. That is all" (301). Lau's "Gentleman" there is *jūnzǐ* 君子, often translated "exemplary person" or "superior person"; this claim that the situational "fit" or "appropriateness" of behavior, guided by the interactive phenomenology of *rén* 仁, is the exemplary person's only business is obviously the passage Huang is thinking of in calling *rényì* 仁義 one of Mencius's core concepts.

A more problematic passage is 4B19: "He followed the path of morality [*rényì* 仁義]. He did not just put morality into practice [*rényì* 仁義]" (Lau, 1970/2003), p. 179). This is a difficult distinction to articulate in English, because it hinges on a very subtle shift in Mencius's Chinese: *yóu rényì xìng/xíng, fēi xìng/xíng rényì yě* 由仁義行, 非行仁義也, where *yóu* 由 is "follow[ed]" and *fēi* 非 is "[did] not." *yě* 也 is a final particle literally meaning "also" but used more or less structurally (i.e., nonsemantically) in classical Chinese to end sentences.

The problem is *xing* 行, which can be tonalized either *xìng* (fourth tone, falling), in which case it is a noun encompassing a fairly narrow sense of behavior or conduct, or *xíng* (second tone, rising), in which case it is a much more versatile verb meaning "to behave" or "to conduct oneself," but in a very broad sense, including things like "to walk/go/travel" (and thus by substantive extension the path that is walked or traveled), "to visit" (and thus by substantive extension the *stay* at one's destination, or by further adjectival extension anything *temporary*), "to do/perform" (and thus various adjectival qualities of being able to do things, such as capable, competent, effective, and their nouns, and thus also various verbal expressions of willingness to do something, like "okay" or "will do"). (行 can also be voiced *háng*, meaning a row or rank or series, and profession/al; this voicing is apparently not relevant here.)

The polysemy in the passage might be unpacked something like this: for Mencius *xìng* 行 "behavior, conduct" ideally emerges "naturally" out of the moral training that makes *xìng* 性 "disposition" seem like "human nature" (as it is often translated—see §4.4 for discussion). (*yóu* 由, by the way, can also mean "emerged.") *xíng* 行 as both the path one follows and the physical/moral (literal/metaphorical) following of that path is the *xíng* 行 "doing" or "performing" or *xìng* 行 "behavioral execution" of that *xìng* 性 "disposition," which is also a calm and largely unconscious *xíng* 行 "ability" and "willingness" to follow that path. The fact that the destination one "visits" "temporarily" is also the path one follows makes the following of the path temporary in the sense of constantly emerging, changing, flowing.

The only syntactic feature that helps us organize this semantic plenitude into a distinction between the first clause (*yóu rényì xìng/xíng* 由仁義行) and the second (*fēi xìng/xíng rényì yě* 非行仁義也) is the fact that in the first clause we have 仁義行, with 仁義 first and 行 second, which suggests that 仁義 may be an adjective like "moral" and 行 may be a noun like "path," and in the second clause we have 行仁義, with 行 first and 仁義 second, which suggests that 行 may be an adjective like "temporary" and 仁義 may be a noun like "morality." The implication seems to be that Shùn 舜 really experienced a fitting fellow-feeling, wasn't just putting the outward structure of 仁義 (say, empathetic words and body language combined with proper behavior) into play to ensure his political effectiveness.

The polysemy of this passage is evident in the various translations. Lau's, for example, would appear to offer us a distinction without a difference: how exactly does putting morality into practice differ from following the path of morality? Behuniak (2005, p. 69) follows Lau on "putting into practice," and rather mystifyingly attempts to naturalize Lau's guess, by calling 行 "an allusion to the uniquely Mohist distinction between theory and practice": "His associated humanity and appropriateness emerged [*you* 由] in due course; he did not put associated humanity and appropriateness into practice [*xing* 行]." Since Behuniak doesn't indicate tones in his pinyin transliterations, it's hard to know exactly how he's getting an allusion to a Mohist "theory/practice" distinction out of 行; presumably he is thinking of *xìng* (falling tone), which can mean behavior or conduct, rather than *xíng* (rising tone), which can mean all those other things.

Shun (1997, pp. 157–58) suggests that "the distinction in 4B:19 between acting out of *rényì* 仁義 (*yóu rényì xìng/xíng* 由仁義行) and putting *rényì* 仁義 into practice (*xìng/ xíng rényì* 行仁義) may be interpreted as a distinction between doing what is proper while being so inclined and forcing oneself to do what is proper, with Mencius opposing the latter" (Wade-Giles transliterations replaced with pinyin and Chinese characters). This is, however, problematic, as Shun notes, because elsewhere in the *MZ* (esp. 2A2) forcing oneself to act properly against one's own inclinations is crucial for ethical self-development. Shun suggests that Mencius's instructions here should probably be taken to describe the behavioral ideal rather than how one should act while striving toward that ideal.

9. Having translated *zéi* 賊 as "outrage" in 1B8, Legge (1861/1970, pp. 394–95) here gives us "do violence and injury," Zhao et al. (1993, p. 405) "chopping

and damaging." Having translated it more literally as "steal" and "thief" in 1B8, Hinton (1998, p. 197) here gives us "maul."

10. Specifically, a male scholar who has published two pro-feminist books about men (Robinson, 1992, 1994).

11. Note that the character that Behuniak renders as "clever" is *zhì* 智— what Mencius calls, when it is the fourth of the four shoots, "wisdom." Wisdom is a very good disposition to develop; but even it has to adapt interactively to the propensities of people, things, conditions, and states. Indeed the highest form of wisdom for Mencius is that which responds complexly to changing conditions. In translating *zhì* 智 as "clever" Behuniak follows Lau (1970/2003, p. 57) and refuses the model of Legge (1861/1970, p. 183), who has "wisdom and discernment," and Hinton (1998, p. 45), who has "deep wisdom," presumably because the kind of mindset that has to be reminded to adapt to seasons and propensities is a very low form of "wisdom."

12. Shun (1997, p. 77) notes that Sun Shi (孫奭, 962–1033) likens Mencius's conception of *tiān* 天 "forces" to Laozi's phrase *wú wéi ér bù wéi* 無爲而不爲 from chapter 48 of the *Dàodéjīng* (道德經 "Tao Te Ching"), variously translated as "nothing is done but nothing is undone," or "do nothing but achieve everything." In a sense Mencius has his own *wúwéi* 無為, but in a different context: *wúwéi qí suǒ bùwéi, wúyù qí suǒ bùyù* 無為其所不為, 無欲其所不欲 (7A17), literally "don't do that which not do, don't desire that which not desire." As Shun (144–45) explains, those commentators who take *suǒ bùwéi* 所不為 and *suǒ bùyù* 所不欲 to refer to what *others* don't do or desire tend to assimilate Mencius's advice here to his remarks in 7A4 on *shù* 恕 "the Golden Rule"; most commentators, however, read it as referring to not doing or desiring what *you yourself* don't do or desire.

13. Most of the key concepts Dai Zhen incorporates into his commentary are already present in Mencius:

孟子曰:「萬物皆備於我矣。反身而誠,樂莫大焉。強恕而行,求仁莫近焉。」(7A4)

Mencius said: "All the ten thousand things are provided in me. Revers[ing my gaze back on my own] body/self/morality [*fǎn shēn* 反身] and [finding there evidence of] creativity [*chéng* 誠], [I] enjoy [*lè* 樂] no more greatly. Try to *shù* 恕 and so conduct yourself, to seek *rén* 仁 [there is] no close[r way]."

14. In Chin and Freeman's translation (1990, pp. 99–100):

The sage is guided by his physical desires when he formulates the teaching of mutual production and nourishment. Thus, by regarding others as his own self, he achieves truthfulness (*chung* [*chéng* 誠]); by inferring the feelings of others from how he feels, he achieves reciprocity (*she* [*shù* 恕]); by sharing the grief and joy of others, he achieves humanity; by being motivated by correctness and not by perverseness, one achieves rightness; by being respectful, one achieves propriety; by avoiding mistakes, one achieves wisdom. Truthfulness, reciprocity, humanity, rightness, propriety, wisdom, is there anything that is lacking?

15. I am obliged to John Wang for the research in this paragraph.

16. Given the idealization in many cultures of "personal honor," this is likely to be a controversial claim. The idea behind personal honor is that honor is an individual possession, something the individual earns by behaving honorably, according to a *code* of honor (ticking off items on a checklist), and that the honorable individual can behave honorably and so possess honor even if surrounded by scoundrels, indeed even if s/he is the only honorable person in a whole culture or a whole world of scoundrels. It is understandable that an individual who feels surrounded by scoundrels should find this conception of honor attractive—it makes honor seem attainable even if there is no one around to confer honor—but it is in fact a mystification of the collective valorization of behavior as honorable. Implicit in the notion of personal honor is a supernatural observer (God) or other idealized observer (someone in the distant future, say) who *honors* the individual, which is to say, observes the individual's behavior and recognizes (valorizes) it as honorable. This is effectively a transcendentalization of the honor-conferring collective, in two steps: [1] replace the group with an idealized observer; [2] internalize that observer's imagined valorization as self-esteem.

17. The term Charles Fourier (1772–1837) actually used, as popularized in English by his leading American disciple Albert Brisbane (1809–1890), was "associative humanity," or "associative life":

> A great vision floated before my mind: it was the universal association of humanity on this earth. I saw humanity united in a great whole—united in all the details of its material life: unity of language; unity in the means of communication; unity in all its enterprises, in its weights and measures, in its currency; concert and combination everywhere. I saw this *associative humanity* working with order, with concert, to realize some great purpose. I had a vivid conception of a great function as the destiny of this humanity; I saw the association of our globe and the humanities upon it with the Cosmic Whole to which they belong; I felt an intuitive pride in the great human race and an ambition to serve it—an ambition to be a part, however small or humble, in the vast organism. (quoted in Brisbane, 1893/1969, p. 208; emphasis added)

This is not exactly what Mengzi means by 仁 *ren*, but it's close enough to be suggestive—and thus to warrant Behuniak's use of a modified Fourierist term for the Mengzian concept.

By the turn of the twentieth century, we find William E. Smythe (1900) channeling a Fourierist understanding of associative living into ecological thinking; over a century later, social ecologists in our day are still writing of "associative humanity" as the key to an integrated communal life. One website, for example, calls for a "community-centered education," and defines education as centered in and on "the communal acts of consociation—interdependent and associative humanity and nature" (CEID, 1999, np). In my terms here this would be *ecotic* education emerging out of and aimed at furthering what Naess calls the self-realization of the ecological self.

18. Note also that Behuniak (2005, p. 87) translates *cè yǐn* 惻隱 in the "Child at the Well" passage successively as "compassion," "empathy," and "commiseration"; and in his Afterword, in telling the story of finding himself in Beijing, researching and writing his book, on 9/11, and expressing his fear and horror to the Chinese people in a shop with whom he was watching the disaster unfold on television, he writes, again using a similar series of verbs and nouns for *rén* 仁: "Everyone *related*. The *commiseration* in that shop was palpable. As Mencius says, such feelings manifest themselves directly in the eyes and in the face. I sensed *compassion* all around me. That shop was charged with deep human *sympathy*—an emotional force as electrifying as the thin, granular hum of the old television" (ibid., pp. 129–30; emphasis added).

19. See also Linebarger (1937/1973, p. 73):

> Fourth, [Sun] employed the doctrine of 仁 *ren*, of social-consciousness, which had already been used by the Confucians, and formed the cornerstone of their teaching, as the key to his interpretation. In regard to the individual, this was, as we have seen, consciousness of social orientation; with regard to the group, it was the development of strength and harmony. It has also been translated *humanity*, which broadly and ethically, carries the value scheme with which 仁 *rèn* is connected. (Wade-Giles romanizations replaced with Chinese character and pinyin)

20. Again, in 3A3 Mencius quotes Yang Hu 陽虎 approvingly to the effect that *wéi fù bù rén yǐ, wéi rén bù fù yǐ* 為富不仁矣, 為仁不富矣, lit. "[if you want to] become rich [you can]not [have] fellow-feeling, [if you want to] become fellow-feeling [you can]not [be] rich"—or, in Lau's (1970/2003, p. 105) translation, "If one's aim is wealth one cannot be benevolent; if one's aim is benevolence one cannot be wealthy." What Yang Hu means here is not that wanting to make a lot of money is somehow at odds with a philanthropic impulse, but rather that the urge to get rich is *selfish*, aimed at self-aggrandizement, and so at odds with the impulse to participate in the circulation of fellow-feeling, at sixes and sevens with the group heart-becoming-mind. The reverse is also true: participation in fellow-feeling, in communal affective connectivity, tends to disincline one to make a lot of money while the others in the group remain poor, or, worse, to make a lot of money by profiting from those others.

Chapter 3. Energy Channeled through Body Language

1. *zhī yán* 知言 is sometimes translated "to know teachings"; Behuniak (2005, p. 37), for example, gives us "I understand doctrines [*yan* 言]" and translates Mencius's explanation of that as: "From the biased ones, I understand the blindness. From the extravagant ones, I understand the catch. From the heretical ones, I understand the deviance. From the evasive ones, I understand the poverty." See also Van Norden (2008, pp. 37–38, 41) and Nivison (1996, pp. 121–32). Shun (1997, p. 116) similarly argues that because *yán* 言 is linked in 2A2 with *yì* 義 "rightness," "which [he says] ethical doctrines are about," we should probably read *yán* 言 there as referring to doctrines rather than words.

I submit, however, that my reading of the passage as tracking the morally directed flows of *qì* 氣 "energy" through *xīn* 心 "feeling-becoming-thinking" through the *xìng* 性 "embodiment of virtue as bodily shape and behavior" to the *body language of speech*—and Mencius's ability to track the body language of speech back down through its shaping forces or flows—fits Behuniak's own ecological understanding of Mencius far better than does his more abstract reading/translation of the passage as dealing with doctrinal matters. And, Shun to the contrary, the fact that ethical doctrines are "about" *yì* 義 does not entail that the opposite is true—that *yì* 義 is always "about" ethical doctrines. Indeed if we follow Shun (1997, p. 65) in associating *yì* 義 primarily not with rules (e.g., doctrines) but with an ability to assess the nature of individual situations and adapt to them, then among the primary signs of a situation that the subject "reads" in assessing it we must surely count body and verbal language: *yán* 言 as I read it.

2. The revision of that passage in the second edition of his translation, Kennedy (1991/2007, p. 7), is more forthcoming:

> Rhetoric, in the most general sense, can be regarded as a form of mental or emotional energy imparted to a communication to affect a situation in the interest of the speaker. Help! HELP! **HELP**! utilizes simple rhetorical devices—repetition (a figure of speech) and pitch and volume (features of delivery)—to convey a message whose intent and energy are compelling.
>
> So understood, rhetoric is a feature of all human communication, even of animal communication. Traditional nonliterate societies all over the world—the aboriginal Australians are a good example—use a variety of rhetorical devices in their deliberations and have terms to describe rhetorical genres and procedures.

This revised statement of the rhetoric-as-energy theory has apparently been expanded to reflect his fuller articulation in Kennedy 1992.

3. "Choosing to single out certain things for presentation in a speech draws the attention of the audience to them and thereby gives them a *presence* that prevents them from being neglected" (Perelman, 1982, p. 35). For his "techniques of

presence," see Perelman (ibid., pp. 36–40) and Perelman/Olbrechts-Tyteca (1969, pp. 144–48). In the earlier work, Perelman (1969, p. 144) tends to speak of "creating emotion": "While a rapid style is effective in reasoning, a slow style creates emotion."

4. By "somatic orientation" I mean not just a body state but a social feeling, or what Teresa Brennan (2004, p. 5) calls an evaluative affect: "By an affect, I mean the physiological shift accompanying a judgment." It is not, in other words, enough to feel something; it must be a socially valenced and directed feeling, an affective form of evaluative social pressure.

5. For Sinologists' readings of *MZ* 2A2, see, e.g., Riegel (1980), Nivison (1996, pp. 127–28), Shun (1997, pp. 72–76, 115–18), Chan (2002a), and Heng (2002).

6. Shun (1997, p. 159) writes:

> Commentators agree that the mention of the four limbs refers to one's outward conduct, but they disagree about the interpretation of the reference to "understanding without speaking." Chao Ch'i [Zhao Qi 趙岐, 108–201 CE] (C) takes it to mean that even if one does not speak, others will understand one's four limbs in the sense of understanding the way one conducts oneself. Chu Hsi [Zhu Xi 朱熹, 1130–1200] (MTCC; YL 1444) takes it to mean that one's four limbs can understand one's intentions, even though one does not speak and issue orders to the four limbs. Yü Yüeh [Yu Yue 俞樾, 1821–1907] (MTPI) objects to Chu Hsi [Zhu Xi]'s interpretation on the grounds that what Chu Hsi [Zhu Xi] takes to be the meaning of "understanding without speaking" is true of everyone and has nothing specifically to do with the ethical attributes. He also rejects the alternative proposal that others can understand one's four limbs without the four limbs speaking, on the ground that the four limbs cannot speak. His own proposal is to emend the text to eliminate the reference to the four limbs. Yü Yüeh [Yu Yue]'s objection against Chu Hsi [Zhu Xi]'s interpretation might not have force, since Chu Hsi [Zhu Xi]'s point might well concern the effortlessness of the ethical conduct of someone with the ethical attributes (the four limbs move properly without one's having to make an effort), which is the way Chang Shih [Zhang Shi 张栻, 1133–1180] interprets the passage. But Chao Ch'i [Zhao Qi]'s interpretation is also possible, and there seems insufficient textual evidence to adjudicate between these interpretations. Still, whichever interpretation we adopt, the passage implies that the ethical attributes are manifest in one's body.

7. Mencius mentions the flood-like *qì* 氣 by way of explaining how he learned not to let his heart be stirred by fear (*bùdòngxīn* 心不動: 2A2). As Birdwhistell (2007, pp. 116–21) notes, this is the traditional masculine (warrior) ideal, but in Mencius's metaphorical world it draws its emotional power from the realm of the feminine, which as a patriarchal philosopher Mencius must rhetorically foreclose:

Thus the very designation of this kind of *qi* as flood-like serves both to enable one to recognize that the origins of morality and moral sprouts are widely regarded as female related and then to forget that one has ever recognized this association. One needs to forget because of the danger to society of women's perceived uncontrollability. (121)

8. Developing a similar model out of Saussurean difference, Pierre Bourdieu (1979/1984) argues that these slight shifts are what builds "distinction" (differentiation) into *habitus* or group disposition (*hexis*)—which, as the roots of *hexis* in *ekhein* "to have" remind us, has the effect of stabilizing (but never fossilizing) change (see Robinson, 2013b, pp. 107–14; 2015, section 6.4). Raymond Williams's (1977, p. 132) concept of "structures of feeling" adds a similar twist to Gramscian hegemony (see Robinson, 2008, pp. 221–23).

9. Note that "to grow" is a "circular" verb very much like *pistis* and *doxa* in Greek, and like *zhì* 治 and *wén* 聞 in Chinese: the same verb is used to describe both the (transitive) action performed by the horticulturalist and the (intransitive) action performed by the tree, and in a very real sense it is the same action, and it is actually *performed* by neither—it just happens.

Chapter 4. The Circulation of Social Value

1. Mencius writes in Chinese:

中天下而立, 定四海之民, 君子樂之, 所性不存焉。君子所性, 雖大行不加焉, 雖窮居不損焉, 分定故也。君子所性, 仁義禮智根於心[.]

2. Hinton writes on his website (in the third person) of his translations of Laozi, Zhuangzi, Confucius, and Mencius:

Hinton's experience translating a wide range of ancient Chinese poets makes these sing in English as never before. But these new versions are not only inviting and immensely readable, they also apply much-needed consistency to key terms in these texts, lending structural links and philosophical rigor heretofore unavailable in English. No previous translation of these works, whether scholarly or literary, has taken pains to recreate the Chinese philosophical worldview on its own terms. In fact, they have failed even to translate the key philosophical terms in a consistent way. (http://www.davidhinton.net/Pages/Profile.html; accessed 17 April 2011)

3. In Hinton's case this adherence to static innate nature is somewhat strange, in fact, given that on his website he describes his own thinking as deep-

ecological in orientation, an orientation that is far closer to the Mencius expounded by Dai Zhen and his followers than to this image of a "given human nature" that is "complete in itself."

4. Here is a table showing how our various translators have handled these terms in English:

	cèyǐn 惻隱	xiūwù 羞惡	cí ràng 辭讓	gōngjìng 恭敬	shìfēi 是非
Collie	compassion	shame and hatred	humility and modesty	reverence and respect	right and wrong
Legge	commiseration	shame and dislike	modesty and complaisance	reverence and respect	approval and disapproval
Dobson	distress at the suffering of others (2A6), pity (6A6)	shame and disgrace (2A6), shame (6A6)	deference to others	respect	right and wrong
Lau	Compassion	shame	courtesy and modesty	respect	right and wrong
Zhao et al.	compassion	shame	modesty	respect	right and wrong
Hinton	compassion	conscience	courtesy	reverence	right and wrong
Van Norden	compassion	disdain	deference	respect	approval and disapproval
Bloom	pity and compassion (2A6), pity and commiseration (6A6)	shame and aversion (2A6), shame and dislike (6A6)	modesty and compliance	respectfulness and reverence	right and wrong

5. For a contrary reading of the *shìfēi zhī xīn* 是非之心 "heart of approval and disapproval" as rational moral judgment, see Kim (2014). Kim's argument, contra those (Wong, 1991 and Nivison, 1996 are singled out) who would see in Mengzi no distinction between reason and emotion, is that Mengzi uses the binary syntax of the 是非之心 *shìfēi zhī xīn* throughout to distinguish right from wrong on patently rational grounds:

> To summarize, I have argued that Mengzi's *shìfēi zhī xīn* is a kind of judgment by examining the way *shì* 是 and *fēi* 非 are used in the

Mengzi. We have first seen that *shi* is used in the sense of "this" in the basic pattern of "*shi* 是 A *ye* 也" (This is A), which refers to the activity of making a judgment about the nature or identity of an object and submitting it as a reason for one's evaluative attitude toward a certain event or a state of affairs. Next, we have seen that *shi* and *fei* sometimes function as a copula and its negation in such grammatical patterns as "A *shi* 是 B *zhi* 之 *lei* 類 *ye* 也" (A is of the same category as B) and "A *fei* 非 C *zhi* 之 *lei* 類 *ye* 也" (A is not of the same category as C), and that their usage in these patterns shows that Mengzian moral reasoning involves a more complicated judgmental activity of comparing more than two things and making discriminations among them according to their characteristic features. And finally, we have seen that *shi* and *fei* can refer to the quality of rightness or wrongness of certain actions, and that when one declares one's or someone else's action to be right or wrong, one is reasonably expected to provide a reason for holding that view. And this fact, that one is expected to provide a reason for taking a position about whether an action is right or wrong, and that normally one provides one's best reason when requested to do so, in turn shows that *shifei zhi xin,* or one's taking a position about the rightness (*shi* 是) or wrongness (*fei* 非) of a certain action, is a voluntary judgment rather than a feeling. (Kim, 2014, p. 57)

Or, as Kim (ibid., p. 71n7) adds in a note: "Mengzi has an important reason to postulate some sort of primacy of practical reason over emotions and . . . this in turn involves a clear conceptual distinction between reason and emotion in his ethical thought."

I would submit that Kim's argument is right (not wrong), as far as it goes. The problem with it is that it is predicated on the assumption that there are two possible constructions of reason and emotion in Mengzi: either they are identical or they are separate. This binary gate is familiar from Western philosophy, of course, but alien to Mengzi's thought, in which reason *emerges out of* emotion and never separates from it. Hence my translation of 心 *xin* as "heart-becoming-mind" or "feeling-becoming-thinking."

6. Speaking of ideological pressures, note Dobson's "If a man does what is evil he is guilty of the sin of denying his natural endowment" (1963, p. 113). Not even the two Christian missionaries among the translators, Collie and Legge, Christianize Mencius this blatantly. Dobson's problem, at least on the textual surface, is that he translates *zuì* 罪 not as "blame" or "fault," like the rest of the translators, but as "sin," and then finds himself driven to construct a plausible co-text for "sin," namely "he is guilty of the sin of denying his natural endowment." This is quite an embellishment of *fēi cái zhī zuì* 非才之罪, literally "not ability's fault." And, while he's at it, he goes ahead and Christianizes *bùshàn* 不善, lit. "not good," as "evil."

7. Note that, unlike *doxa*, *wén* 聞 cannot be translated as "face." The only face-word Mencius uses, *miànmù* 面目, appears only once (*MZ* 3A5), in the mythic

story he tells about the sons who have "buried" their dead parents by throwing them in a ditch: as they walk past the rotting bodies, their faces (*miànmù* 面目) spontaneously break into a sweat. The sweat signals to the sons that they have done wrong in not burying their parents, and must right that wrong. This is face as social communication, but not as social value.

8. The other key verb in that passage is *lanthanō*, which is also circular: it is "to be hidden from one" or "to escape notice," but also "to be unaware of, not to know about," often used adverbially ("unwittingly," "unawares"), so that either I don't notice it or it escapes my notice. "Notice," then, becomes the circulatory median point between you and me: to the extent that we both notice the same thing, pay attention to the same thing, we circulate perception, directed awareness, and thus also the potential for assigning social value to that thing. To the extent, on the other hand, that the thing drops out of our perceptual circulation, it becomes "hidden from" or "secret to" us, and unavailable for the construction of social meaning and value. It is, of course, possible for me to notice something that you miss, and vice versa; but Aristotle is specifically talking here of the drawing of *group* attention to a thing. It's not so much a matter of whether I notice it and you miss it, or you notice it and I miss it, as it is of whether the group is or is not in a position to take it into its economic considerations, to assign it a positive or negative social value.

Note too that the "benefit" to be obtained there is a *pathos, eu paskhein*, "to suffer good," which is "chosen" more (*hairetōteron*) than *eu poiein*, "to do good." "Choosing" would seem to be more a doing than a suffering, more a "poetic" making or creating than a being-moved-from-without (or, for that matter, a being-moved-from-within or emotion); but obviously doing and being-done-to are closely interrelated here, related circularly, as part of the circulation of doing through bodies in groups. Good can only be a "benefit" that can be actively created (*eu poiein*) by some and passively received and experienced (*eu paskhein*) by others if the other members of the group are on the doing end of the good that is suffered-from-without by one (or by several, or all).

9. Other translations:

What can be said, then, of the respect you feel for carpenters and carriage-wrights and your lack of respect for Humanity and Justice? (Dobson, 1963, p. 95)

Why do you place more value on the carpenter and the carriage-maker than on a man who practices morality? (Lau, 1970/2003, p. 131)

10. I'm not sure exactly what Garver means by honor—whether for example David Konstan's (2007, p. 74) stricture is apposite when he warns us against associating Aristotelian "honor" with "the complex of honour and shame that has become popular in so-called Mediterranean anthropology of the past two or three decades, with its particular emphasis on the need to control the sexual comportment of the

women in one's family. Athenian literature of the classical period," he adds, "offers little evidence of an obsessive preoccupation with dishonor in this narrow sense of defilement." Perhaps this is not what Garver means; but given his assertion that "modern man" is *not* particularly concerned with honor, I assume he has some such narrow definition in mind.

11. For other references to *atimia*, see 1.13.10 (1374a14), 1.13.12 (1374a23), 2.6.13 (1384a19). Other prefixed variants on *timē* include *ta entima* "honored things" and its variants (*entimotera, entimotēs*), at 2.11.1–3 (1388a32, 1388b4, 1388b9) and 2.15.2 (1390b16–21); and *epitimeō* "to censure, to blame, to disparage" and its variants (*epitimēsis, epitimai*), at 1.1.12 (1355a24), 1.11.27 (1371b29), 2.23.7 (1398a13), and 3.14.2–3 (1415a34).

12. *Timai* is elsewhere contrasted with *atimiai* ("dishonors and honors" [1.13.12, 1374a23, Kennedy, p. 99]), and the collocation *ta protreponta kai timōnta* (1.9.38, 1368a16) is variously translated as "incitements and honors" (Kennedy, 1991/2007, p. 81), "distinctions which are an encouragement of honour" (Freese, 1926, p. 103), "special incentives to achievement, and honors for it" (Cooper 1932, p. 53), and "observances . . . to encourage or honour such achievements" (Roberts, 1941/1984, p. 2177).

13. See also 2.2.22 (1379b24) on further causes of anger among the ambitious, 2.6.15–17 (1384a28, 30, 33) and 2.6.25 (1385a7) on causes of shame, 2.9.14–15 (1387b10, 11, 14) on causes of indignation, and 2.10.4 (1388a1) and 2.10.5 (1388a9) on causes of envy. Other appearances of *philotimoi* and its variants (*philotimia, philotimountai, philotimoteroi*) can be found at 1.5.9 (1361a39, 1361b3), 1.6.30 (1363b2), 2.10.6 (1388a15), 2.12.5–6 (1389a11, 12), 2.15.2 (1390b16–21), and 2.17.2 (1391a22).

14. Cope (1877, 2, p. 125) actually suggests "And those who have a pre-eminent reputation for anything, and especially for wisdom or happiness."

15. It is not quite clear to me how being "*exceptionally* honored for something, and especially for wisdom or happiness" (2.10.3, 1387b30) makes people envious, as that first clause seems to say, and as Cope (1877, 2, p. 125) affirms and all four translators reflect. It seems far likelier to me, based not only on social experience but on the next three sentences as well, that those who are "exceptionally honored for something, and especially for wisdom or happiness," are the *targets of others' envy* rather than themselves envious of others. What people envy, after all, is precisely that honor or that reputation these people already have for being wise or happy. The ambitious, who in the next sentence are said to be more envious than the unambitious, are those who are *striving* to be so honored—not, presumably, those who have already achieved the pinnacle of social esteem. (It's possible to imagine *hoi timōmenoi* feeling anxiety or fear that they might lose that esteem, or perhaps jealousy of another who is equally esteemed; but Aristotle does not theorize such cases.) In fact Aristotle doesn't actually say that *hoi timōmenoi* are envious; that is only implied by the series he is developing, an elisive stylistic device he uses all through the *TR*, and especially in the *pathē* chapters, stating "they are envious who . . ." in the beginning and then eliding that phrase in all

future instances. (Cooper and Roberts tend to reframe the sentences from which the implied repetition has been elided so that the repetition is overt; Freese, sticking more closely to the Greek, tends to elide it as well; and Kennedy always gives the elided repetition in square brackets.) This elisive device makes me wonder whether Aristotle's attention didn't just slip here, so that in the middle of his series he started thinking about a nonparallel case that he had neglected to mention earlier (they are envious who, they are envious who, they are envious who, oh and also there are these people who *arouse* envy) and neglected to change his syntax accordingly. *hoi timōmenoi epi . . . sophiai ē eudaimoniai* are the possessors of the honor and the reputation that the ambitious envy and strive to attain; it is reasonable to assume that this ideal occurred to him, and he wrote it into his paragraph without going back and fixing his syntax.

16. The Chinese is 仁則榮, 不仁則辱, literally "fellow-feeling then honor, no fellow-feeling then disgrace."

17. Mencius uses *róng* 榮 in a similar way in 7A32, where if the ruler has an exemplary person (*jūnzǐ* 君子) as his advisor and heeds his advice, there will follow (*zé* 則) *ān fù zūnróng* 安富尊榮, peace, wealth, and honor/glory.

18. The two translations not accommodated in the table, and thus implicitly "off the map" of Mencius interpretations, are Dobson's "disgrace" and Hinton's "conscience." "Disgrace" would assimilate *wù* 惡 to *rǔ* 辱; but note that in English it's possible to *be* disgraced, and even to *feel* disgraced, without feeling shame (one can feel aggrieved or resentful, for example, if one believes the disgrace is unearned). Hinton's "conscience" is interesting in its radical assimilation of shame to a modern Western view of the internalized sense of moral rightness that guides our behavior. Shame seems extremely negative to us in the West today, even sick and destructive; certainly the high value we place on self-esteem would militate against a warmly positive construction placed on it. That shame as a *temporary* state arising out of a sense of having done something terrible is an extremely powerful tool for self-transformation, however, should be obvious to all but the most avid defenders of self-esteem; and certainly that is how the Confucian tradition has always seen it, from Confucius himself until today. Hinton, as we've seen (chapter 4, note 2), is also the English translator of the Confucian Four Books who boasts on his website that "No previous translation of these works, whether scholarly or literary, has taken pains to recreate the Chinese philosophical worldview on its own terms" (http://www.davidhinton.net/Pages/Profile.html, accessed 17 April 2011).

19. Note also that in 2A7, Van Norden renders Confucius's word for shame (or disgrace)—*chǐ* 恥, which we saw Shun (1997, p. 59) arguing should be translated "disdain"—as "ashamed": "This is to be the lackey of other people. To be the lackey of other people yet to be ashamed of being a lackey is like being a bow-maker yet to be ashamed of making bows, or to be an arrow-maker yet to be ashamed of making arrows."

20. This group orientation also solves what Nivison (1996, chs. 3, 7) calls "the paradox of virtue," namely that in order to (learn/decide to) act virtuously, or to submit to training in virtue, I must already be virtuous:

> To say, as Mencius seems always to assume, that I am morally responsible for my moral dispositions seems to lead to a regress: if I ought to do A, then I ought to come to want to do A, and so, I ought to come to want to come to want to do A, and so on. If I accept Mencius's view, I have to find some way of stopping the regress without destroying the point, or else show that the regress is acceptable without embarrassment. (Ibid., p. 114)

But Mencius never even implies that I am ever in a position to think these things, let alone try to make a moral decision, as a stand-alone individual in a social vacuum. I don't have to stop the regress; if there is (or ever was) a regress, it was long since stopped by the group. I would venture to suggest, in fact, that the reason this issue never comes up for Mencius is that there simply is no regress. The motivation to act morally is always there, always everywhere around us, in the groups to which we belong; all we have to do is surrender to them. In the "casuistic" cases I discuss in §3.9, where Mencius defends his decision to deviate from the normative pressures of the group in specific cases, he always offers as his justification not [a] a private rational decision to deviate but either [b] other regulatory pressures brought to bear by the same group, which the critic had failed to notice, or [c] the regulatory pressures of another (usually higher) group, especially the group of sages, from Yao and Shun through Confucius to himself. The kind of rationalistic regress Nivison imagines would be the product of a *logical* response to morality; Mencius by contrast group-feels his way to every decision, and urges us to do the same.

21. That Miller is close to articulating a somatic theory of "schooling" here but doesn't quite realize how close she is becomes clear in her first chapter, as she works to establish the collectivist *ēthos* of ancient Greek culture and to distinguish it from our own individualistic *ēthos*:

> As Rui Zhu [Zhu Rui 朱睿] says of our current view that motives always arise from discrete inner selves, "There was no distinction between private life and public life [in Aristotle's Athens], as there is today. There was no such concept as the 'invasion of privacy,' perhaps because *no Athenian felt that he had a private life that was to be kept distinct from his public life*" (232, emphasis added). Thus, a "non-technical" proof of character is one unframed by cultural scripts, whatever its content.
>
> Of course, the word "felt" in Zhu's comment projects onto individual Athenians a model of universal individualism that long postdates their cultural norms. (47)

Miller's apparent assumption there that talk of "feeling" necessarily entails "universal individualism" suggests that she hasn't fully explored the icotic organization of reality and identity through the circulation of social feelings of approval and disapproval. Her reading of Zhu's "no Athenian felt that he had a private life" is complicated by Zhu's negative, of course—even if we take talk of feeling to imply the individualistic origins of feelings, the fact that Zhu insists that Athenians *lacked* that feeling of privacy makes it clear that he is not projecting onto Athenians "a model of *universal* individualism that long postdates their cultural norms." If he's patently *not* projecting that feeling onto Athenians, that fact undermines any universalism that Miller or you or I (as ideosomatically conditioned for individualism) might want to project onto his claim. But even in the affirmative, her assumption would be problematic: even if Zhu had said that, for instance, "every American today feels s/he has a private life that is to be kept distinct from her or his public life," it would not follow that that feeling is individual in origin. The culture of privacy may *stress* the value of the individual, but it is nevertheless collectively organized, through the circulation of normative social approval for the separation of "private life" from "public life." (And even that feeling is not universal, even in American culture: we still assume that a politician has no right to a private life, for instance—that a politician's life must be entirely transparent to public scrutiny.)

22. For uses of *dokeō* as statements of apparent fact, see 1.2.1 (1355b33), 1.2.11 (1356b28), 1.2.19 (1358a1), 1.5.9 (1361a33), 1.5.17 (1362a12), 1.6.10 (1362b17), 1.7.13 (1364a17), 1.9.3 (1366a36), 1.9.38 (1368a15), 1.9.39 (1368a26), 1.10.13 (1369b4), 2.6.23 (1384b25), 2.19.1 (1392a10), 2.25.2 (1402a34), 3.8.1 (1408b23), and 3.18.7 (1419b3).

23. For uses of *dokeō* as statements of a group opinion that is also a false appearance, see 1.4.12 (1360a30), 1.9.29 (1367b2), 1.12.26 (1373a11), 1.15.7 (1375b3), 2.6.7 (1383b26, 28), 2.23.24 (1400a24), 2.24.3 (1401a25), 3.18.5 (1419a21).

24. For uses of *dokeō* as statements of a group opinion that seems true, see 2.17.5 (1391a33), 2.21.11 (1395a11), 2.23.22 (1400a5, 6), 2.24.7 (1401b23), 2.24.11 (1402a20), and 2.25.8 (1402b14).

25. For uses of *dokeō* as statements of unmarked group opinion, see 1.5.11 (1361b13), 1.9.30 (1367b12), 1.10.3 (1368b9), 1.10.16 (1369b8), 1.12.7 (1372a30), 1.12.9 (1372b1), 1.15.26 (1376b32), 2.2.12 (1379a32), 2.3.4 (1380a13), 2.3.7 (1380a27), 2.6.3 (1383b18), 2.6.19 (1384b2), 2.6.23 (1384b24), 2.9.3 (1386b16), 2.9.10 (1387a24, 25), 2.13.10 (1390a3), 2.17.5 (1391a32), 2.22.3 (1395b32), 2.22.6 (1396a14), 2.23.22 (1400a8), 2.24.7 (1401b27), 2.24.11 (1401b27), 2.25.8 (1402b15), 3.1.5 (1401a1), 3.1.9 (1404a23), 3.12.4 (1413b32, 1414a1, 5), and 3.14.10 (1415b22).

26. For uses of *dokeō* as statements of individual opinion, see 1.10.11 (1369a30), 1.11.28 (1371b30), 2.1.4 (1378a1), 2.4.20 (1381b13), 2.5.14 (1382b35), 2.6.20 (1384b35), 2.10.3 (1387b34), 2.13.10 (1390a3), 2.23.12 (1398b33), and 3.18.6 (1419a32s).

27. For uses of *dokeō* as advice on how to present the right image, see 1.9.32 (1367b27), 1.11.27 (1371b28), 1.13.13 (1374a26), 2.1.6 (1378a12, 14), 2.2.12 (1379a32), 2.2.26 (1379b36), 2.22.8 (1396a27), 3.2.4 (1404b19), 3.7.9 (1408b3), 3.11.6 (1412b2), 3.15.3 (1416a17), and 3.18.4 (1419a17).

28. One possible explanation here is that Kennedy (like most of the other English translators) has misread the Greek, which is in fact ambiguous: my colleague

Jonathan Fenno suggests that the subject of *doxei* could well be different from the subject of the infinitive, yielding "and to praise what (some)one will seem/feign to ask for." This reading would free *doxei* from the burden of encouraging manipulation.

29. By using the infinitive *ekhein* rather than the indicative *ekhousin* in *hōste hoi heteroi ou ta hautōn ekhein* Aristotle implies potentiality, which I've rendered with the conditional "might"; the uncertainty implied there might be taken to imply *dokei* "seem" as well. More pressingly, though, Aristotle often elides the predicate in a long list of syntactically parallel structures, and the predicate in previous structures in this spot is *dokei*.

30. It is instructive to remember that "paradox" is morphologically that which is "beside/beyond opinion/expectation." Aristotle says, for example, that we are often angered (*lupei*) or delighted (*terpei*) when something happens that is sharply contrary to our expectations (*to polu para doxan*, 2.2.11, 1379a23)—that our emotional response, positive or negative, is heightened by (literally in Greek) "the very much alongside expectation." Actually, it's more than that: *para* there is a *moving* alongside, a *going* past or by. There's a kinesthetic thrust to the blow that we feel to our doxic expectations. We can feel our expectations being derailed. And that, significantly enough, is the origin of paradox: that kinesthesia of expectations being derailed.

But the entelechy of paradox also involves mentalization, logicalization. It begins in the kinesthesia of the derailment of expectations, in the jolt that comes from an event that defies collective norms and expectations; but that bump is eventually "purified" or "perfected" in or as a logical schema. In *TR* 3.11, for example, Aristotle notes that good riddles please us "when there is a paradox [*paradoxon*] and not, as he [Theodorus] says, in opposition to previous opinion [*pros ten emprosthen doxan*]" (3.11.6, 1412a25; Kennedy, 1991/2007, p. 223). But what is the *doxa* that the paradox is contrary to if not the *doxa* of previous opinion? If conventional expectations about the nature of reality make a paradoxical riddle or statement surprising and disturbing, and that affective/kinesthetic disturbance is the source of the pleasure we take in such paradoxes, what could it possibly mean for a riddle to be paradoxical *without* flying in the face of "previous opinion" (*emprosthen doxan*)? Indeed Roberts (1941/1984, p. 2254) translates that passage "In these the thought is startling, and, as Theodorus puts it, does not fit in with the ideas you already have": *paradoxon* is not a logical structure there but a surprise, a startlement, at the thought's failure to "fit in with the ideas you already have."

31. For *eikos* and *eikotos*, see 1.2.14 (1357a32), 1.2.15 (1357a34, 37), 1.2.18 (1357b21), 1.3.7 (1359a8), 1.9.33 (1367b31), 1.11.12 (1370b27), 1.11.16 (1371a13), 1.15.17 (1376a18, 20, 21, 22), 2.16.2 (1391a7), 2.19.24–25 (1393a7, 8), 2.25.13 (1403a7), 3.3.3 (1406a17), 3.17.10 1418a22).

For *epieikes* and its variants, see 1.2.3 (1356a6), 1.5.16 (1361b38), 1.12.14 (1372b18), 1.12.29 (1373a17), 1.15.18 (1376a28), 2.1.6 (1378a12), 2.3.12 (1380b5), 2.8.7 (1385b35), 2.9.4 (1386b32), 3.14.7 (1415a40), 3.17.12 (1418a40), 2.23.17 (1399b2), 3.2.12 (1405b4).

Eikos-words in the *TR* also include *aeikizei*, in *kōphen gar dē gaian aeikizei meneainōn* (2.3.16, 1380b30), "for it is *unseemly* to rage at senseless clay" (Kennedy, 1991/2007, p. 123), and *proeikazontes* in *proskhrōntai de pollakis kai ta genomena anamimnēskontes kai ta mellonta proeikazontes* (1.3.4, 1358b20), "both reminding [the audience] of the past and projecting the course of the future" (Kennedy, ibid., pp. 48–49). Negating *ta eikota* with *a-* makes it deviate from community norms for appropriate behavior ("unseemly"); casting it into the future with *pro-* makes the future conform to current communal expectations.

32. For a discussion of Aristotle and Lacan that triangulates with Kant, see Metzger (1995, ch. 4).

33. For critiques of the notion, a staple of writing-studies readings of Aristotle's *TR* (see Corbett, 1965, pp. 45–70; Kinneavy, 1971, pp. 236–53; Brandt et al., 1969, pp. 14–17; Green, 1980, pp. 623–25; Gage, 1984, pp. 156–57; Raymond, 1984, p. 142), that the enthymeme is a kind of truncated syllogism designed for less-educated people, see Gaines (2008, pp. 12–18) and Walker, 2000, pp. 168–84 (a revised reprint of Walker, 1994). Gaines's (2008, p. 16) argument against this position is that, while it is "certainly consistent with Aristotle's view," it "bleeds out" of the Aristotelian enthymeme most of what is most Aristotelian about the enthymeme: "its formal relation to special and common topics, its material relation to signs, necessary signs, and probabilities, and, more generally, the intellectual apparatus that Aristotle erects around the enthymeme to guide its potential user." Walker's (2000, p. 170) critique is that calling the enthymeme a truncated syllogism tends to construct the Aristotelian syllogism in terms of "what 'syllogism' and 'logic' have generally meant in modern, Western culture," namely "formalized, propositional reasoning," whereas in fact "the nontechnical meaning of 'syllogism' in ancient Greek seems to be nothing more than ordinary, informal reasoning and inference and . . . , in the context of discussion and debate, this meaning includes informal (as well as formal) reasoning/inference from probable assumptions or received opinions granted by one's audience. If, then, 'syllogism' can be used in such a sense with reference to everyday thought and discourse, why use 'enthymeme' to name the same thing? By carelessly invoking 'enthymeme' as 'the rhetorical syllogism,' one may make a distinction without a difference" (ibid., p. 171). As we've seen (§1.2, §2.8) Walker's (ibid., p. 174) reading of enthymeme is grounded in its *thumos*-root, and thus in affect: "it is this 'in-thymatic' kind of rationality that makes it possible for one to judge whether a person's emotional responses to a given situation are 'reasonable' (or simply intelligible) or not *under the circumstances*, and that makes emotional response at least potentially amenable to persuasion." I would agree completely, but suspect that Aristotle might not: "And when you would create pathos, do not speak enthymemes; for the enthyme either 'knocks out' [*ekkrousei*; knocks out, drives back, repulses] the pathos or is spoken in vain" (*TR* 3.17.8, 1418a; Kennedy, 1991/2007, p. 243). Interesting to think of *logos* and *pathos* as boxers in the ring or as enemies on the battlefield, and *logos* (according to Aristotle) either winning or vitiating the enthymeme by being defeated.

Glossary

Affective self: the felt self, which can expand to include one's home, neighborhood, country, landscape (see **ecological self**), or anything else, or shrink to exclude one's own body. See ***shēnxīn*** 身心.

Affective-becoming-conative-becoming-cognitive: describing the emergence out of affect of pressure on others to act in a certain way (**conation**), and then increasingly "mental" mappings or imagings of body states. See ***xīn*** 心, **feeling-becoming-thinking, heart-becoming-mind, body-becoming-mind.**

Becoming-communal: a conception of **ecosis** or **ethecosis** or **ecotic self-realization** as the coherent collectivization of individuals through the **becoming-normal**/conformative functioning of the **somatic exchange.**

Becoming-good: a conception of **ecosis** or **ethecosis** or **ecotic self-realization** as the coherent collectivization of individuals as "good" members of the group (*ēthos* or character as adherence to group norms).

Becoming-human: a conception of **ecosis** or **ethecosis** or **ecotic self-realization** as the coherent collectivization of individuals as "truly human" (true "humanity" as adherence to group norms).

Becoming-normal: a conception of **ecosis** or **ethecosis** or **ecotic self-realization** as the coherent collectivization of individuals around group norms.

Becoming-persuasive: a conception of **icosis** or **doxicosis** as the group **affective-becoming-conative presencing** or **energizing** of opinion so that it is **ecotized** as **persuasivity.**

Becoming-real-seeming: a conception of **icosis** or **doxicosis** as the group **affective-becoming-conative** construction of reality out of **ecotized** opinion.

Becoming-truthy: a conception of **icosis** or **doxicosis** as the group **affective-becoming-conative** construction of truth out of **ecotized** opinion.

Body language: the display on the stage of the body, as gesture, tone of voice, facial expression, posture, proxemics, etc., of inwardly felt emotion. The primary **mimetic** channel of the **somatic transfer**, and thus of the **somatic exchange**. See also **hupokrisis, presence.**

Body-becoming-mind: the theory that mind emerges evolutionarily out of the homeostatic self-monitoring (self-mapping) of the body; see also **feeling-becoming-thinking, heart-becoming-mind.**

Circulatory: referring to the theory that **evaluative affect** is transmitted **mimetically** and very rapidly from body to body, and thus occupies all the bodies in a group **iteratively** in a nonlinear sequence that can also be described as **reticulatory**.

Conation: motivation; the third part of the classical soul, along with affect and cognition. Understood here primarily in a transpersonal sense, so that I feel your **evaluative affect** (and you feel mine) as motivational—especially normative/conformative—pressure; see **somatic exchange**.

Conditions: an English translation of *mìng* 命 (literally "fate" or "decree"), based on the observation that Mencius tends to use *mìng* 命 to mean "external" conditions that are not obviously controlled by human beings. See **forces, tiān** 天.

Counterideosomatic: referring to the resistant or dissident organization of **idiosomatic** impulses into an oppositional regime that seeks to displace the **ideosomatic** regulation of any given group.

dào 道: can mean road, path, way, course; when used by Confucian thinkers to mean the organized social/behavioral/ethical ideal, usually capitalized as **the Way**. Here theorized as the **ethecosis** of **exemplary persons**, ideally experienced directly, through membership in such a group, but may also be experienced through books like the *Analects* and the *MZ*.

Deep ecology: an ecological philosophy (ecosophy) developed by Arne Naess, grounded in the **ecotic self-realization** of the (collective) **ecological self**.

Disposition: an English translation of **xìng** 性, which is also traditionally translated "(human) nature." As Mencius conceives it, disposition is rooted in (grows out of) **xīn** 心 (**feeling-becoming-thinking**), but its growth is shaped by both **mìng** 命 (**conditions**) and the **ethecotic** cultivation of **qì** 氣 (configurative **energy**).

Doxa: Attic Greek for both "persuading" and "believing," thus translatable ecologically as **opinion-becoming-reputation**. See **doxosis, doxicosis**.

Doxicosis: the **ecotic becoming-persuasive (becoming-truthy, becoming-real-seeming)** of people's **opinions**. Derived from *ta dokounta* (the seemings, **doxosis**) + *ta eikota* (the plausibilities, **icosis**), with *to pithanon* (**persuasivity**) as the glue that holds the two together. The **deep ecology** of **rhetoric**.

Doxosis: an ecological translation of *ta dokounta*, "the seemings," based in the assumption that things don't just seem certain ways on their own, but are *assigned* seemings through the **somatic exchange**; see also **doxicosis, ecosis, ethecosis**.

Ecological self: Arne Naess's term for the **affective self** when expanded beyond the social (the home, the group of friends, the neighborhood, the country, etc.) to encompass the landscape, or nature. An interactive construct, a collectivized self, not a solipsistic projection. When Naess grounds **deep ecology** in **self-realization**, this is the "self" that he means.

Ecosis: the interactive (group **affective-becoming-conative-becoming-cognitive**) process by which individuals collectively reshape themselves as members of a coherent normative group (**becoming-normal**), and define the norms that structure their behavior as "the good" or "morality" or "character" (**becoming-good**), or as "humanity" or "the human" (**becoming-human**). As a process that no individual can control, and that often seems to be performed by impersonal and even transhuman **forces**, a (social) form of **tiān** 天. What Arne Naess calls the **self-realization** of the **ecological self**. See also **ethecosis, icosis**.

Ecotic: referring to **ecosis**.

Ecotic-becoming-icotic: referring to the emerging of **icotic persuasivity** (**becoming-persuasive, becoming-truthy, becoming-real-seeming**) out of the **becoming-communal** of **ecosis**.

Ecotize: to process **ecotically**, collectively, conformatively, through the **somatic exchange**.

Emotional-becoming-moral: an unpacking of Mencius's belief that the path of morality (*rényì* 仁義) is rooted in (grows **ethecotically** out of) *xīn* 心 (**feeling-becoming-thinking, heart-becoming-mind**).

energeia: probably an Aristotelian coinage, from *en* "in" + *ergon* "work," thus "in-working" or "en-acting"; used by Aristotle synonymously with **entelekheia** to mean "actuality." The source of the English word **energy**.

Energy: a loose English translation of **energeia** (also translated as "actuality": see **entelekheia**) as well as of *qì* 氣 (also translated expansively by Porkert as "configurative energies"). George Kennedy argues that **rhetoric *is* energy**; drawing on Perelman's theory of the **techniques of presence**, Jeffrey Walker argues that for Aristotle **rhetoric** is **presenced** or energized with **body language**.

Entelechy: the standard English translation of **entelekheia**.

entelekheia: Aristotle's coinage for the tendency of things to actualize their potential. Built out of the roots for "the having of an end within" (*en* "in" + *telos* "end" + *ekhein* "to have"), with the idea that the end or perfection or completeness is not some perfect stable state toward which potentiality (*dunamis*) distantly points but rather is constantly *emerging from within*, and specifically emerging out of work, out of a generative energetic working-through. Aristotle himself uses the term synonymously with **energeia** to mean *actuality*.

enthuměma: Aristotle's coinage for the basic structure of practical reasoning. One of the elements of *to endekhomenon pithanon* "the available **persuasivity**" that the rhetor is to "see" or "observe" in *TR* 1.2. Defined structurally in logic as an "incomplete syllogism," one in which the universal (minor) premise is left unstated, because it is technically something that everyone knows. Built morphologically out of the roots for "in passion" or "in courage" (*en* + **thumos**); Jeffrey Walker argues that the best translation of *enthuměma* is actually "encouragement," because it effectively channels passion-as-pressure (**affect-becoming-conation**) to the audience.

Enthymeme: the standard English translation of **enthuměma**.

Ethecosis: **ecosis** conceived specifically as a **becoming-communal** organization of "character" (*ēthos*), and character specifically as organized by group norms (**becoming-normal, becoming-human**). Whereas "ethics" is the organization of behavioral and attitudinal choices (and thus character/*ēthos*) from the individual's point of view, ethecosis is that same organization from the group's point of view.

Ethecotic: referring to **ethecosis**. "Ethical" in a collectivist purview.

Evaluative affect: the channeling of affect into behavioral (especially normative/conformative) pressure channeled through the **somatic exchange**. **Affect-becoming-conation**, or what Mencius calls the **heart of approval and disapproval** (*shìfēi zhī xīn* 是非之心). See **somatic, somatic transfer**.

Exemplary person: an English translation of *jūnzǐ* 君子, also translated "superior person" and "gentleman."

Face: as theorized by Erving Goffman (1955/1967, p. 5), "the positive **social value** a person effectively claims for himself by the line others assume he has taken during a particular contact." An English translation of Chinese *miànzi* 面子, from *miàn* 面, the physical face, which is theorized by Mencius as a display site only for **dispositional body language**, not for **social value**.

Feeling-becoming-disposition: an ecological condensation of Mencius's belief that **disposition** (*xìng* 性) is rooted in (emerges or grows **ethecotically** out of) *xīn* 心 (**feeling-becoming-thinking, heart-becoming-mind**).

Feeling-becoming-thinking: an ecological translation of *xīn* 心 (literally "heart"). Rooted in the neo-Jamesian neurophysiological tradition, according to which emotion is a homeostatic mapping of "lower" body states (like appetite), feeling is a becoming-mental mapping of emotion, and "mind" is a mapping of social feelings. See also **heart-becoming-mind**.

Feeling-becoming-thinking-becoming-knowing-becoming-truth: an unpacking of the entelechial process by which groups organize affectively invested or **energized beliefs** and **opinions** as normative truth-constructs (**doxicosis**). See also **persuading-becoming-believing-becoming-valuing-becoming-knowing-becoming-truth**.

Fellow-feeling: an English translation of *rén* 仁, Mencius's supreme virtue. The translation is based on the observation that the Chinese term's semantics is not exhausted by the "associated humanity" (Behuniak) or "co-humanity"

(Ritchie) implied by its etymology, but contains a strong component of **shared affect** as well. According to Mencius, it is produced by the **heart of compassion**. See also *rényì* 仁義.

Forces: an English translation of *tiān* 天 (literally "heaven" or "the sky"), based on the observation that Mencius tends to use *tiān* 天 to mean any forces that are not obviously controlled by human beings. See **conditions, mìng** 命.

Four shoots: an English translation of *sì duān* 四端 (also translated "four germs," "four sprouts," "four beginnings"), the four primary virtuous dispositions that are rooted in, and grow out of, *xīn* 心 (especially **shared affect**): *rén* 仁 (**fellow-feeling**), *yì* 義 (**rightness**), *lǐ* 禮 (**ritual propriety**), *zhì* 智 (**wisdom**). Here theorized as collectivist (interactive, **ecotic**) virtues.

Heart of approval and disapproval: an English translation of *shìfēi zhī xīn* 是非之心 (literally "heart of is isn't"); also translated as "the heart of right and wrong." See **evaluative affect, somatic exchange**.

Heart of compassion: an English translation of *cèyǐn zhī xīn* 惻隱之心 (literally "heart of secret sorrow"; usually taken to indicate the vicarious experience of someone else's distress). According to Mencius, produces *rén* 仁 (**fellow-feeling**).

Heart of shame: an English translation of *xiūwù zhī xīn* 羞惡之心; also translated by Van Norden as "feeling of disdain." The larger composite concept can be described ecologically as **shame-becoming-disdain**.

Heart-becoming-mind: an ecological translation of *xīn* 心 (literally "heart"), rooted in the neo-Jamesian neurophysiological tradition, according to which emotion is a homeostatic mapping of "lower" body states (like appetite), feeling is a becoming-mental mapping of emotion, and "mind" is a mapping of feelings; see also **feeling-becoming-thinking**.

Hupokrisis: Aristotle's term for "acting"; the origin of the English terms "hypocrisy" and "hypocritical." In **rhetorical** studies, technically translated "delivery"; here theorized as **body language**.

Icosis: derived from Aristotle's term *eikos* "plausible," *ta eikota* "the plausibilities," icosis is the process by which group opinions are "plausibilized" through *pistis* **"persuasion-becoming-belief"** as truth or reality. A socio-ecological theory of the social construction of reality, grounded in the **affective-becoming-conative-becoming-cognitive** circulation of felt pressures to conform to group norms. See also **doxicosis, ecosis**.

Icotic: referring to **icosis**.

Identification: as theorized by Kenneth Burke, the process or state in which the **affective selves** of two or more people merge, forming a felt "consubstantiality." As Arne Naess retheorizes it, it can involve the merging of the **ecological selves** of humans and nonhuman entities as well. The condition of possibility for **ecosis** and **icosis**, as well as the **ethecotic** Mencian **four shoots**, especially *rén* 仁 **(fellow-feeling)**.

Ideosomatic: **somatically** collectivizing, normative, conformative, regulatory; referring to **ecosis, ethecosis, icosis, doxicosis**.

Idiosomatic: **somatically** individualizing, deviant, arising out of the biological fact that we inhabit different bodies, look at the world through different eyes, and therefore tend to have different experiences, and thus to **iterate** collective **forces** in different ways. The stray impulses that **ecosis, ethecosis, icosis, doxicosis** attempt to organize; may be organized into **counterideosomatic** resistance.

Iterations: as theorized by Derrida (1971/1988), individual repetitions of "the same" that subtly but significantly alter the same, producing a tentative stability that is always being slightly destabilized, and thus must constantly be restabilized.

Iterative, iterate, iterability: referring to **iterations**.

Iterecotic: referring to the multiple **iterations** by which groups **circulate** or **reticulate** the **evaluative affects** or **affective-becoming-conative** impulses that organize their members as a coherent **becoming-communal (becoming-normal, becoming-good, becoming-human)** group. See also **itericotic**.

Itericotic: referring to the multiple **iterations** by which groups **circulate** or **reticulate** and **energize** or **presence** the **evaluative affects** or **affective-becoming-conative** impulses that organize their members' *doxal* **opinions** (what their members tell each other, and hear each other saying;

see ***wén*** 聞) as a coherent **becoming-persuasive (becoming-truthy, becoming-real-seeming)** account of truth, fact, reality, justice, or identity. See also **iterecotic**.

jūnzǐ 君子: **exemplary person.** Literally "ruler's son," translated by Lau as "gentleman": Confucius's radical idea was that nobility is something one does not inherit but grows into **ethecotically**, by following **the Way** (*dào* 道).

lǐ 禮: a key Confucian term (one of the **four shoots**) variously translated into English as "the rites," "ritual form," "ritual observances," or "**ritual propriety**." Here theorized as a form of **ethecotic** social memory, or the **ideosomatic** regulation of groups.

Mimesis: see **somatic mimesis**.

míng 命: "external" **conditions** that are not obviously controlled by human beings; see **forces, *tiān* 天**.

MZ: abbreviation for *Mengzi* (孟子), also called in English the *Mencius*.

Opinion-becoming-reputation: an ecological translation of **doxa**. The **doxicotic** process by which groups convert what they *think* into an apparent truth or fact about a person, or even a "property" of that person. See also ***wén*** 聞.

Ordinary-becoming-exemplary: an unpacking of the Mencian thinking behind the emergence of the kind of exemplary *community* that is **ethecotically** productive of **exemplary *persons*** (and that is often referred to by the shorthand of "the Way," *dào* 道) out of ordinary social interaction.

Panicked moralism: an adaptation of Judith Butler's term "panicked heterosexuality" to account for the low-level morality represented by the **heart of shame** (or the heart of **shame-becoming-disdain**), which moves the social actor from shameful or disgraceful behavior toward a negative (prohibition-laden, censorious) morality; the "panic" refers to the (never quite successfully suppressed) moralist's fear that s/he will backslide from a precarious moral uprightness back down into disgrace and shame.

Persuading-becoming-believing: an ecological translation of *pistis*, which in Attic Greek means both persuading and being persuaded (or believing), and thus also persuasion as the attempt to make someone believe (including proofs and arguments, which Aristotle calls *pisteis*) and the belief that ideally results. Theorized here as a **circulatory** or **reticulatory** group speech act that is saturated in **persuasivity** (*to pithanon*).

Persuading-becoming-believing-becoming-valuing-becoming-knowing-becoming-truth: an unpacking of the **entelechy** (theorized here as **doxicosis**) by which *doxa* is **icotically** transformed into a collective truth-construct that is persuasive enough to be considered truth, reality, identity. See also **feeling-becoming-thinking-becoming-knowing-becoming-truth**.

Persuasivity: an English translation of Aristotle's *to pithanon*, especially in *TR* 1.2 *to endekhomenon pithanon* "the available persuasivity"; see also **becoming-persuasive**.

Phenomenology: as theorized by Edmund Husserl, and later by Martin Heidegger and Maurice Merleau-Ponty, the experience (or "**feeling-becoming-thinking**") of living in the world, in the body. Phenomenology is sometimes misunderstood as a *subjective* experience of the world; in fact it is radically interactive, and the various phenomenologies theorized here—**fellow-feeling**, love, loyalty, happiness, **persuading-becoming-believing**, **opinion-becoming-reputation**, and so on—are not only interactive but **ecotic/icotic**.

Presence, techniques of: Chaim Perelman's term for **rhetorical** effects achieved prosodically and through other forms of **body language** to intensify the effect of the words being spoken on listeners.

qì 氣: a "configurative **energy**" that may be channeled physiologically, as a fluid similar to blood, but may also take **phenomenological** forms.

qíng 情: characteristic tendencies that are hard to change; similar to *xìng* 性, which are characteristic tendencies that can be improved or degraded.

rén 仁: **fellow-feeling** (the sharing of other people's feelings); commonly thought of as Mencius's primary virtuous **disposition**; actually a collective or interactive **phenomenology**. Traditionally translated into English as "benevolence," more recently as "humanity" or "humaneness"; since these English terms all reflect individual virtues, and *rén* 仁 is relational, interactive, Behuniak translates it "associated humanity," Ritchie "co-humanity."

One of the **four shoots**.

rényì 仁義: a fitting **fellow-feeling**, or a fellow-feeling that best fits the occasion. Mencius's core conception of "the path of morality" (Lau's translation); two of the **four shoots**. See also *rén* 仁, *yì* 義, and **rightness**.

Reticulatory: referring to the theory that **evaluative affect** is transmitted **mimetically** and almost instantaneously from body to body, and thus occupies all the bodies in a group **iteratively** in a nonlinear sequence that can also loosely be described as **circulatory**.

Rhetoric: traditionally defined as the art of persuasion, and reduced to a collection of rhetorical *forms* (proofs and arguments, tropes and figures, *topoi*, etc.); here studied ecologically as the flow of regulatory **affect-becoming-conation (persuasivity, energy, presencing)** through groups for purposes of motivating and mobilizing desired group behavior, and thus as **doxicosis**.

Rightness (, situational): an English translation of *yì* 義; also translated "righteousness." One of the **four shoots**.

Ritual propriety: an English translation of *lǐ* 禮; also translated "the rites," "ritual form," "ritual observances." One of the **four shoots**.

Self-realization: the "realizing [of] inherent potentialities" of the **ecological self**; Arne Naess's central concept of **deep ecology**. See Aristotle's **entelechy/entelekheia** and Mencius's **Way/***dào* 道. Theorized here as ecosis and **ethecosis**, as **becoming-human** and **becoming-communal**.

Shame-becoming-disdain: an expanded English translation of *xiūwù* 羞惡 (see **heart of shame**), based on the observation that some commentators and translators take it to mean shame, others disdain, and that in either case the translation chosen tends to include the other term implicitly as part of an entelechial movement. Disgrace produces shame; shame is such an unpleasant emotion that, to ward it off, the social actor develops disdain for shameful behaviors. This process ideally leads the social actor up onto the **ethecotic Way** (*dào* 道). See also **panicked moralism**.

Shared affect: feelings, attitudes, and beliefs that are **circulated** or **reticulated** through the **somatic exchange**. When what is shared is **evaluative**

affect, trading on **social value**, its circulation/reticulation has a regulatory effect, conforming member feelings, attitudes, and beliefs to group norms (**becoming-normal**). The vehicle of the **somatic transfer**, and thus of **ecosis, ethecosis, icosis, doxicosis**. At the core of Mencius's conception of *rén* 仁 (**fellow-feeling**); but then all **four shoots** are here theorized as steeped in shared affect.

shēnxīn 身心: the psychosomatic body; the body (or self) as felt. In Taiwan used as a translation of **somatic**. See **affective self, ecological self,** *xīn* 心.

Social value: the key **ethecotic** currency used by groups (communities, societies) to organize the behavior, **feeling-becoming-thinking**, and **becoming-real-seeming** of their members. Variously called *doxa* and *timē* by Aristotle, *zūn* 尊 and *róng* 榮 by Mencius. Theorized here in terms of Goffman's understanding of **face**. Social devaluation is a powerful threat variously called *adoxia* (loss of reputation) and *atimia* (disgrace) by Aristotle, *rŭ* 辱 (disgrace) by Mencius; ideally devaluation should activate the **heart of shame** (*aiskhunē/xiūwù* 羞惡), because that is such an unpleasant emotion that it will ideally lead the social actor back onto the **ethecotically** desirable path (*dào* 道). See also **shame-becoming-disdain**.

Somatic: referring to [a] the neurophysiological storage and signaling of lessons learned through experience in and through the autonomic nervous system, as **somatic markers**; [b] the **somatomimetic transfer** of somatic states (**evaluative affects**) from body to body; and [c] the resulting **somatic exchange**.

Somatic exchange: the cycling of **evaluative affects** through the **somatic transfer** in two directions, *inward* (the **somatomimetic** internalization of other people's affective states as one's own **conation**) and *outward* (the display of one's own affective states on the stage of one's own body, as **body language**, where it can be read and internalized by others as their own conation).

Somatic marker: as theorized by Antonio Damasio, a **somatic response** that "biases" decision-making in favor of the organism's own past experiential learning.

Somatic mimesis, somatomimesis: the theory that our bodies almost instantaneously (within 300 milliseconds) simulate the **evaluative affect** currently or potentially being experienced by other people, by either seeing/hearing or imagining their **body language**. See **somatic response, somatic transfer, somatic exchange**.

Somatic response: a feeling produced by the autonomic nervous system (a constriction in the chest or throat, chills down the spine, sweaty or tingly palms, a rumbling in the stomach, etc.) that, as Antonio Damasio theorizes, serves as a **somatic marker** of some experiential lesson that should serve homeostasis by guiding decision-making.

Somatic transfer: the **somatomimetic** simulation in one's own body of a body state (especially an emotion) either currently or potentially being experienced by someone else, so that the body state seems to be "transferred" from one body to another.

Telling/hearing-becoming-reputation: an expanded English translation of **wén** 聞.

thumos: Greek noun used by Homer to mean a warrior's "valor" in battle; adapted for philosophical use by Plato in the sense of "spiritedness," the kind of passionate adherence to community values that makes soldiers behave honorably, and the "middle" part of the Platonic soul, midway between reason and the appetites. Built by Aristotle into his coinage ***enthumēma***. Cf. Mencius's terms *xuéqì* 血氣 "blood-*qì*, valor," and *yù* 欲 "passion."

tiān 天: literally "heaven" or "the sky"; in Confucian thought, any "**forces**" that are not obviously controlled by human beings. See **conditions, *míng*** 命.

TR: abbreviation for Aristotle's *tekhnē rhetorikē*; also called in English *The Art of Rhetoric*.

Value: see **social value**.

Way, the: an English translation of ***dào*** 道. Here theorized as the **ethecosis** of **exemplary persons**, ideally experienced directly, through membership in such a group, but may also be experienced through books like the *Analects* and the *MZ*.

wén 聞: Chinese for "hearing," but also "being heard," and thus "telling" and "being told," and the news that is told and heard, and the state of being well-informed about the news, and the reputation that results. See ***doxa, opinion-becoming-reputation***.

Wisdom: an English translation of ***zhì*** 智; one of the **four shoots**.

xīn 心: the "heart" as **feeling-becoming-thinking**, or **heart-becoming-mind**. For Mencius the metaphorical soil in which the **four shoots** are rooted. See **evaluative affect, somatic transfer**.

xìng 性: Mencius's primary term (along with ***qíng*** 情) for a "'**disposition**' that arises in the process of transaction within a set of localized conditions, and this process results in the formation of something aesthetically distinct" (Behuniak, 2005, p. xvi).

yì 義: a situational "rightness" or "fittingness"; a sense of a situation that is attuned to what others are feeling and expect; behavior that fits a situation perfectly. May also carry over from one situation (especially one involving **exemplary persons**) to another (an ordinary one); the reconstruction of this carry-over as an **ethecotic** ideal produces an **ordinary-becoming-exemplary entelechy**. See also ***rényì*** 仁義.

References

Adolphs, Ralph. (2002). Neural mechanisms for recognizing emotion. *Current Opinion in Neurobiology*, 12, 169–78.
Adolphs, Ralph, Tranel, Daniel, & Damasio, Antonio. (1994). Impaired recognition of emotion in facial expressions following bilateral damage to the human amygdala. *Nature, 372,* 669–72.
Adolphs, Ralph, Tranel, Daniel, & Damasio, Anotonio. (1998). The human in social judgment. *Nature, 393,* 470–74.
Adolphs, Ralph, Damasio, Hannah, Tranel, Daniel, Cooper, Gregroy, & Damasio, Antonio. (2000). A role for somatosensory cortices in the visual recognition of emotion as revealed by 3-d lesion mapping. *The Journal of Neuroscience, 20,* 2683–90.
Agamben, Giorgio (1990/1993). *The coming community.* (Michael Hardt, trans.). *Theory out of bounds*, vol. 1. Minneapolis, MN, & London, UK: University of Minnesota Press.
Ames, Roger T. (1991). The Mencian conception of *ren xing*: Does it mean "human nature"? In Henry Rosemont Jr. (Ed.), *Chinese texts and philosophical contexts: Essays dedicated to Angus C. Graham* (pp. 143–75). La Salle, IL: Open Court.
Ames, Roger T. (1993). The meaning of body in classical Chinese philosophy. In Thomas P. Kasulis with Roger T. Ames & Wimal Dissanayake (Eds.), *Self as body in Asian theory and practice* (pp. 157–77). Albany, NY: State University Press of New York.
Ames, Roger T. (2002a). Mencius and a process notion of human nature. In A. K. L. Chan (Chan Kam-Leung 陳金樑) (Ed.). *Mencius: Contexts and interpretations* (pp. 72–90). Honolulu, HI: University of Hawai'i Press.
Ames, Roger T. (2002). Thinking through comparisons: Analytical and narrative methods for cultural understanding. In Steven Shankman & Stephen W. Durrant (Eds.), *Early China / Ancient Greece: Thinking through comparisons* (pp. 93–110). Albany, NY: State University of New York Press.
Annas, Julia. (1981). *Introduction to Plato's Republic.* Oxford, UK: Clarendon.
Aristotle. (1957). *politika.* W. D. Ross (Ed.). Oxford, UK: Clarendon.
Aristotle. (1959). *tekhnē rhetorikē.* W. D. Ross (Ed.). Oxford, UK: Clarendon.

Arnhart, Larry. (1982). *Aristotle on political reasoning: A commentary on the Rhetoric*. DeKalb, IL: Northern Illinois University Press.

Austin, J. L. (1940/1961). The meaning of a word. In Austin, *Philosophical Papers* (pp. 55–75). Oxford, UK: Oxford University Press.

Austin, J. L. (1962/1975). *How to do things with words*. J. O. Urmson & Marina Sbisà (Eds.). Cambridge, MA: Harvard University Press.

Bakhtin, Mikhail. (1934–1935/1981). Discourse in the novel. C. Emerson & M. Holquist (Trans.). In M. Bakhtin, *The dialogic imagination* (259–422). M. Holquist (Ed.). Austin, TX: University of Texas Press.

Barnes, Jonathan. (Ed.) (1984). *The complete works of Aristotle*. Princeton, NJ: Princeton University Press.

Behuniak, James, Jr. (2005). *Mencius on becoming human*. Albany, NY: State University of New York Press.

Birdwhistell, Joanne D. (2007). *Mencius and masculinities: Dynamics of power, morality, and maternal thinking*. Albany, NY: State University of New York Press.

Bloom, Irene. (1994). Mencian arguments on human nature (*jen-hsing*). *Philosophy East and West, 44(1)*, 19–53.

Bloom, Irene. (1997). Nature and biological nature in Mencius. *Philosophical Nature, 47(1)*, 21–32.

Bloom, Irene. (2002). Biology and culture in the Mencian view of human nature. In Alan K. L. Chan (Chan Kam-Leung 陳金樑) (Ed.), *Mencius: Contexts and interpretations* (pp. 91–102). Honolulu, HI: University of Hawai'i Press.

Bloom, Irene. (Trans.) (2009). *Mencius*. New York, NY: Columbia University Press.

Boodberg, Peter. A. (1953). The semiasiology of some primary Confucian concepts. *Philosophy East and West, 2(4)*, 317–32.

Bookchin, Murray. (1994). Will ecology become "the dismal science"? In M. Bookchin, *Which way for the ecology movement: Essays* (pp. 21–29). Edinburgh, Scotland, and San Francisco, CA: AK Press.

Bourdieu, Pierre. (1979/1984). *Distinction: A social critique of the judgement of taste*. Richard Nice (Trans.). London, UK, & New York, NY: Routledge & Kegan Paul.

Brandt, William. J., Beloof, Robert, Nathan, Leonard, & Selph, Carroll E. (1969). *The craft of writing*. Englewood Cliffs, NJ: Prentice-Hall.

Brennan, Teresa. (2004). *The transmission of affect*. Ithaca, NY: Cornell University Press.

Brisbane, Redelia. (1893/1969). *Albert Brisbane: A mental biography with a character study*. New York, NY: Franklin.

Brooks, E. Bruce, & Brooks, A. Takeo. (2002). The nature and historical context of the *Mencius*. In Alan K. L. Chan (Chan Kam-Leung 陳金樑) (Ed.). *Mencius: Contexts and interpretations* (pp. 242–81). Honolulu, HI: University of Hawai'i Press.

Brown, Penelope, & Levinson, Steven. (1987). *Politeness: Some universals in language usage*. Cambridge, UK: Cambridge University Press.

Buckley, Theodore. (Trans. and Ed.) (1885). *Aristotle's Treatise on Rhetoric, literally translated from the Greek, with an analysis by Thomas Hobbes, and a series of questions. Also The Poetic of Aristotle, literally translated, with a selection of notes, an analysis, and questions.* London, UK: Henry G. Bohn.

Burke, Kenneth. (1945/1969). *A grammar of motives.* Berkeley, CA: University of California Press.

Burke, Kenneth. (1950/1969). *A rhetoric of motives.* Berkeley, CA: University of California Press.

Burnyeat, M. F. (1981). Aristotle on understanding knowledge. In E. Berti (Ed.), *Aristotle on science: The posterior analytic* (pp. 97–139). Padua, Italy: Editrice Antenore.

Butler, Judith. (1989). Foucault and the paradox of bodily inscriptions. *Journal of Philosophy, 86(11),* 601–607.

Butler, Judith. (1991). Imitation and gender insubordination. In Diana Fuss (Ed.), *Inside/Out: Lesbian theories, gay theories* (pp. 13–31). London, UK, & New York, NY: Routledge.

Carpenter, William B. (1874). *Principles of mental physiology, with their applications to the training and discipline of the mind, and the study of its morbid conditions.* New York, NY: Appleton.

CEID (Center for Educational Innovation and Development). (1999). Community centered learning. http://www.ecosage.com/plan97/ceid/comctred.htm; accessed 23 February 2011.

Chan, Alan K. L. (Chan Kam-Leung 陳金樑). (2002a). A matter of taste: *Qi* (vital energy) and the tending of the heart (*Xin*) in *Mencius* 2A2. In Alan K. L. Chan (Chan Kam-Leung 陳金樑) (Ed.), *Mencius: Contexts and interpretations* (42–71). Honolulu, HI: University of Hawai'i Press.

Chan, Alan K. L. (Chan Kam-Leung 陳金樑). (Ed.) (2002b). *Mencius: Contexts and interpretations.* Honolulu, HI: University of Hawai'i Press.

Chan, Wing-tsit (陳榮捷). (1955). The evolution of the Confucian concept *jên*. *Philosophy East and West, 4* (January), 295–319.

Chan Wing-tsit (陳榮捷). (1963). *A sourcebook in Chinese philosophy.* Princeton, NJ: Princeton University Press.

Cheng, Chung-ying. (Cheng Zhongying 成中英). (1991). *New dimensions of Confucian and neo-Confucian philosophy.* Albany, NY: State University of New York Press.

Chin, Ann-Ping, & Freeman, Mansfield. (1990). *Tai Chen on Mencius: Explorations in words and meaning.* New Haven, CT: Yale University Press.

Chong, Kim-Chong (庄锦章). (1999). The practice of jen. *Philosophy East and West, 49(3),* 298–316.

Chowka, Peter Barry. (Interviewer and Photographer) (1977/1980). The original mind of Gary Snyder. In William Scott McLean & Gary Snyder (Eds.), *The real work: Interviews and talks, 1964–79* (pp. 92–137). New York, NY: New Directions.

Collie, David. (Trans.) (1828). The Shang Mung and the Hea Mung. In *The Chinese classical work commonly called the Four Books* (pp. 171–352). Malacca, Malaysia: Mission Press.

Confucius (Kongzi 孔子). 論語 (*Lúnyǔ, The analects*). http://www.confucius.org/lunyu/langc.htm; accessed 11 February 2011.

Connors, Robert J., Ede, Lisa S., & Lunsford, Andrea A. (Eds.) (1984). *Essays on classical rhetoric and modern discourse.* Carbondale, IL: Southern Illinois University Press.

Cooper, John M. (1984). Plato's theory of human motivation. *History of Philosophy Quarterly, 1(1)* (January), 3–21.

Cooper, Lane. (Trans. & Ed.) (1932). *The Rhetoric of Aristotle.* New York, NY: Appleton-Century-Crofts.

Cope, Edward Meredith. (1877). *The Rhetoric of Aristotle with a commentary.* Three volumes. Revised by John Edwin Sandys. Cambridge, UK: At the University Press.

Corbett, Edward P. J. (1965). *Classical rhetoric for the modern student.* London, UK, and New York, NY: Oxford University Press.

Cornford, F. M. (1907). *Thucydides Mythohistoricus.* London, UK: Routledge & Kegan Paul.

Damasio, Antonio R. (1994). *Descartes' error: Emotion, reason, and the human brain.* New York, NY: Putnam.

Damasio, Antonio R. (1999). *The feeling of what happens: Body and emotion in the making of consciousness.* New York, NY: Harcourt.

Damasio, Antonio R. (2003) *Looking for Spinoza: Joy, sorrow, and the feeling brain.* New York, NY: Harcourt.

De Bary, Wm. Theodore. (1993). *Waiting for the dawn: A plan for the prince; Huang Tsung-Hsi's* Ming-I-Tai-Fang Lu. New York, NY: Columbia University Press.

Deleuze, Gilles, & Guattari, Félix. (1972/1983). *Anti-Oedipus.* Vol. 1 of *Capitalism and schizophrenia.* 1972. Robert Hurley, Mark Seem, & Helen R. Lane (Trans.). London, UK: Athlone Press.

Dobson, W. A. C. H. (Trans.) (1963). *Mencius: A new translation arranged and annotated for the general reader.* Toronto, ON: University of Toronto Press.

Edbauer, Jenny. (2005). Unframing models of public distribution: From rhetorical situation to rhetorical ecologies. *Rhetoric Society Quarterly, 35(4)* (Fall), 5–24.

Eno, Robert. (2002). Casuistry and character in the *Mencius*. In Alan K. L. Chan (Chan Kam-Leung 陳金樑) (Ed.), *Mencius: Contexts and interpretations* (pp. 189–215). Honolulu, HI: University of Hawai'i Press.

Foucault, Michel. (1975/1977). *Discipline and punish: The birth of the prison.* A. Sheridan (Trans.). New York, NY: Pantheon.

Freese, John Henry. (Trans.) (1926). Aristotle, *The "art" of rhetoric.* London, UK: Heinemann.

Friedman, Howard S. (1979). The interactive effects of facial expressions of emotion and verbal messages on perceptions of affective meaning. *Journal of Experimental Social Psychology, 15(5),* 453–69.

Friedman, Howard S., & Riggio, Ronald E. (1981). Effect of individual differences in nonverbal expressiveness on transmission of emotion. *Journal of Nonverbal Behavior, 6(2)* (Winter), 96–104.

Friedman, Howard S., Prince, Louise M., Riggio, Ronald E., & DiMatteo, M. Robin. (1980). Understanding and assessing nonverbal expressiveness: The Affective Communication Test. *Journal of Personality & Social Psychology, 39(2)* (August), 333–51.

Gage, John T. (1984). An adequate epistemology for composition: Classical and modern perspectives. In Robert J. Connors, Lisa S. Ede, & Andrea A. Lunsford (Eds.), *Essays on classical rhetoric and modern discourse* (pp. 152–69). Carbondale, IL: Southern Illinois University Press.

Gaines, Robert N. (2008). Aristotle's *Rhetoric* and the contemporary arts of practical discourse. In Alan G. Gross & Arthur E. Walzer (Eds.), *Rereading Aristotle's Rhetoric* (pp. 3–23). Carbondale, IL: Southern Illinois University Press.

Gardner, Daniel K. (Trans. & Ed.) (2007). *The Four Books: The basic teachings of the later Confucian tradition*. Indianapolis, IN: Hackett.

Garver, Eugene. (2008). The contemporary irrelevance of Aristotle's *Practical Reason*. In Alan G. Gross & Arthur E. Walzer (Eds.), *Rereading Aristotle's Rhetoric* (pp. 57–73). Carbondale, IL: Southern Illinois University Press.

Goffman, Erving. (1955/1967). On face-work: An analysis of ritual elements in social interaction. *Psychiatry: Journal of Interpersonal Relations, 18*(3), 213–31. Reprinted in Goffman, *Interaction ritual* (pp. 5–46). Garden City, NY: Doubleday.

Gosling, J. C. B. (1973). *Plato*. London, UK: Routledge & Kegan Paul.

Graham, A. C. (1967/1999). *Disputers of the Tao: Philosophical argument in ancient China*. Chicago, IL: Open Court.

Green, Lawrence D. (1980). Enthymematic invention and structural prediction. *College English, 41*, 623–34.

Hall, D. L. (1982). *Eros and irony*. Albany, NY: State University of New York Press.

Hang, Thaddeus T'ui-Chieh (Xiang Tuijie 項退結). (1974). Jen experience and Jen philosophy. *Journal of the American Academy of Religion, 42* (March), 53–65.

Haskins, Ekaterina V. (2004a). Endoxa, epistemological optimism, and Aristotle's rhetorical project. *Philosophy and Rhetoric, 37(1)*, 1–20.

Haskins, Ekaterina V. (2004b). *Logos and power in Isocrates and Aristotle*. Columbia, SC: University of South Carolina Press.

Hatfield, Elaine, Cacioppo, John T., & Rapson, Richard L. (1994). *Emotional contagion*. Cambridge, UK: Cambridge University Press.

Havelock, Eric A. (1963). *Preface to Plato*. Cambridge, MA: Belknap Press of Harvard University Press.

Hawk, Byron. (2007). *A counter-history of composition: Toward methodologies of complexity*. Pittsburgh, PA: University of Pittsburgh Press.

Heidegger, Martin. (1927/2001). *Sein und Zeit*. Tübingen, Germany: Max Niemeyer.

Heng, Jiuan. (2002). Understanding words and knowing men. In Alan K. L. Chan (Chan Kam-Leung 陳金樑) (Ed.), *Mencius: Contexts and interpretations* (pp. 151–68). Honolulu, HI: University of Hawai'i Press.

Hinton, David. (Trans.) (1998). *Mencius*. Berkeley, CA: Counterpoint.
Holland, Virginia. (1959). *Counterpoint: Kenneth Burke and Aristotle's theories of rhetoric*. New York, NY: Philosophical Library.
Holquist, Michael. (1990). *Dialogism: Bakhtin and his world*. London, UK: Routledge.
Huang, Chun-chieh. (Huang Junjie 黃俊傑). (2001). *Mencian hermeneutics: A history of interpretations in China*. Piscataway, NJ: Transaction.
Hughes, Richard. (1965). The contemporaneity of classical rhetoric. *College Composition and Communication, 16(3)* (October), 157–59.
Ingarden, Roman. (1931/1974). *The literary work of art: An investigation on the borderlines of ontology, logic, and theory of literature*. G. G. Grabowicz (Trans). Evanston, IL: Northwestern University Press.
Jung, Hwa Yol. (1966) *Jen*: An existential and phenomenological problem of intersubjectivity. *Philosophy East & West, 16(3–4)*, 169–88.
Jung, Hwa Yol. (1969). Confucianism and existentialism: Intersubjectivity as the way of man. *Philosophy and Phenomenological Research, 30(2)* (December), 186–202.
Kennedy, George A. (1992). A hoot in the dark: The evolution of general rhetoric. *Philosophy and Rhetoric, 25(1)* (1992): 1–21.
Kennedy, George. (Trans. & Ed.) (1991). Aristotle, *On rhetoric: A theory of civic discourse*. First edition. Oxford, UK: Oxford University Press.
Kennedy, George. (Trans. & Ed.) (1991/2007). Aristotle, *On rhetoric: A theory of civic discourse*. Second edition. Oxford: Oxford University Press.
Kim Myeong-seok. (2014). Is there no distinction between reason and emotion in Mengzi? *Philosophy East & West, 64(1)*, 49–81.
Kinneavy, James. L. (1971). *A theory of discourse: The aims of discourse*. Englewood Cliffs, NJ: Prentice-Hall.
Konstan, David. (2007). *The emotions of the ancient Greeks: Studies in Aristotle and classical literature*. Toronto, ON: University of Toronto Press.
Lakoff, George. (1990). *Women, fire, and dangerous things: What categories reveal about the mind*. Chicago: University of Chicago Press.
Lau, D. C. (劉殿爵). (Trans.) (1970/2003). *Mencius*. Hong Kong: Chinese University Press.
Legge, James. (Trans.) (1861/1970). *The works of Mencius*. New York, NY: Dover.
Lindsay, Stan. (1998). *Implicit rhetoric: Kenneth Burke's extension of Aristotle's concept of entelechy*. Lanham, MD: University Press of America.
Linebarger, Paul Myron Anthony. (1937/1973). *The political doctrines of Sun Yat-sen: An exposition of the* San Min Chu I. Reprint. Baltimore, MD: Johns Hopkins University Press.
Lloyd, G. E. R. (1990). *Demystifying mentalities*. Cambridge, UK: Cambridge University Press.
Martinich, A. P., & Xiao, Yang. (2010). Ideal interpretation: The theories of Zhu Xi and Ronald Dworkin. *Philosophy East and West, 60(1)* (January), 88–114.
Massumi, Brian. (2002). *Parables for the virtual: Movement, affect, sensation*. Durham, NC: Duke University Press.

Mencius (Mengzi 孟子). 孟子 (*Mèngzǐ, Mencius*). http://www.with.org/classics_mencius_ch.html; accessed 26 August 2010.

Metzger, David. (1995). *Lost cause of rhetoric: The relation of rhetoric and geometry in Aristotle and Lacan*. Carbondale, IL: Southern Illinois University Press.

Miller, Susan. (2008). *Trust in texts: A different history of rhetoric*. Carbondale, IL: Southern Illinois University Press.

Moon, Gretchen Flesher. (2003). The pathos of *pathos*: The treatment of emotion in contemporary composition textbooks. In Dale Jacobs & Laura R. Micciche (Eds.), *A way to move: Rhetorics of emotion and composition studies* (pp. 33–42). Portsmouth, NH: Boynton/Cook.

Naess, Arne. (1995). The systematization of the logically ultimate norms and hypotheses of ecosophy T. In Alan Drengson & Yuichi Inoue (Eds.), *The deep ecology movement: An introductory anthology* (pp. 31–48). Berkeley, CA: North Atlantic Books.

Naess, Arne, with Per Ingvar Haukeland. (2002). *Life's philosophy: Reason and feeling in a deeper world*. Roland Huntford (Trans.). Athens, GA, & London, UK: University of Georgia Press.

Nelson, Erick (1985). An examination of thumos in the Republic. MA thesis, Claremont Graduate School. http://www.ericknelson.net/Apol/Epistemology/Thumos.htm; accessed 17 April 2011.

Nivison, David S. (1996). Philosophical voluntarism in fourth century China. In David S. Nivison & Bryan W. Van Norden (Eds.), *The ways of Confucianism* (pp. 121–32). Chicago, IL: Open Court.

Nussbaum, Martha C. (1986/2001). *The fragility of goodness: Luck and ethics in Greek tragedy and philosophy*. Cambridge, UK: Cambridge University Press.

Oakeshott, Michael. (1962). *Rationalism in politics*. London: Methuen.

Pang, Pu. (龐朴). (1999). Between Confucius and Mencius: Confucian discourse on *Xin* and *Xing* in the Chu strips. In Jian Guanghui (Ed.), *Guodian Chujian Yanyiu* (pp. 22–35). Series in Chinese Philosophy, vol. 20. Liaoling Province Education Publishing Company.

Pang, Pu. (龐朴). (2009). Some conjectures concerning the character *ren*. *Contemporary Chinese Thought, 40(4)*, 59–66.

Perelman, Chaim, & Olbrechts-Tyteca, L. (1969). *The new rhetoric: A treatise on argumentation*. John Wilkinson & Purcell Weaver (Trans.). Notre Dame, IN: University of Notre Dame Press.

Perelman, Chaim. (1982). *The realm of rhetoric*. William Kluback. (Trans.). Notre Dame, IN: University of Notre Dame Press.

Porkert, Manfred. (1974). *The theoretical foundations of Chinese medicine: Systems of correspondence*. East Asian Science Series, vol. 3. Cambridge, MA: MIT Press.

Rackham, H. (Trans.) (1932). Aristotle, *The politics*. London, UK: Heinemann & New York, NY: Putnam.

Rackham, H. (Trans.) (1935/1996). Aristotle, *The Athenian constitution, The Eudemian ethics, On virtues and vices*. Cambridge, MA, & London, UK: Harvard University Press.

Raymond, James C. (1984). Enthymemes, examples, and rhetorical method. In Robert J. Connors, Lisa S. Ede, & Andrea A. Lunsford (Eds.), *Essays on classical rhetoric and modern discourse* (pp. 140–151). Carbondale, IL: Southern Illinois University Press.

Renault, Olivier. (2010). Thumos's function in Plato's *Republic*. International Plato Society IX Symposium Platonicum: Plato's *Politeia*. Keio University, Tokyo, 2–7 August, 2010. http://phil.flet.keio.ac.jp/ips2010/pdf/Renaut_en_ips2010abst.pdf; accessed 14 June 14 2011.

Richie, Jeffrey. (2003/2005). Mencius (c. 372–289 BCE). Internet Encyclopedia of Philosophy. http://www.iep.utm.edu/mencius/; accessed 27 February 2011.

Riegel, Jeffrey. (1980). Reflections on an unmoved mind: An analysis of *Mencius* 2A2. In Henry Rosemont Jr. & Benjamin I. Schwartz (Eds.), *Journal of the American Academy of Religion, 47(3)*, Thematic Issue S, 433–57.

Roberts, W. Rhys (Trans.) (1941/1984). Aristotle, *Rhetoric*. In Jonathan Barnes (Ed.), *The complete works of Aristotle* (pp. 2152–69). Princeton, NJ: Princeton University Press.

Robinson, Douglas. (1991). *The translator's turn*. Baltimore, MD: Johns Hopkins University Press.

Robinson, Douglas. (1992). *Ring Lardner and the Other*. Oxford, UK, & New York, NY: Oxford University Press.

Robinson, Douglas. (1994). *No less a man: Masculist art in a feminist age*. Bowling Green, OH: Popular Press.

Robinson, Douglas. (2001). *Who translates? Translator subjectivities beyond reason*. Albany, NY: State University of New York Press.

Robinson, Douglas. (2003). *Performative linguistics: Speaking and translating as doing things with words*. London, UK, & New York, NY: Routledge.

Robinson, Douglas. (2006). *Introducing performative pragmatics*. London, UK, & New York, NY: Routledge.

Robinson, Douglas. (2008). *Estrangement and the somatics of literature: Tolstoy, Shklovsky, Brecht*. Baltimore, MD: Johns Hopkins University Press.

Robinson, Douglas. (2011). *Translation and the problem of sway*. Amsterdam, the Netherlands, and Philadelphia, PA: John Benjamins.

Robinson, Douglas. (2012). *First-year writing and the somatic exchange*. New York, NY: Hampton Press.

Robinson, Douglas. (2013a). *Displacement and the somatics of postcolonial culture*. Columbus, OH: Ohio State University Press.

Robinson, Douglas. (2013b). *Feeling extended: Sociality as extended body-becoming-mind*. Cambridge, MA: MIT Press.

Robinson, Douglas. (2013c). *Schleiermacher's icoses: Social ecologies of the different methods of translating*. Bucharest, Romania: Zeta Books.

Robinson, Douglas. (2015). *The dao of translation: An east-west dialogue*. London, UK, & Singapore: Routledge.

Rorty, Amélie Oksenberg. (1996). Structuring rhetoric. In Rorty (Ed.), *Essays on Aristotle's "Rhetoric"* (pp. 1–33). Berkeley & Los Angeles, CA: University of California Press.

Sachs, Joe. (1995). *Aristotle's Physics: A guided study.* New Brunswick, NJ: Rutgers University Press.

Schaberg, David. (2002). The logic of signs in early Chinese rhetoric. In Steven Shankman & Stephen W. Durrant (Eds.), *Early China / ancient Greece: Thinking through comparisons* (pp. 155–86). Albany, NY: State University of New York Press.

Schankula, H. A. S. (1971). Plato and Aristotle: εὐδαιμονία, ἕξις OR ἐνέργεια? *Classical Philology, 66(4),* 244–46.

Schore, Allan N. (2003a). *Affect dysregulation and disorders of the self.* New York, NY: Norton.

Schore, Allan N. (2003b). *Affect regulation and the repair of the self.* New York, NY: Norton.

Shaviro, Steven. (2003). *Connected, or, what it means to live in the network society.* Minneapolis, MN: University of Minnesota Press.

Sherman, Nancy. (1989). *The fabric of character: Aristotle's theory of virtue.* Oxford, UK: Clarendon Press.

Shun, Kwong-Loi (信廣來). (1997). *Mencius and early Chinese thought.* Stanford, CA: Stanford University Press.

Shun, Kwong-Loi (信廣來). (2002). Mencius, Xunxi, and Dai Zhen: A study of the *Mengzi ziyi shuzheng*. In Alan K. L. Chan (Chan Kam-Leung 陳金樑) (Ed.), *Mencius: Contexts and interpretations* (pp. 216–41). Honolulu, HI: University of Hawai'i Press.

Smythe, William E. (1900). *The conquest of arid America.* New York, NY, & London, UK: Harper.

Snyder, Gary. 1995. Ecology, place and the awakening of compassion. In Alan R. Drengson & Yuichi Inoue (Eds.), *The deep ecology movement: An introductory anthology* (pp. 237–41). California: North Atlantic Books.

Surowiecki, James. (2004). *The wisdom of crowds: Why the many are smarter than the few and how collective wisdom shapes business, economies, societies and nations.* Garden City, NY: Doubleday.

Syverson, M. A. (1999). *The wealth of reality: An ecology of composition.* Carbondale, IL: Southern Illinois University Press.

Terada, Rei. (2001). *Feeling in theory: Emotion after the "death of the subject."* Cambridge, MA: Harvard University Press.

Tiwald, Justin. (2010). Is sympathy naïve? Dai Zhen on the use of *shu* to track well-being. In Kam-por Yu, Julia Tao, & Philip J. Ivanhoe (Eds.), *Taking Confucian ethics seriously: Contemporary theories and applications* (pp. 145–62). Albany, NY: State University of New York Press.

Toulmin, Stephen. (1958). *The uses of argument.* Cambridge, UK: Cambridge University Press.

Tu, Wei-ming (Du Weiming 杜維明). (1981). *Jen* as a living metaphor in the Confucian *Analects*. *Philosophy East and West, 31(1),* 45–54.

Van Norden, Brian W. (Trans.) (2008). *Mengzi: With selections from traditional commentaries.* Indianapolis, IN: Hackett.

Walker, Jeffrey. (1994). The body of persuasion: A theory of the enthymeme. *College English, 56(1),* 46–65.

Walker, Jeffrey. (2000). *Rhetoric and poetics in antiquity.* London, UK, & New York, NY: Oxford University Press.

Walker, Jeffrey. (2008). *Pathos* and *katharsis* in "Aristotelian" rhetoric: Some implications. In A. G. Gross & A. E. Walzer (Eds.) *Rereading Aristotle's* Rhetoric (pp. 74–92). Carbondale, IL: Southern Illinois University Press.

Wardy, Robert. (2006). *Aristotle in China: Language, categories and translation.* Cambridge, UK: Cambridge University Press.

Weber, Max. (1922/1947). *Theory of social and economic organization.* 1922. Talcott Parsons (Ed.). A. R. Anderson & Talcott Parsons (Trans.). London, UK, & New York, NY: Oxford University Press.

Whitehead, Alfred North. (1925). *Science and the modern world.* New York, NY: New American Library.

Williams, Raymond. (1977). *Marxism and literature.* London, UK, & New York, NY: Oxford University Press.

Zhang, Qianfang (张千帆). (2010). Humanity or benevolence? The interpretation of Confucian *ren* and its modern implications. In K-p. Yu, J. Tao, & P. J. Ivanhoe (Eds.), *Taking Confucian Ethics Seriously: Contemporary Theories and Applications* (pp. 55–72). Albany, NY: State University of New York Press.

Zhao, Zhentao (趙甄陶), Zhang, W. (张文庭), & Zhou, D. (周定之). (Trans.) (1993). *Mencius.* 濟南：山東友誼書社 (Jǐnán, China: Shāndōng Friendship Press).

Zhu, Rui (朱睿). (2004). Distinguishing the public from the private: Aristotle's solution to Plato's paradox. *Histories of Political Thought, 25(2),* 231–42.

Index

References to Chapters and
Sections in the *Mencius*

1, 20, 29
1–3, 43
1A1, 19, 69, 264
1A3, 19, 256
1A4, 264
1A5, 19, 68, 256
1A6, 19, 82
1A7, 2, 27, 67, 68, 73, 219, 256
1B1, 19
1B3, 85
1B5, 256
1B7, 256, 264
1B8, 70, 72, 266–7
1B9, 19
1B10, 19, 111
1B11–12, 68
1B12–16, 19
1B15, 68
2, 20, 31
2A1, 68
2A2, 18–9, 29, 30–1, 78, 82–3, 99–100, 108–9, 141–6, 187, 266, 270, 271
2A4, 31, 99
2A4–5, 256
2A5, 256, 264
2A6, 31, 73, 74, 76–7, 82, 93, 143, 179, 188
2A7, 31, 96–7, 185, 195, 218, 277

2B2, 69, 264
2B4, 27
2B9, 69
3, 20
3A3, 256, 264, 269
3A3–4, 27, 68
3A4–8, 263
3A4–5, 32
3A5, 32, 68, 147, 188, 274–5
3A6, 20
3B1, 210
3B3, 194
3B4, 265
3B8, 256
3B9, 69, 97
4, 20, 31
4–7, 43
4A1, 68, 69, 74, 101, 160, 162
4A1–3, 31, 99, 218
4A2, 71, 93
4A4, 31, 63–7
4A8, 31, 99, 100–1
4A9, 31, 102
4A12, 65, 111, 185, 218
4A14, 68
4A15, 31, 144
4A17, 146, 149
4A18, 144
4B19, 69
4B24, 74
4B27, 146, 149
4B33, 210

308   Index

5, 20
5A, 248
5A2, 146, 149
5A3, 68
5A5–6
5A6, 72, 98, 248–9
5A7, 19
5B1, 74
5B4, 146, 149
5B6, 147, 149
5B7, 97, 160
5B33, 61
6, 32
6A1, 72
6A1–6, 20, 31, 69
6A2, 82, 84
6A4, 54, 166, 262
6A6, 31, 179
6A7, 185, 218
6A8, 31, 69, 72–3, 82, 187
6A9, 82
6A10, 210
6A11, 31, 95, 97–8
6A15, 31, 77, 79, 167, 185
6A16, 185, 195, 218
6A16–17, 69
6A17, 160
6A18, 99
6A19, 82
6B1, 20
6B2, 27, 219
6B4, 19, 69
6B5, 147, 149
6B11, 68, 82, 84
6B13, 160
6B15, 31, 144–5
7, 20, 32
7A1, 31, 178, 186, 218
7A2, 186
7A4, 267
7A5, 27
7A7, 208
7A9, 186
7A14, 256

7A15, 188
7A19, 168
7A20–1, 168
7A21, 31, 69, 82, 143–4, 168–75, 264
7A22, 68
7A30, 168
7A32, 277
7A33, 69, 265
7A40, 83, 99
7A42, 31, 187, 219, 219
7A45, 2
7B1, 99
7B3, 68
7B13, 99
7B16, 93
7B24, 185, 218
7B31, 74
7B33, 168
7B36, 74

References to Chapters and Sections in Aristotle's *Rhetoric*

1.1, 43, 132
1.1.3, 128
1.1.9, 262
1.1.10–11, 262
1.1.11, 11
1.1.12, 276
1.2, 129
1.2.1, 104–6
1.2.1, 279
1.2.2, 103
1.2.3, 10, 54, 280
1.2.3–6, 104
1.2.4, 54, 103–4
1.2.5, 103–4
1.2.7, 103, 105–6, 262
1.2.8, 56
1.2.8–10, 103
1.2.11, 103–6, 232, 279
1.2.12, 103

Index

1.2.13, 103–4, 242
1.2.14, 280
1.2.14–18, 103
1.2.15, 280
1.2.18, 280
1.2.19, 262, 279
1.3.1, 18
1.3.4, 281
1.3.7, 280
1.4.12, 222, 279
1.5.9, 199, 202, 276, 279
1.5.11, 222, 279
1.5.16, 280
1.5.17, 279
1.6.10, 199, 279
1.6.30, 262, 276
1.7, 191
1.7.13, 279
1.7.30, 199
1.7.41, 262
1.8.7, 262
1.9.1, 54
1.9.3, 279
1.9.29 224, 279
1.9.30, 226, 279
1.9.32, 226, 279
1.9.33, 280
1.9.38, 276, 279
1.9.39, 224, 279
1.10, 162
1.10.3, 279
1.10.4, 194, 197, 200, 206, 211
1.10.7, 163
1.10.11, 279
1.10.13, 279
1.10.16, 279
1.11.12, 280
1.11.16, 280
1.11.18, 202
1.11.27, 276, 279
1.11.28, 279
1.12.7, 279
1.12.9, 222, 279
1.12.14, 230, 280

1.12.15, 230
1.12.26, 279
1.12.29, 280
1.13.10, 276
1.13.11–19, 227–30
1.13.12, 276
1.13.13, 279
1.14.3, 199
1.15.1, 262
1.15.3–6, 230–1
1.15.7, 279
1.15.17, 280
1.15.18, 280
1.15.26 225, 279
1.15.33, 262
2, 38
2.1.4, 225, 279
2.1.6, 223, 279, 280
2.2.3, 192
2.2.3–4, 194
2.2.6, 197–8
2.2–11, 11, 37, 202
2.2.12, 279, 279
2.2.16, 202
2.2.22, 276
2.2.26, 279
2.3.4, 223, 279
2.3.7, 223, 279
2.3.12, 280
2.3.16, 281
2.4, 196
2.4.2–3, 137
2.4.20, 223, 279
2.4.24, 200
2.5.14, 222, 279
2.6.3, 279
2.6.7, 225, 279
2.6.13, 276
2.6.14–18, 140
2.6.15–17, 276
2.6.19, 279
2.6.20, 224–5, 279
2.6.23, 223, 279
2.6.25, 276

2.7, 125
2.8.1, 137
2.8.7, 280
2.8.12–15, 138
2.9.3, 279
2.9.4, 280
2.9.7, 137
2.9.10, 226, 279
2.9.14–15, 276
2.9.19, 230
2.10.3, 200, 276–7, 279
2.10.4–6, 276
2.11.1, 230
2.11.1–3, 276
2.11.7, 262
2.12.5–6, 276
2.12–17, 163
2:12–23, 37
2.13.10, 224, 279
2.15.2, 276
2.16.1, 199
2.16.2, 280
2.17.2, 276
2.17.5, 279
2.18.2, 262
2.19.1, 279
2.19.24–25, 280
2.20.1, 262
2.21.11, 226, 279
2.22.3, 223, 279
2.22.6, 279
2.22.8, 279
2.23.7, 276
2.23.12, 223, 279

2.23.17, 280
2.23.22, 224, 234–40, 279, 279
2.24.3, 279
2.24.7, 224, 279
2.24.10, 226–7, 231–3, 241–5
2.24.11, 279
2.25.2, 279
2.25.8, 279
2.25.13, 280
3.1.1, 262
3.1.3–5, 131
3.1.5, 131
3.1.9, 279
3.2.4, 279
3.2.12, 280
3.3.3, 280
3.7.3–5, 133
3.7.9, 279
3.8.1, 279
3.11.6, 279–80
3.12.4, 279
3.13.2, 262
3.13.4, 262
3.14.2–3, 276
3.14.7, 280
3.14.10, 279
3.15.3, 279
3.16.4, 262
3.17.1, 262
3.17.10, 280
3.17.12, 280
3.17.14, 262
3.17.16, 262
3.18.4–7, 279

Name and Subject Index

Adolphs, Ralph, 134–5
Affect, 9; -becoming-conation (-becoming-cognition), vii, 1, 3, 4, 14, 38, 81, 104, 121, 128–9, 148, 197, 212, 240, 256; evaluative (Brennan), 3, 271; Massumi on, 9, 15–7; shared, 90, 91, 133–4, 136–41, 211
Affective(-becoming-conative) ecology, 1–6, 8, 17, 38, 105, 126, 148, 240, 247
Affective self (*shēnxīn* 身心), 61–2, 108, 253
Agamben, Giorgio, 225
ài (愛 love, Mencius), 2, 64–5, 67, 71, 107, 153
aiskhunē (shame, Aristotle), 48, 211–7
Ames, Roger T., viii, 19, 32, 44–5; and Sino-Hellenic oppositions, 33, 36, 108
Analects (*Lunyu* 《論語》, Confucius), 21, 68, 69–70, 84, 89, 96, 111, 155, 184, 218, 220, 249
Anti-Oedipus (Deleuze and Guattari), 118
Aristotle, vii–ix, 3, 4, 5–15, 16, 18, 49, 114; on catharsis, 127–8, 139; and democracy, 28–9; on *doxa* as the circulation of social value, 157–67; on *doxa* as face, 189–92, 198, 211–5; and *doxa* as feeling-becoming-thinking, 165–7; and doxicosis, 240–5; and emotional flooding, 75–6; on energizing of rhetoric, 78–9; on *energeia/ entelekheia*, 84, 109–11, 130, 182–4, 188; on *energeia doxēs* (energizing of opinion), 192–5, 196–7; and energy (Kennedy) as charisma (Miller), 124–6; and entelechial thinking, applied to Mencius, 34, 110–1, 172, 182, 188; and (eth)ecosis, 247–8, 254–8; on *eudaimonia* (happiness), 59–61; and Goffman on face, 211–7; on humans as social animals, 95; and identification (Burke), 57–62; and Lacan/Kant, 281; and *oikos/ eikos* puns, 6, 259; on paradox, 280; on *pathos*, 10, 103–4, 106, 126–33, 138, 163–4, 275, 276, 281; on persuasion, 53, 54–62; on persuasive structures (*pisteis*), 26, 51–2; on *philia* (friendship), 59–61, 70–1, 91, 95; on *pistis* (persuading-becoming-believing), 66; and polarism, 45–7; as proto-social-constructivist, 233; on shame, 210–8; on shared affect, 133–4, 136–41; and Sino-Hellenism, 33–44; and somatics, 10–15; and *thumos* (valor), 14, 41–2, 48, 54, 84–7, 63, 163; on *thumos* and the enthymeme, 41, 128–9, 281; on *timē* (honor) as value 158, 197–203; and Western ontology, 96; on *to*

Aristotle *(continued)*
  endekhomenon pithanon (the available persuasivity), 73, 102–6; and vitalism, 84, 118–24
Associated humanity: in Fourier/Brisbane, 92, 268; in Mencius (*rén* 仁, Behuniak), 23, 25, 92–3, 94–5, 188, 247, 266
Augustine, 12, 158
Austin, J.L., 56–7; on paronymy, 159–61

Bakhtin, Mikhail, 45, 161
Becoming-: -communal, 5, 9, 49, 58, 81–2, 92, 97, 134, 154, 158, 202, 241, 251, 258; -exemplary, 210, 218, 240; -fair, 5; -good, 4, 49, 134, 240, 247, 251, 258; -human (Mencius/Behuniak), 4, 27, 93; -normal, 4, 134, 240, 251, 258; -moral 93; -persuasive, 6, 26–7, 105, 158, 189, 240, 251, 258; -rational, 53; -real-seeming, 6, 233, 258; -true, 5, 233; -truthy, 6, 258
Behuniak, James, Jr., viii, 4, 8, 23–4, 25, 27, 76–9, 81, 82–3, 99, 108, 120, 142, 147–8, 168, 184–5, 188, 220, 256, 266, 267, 269; on Aristotle, 34; and Fourierism, 92, 268; on *rén* (仁 associated humanity), 92–5; on *zhī yán* (知言 knowing speech, Mencius), 270
Benevolence (*rén* 仁, Mencius), 24–5, 48, 69–72, 91–5, 162, 251, 264; *see* fellow-feeling, humanity/humaneness
Birdwhistell, Joanne D., 24–5, 32, 75–6, 84, 99, 146, 207–8, 210, 264; on the flood-like *qì* (*hàorán zhī qì* 浩然之氣, Mencius), 271
Blood-*qì* (*xuèqì* 血氣, Dai Zhen), 48, 54, 73, 84–5, 87–91, 96, 129
Bloom, Irene, 69, 91, 94, 162, 167, 176, 178, 181–3, 195, 204–5, 219, 273; and disputation with Ames, 32

Body language, 31, 48, 79, 105, 109, 121, 134, 139, 198, 212, 214–5, 216–7, 240; and dispositional training, 142–6; energized, 202; simulated, 15; of speech (*zhī yán* 知言, knowing speech, Mencius), 30, 48, 108–9, 270; *see hupokrisis*
Body of persuading-becoming-believing (*sōma tēs pisteōs*, Aristotle), 128, 130
Body-becoming-(morality-becoming-)mind, 107, 175, 213, 242
Boodberg, Peter, 108
Book of Rites (*Liji*《禮記》), 147
Bookchin, Murray, 49, 76, 253, 254, 256
Bourdieu, Pierre, 164, 272
Brennan, Teresa, 9, 271
Brisbane, Albert, 268
Brooks, E. Bruce, and A. Taeko Brooks, 19–20, 29–32, 43–4
Brown, Penelope, and Steven Levinson, 214
Buber, Martin, 45
Buddhism, 21; Zen, vii, 76
bùrén (不仁 inhumanity, sociopathology, Mencius), 93, 97, 99
bùrěn (不忍 inability to bear other people's suffering, Mencius), 48, 53, 71, 73, 107
Burke, Kenneth, 2, 26, 42, 120, 188; on identification, 14, 48, 53, 57–62, 68, 107
Burnyeat, M.F., 256
Butler, Judith, 14, 53, 208

Carpenter Effect, 16, 134
Carpenter, William B., 134
Cassiodorus, 164
Categories (Aristotle), 39, 40, 159
Catharsis (Aristotle), 139
cèyǐn zhī xīn (惻隱之心 heart of compassion, Mencius), 74–5, 77, 95, 107, 149, 176, 269; *see also* four hearts

Chan Wing-tsit (陳榮捷), 69, 91
Character, 4, 6–8, 46, 248, 251, 278; and body language, 144; as charisma (Weber), 126; as *dé* (德, Mencius), 8, 23, 125; as *doxa* (Plato/Aristotle), 46, 159, 201; as *ēthos* (Aristotle), 8–11, 54–5, 106, 141, 163, 190; as *hexis* (Aristotle), 163–4; and *rén* (仁, Mencius), 68–9, 94; as situational "line" (Goffman), 189–90; as *thumos/andreia* (Plato/Aristotle), 85–7
Charismatic signifiers (Miller), 124, 126
Charmides (Plato), 259
Cheng Zhongying (成中英), 34–5, 36, 38, 42
chǐ (耻 shame, Confucius), 205
Chiang Kai-shek (蔣中正), 22
Child at the Well (Mencius), 74, 76–7, 93
Chin, Ann-Ping, and Mansfield Freeman, 77, 89, 90, 267–8
Cicero, Marcus Tullius, 26, 104
Circularity, of *doxa* (opinion-becoming-reputation, Aristotle), 157–64; of "to grow," 272; of *oligōria* (slighting, Aristotle), 197; of *pistis* (persuading-becoming-believing, Aristotle), 53, 54–7, 66; of *wén* (聞 hearing-becoming-reputation, Mencius), 157–8, 160–2, 165–6; of *zhì* (治 governing, Mencius), 53
Circulation through groups, 104, 179; of affective intensities, 37–8; of body states, 217; of energy, 2; of exemplarity, 218; of face-loss, 216; of the (*sì duān* 四端, Mencius), 251; of reality-images, 233; of social value, 49, 87, 157–66, 202
Co-humanity (*rén* 仁, Mencius/Richie), 92–5
Colbert, Stephen, 5, 227
Collectivism, 53
Collie, David, 66, 69, 70–2, 77–8, 91, 93–4, 98, 169–74, 176, 178, 180, 183, 185, 204–5, 264, 273, 274
Communicative triangle (Aristotle), 18
Compassion, 31, 95, 188; as *bùrěn* (不忍, Mencius), 74–5, 99, 107; in deep ecology (Naess/Snyder), 76; and gender (Birdwhistell), 25, 75, 84, 207–8, 210; heart of (*cèyǐn zhī xīn* 惻隱之心, Mencius), 74–5, 93, 95, 107, 149, 176–7, 179, 220, 269, 273
Conditions (*ming* 命 in Mencius, *kath' hekaston* in Aristotle), 8, 82, 120, 167, 178
Confucian Way (*rúdào* 儒道), 219–20, 241, 258
Confucianism, vii–viii, 21, 48, 78, 92, 96, 98, 147, 150, 153–4, 171, 184, 249, 257
Confucius (Kongzi 孔子), viii, 18–9, 42, 69–70, 71, 76, 84, 96–7, 111, 122, 150, 178, 184, 205, 220, 249, 257, 264, 272, 277–8
Connerton, Paul, 148–53
Cooper, Lane, 52, 55–6, 85–6, 163–4, 192, 199–202, 230, 276–7
Cope, E.M., 193, 201, 234, 236–7, 239, 276
Cornford, F.M., 44–5
Crowd phenomenology/sourcing, 161–2
Cultivating energy (養氣 *yǎng qì*, Mencius), 30, 48, 109, 145–6; *see also* knowing speech

Dai Zhen (戴震), xi, 22, 267, 273; on *rén* (仁), 92, 95; on the two hearts in Mencius, 77; on *xuèqì* (血氣 blood-*qì*), 73, 77, 84–5, 87–91, 96
Damasio, Antonio R., 15, 79, 81, 134–5, 219
dào (道 path, way), 31, 83, 94, 185–6, 187; Confucian, 219–20, 241, 256, 258

Daodejing (《道德經》, Laozi), 158, 267
Daoism, 21, 83, 184
Darwin, Charles, 117, 118, 123
Das Man (Heidegger), 179
dé (德 character, virtue), 125–6
Deep ecology, vii–viii, ix, 49, 76, 107, 150, 152, 247, 253, 272–3; as energy-exchanges (Snyder), 48; of ethical growth, 7–8, 81–4, 189; of rhetoric, viii, 1–3, 7–8, 18, 29, 48, 53, 75–6, 104, 240, 247, 257–8; of social interaction, 51, 107–8, 147
Deference, 90, 257, 273; heart of (*gōngjìng zhī xīn* 恭敬之心, Mencius), 149, 176, 178–9, 220; *see also* four hearts
Deleuze, Gilles, 16, 118
Democracy, 10, 22, 27–8, 254, 256, 262; anti-, 131–4, 161–2; as persuasion, 43; in Plato, 85
Derrida, Jacques, 15, 151
Descartes, René, 62, 108, 158, 193
Ding-an-sich (thing-in-itself, Kant), 239
Discipline and Punish (Foucault), 14
Discursivism, 13–14
Displacement and the Somatics of Postcolonial Culture (Robinson), ix, 136, 216
Disposition, 2, 8, 9, 30, 48, 53, 70, 71, 101, 105, 111, 143, 146, 154, 165, 167–75, 180–2, 219, 257; feeling-becoming-, 97, 145; as the four shoots (*sì duān* 四端, Mencius), 73, 75, 98, 107–8, 264; as *hexis* (Aristotle), 8, 37–8, 103–6, 110, 125, 163–4, 203, 272; as the basis of *lǐ* (禮 ritual propriety, Mencius), 109, 146; Miller on, 221; Nivison on, 277–8; as *qíng* (情, Mencius), 180–2; as *taxis* (Aristotle), 127; -to-let-things-emerge (*wù zhù zhǎng* 勿助長 "don't help grow," Mencius), 108; as training the body (Mencius), 14, 111, 143–5, 257; of *xīn* (心 feeling, Mencius), 78, 97, 146, 148; as *xìng* (性 Mencius), 8, 23, 49, 78–9, 91, 167, 168, 174, 185, 188, 258, 266, 267
Dispositions Arise from Conditions (*Xing Zi Ming Chu* 性自命出), 168, 184
Disputers of the Tao (Graham), 40
Dobson, W.A.C.H., 66, 69, 91, 176, 178, 181–3, 204–5, 273–5, 277
Doctrine of the Mean (中庸 *Zhongyong*), 21, 178
dokeō (think, seem, Aristotle), 40, 46, 132, 191–4, 221–6, 280; *see also doxa*
"Don't help grow" (*wù zhù zhǎng* 勿助長), 83, 187; as a disposition, 108
doxa (opinion-becoming-reputation), 7, 40–2, 47, 62, 241, 272; in Aristotle, 41–2, 47, 49, 62, 121, 124, 140–1, 157–8, 211, 240–1; -becoming-*epistēmē*, 124, 243, 256; and *dokeō*, 40, 46, 132, 191–4, 221–6; and doxicosis, 126, 129, 152, 158, 189; energized, 192–7; as face, 49, 189–92, 196–7, 198, 211–6, 274; as feeling-becoming-thinking, 165–7, 192; and paradox, 132, 280; in Plato, 46–7; as polaristic, 46–7; as social value, 193; and *timē* (honor, Aristotle), 201–3; and *wén* 聞 (hearing-becoming-reputation, Mencius), 158–67, 274; *see also endoxa*, doxosis, doxicosis, social value
Doxicosis, 7–8, 18, 49, 54, 126, 129, 158, 195, 221, 240–5, 247, 251, 254–5, 258; derived from Aristotle, 240–5; in governance, 152, 248, 250–2, 254–8; and identification, 14; in Mencius, 18, 20, 25–8; and pragmatism, 241
Doxosis (*ta dokounta*, Aristotle), 202, 215, 225, 234, 236, 239, 240, 245, 258
Dualism, 44–6; *see also* polarism

Ecological self (Naess), vii, 5, 49, 62, 68, 252–3, 256, 269

Ecology, 5, 34, 53–4, 62, 73, 76, 254, 269; affective(-becoming-conative), 1–6, 8, 17, 38, 105, 126, 148, 240, 247; biological, 81–4, 117; and circulation, 55; of conditions, 9, 37, 120, 189; as (dox)icosis, 57, 221, 232, 240, 247, 252; as entelechy, 4–6, 42, 110–1, 240; as (eth) ecosis, 9, 195, 203, 211, 251–2, 258, 264; and flows of persuasivity, 47, 57, 146, 247, 270; of rhetoric, 1–3, 7–8, 18, 29, 38, 40–1; social-constructivist, 232–3; of social value, 3, 4, 7, 9, 18, 117, 126, 147–8, 154, 203; somatic, vii–viii, 15, 33; vitalistic, 9, 122; *see also* deep ecology, ecological self
"Ecology, Place, and the Awakening of Compassion" (Snyder), 76
Economics (Xenophon), 259
Ecosis, ix, 5–9, 14, 58, 92, 97, 120, 125–6, 133, 134, 151, 164, 227, 240, 247, 252, 264; in Aristotle, 247–8, 254–8; -becoming-icosis, 104; as circulation of affect, 66, 93; of face, 211; as flow of feeling into thinking, 79; and friendly feeling, 70; and ritual propriety (*lǐ* 禮, Mencius), 152–5; in Mencius, 18–23, 195, 247–52, 255–8; nightmarish, 101; of shame-becoming-disdain (*xiūwù* 羞惡, Mencius), 209, 214; of social value, 3–4, 6, 9, 38, 49, 87, 147–8, 154, 203, 247, 251, 275; and the somatic exchange, 152, 158, 220, 258; and *wúwéi* (無為, Laozi), 83; *see also* ethecosis
Edbauer, Jenny, 1, 240
eikos (plausible, Aristotle), x, 5–6, 47, 133, 189, 259, 280–1; and icosis, 227, 231–4, 238–9, 280–1; *see also ta eikota*
Einfühlung (empathy, Lotze), 95
Empathy (*cèyǐn* 惻隱, Mencius), 269; *see also* compassion

endoxa (commonplace beliefs, Aristotle), 13, 138; *see also doxa*
Energizing: of body language (presencing, Perelman), 198, 202; of opinion (*energeia doxēs*, Aristotle), 189, 192–5, 196–7; of rhetoric through contagious body language/shared affect, 257–8; of telling/hearing (*wén* 聞, -becoming-reputation, Mencius), 240
Energy, 1, 30, 41–2, 47, 78–9, 86, 109, 114, 121, 130, 157; as charisma (Miller), 124, 126; as *energeia* (Aristotle), 41–2, 47, 48, 59, 84, 109, 193, 257; *energeia doxēs* (energizing of opinion, Aristotle), 189, 192–5, 196–7, 216; and *entelekheia* (entelechy, Aristotle), 109–11, 123; activated by feeling (*pathos*, Aristotle/Walker), 126, 130–1, 146; Kennedy on, 109, 112–8, 134, 148, 194, 252, 270; as *qì* (氣, Mencius), 9, 30, 47–8, 81, 84, 108–9, 111, 120, 146, 257, 270; transfer of from body to body, 112–3, 123, 124, 133–4, 141; vitalistic, 122–3
Energy-exchange (Snyder), 2, 37, 48
Eno, Robert, 34
Entelechy/*entelekheia* (Aristotle), vii, 4, 6, 16, 41–2, 48, 59, 106, 109, 120, 121, 182–4, 188, 192, 196, 217–8, 242; and energy/*energeia*, 109–11, 123; of *thumos* (valor), 87
Enteroception, 217
Enthymeme/*enthumēma*, 14, 26, 38, 51, 56, 85, 105, 128, 130, 281; applied to Mencius, 34, 110–1, 172, 182, 188; in reasoning, 36–7
Epideictic, 254–5
epieikeia (fairness, Aristotle), 5, 230
epistēmē (knowledge, Aristotle), 41–2, 47, 122, 124, 140, 152, 231, 233, 263; Burnyeat on, 256; *doxa-*

epistēmē (continued)
  becoming-, 243; as the *epistēta*, 140; see also *doxa*
Estrangement and the Somatics of Literature (Robinson), ix, 95, 216, 272
Ethecosis, 7–9, 17, 27, 49, 147, 152–5, 156, 168, 210, 219, 247, 251–2, 254–6; -becoming-doxicosis, 9; and becoming-exemplary, 154–5, 195, 210; counter-, 207; of the four shoots (*sì duān* 四端, Mencius), 251–2; Mencius on, 18, 20, 23, 25, 27–8, 81–2, 143, 152–3, 219–20, 250; and the self, 253; as the Self-realization of the ecological self (Naess), 256; of shame-becoming-disdain (*xiūwù* 羞惡, Mencius), 207, 210; as social regulation, 252; as the somatic exchange, 254
ēthos (character, Aristotle), 7, 104, 106, 128, 141, 146, 278; and face, 212, 214; and permeable shared identity, 58; see also ecosis, ethecosis
eudaimonia (happiness, Aristotle), 59–61, 107, 111, 252; see also *lè*
Eudemian Ethics (Aristotle), 61, 134
Exemplarity, 210, 256, 258; see also becoming-
Exemplary person (*jūnzǐ* 君子, Mencius), 265

Face, 55, 81, 86, 90, 140, 263; as *doxa* (Aristotle), 46, 49, 189–93, 196, 215, 274; as emotion, 212–5; in Mencius, 274–5; as *miànzi* (面子), xii, 143, 213, 275; as self-esteem, 215; and shame, 211–6; as social regulation (Goffman), 49, 141, 158, 189–92, 198, 211–5; as social value, 190–2, 197, 201, 212–5, 258; as a stage for emotion and disposition, 103, 135, 143, 175, 213–7, 269

Face-Threatening Event (FTE, Brown and Levinson), 214, 216
Faithfulness (*xìn* 信, Mencius), 65
Fame, 46, 49, 160, 165–6, 200
fǎn (反 to reverse/invert, Mencius), 63, 217
Feeling: as becoming-cognitive mapping of emotion, 80–1; -becoming-disposition, 97; structures of (Williams), 272
Feeling-becoming-thinking (*xīn* 心), 9, 62, 76–81, 83–4, 96, 99, 145, 185, 274; in *doxa* (Aristotle), 165–7; as group fellow-feeling (*rén* 仁, Mencius), 68–73, 97, 102, 198
Feeling Extended (Robinson), ix, 136, 272
Fellow-feeling (*rén* 仁, Mencius), 2, 9, 47, 88–90, 91–8, 107, 111, 143, 145, 153, 155, 162, 166–7, 175, 176, 185, 188, 202, 203–4, 251–2, 255–6, 266, 269, 277; as collective *xīn* (心), 48, 53, 67–73, 82, 84, 91–8, 107, 145–6; in the ruler, 31, 98–102, 255–6; government (*rén zhèng* 仁政, Mencius), 24–6, 54, 67, 73, 98–102, 152; as *tiān zhī zūn* (天之尊 "heaven's honors," Mencius), 96–7, 185, 195, 210, 218; see also four shoots
First-Year Writing and the Somatic Exchange (Robinson), ix, 100, 136, 216
Five relationships (*wǔlún* 五倫, Mencius), 31–2, 149, 252
Flood-like *qì* (*hàorán zhī qì* 浩然之氣, Mencius), 75, 78, 83, 108–9, 119, 141, 145, 271–2
Foucault, Michel, 13–4
Four hearts: of approval and disapproval (是非之心 *shìfēi zhī xīn*, Mencius), 176, 273–4; of compassion (惻隱之心 *cèyǐn zhī xīn*, Mencius), 74–5, 107, 149, 176,

177–8, 269; of deference (*gōngjìng zhī xīn* 恭敬之心, Mencius), 149, 176, 178–9, 220; of shame (羞惡之心 *xiūwù zhī xīn*, Mencius), 176, 178–9, 204–10
Four shoots (*sì duān* 四端, Mencius), 31, 49, 73, 82–3, 98, 143–4, 149, 167, 175–84, 204, 220, 258, 267; as circulatory, 251
Fourier, Charles, 92, 256, 268
Freese, John Henry, 52, 54–6, 106, 137–8, 163–4, 193, 199–202, 277
Freud, Sigmund, 114, 177, 253
Friedman, Howard, 134
Friendly feeling (*to philein*, Aristotle), 59, 62, 65, 70–1, 91, 95, 107, 111, 134, 137, 141, 202, 252
Friendship: as *philia* (Aristotle), 59, 62, 91, 95, 107, 134, 137, 196, 229, 252, 255–6; as *péngyou* (朋友, Mencius), 65, 111, 252; as virtue friendship (Aristotle), 61

Gaines, Robert N., 281
Gandhi, Mahatma, vii
Gardner, Daniel K., 181–3
Garfinkel, Harold, 151
Garver, Eugene, 197–9, 275–6
gēn (根 root, Mencius), 31, 82, 108, 143, 169, 171, 174–5
Goffman, Erving, 49, 151; on face, 158, 189–92, 198, 211–7
Golden Rule (*shù* 恕, Mencius), 68, 88–9, 107, 267
Gorgias (Plato), 105, 127, 131, 241
Govern (*zhì* 治, Mencius), x, 31, 47, 48, 53, 62–7, 102
Graham, A.C., 34, 40, 120, 173
Gramsci, Antonio, 272
Great Learning (*Da Xue* 《大學》), 21
Guattari, Félix, 118
Guodian strips (郭店楚簡), 23, 168

Habitualization, 256–7

Habitus (Bourdieu), 164; as group disposition, 272
Hall, David L., 44–6, 108
Han Fei (韓非), 18, 36, 37
hàorán zhī qì (浩然之氣 flood-like *qì*, Mencius), 78, 83, 108–9, 145
Happiness: as *eudaimonia* (Aristotle), 59–61, 107, 111; as *lè* (樂 Mencius), 90, 107
Haskins, Ekaterina, 12
Hatfield, Elaine, 134
Havelock, Eric, 46–7, 62, 157–9
Hawk, Byron, 122
Heart-becoming-mind (*xīn* 心), 9, 53, 62, 68, 73, 76–9, 81, 83–4, 145, 147, 153, 154, 156, 162, 167, 168, 176–7, 270, 271, 274; and the affective self (*shēnxīn* 身心), 62, 107–8, 146, 253; compassionate (*bùrěn zhī xīn* 不忍之心, Mencius), 48, 53, 71, 73–5, 107; as group fellow-feeling (*rén* 仁, Mencius), 31, 48, 53, 67–73, 91–3, 95, 97, 99, 107; and human goodness, 183–6, 218, 229–30; as the root (*gēn* 根, Mencius) of the four shoots (*sì duān* 四端, Mencius), 31, 82, 108, 143, 169, 171, 174–5; steering *doxa*/*wén* 聞 (reputation), 166; *see also* four hearts
Hegel, G.W.F., 79, 139
Hegemony (Gramsci), 272
Heidegger, Martin, 179
Heterosexuality, panicked (Butler), 53, 208–9
hexis (disposition, Aristotle), 8, 110; and *habitus* (Bourdieu), 164, 272
Hinton, David, 66, 69, 72, 91, 94, 142, 169, 171–4, 176, 178, 181–3, 204, 265, 267, 277; on his fidelity to poetry and Chinese thought, 272–3
Holland, Virginia, 59
Honor, 3, 31, 55, 96–7, 154, 158, 166, 268, 275–6; and money,

Honor *(continued)*
198–9; as *timē* (Aristotle), 48, 49, 85–6, 140, 197–203, 221, 226–7; and warrior cultures, 197–9, 268; as *zūn* 尊/*róng* 榮 (Mencius), 48, 88, 90, 96–7, 148, 185, 194–7, 203–4, 210, 218
Hou Wailu (侯外廬), 249
Huang Junjie (黃俊傑), viii, 20–3, 72, 261, 265
Hughes, Richard, 119–21, 123
Human nature (*rénxìng* 人性, Mencius), 31, 34, 72, 158, 168, 170, 172, 174, 175, 181–3, 219, 258, 266, 273; see also *qíng*, *xìng*
Humanity/humaneness (*rén* 仁), 24–5, 48, 69–70, 91–5; *see also* benevolence, fellow-feeling
Hume, David, 198
hupokrisis (acting, body language, Aristotle), 48, 105, 109, 116, 130–3, 134, 139, 140

Icosis, ix, 6–9, 121, 124, 133, 152, 158, 227, 240–5, 252, 256, 258; counter-, 241; as energizing opinion, 189, 192, 195; and *hupokrisis* (acting), 134; iter-, 152, 157, 255; of persuasivity, 57, 104, 129, 165, 189, 203, 220, 247, 258, 278; and seemings, 242–5; of social value, 33, 53, 156–7, 164, 188, 195; and the somatic exchange, 15, 164
Identification, 46, 141, 252, 257; as theorized by Burke/Naess, 2, 14, 48, 53, 57–9, 61–2, 68, 74, 107; affective, 76, 84; circulated through groups, 104; as consubstantiality (Burke), 14, 59; and exemplarity, 218; as persuasivity, 104; in Plato, 46
Illocutionary force (Austin), 56–7
"In the Penal Colony" (Kafka), 14
Individualism, panicked, 53

Ingarden, Roman, 161
Intimacy (*qīn* 親, Mencius), 64–5
Introducing Performative Pragmatics (Robinson), 151
Iser, Wolfgang, 161
Isocrates, 255
Iterability (Derrida), 15, 151
Itericosis, 152, 155, 157, 255
Ivanhoe, P.J., 34

James, William, 81
Jauss, Hans Robert, 161
jūnzǐ (君子 exemplary person, Mencius), 265

Kafka, Franz, 14
Kant, Immanuel, 32, 239; and Aristotle/Lacan, 281
kataphronēsis (contempt, Aristotle), 209
Kennedy, George, 18, 52, 54, 106, 131, 132, 133, 138, 140, 162, 163–4, 189, 192, 193, 198–203, 206, 211, 222–8, 237–9, 241, 277, 280; on Aristotle's emotions, 103; on energy as charisma (Miller), 124–6; on rhetoric as energy, 48, 109, 112–8, 134, 141, 148, 194, 252, 270
kharis, ekhō (gratitude, Aristotle), 124–5; *see also* charismatic signifiers
Kim Myeong-seok, 273–4
Knowing speech (*zhī yán* 知言, Mencius), 30, 48, 108–9; *see also* cultivating energy
Konstan, David, 125, 189, 196, 275–6

Lacan, Jacques, 75, 239; and Aristotle/Kant, 281
Lamarck, Jean-Baptiste, 118
Laozi (老子), 76, 158, 267, 272
Lau, D.C. (劉殿爵), 18–9, 21, 63, 64, 66, 68, 69, 70–3, 74–6, 77–8, 79, 91, 93–4, 97, 98, 100, 101, 102, 107, 142, 145, 167, 173–4,

176, 178, 179, 181–3, 204–5, 250, 267, 273, 275
Laws (Plato), 259
lè (樂 happiness, Mencius), 90, 107; see also *eudaimonia*
Legge, James, 66, 69, 70–2, 77–8, 91, 93–4, 98, 100, 162, 170–4, 176–7, 178, 179, 181–3, 185, 195, 204–5, 207, 264, 266, 267, 273, 274
lǐ (理 pattern, Zhu Xi), 78
lǐ (禮 ritual propriety, Confucius/Mencius), 31, 49, 88, 90, 97–8, 107–8, 146–56, 176, 251, 257; see also *sì duān*
Lindsay, Stan, 105
Linebarger, Paul, 95–6, 269
Literary Work of Art, The (Ingarden), 161
Lloyd, Geoffrey, 35, 39
logos (Aristotle), 5, 104, 127–9, 281
Lotze, Rudolph, 95
Love, 123, 129, 256; as *ài* (愛, Mencius), 2, 63–5, 67, 69, 71, 75, 107, 153, 188, 263; in Aristotle, 60, 140, 199–202; as *qíng* (情, Mencius), 180; see also *rén*
Loyalty, 61, 256; as *zhōng* (忠, Mencius), 71, 88–9, 107, 153; see also *rén*

Ma Yo Yo (马友友), 166
Magna Moralia (Aristotle), 60
Massumi, Brian, 9, 12–3, 15–7
"Meaning of a Word, The" (Austin), 159
"Meaning of Body in Classical Chinese Philosophy, The" (Ames), 44–5
Mencius (《孟子》), 7, 32, 42–4, 73, 155, 158, 168, 173; historical core of (Brooks and Brooks), 18–20, 29–32, 43–4; as rhetorical theory, 18–29; read by Tang, 23
Mencius (孟子), vii–ix, 2, 4, 7–10, 49, 107–9, 124, 164–89, 197; and Aristotle on entelechy, 34, 110–1, 172, 182, 188; on bioecological metaphors, 53–4; on *bùrěn* (不忍 inability to bear other people's suffering), 48, 53, 71, 73–6, 107; on conditions (*mìng* 命), 8, 23, 49, 82–4, 120, 155, 167–8, 178, 184–7, 190, 192–3, 218, 220, 248–52, 258; on cultivating energy (*yǎng qì* 養氣), 30, 48, 109, 145–6; and democracy, 10, 22, 27–8, 254, 256, 262; on disposition (*xìng* 性), 8, 32, 49, 78, 79, 143, 15, 185, 188, 258, 266; in disputation with Gaozi, 31, 72, 166–7, 179, 183–4; and ecosis, 247–52, 255–8; on energy (*qì* 氣), vii, 9, 47, 48, 84, 98, 148, 156, 270; on the flood-like *qì* (*hàorán zhī qì* 浩然之氣), 75, 78, 83, 108–9, 119, 141, 145, 271–2; on forces (*tiān* 天), 31, 49, 53, 83, 98, 119, 153–5, 167, 184–8, 193, 195, 218, 258, 267; on the four hearts, 31, 49, 74, 149, 167, 175–84, 204, 220, 258; as historical/literary figure, 29–32; on honor (*zūn* 尊/*róng* 榮), 48, 88, 90, 96–7, 148, 185, 192–7, 203–4, 210, 218; 203–4; on human goodness, 179–84; and the human-as-plant metaphor, 81–4; on knowing speech (*zhī yán* 知言), 30, 48, 108–9, 141–6; on persuasion, 53; on *rén* (仁 fellow-feeling), 2, 9, 47, 88–90, 91–8, 107, 111, 143, 145, 153, 155, 162, 166–7, 175, 176, 185, 188, 202, 203–4, 251–2, 255–6, 266, 269, 277; on *rén zhèng* (仁政 government as persuasion), 24–6, 54, 67, 73, 98–102, 152; on rhetoric, 18–29; on ritual propriety (*lǐ* 禮), 31, 49, 88, 90, 97–8, 107–8, 146–56, 176, 251, 257; on shame (*xiūwù* 羞惡), 48, 176, 178–9, 197, 204–10, 218–20, 258, 273,

Mencius *(continued)*
277; and Sino-Hellenism, 33–44; on slighting (*qīng* 輕), 192–6, 209–10; and somatics, 9–10; on *tiān* (天 forces) as the somatic exchange, 218; vitalism, 84, 119–23; on *wén* (聞 reputation), 69, 157–8, 160–2, 165–6, 188, 190, 265; on *xīn* (心 feeling), 9, 31, 53, 73, 76–81, 92, 99, 156, 175, 185, 229, 230, 270; and *xuèqì* (血氣 blood-*qì*), 84–5, 87–91; on *zhì* (治 govern), x, 31, 47, 48, 53, 62–7, 257
Metaphysics (Aristotle), 110
Miller, Susan, 117, 118; on charismatic signifiers, 48, 104, 105, 109, 125–6, 220–1, 240, 278–9
mìng (命, Mencius), 176, 189; as "conditions," 8, 23, 49, 82–4, 120, 155, 167–8, 178, 184, 186–7, 190, 192–3, 218, 220, 248, 252, 258; as "fate/ordinance/decree," 23, 184, 248, 250; see also *tiān*
Mirror neurons, 64, 219
Mohism, 36, 219, 266
Mou Zongsan (牟宗三), 22, 173
Mozi (墨子), 219

Naess, Arne, vii, 2, 5, 49, 58, 68, 74, 120; on the ecological self, vii, 5, 49, 62, 68, 252–4, 256, 269; on identification, 2, 48, 53, 58, 62, 68, 74, 76, 107, 252
Nelson, Erick, 84–7
Neo-Jamesian neurophysiology, 80–1
Nicomachean Ethics (Aristotle), 59–60, 134
Nivison, David, 89, 92–3, 125–6, 270, 271, 273, 277–8, 290
No Less a Man (Robinson), 267
Nussbaum, Martha, 256

Oakeshott, Michael, 148, 153
Objectivism, 12–4, 46–7, 158, 233, 236, 244; as icotic, 129, 241

oikos (household, community), x, 5–6, 47, 133, 227, 259; and puns with *eikos*, 6, 259
oligōria (slighting, Aristotle), 209; *doxēs* (contempt for public opinion, Aristotle), 192, 195–7, 206, 211
On Christian Doctrine (Augustine), 12
On the Soul (Aristotle), 139–40
Opinion-becoming-reputation: see *doxa*, reputation
Organon (Aristotle), 36, 39
Orientalism, 33, 42
Ox Mountain (牛山 Niu Shan, Mencius), 31, 72–3, 82–3, 120, 187

Pang Pu (龐朴), 168
Panicked: heterosexuality (Butler), 108–9; individualism, 53; moralism, 209–10
Paradox, 280
Parmenides, 96
Pathetic fallacy (Ruskin), 253
pathos (emotion, Aristotle), 10, 103–4, 106, 126–33, 138, 163–4, 275, 276, 281; and permeable shared identity, 58–9, 141, 146
Paul of Tarsus, 12
Perelman, Chaim, 78–9, 130–1, 139, 270–1
Performative Linguistics (Robinson), 57–8
Performativity, 141, 151
Perlocutionary effect (Austin), 56–7
Persuading-becoming-believing (*pistis*, Aristotle), 52–4, 62, 117; -becoming-valuing-becoming-knowing, 221; as the energizing of opinion (*energeia doxēs*, Aristotle), 193; as energy (Kennedy), 252
Persuasivity (*to pithanon*, Aristotle), vii, 1–2, 6, 9, 18, 47–9, 124, 158, 234, 238, 247, 257, 262; channeled through body language (*hupokrisis*, Aristotle), 40, 54, 57, 73, 102–6, 107, 112, 114, 117, 129, 131, 134, 240; and (dox)icosis, 49, 189, 192,

202, 220, 240, 251; flows of, 47, 240, 255; in governance, 98–102, 152; and *rén* (仁, Mencius), 257; *see also* pistis
Phaedo (Plato), 60
phainomena (appearances, Aristotle), 138, 140
philia (friendship, Aristotle), 59–61, 62, 91, 95, 107, 111, 252
Physical body (*shēntǐ* 身體), 62, 108
pistis (persuasion-becoming-belief, Aristotle), x, 40, 46–8, 52–4, 117, 262; as argument/means of persuasion, 10, 54–6, 104–5; as circular, 53, 66, 257, 272; collective agent of, 62, 102, 146; and doxicosis, 189; as polaristic, 46–7; and *zhì* (治 govern, Mencius), 66, 107, 157
Plato, viii, 4, 6, 30, 38, 42–4, 45, 46–7, 60, 78, 96, 113, 122, 131, 132, 158–9, 163, 224, 226, 233, 239–40, 241, 244; and copy theory, 139; and *oikos-eikos* puns, 259; on *thumos*, 85–7
Polarism, 44–7, 54–5, 57; *see also* dualism
Politics (Aristotle), 43, 127, 259
Porkert, Manfred, 146
Preface to Plato (Havelock), 46
Presencing (Perelman), 48, 78–9, 121, 130–1, 139, 157, 240, 270–1
Propensity (*shì* 勢, Mencius), 83, 108, 175
Proprioception, 217

qì (氣 energy, Mencius), vii, 9, 47, 48, 98, 148, 156, 270; flood-like (*hàorán zhī qì* 浩然之氣, Mencius), 75, 78, 83, 108–9, 119, 141, 145, 271–2
qīn (親 intimacy, Mencius), 2, 64–5, 67, 263
qíng (情 characteristic tendencies, Mencius), 179–82, 192–4, 195–6; see also *xìng*

qīng (輕 slighting, Mencius), 195–6, 209–10
Queer theory, 209
Quintilian, 26, 104

Reader-response theory, 161
Real (Lacan), 239
rén (人 human), 65–8, 75, 88, 92–7, 176, 179, 188, 248–50, 262, 263; *bùrěn rén* (不忍人 compassionate person, Mencius), 75, 99, 107; *rén lún* (人倫, human relationships, Mencius), 263–4; *rén rén* (仁人 fellow-feeling person, Mencius), 68–70, 95; *rén xīn* (人心 human feeling, Mencius), 31; *rénxìng* (人性 human nature, Mencius), 31, 34, 72, 158, 168, 170, 172, 174, 175–6, 219, 258, 266, 273; *rén zhī zūn* (人之尊 human honor, Mencius), 195, 210, 218
rén (仁, Mencius), 2, 9, 31, 47, 48, 53, 125, 251–2, 255–6, 266, 269, 277; as associated humanity (Behuniak), 25, 92–3, 94–5; as benevolence, 24–5, 48, 69–72, 91–5, 162; as *bùrěn* (不忍 inability to bear other people's suffering), 73–6; as *cèyǐn zhī xīn* (惻隱之心 heart of compassion), 75; as co-humanity (Richie), 92–3, 94–5; as exemplary humanity, 188; as fellow-feeling, 2, 9, 47, 88–90, 91–8, 107, 111, 143, 153, 155, 162, 166–7, 175, 176, 185, 188, 202, 203–4, 251–2, 255–6; and Fourierist associative humanity/life, 268; as Golden Rule (Confucius), 68–70; as group *xīn* (心 feeling-becoming-thinking), 67–73, 91–8, 107, 145–6; and *habitus* (Bourdieu), 164; humanity/humaneness, 24–5, 48, 69–70, 91–5; ruler as fellow-feeling teacher, 99–100; as *tiān zhī zūn* (天之尊 "heaven's honor,"

rén (continued)
Mencius), 96–7, 185, 195, 210, 218; as utopian anarchy, 256; see also *sì duān*

rén zhèng (仁政 persuasive government, Mencius), 24–6, 54, 67, 73, 98–102, 152

rényì (仁義, morality, Mencius), 69, 72–3, 88, 97, 264–6, 272

Republic (Plato), 46–7, 85–7, 132

Reputation, 47, 49, 55, 86, 111, 190, 203, 276–7; as *doxa/dokeō* (Aristotle), 7, 40, 46, 62, 140, 157–66, 189, 197, 200–2, 211, 221–2, 224; as face (Goffman), 189–90, 202, 211–5; as *wén* (聞, Mencius), 69, 157–8, 160–2, 165–6, 188, 265

Reticulation of affect, 2–4, 41, 55, 63–4, 107, 147, 157, 179, 216, 251

Rezeptionsästetik (reception aesthetics), 161

Rhetoric, The Art of (Aristotle), 7–8, 10, 36, 41, 42–4, 45, 58, 112; and democracy, 28–9; read in terms of persuasive structures, 26, 51–2, 129

Rhetoric of Motives (Burke), 26, 58

Richie, Jeffrey, 92–3, 94–5

Rightness (*yì* 義, Mencius), 82, 90, 97, 107, 170, 172, 176, 178, 186, 195, 208–10, 251, 263, 264, 270; see also four shoots

Ring Lardner and the Other (Robinson), 267

Ritual propriety (*lǐ* 禮, Mencius), 31, 49, 63–4, 67, 82, 88, 90, 97–8, 107–9, 143, 146–56, 171, 175–6, 251, 257; see also four shoots

Roberts, W. Rhys, 52, 55–6, 106, 137, 163–4, 199–202, 224, 227, 230, 276, 277, 280

róng (榮 honor, Mencius), 48, 197, 203–4

Root, 56, 59, 95, 109–10, 119, 122, 128, 272, 281; as *gēn* (根, Mencius), 31, 82, 108, 143, 169, 171, 174–5

Rorty, Amélie Oksenberg, 10–11, 14, 18

Ruskin, John, 253

Saussure, Ferdinand de, 272

Schaberg, David, 35–8

Schleiermacher's Icoses (Robinson), ix, 136, 216

Schwartz, Benjamin, 34, 120

"Second Coming, The" (Yeats), 144

Self-realization (Naess), vii, 2, 5–6, 58, 68, 87, 218, 252, 256, 269

sēmeion (sign, Aristotle), 37, 103, 105–6, 202, 221, 225–6, 281

Shame, 7, 86, 132, 152, 154, 158, 275; as *aiskhunē* (Aristotle), 48, 140–1, 194, 197, 202, 210–8, 276; and gender, 84; and loss of face (Goffman), 49, 211–7; as *xiūwù* (羞惡, Mencius), and disdain, 48, 176, 178–9, 204–10, 218–20, 258, 273, 277

shēntǐ (身體, physical body), 62, 108

shēnxīn (身心 affective self), 62, 107–8, 146, 253

Sherman, Nancy, viii, 8, 15, 59, 60, 134, 248

shì (勢 propensity), 95, 108

shìfēi zhī xīn (是非之心 heart of approval and disapproval, Mencius), 176, 178–9, 273–4

shù (恕 Golden Rule, Mencius), 88–90, 107, 267

Shun (舜), 147, 149–50, 248, 250–1, 266, 278

Shun Kwong-loi (信廣來), viii, x, xi, 73, 75, 78, 83, 84, 89, 143, 167–8, 173–5, 177, 179–80, 183, 184–8, 205–6, 208–10, 219, 249, 256, 266, 267, 270, 271, 277

sī (思), 168, 249; as thinking (Mencius), 77–81

sì duān (四端 four shoots, Mencius), 31, 73, 82–3, 97, 143
Signs, 12, 13, 79, 103, 112–4, 116, 186, 213–4, 270, 275; as charismatic signifiers (Miller), 124, 126; as *sēmeia* (Aristotle), 37, 103, 105–6, 200, 202, 221, 225–6, 281
Sino-Hellenism, 33–44; and Orientalist gender hierarchies, 75
Slighting: as *oligōria* (Aristotle), 158, 193–4, 197, 206, 211; as *qīng* (輕, Mencius), 195–6, 209–10, 211
Smythe, William E., 269
Snyder, Gary, 48
Social ecology, vii, 5, 33, 84, 104, 254; of affective value, 117, 203; and associative humanity, 269; of ethecosis, 189, 203, 252; as entelechy, 4, 6, 111; of face, 211–7; of *lǐ* (禮 ritual propriety, Mencius), 147; of persuasivity, 18; of plausibilization (doxicosis), 47, 240, 252
Social regulation, vii, 85, 112, 152, 179, 220, 252, 258
Social value, 86, 156, 189, 193; affectively charged, 126; ecology/circulation of, 3–4, 6, 9, 38, 49, 87, 147–8, 154, 247, 251, 275; and face, 189–93, 258, 275; and honor (*timē*, Aristotle), 197–203, 221; icosis of, 6, 156; as work, 258
Socioeconomic policy (Mencius), 254, 256
Socrates, 30, 43, 105, 241
sōma tēs pisteōs (body of persuading-becoming-believing, Aristotle), 128–9
Somatic, 9–18; in Aristotle, 10–15, 138–41; charisma (Miller), 126; contagion, 63, 141, 251; counterideo-, 211, 241; ecology, vii–ix, 15, 33; entelechy, 221, 225; evaluative affect (Brennan), 3, 271; exchange, vii, 2, 15–6, 18, 158, 215–21, 225, 240, 254–5, 258; icosis, 225, 233, 241, 254–5, 258; ideo-, 14, 152, 154–6, 217, 221, 233, 254–5, 279; idio-, 152, 255; markers (Damasio), 79, 81, 214, 216–7, 219–20; in Mencius, 9–10; mimesis/transfer, 9, 15, 133–41, 216–7, 219, 220; persuasion, 129; pressure, 211, 213, 221, 271; response, 213; signaling, 32; shame, 211–21; theory, vii–viii, 9–18, 220, 233, 278
Somatic-marker hypothesis (Damasio), 79, 81, 214, 216–7, 219–20
Sophistical Refutations (Aristotle), 36
Speech act, 47, 51, 56–8, 66; collective, 48, 129, 194; embodied, 141
Spinoza, Baruch, vii, 252
Structures of feeling (Williams), 272
Summa Theologica (Thomas), 12
Sun Yat-sen (孫逸仙), 22, 95
Syllogistic, 106, 231, 243; and the enthymeme (Aristotle), 36–8, 41–2, 242, 281; quasi-, in emotion, 127

ta dokounta (the seemings, doxosis, Aristotle), 49, 226, 234, 236–41, 258
ta eikota (the plausibilities, icosis, Aristotle), 5, 47, 49, 105–6, 121, 226–7, 232–4, 237–41, 258–9, 281
Tai Shi (《泰誓》), 251
Tang Junyi (唐君毅), 22, 23
Thomas Aquinas, 12, 110, 158
thumos (anger, spirit, valor), 14, 41–2, 48, 54, 84–7, 63, 163; and the enthymeme, 41, 128–9, 281
tiān (天, Mencius), 176, 189–90, 192, 229, 230; as "forces," 31, 49, 53, 83, 98, 119, 153–5, 167, 184–8, 193, 195, 218, 258, 267; as "heaven," 23, 34, 63, 68, 96–7, 119, 153, 167, 169–73, 184, 185, 195, 210, 218, 248–51; as the

tiān (continued)
somatic exchange, 218; *zhī dào* (天之道 the way of *tiān*, Mencius), 218; *zhī zūn* (天之尊 heaven's honor, Mencius), 185, 195; see also *mìng*
timē (honor, Aristotle), 47, 48, 55, 85–6, 140, 197–203, 221, 276
to philein (friendly feeling, Aristotle), 59–62, 85, 91, 95, 107, 111, 134, 137, 202, 252
to pithanon (persuasivity, Aristotle), vii, 2, 6, 9, 40, 48, 49, 54, 57, 73, 102–6, 107, 112, 226, 234–40, 258
to theōrēsai (observation, Aristotle), 104–6
Topics (Aristotle), 36, 37
topoi (commonplaces, Aristotle), 26, 37, 51
Toulmin, Stephen, 242–3
Training, 14; of the body-becoming-mind, 108, 111, 143–5, 168, 257, 266; of plants, 143; rhetorical, 27, 28; thumotic, 87; in virtue, 277
Translation and the Problem of Sway (Robinson), ix, 216
Translator's Turn, The (Robinson), ix, 152
Trust, 82, 165; and gender, 75; and *pistis* (Aristotle), 55–6, 103, 262; and persuasion (Miller), 117, 124, 126, 220–1, 240; as *xìn* (信, Mencius), 65, 71, 107, 263
Truthiness (Colbert), 5–7, 9, 47, 49, 161, 191, 221, 227, 233, 236–7, 240, 245, 247, 258

Uprightness (正 *zhèng*, Mencius), 64, 88, 90, 144, 149, 166

Van Norden, Bryan W., 9, 19, 66, 69, 70–2, 91, 98, 162, 176–7, 178, 179, 181–3, 195, 270; on the five relationships, 263–4; and the pear tree, 153, 173; reliance on Aristotle, 172–3, 182–3, 219; reliance on Zhu Xi, 10, 78, 85, 153, 171, 182; on shame and disdain, 204–5, 208–10, 273, 277
Vitalism, 9, 16, 42, 109, 112–3, 118–23, 185, 192, 257; and affect/vitality, 16–7; and *energeia* (Aristotle), 84, 121, 257; and vital energy (*qì* 氣, Mencius), 48, 84, 119–20, 146, 257

Walker, Jeffrey, viii, 118, 126–31, 254; on enthymemes as encouragement, 14, 128, 281; on *mokhtheō*, 131; on presencing (Perelman), 48, 109, 116, 130
Wardy, Robert, 38–40
Warrant (Toulmin), 242
wén (聞 hearing-becoming-reputation, Mencius), 47, 49, 69, 157–8, 160–2, 165–6, 265, 274; as "hearing," 188
Whatever singularity (Agamben), 225
Whitehead, Alfred North, 44–5
Who Translates? (Robinson), 161
Williams, Raymond, 272
Wisdom (*zhì* 智, Mencius), 82, 88, 90, 96–8, 107, 176; see also four shoots
wù zhù zhǎng (勿助長 "don't help grow," Mencius), 83, 108, 187
wǔlún (五倫 five relationships, Mencius), 31–2, 149, 154, 252, 258
wúwéi (無為 don't act, Laozi), 83, 267

Xenophon, 6, 259
xìn (信 faithfulness/trust, Mencius), 65, 71, 107, 263
xīn (心 heart-becoming-mind, Mencius), 9, 31, 53, 73, 76–81, 92, 99, 156, 175, 185, 229, 230, 270; as affect-becoming-conation-becoming-cognition, 84; *bùrěn*

zhī xīn (不忍之心 compassionate heart, Mencius), 48, 53, 71, 73–5, 107; collective, as internal, 167–8; and human goodness, 183–6, 218, 229–30; as rén (仁 fellow-feeling, Mencius), 9, 68, 89, 91–8, 99, 101, 107, 179, 257, 269; as the root (gēn 根, Mencius) of the four shoots (sì duān 四端, Mencius), 31, 82, 108, 143, 169, 171, 174–5; as (shaping) disposition, 75, 78–9, 91, 97, 101, 108, 111, 145, 146, 167, 168–75, 180–84, 185, 258; and shēnxīn (身心 the affective self), 62, 107–8, 146, 253; as somatic markers (Damasio), 79, 81; as the source of lǐ (禮 ritual propriety), 147, 153, 154; steering doxa/wén 聞 (reputation), 166; see also four hearts

xīn sī (心思 the heart thinks, Mencius), 77–81

xìng (性, Mencius): as "disposition," 8, 32, 49, 78, 79, 143, 15, 185, 188, 258, 266; as innate "nature," 34, 72, 120, 158, 167–75, 186, 188, 232, 258, 266; and qíng (情 characteristic tendencies, Mencius), 180–3; as verb, 31, 167–75, 270

xíng (行 conduct, Mencius), 248, 265–6

xiūwù (羞惡 shame-becoming-disdain, Mencius), 176, 178–9, 204–10, 218–20, 258, 273, 277

xuèqì (血氣 blood-qì, valor, Dai Zhen), 48, 54, 73, 84–5, 87–91, 96, 129

Xunzi (荀子), 18, 31, 36, 37, 219

yǎng qì (養氣 cultivating energy, Mencius), 30, 48, 109; see also zhī yán

Yao (堯), 248, 250–1, 278

Yeats, W.B., 144

yì (義 rightness), 82, 90, 97, 107, 155, 176, 178, 186, 209, 251, 270; see also sì duān

yīnyáng (陰陽), 84

Zhang Qianfang (张千帆), 24–5, 27, 28, 67, 98

Zhao Zhentao (赵甄陶), Zhang Wenting (张文庭), and Zhou Dingzhi (周定之), 66, 69, 70–2, 93–4, 98, 100, 176, 178, 181–3, 204–5, 264, 266, 273

zhèng (正 uprightness, Mencius), 88, 90, 144

zhì (智 wisdom, Mencius), 88, 90, 96–8, 107, 176, 251, 267; see also sì duān

zhì (治 govern, Mencius), x, 31, 47, 48, 53, 62–7, 257; collective agent of, 102, 107, 157, 160

zhī yán (知言 knowing speech, Mencius), 30, 48, 108–9, 270; see also yǎng qì

zhōng (忠 loyalty, Mencius), 71, 88–9, 107, 153

Zhongyong (《中庸》 *Doctrine of the Mean*, Confucius), 21, 178

Zhu Xi (朱熹), xi–xii, 10, 85, 108–9, 271; and dualism, 22; on lǐ 理 (the Pattern), 78; on inborn human nature, 168, 171, 173, 181–2; on political quietism, 21, 153, 174; on shame/disdain (xiūwù 羞惡, Mencius), 208–9

Zhu Yuanzhang (朱元璋), 21

Zhuangzi (莊子), 76, 272

zūn (尊 honor, Mencius), 96–7, 195–6, 197, 218